Parishes of th

i.m. Margaret Vincent

I took for emblem the upland moors and the rocky
Slopes above them, bitter parishes
Of the buzzard.

'Llanafan Unrevisited' by T. Harri Jones (1963)

Parishes of the Buzzard

Ruth Bidgood

Gold Leaf Publishing

© Ruth Bidgood 2000

ISBN 0 907117 80 5

Published by Goldleaf Publishing, 3 Crown Street, Port Talbot, SA13 1BG

Printed in Great Britain by CIT Brace Harvatt,
Haverfordwest, Pembrokeshire, SA61 1XF

Contents

Foreword

This book is about Abergwesyn, a remote village in the mid-Welsh hills: a village that is still alive, though its churches, schools and inns are gone, its every valley holds ruined houses and disused fields, and many of its farms and sheepwalks have been lost to forest and reservoir. The two parishes of Abergwesyn, Llanddewi and Llanfihangel, still appear on diocesan lists, despite their lack of churches. As civil parishes they have ceased to exist; in 1985 Abergwesyn was divided between Llanwrtyd and Treflys (Llangamarch).

The book is not an exercise in nostalgia. I have gathered together fact and tradition, developed some themes from Abergwesyn's history, not to lament but to celebrate a village typical of rural Wales yet individual to the point of eccentricity.

I am greatly indebted to a host of helpers: scholars and research workers who have generously spared time from their own work to make valuable suggestions for mine: library and record-office staff who have patiently dealt with my queries: local friends who have shared with me their knowledge of the district. To all who have helped my warm thanks are given. In particular I must mention Mr David Jones of Abergwesyn Post Office, for constant help over many years: Mrs J.M. Vincent, for generous assistance with the production of the book: and also the following: Mr G.F. Bartle: Martin Bidgood: Mrs I. Blake (NSPRE): Mr Mervyn Bourdillon: Mr B.D. Clarke: Mrs H. Davies: Dr J. Davies: Mrs M.A. Evered: Mr B. Gibbins: Mr C. Hill: Mr. J.R. Hope: Major-General R. Stedman Lewis: Mr S. Meredith: Dr R.J. Moore-Colyer: Mr D.R. Morgan: Mr Peter Owen and family, for information from the unpublished papers of David Lewis Wooding: Professor William Rees: Miss D. Sanders: Mr R. Thomas: Mr J.L.M. Yates: staff of the National Library of Wales, the National Museum of Wales and the Public Record Office: and *Country Quest*, for the use of material from articles of mine first published in its pages.

Introduction: A Land Apart

The ancient lordship and Hundred of Buellt or Builth remains today, as it has always been, separate in spirit if not in fact from the rest of the modern county of Powys, and even from Brycheiniog, to which, as the county of Brecknock, it was joined by the Act of Union (1536). Deep in the hill-country of Buellt lies the most remote and most beautiful of its villages, the two ancient parishes of Llanddewi Abergwesyn and Llanfihangel Abergwesyn, thirty-four square miles of moor and valley.

Cars coming over the mountain road from Tregaron sometimes stop at the junction by Pentwyn farmhouse, at the signpost that says 'Llanwrtyd 5 miles, Beulah 5½ miles'. Puzzled drivers ask the way to 'Abergwesyn village', finding it hard to accept that they are already in it. The Ordnance Survey map marks Abergwesyn just downstream, literally at the aber (confluence) of Gwesyn and Irfon, but to a lowland eye the place seems hardly to exist. In shape and character it conforms to the old Welsh hill-pattern of isolated farmsteads, loosely linked. Local people feel more kinship with the mountain men of Llanddewi Brefi and Tregaron to the west, those of the Claerwen and Elan valleys to the north, or of Rhandirmwyn and Cilycwm to the south-west, than with those of old Brycheiniog, the larger south-eastern part of one-time Breconshire. Dwellers in the lordship of Buellt over the centuries shared with the hill people of Elenydd (the mid-Cambrian massif) the rigours of a hard and challenging land. Men lived their lives within tight bonds of work, kinship and neighbourhood. Trust was not lightly given, nor, if it should be betrayed, did the betrayal go unpunished.

Politically, Buellt was often separate from Brycheiniog. Tradition says that, together with the western part of what was later to be called Radnorshire, it was ruled over by nine generations of descendants of the fugitive Vortigern. Maps of pre-Norman Wales in William Rees' 'Historical Atlas' show it frequently grouped with the area to its north and north-east, Rhwng Gwy a Hafren (Between Wye and Severn), rather than with Brycheiniog. In Norman times we find it de Braose land when Brecon was Newmarch, later linked with Brecon under the de Braoses, but then divided from it as an acquisition of Llywelyn the Great. It was a lordship of the English Crown when Brecon was de Bohun territory. At the time of Glyndwr's rising Buellt was Mortimer (Yorkist), Brecon Lancastrian. The Wars of the Roses found Buellt, like Maelienydd, a land of the Duke of York, while Brecon was Buckingham country. In

Henry VIII's reign Buellt was again a lordship of the Crown, and finally yoked in 1536 with Brycheiniog as the county of Brecknock. Nowadays Breconshire, Radnorshire and the more northerly Montgomeryshire have all been swallowed up in Powys, which bears the name of an old kingdom but has very different boundaries from the ancient ones. Within these arbitrary bounds the old lordship of Buellt preserves its identity, remaining something of a land apart.

Abergwesyn has seen many changes this century: the shift of balance in population and language towards English-speaking incomers who, mainly, have arrested depopulation, the planting of the forests, the drowning of a large part of the upper Tywi valley by Llyn Brianne, the coming of tourism on a larger scale than ever before. Its people have known the divided mind which made them welcome the work brought by the Forestry Commission and the Economic Forestry group in the planting days, yet weep for the vanishing of old farms 'planted to the door': the split heart that welcomes all newcomers of good will, yet feels the pain of loss of the 'old days', the Welsh way of life, the hard work, bitterly hard, of the hill farms, and the vigorous enjoyments that went some way to sweeten labour. Under the surface of new life, old tides run. Those native to the place share knowledge, attitudes, responses not easily come at by the most welcome of incomers. In many ways this is still a secret land, that remembers more than it tells.

In so far as there is a 'village' of Abergwesyn, it is divided nowadays between two nodal points. The first is at the junction of the Tregaron road with the loop-road from Llanwrtyd to Beulah. Here opposite Dôliâr bungalow is Pentwyn, once the Grouse Inn as well as a farmhouse. In the heyday of the drovers, two more taverns stood nearby. Here too behind the farmhouse was the old shoeing enclosure where the cattle were fitted with fresh *ciws* (iron shoes) for the long road to England. Nearer the river was the village pound. There are two yew-shaded churchyards, one either side of the river Irfon; Llanddewi church is in ruins, Llanfihangel is gone. Nearby are the little Independent chapel of Moriah, and two cottages.

The other cluster of buildings which might nowadays claim to be 'Abergwesyn village' is about three quarters of a mile from Pentwyn towards Beulah, past two more houses and a disused school. Opposite the former Post Office (once combined with a shop) is a house on the site of an old mill; the Post Office garden lies where the mill-pond used to be. Nearby is a bungalow by the site of a former smithy. Two farmhouses are visible on the hill slopes, and further up the Gwesyn valley stands one more isolated house inhabited part-time.

But to think of either or both of these little groups as Abergwesyn would leave out the farmhouses and cottages glimpsed from the road up the Irfon valley from Llanwrtyd and on down the Cnyffiad valley to Beulah. It would leave out another chapel, Pantycelyn, and the gentry houses of Llwynderw (recently a hotel) and Llwynmadog. It would take no account of the great sweep of the hills through the two old parishes, mile after mile of moorland, sheepwalk and forest, and the cairned mountain Drygarn Fawr, rearing itself a little higher than the rest of the tableland.

There are the other valleys, too, each individual – bleak, wooded, solemn, gentle, secretive or welcoming. It is chiefly in the valleys along which the road runs that one finds living farms and occupied houses; and the motorist, who sees only these valleys and even there is impressed by the peaceful seclusion of the place, can have little idea of the remoteness of the valleys which can be explored only on foot or horseback. One such valley, that of Camarch, used to be called 'Cwm-cyn-nos' (Valley-before-night) – a valley to get into, or out of, before nightfall. Till the coming to a few of these valleys of forestry roads, they had only paths and cart-tracks, though anciently some of these were as important thoroughfares as today's motor road. Each valley sheltered farmhouses and cottages, and seems to have felt itself a community within a community. Most of the houses are now in ruins; some have been totally destroyed, some, with their gardens and fields, have 'gone under the scum/ Of the forests'. Llyn Brianne has drowned the old Tywi valley lands of Llanddewi's western boundary. These empty valleys, too, with their varied beauties and their inevitable sadness, are Abergwesyn.

1. Beginnings

(i) The Shaping of the Land

Nineteenth century conjectures about the shaping of the hills and valleys of the Abergwesyn area were cast in a romantic mould. The Rev. Rhys Gwesyn Jones, a native of the place, wrote in a Welsh article of 1861 about the raging primeval sea which, he felt, must have swirled into shape the steep craggy hill by Penybont uchaf farmhouse on the way up from Llanwrtyd – Pengraig Dinas Fach, as it is now marked on the map. He said that the river Irfon used, long ago, to run half a mile above its present bed, but that it must have taken the more powerful force of a vast whirlpool around the hill to give it its present sudden dramatic steepness and dome-like shape, like the much larger Sugar-Loaf on the way to Llandovery. The half-moon corrie behind Pwllybô, a little further north by the road to Abergwesyn, Gwesyn Jones attributed to the same agency. The sea dared not leave the bed that God had ordained for it, he claimed, but it surged through the valleys of Abergwesyn, and its path could now be traced by the wrathful grinding of rocks against each other. Perhaps his imagination was not so far astray. If the slow, relentless progress of the great glaciers could be seen on a speeded-up film, the movement of ice through these valleys, and the grinding of the rocks it brought down, might well seem like the flooding-in of a sea. However, geologists now consider the effects of ice on the landscape to be less important than was once supposed. Valleys formed by rivers which cut down almost as far as the present levels were smoothed and polished by the passing of the ice.

A newcomer to Abergwesyn may take the road that winds into the hills from Llanwrtyd, alongside the river Irfon: or the one from Beulah up the delectable Cnyffiad valley, over the pass and down the 'Pitch' into the wide and gentle lower valley of the Gwesyn: or the old drovers' road from Tregaron, braving the asperities of the Nantystalwyn hill and the Devil's Staircase. If he climbs to a vantage-point on any of the hills he will see a panorama of high moorland, range after range of hills whose flattish tops lie mainly at about 1500 feet, rising here and there to over 2000 feet, and topped by Drygarn Fawr with its cairns and triangulation point. Between the ridges plunge the valleys; he will see only their highest slopes, grassy, tree-covered or craggy.

It used to be thought that the levelling of the Central Wales massif into a peneplain was due to marine erosion. It is now believed that this levelling was due to the work of rivers during long periods of constant sea-level. It was far more recently that ice played its part in shaping the landscape. Nowadays the disappearance of the ice from the British Isles is taken as having been a mere 10,000 years ago. Periods of warmth between the four ice ages lasted longer than the centuries which have passed since the most recent departure of the ice; there is no guarantee that it will not return. Each highland mass in Wales had its own ice-sheet. Plynlumon, about twenty miles north of Abergwesyn, had the largest in Central Wales, but the Epynt hills and Drygarn, too, were capped with ice. At periods of great cold, the ice-caps grew larger and linked up. From them ice flowed out in all directions. An ice-sheet covered the land between the present Llanwrtyd Wells and Cefngorwydd, spreading to Penrhiwgoch and the Prysiau farms. There are traces of lateral moraine along the sides of the area. The thawing of the ice caused a lake to form. As vegetation round the edges grew inwards the lake became a marsh and eventually a peat-bog. Stretches of this can be seen now in Waun Rudd and near the old golf course south-east of the Cambrian Factory.

Almost every valley in Abergwesyn bears marks of the passing of the glaciers. Ice modified the shape of the valley through which the Tregaron road leaves Abergwesyn, cutting off the lower slopes of the little tributaries and fashioning them into hanging valleys, from which the gently-sliding stream of the shallow upper section leaps 'like a downward smoke' to join the main river. Further down the Irfon valley, the Pwllybô corrie was the starting point of a tributary glacier. The ice shifted many erratic boulders, the rock of which differs from that of the valleys where they now lie. Boulders in the Cnyffiad river-bed above Trallwm, and two (one of them huge) at a high crossing of tracks between Bryn Clyn and the upper Cnyffiad are of a conglomerate found in narrow bands here and there throughout the Gorllwyn, Drygarn and upper Irfon area. The typical rocks of the Abergwesyn area are Ordovician and Silurian, dating from about 520 to 405 million years ago. But older rocks, some Cambrian and pre-Cambrian, thought to be probably 900 to 550 million years old, are to be found in the conglomerate, which is a cementing together of rounded pebbles of varying sizes and period. They came originally from the beach of a great sea, now generally regarded as part of the Iapetus Ocean, which once separated the old North America from Western Europe. From the beach the pebbles had rolled down the continental shelf and plunged in avalanches to the ocean-bed to form submarine canyons and fan out into a complex of channels on the ocean-floor. In an unimaginably remote antiquity (up to 400 million years ago) today's hill-country north-west of Llanwrtyd lay deep in the ocean, near the bottom of the continental slope. A submarine canyon opened in the ocean-bed near Llanwrtyd, and another near Llanafan fawr. Like the present Pacific Ocean, the Iapetus Ocean was bordered by volcanoes. The only volcanic rocks exposed near Abergwesyn are of the Ordovician period. They are found just to the north of Llanwrtyd in the hills Garn Dwad and Pen y Garn Goch, between which now flows the river Cerdin. In this area the shale contains fool's gold (iron pyrite), which as it decays forms yellow ochre, and hydrogen sulphide gas. Where shale has been crushed by upheavals of the rock-strata the finely-ground iron pyrite gives it a greenish-black appearance. Geologists now consider the abundance of medicinal springs in the district is due not only to the presence of sulphide (whether or not that was originally caused by volcanic action), but to the existence of rock-fractures, permitting water to carry sulphur salts to the surface with the minimum of interference, and enabling the rich water to bubble up easily into springs. Certainly springs follow the fracture-lines, one of which passes through the grounds of the Dôlycoed Hotel.

On the north-west side of Abergwesyn the rocks are Silurian, dating from a period when the ocean was closing up, becoming narrower and shallower, and the sea-floor being crumpled between colliding landmasses into a huge chain of mountains stretching from Florida to northern Norway. To the south of the mountains a desert plain formed, through which great rivers flowed, forming deltas. In part of this plain the Old Red Sandstone, characteristic of most of southern Breconshire, was laid down. North-west Breconshire did not share in the sandstone deposits. Even geologically it is set apart.

The courses of the rivers of north Breconshire are affected by the basic structure of the land. Changes in the direction of their flow can be traced to various combinations of joints, faults, cleavages, folds and idiosyncrasies of lithology. In general, they flow where they find soft or structurally weak rock. O.S. maps show some of these lines of weakness very clearly. For instance, following a north-east to south-west line from near Nantyrhwch (Cwm Cnyffiad) in Abergwesyn one travels along a short length of the Cnyffiad, then the brook Nant Bach Helyg, the lower part of the river Gwesyn, a stretch of the Irfon, the middle reaches of the Culent, and down the Gwrâch into the Tywi valley, which at this point flows south-west as far as Ystradffîn.

(ii) Early Man

No-one knows exactly when Abergwesyn as a place with its own identity was born. From the time when the land took the shape we know today, and climatic conditions made human life in the valleys possible, it is likely that the lure of a little fertile land by the Irfon and its tributaries, and the presence of access-routes through the hills, marked it out for settlement.

Early men left many enigmatic traces of their life on the high moors and sometimes in the valleys of the north-western region of Breconshire. Archaeologists used to think that it was not until the Bronze Age (about 2,000 to 400 years B.C.) that human occupation of this area began. The Stone Age climate made the high moors bleak and unfriendly places, while the valleys that cleft them were, it was said, choked with thick forest, the home of dangerous beasts – forests too dense for the earliest implements to clear. The gentler weather of the Bronze Age brought man the pastoralist to the uplands, which are still studded with his round cairns.

Dr H.N. Savory's article in *Brycheiniog*, vol. XV, a postscript to his earlier one on the archaeology of North-west Breconshire in the first volume of that journal, shows how this original view has been modified. It now seems that after the first Neolithic settlers came by boat up the Wye some time between 3,000 and 2,000 B.C. and occupied the best lands near that river, there may have been a second influx of settlers, penetrating this time the uplands, where some even earlier Neolithic communities may have found their way and survived. The valleys are now thought to have been more lightly wooded, with oak, ash and hazel, than archaeologists used to suppose. However, the so-called chambered tomb or long barrow on Pen y Garn Goch near Llanwrtyd, a structure which used to be considered one of the few local evidences of Neolithic occupation, is now thought to be three round cairns of the Bronze Age linked by the rubble of their collapse.

The district is not without other traces of these earliest North Breconshire men. Neolithic occupation of the easier lands hereabouts is deduced from such finds as a large polished axe found in 1892 at Builth, and a flint axe-head near Beulah. From Abergwesyn itself came two of the undated collections of flints listed by W.F. Grimes in his 'Prehistory of Wales' – one 'consisting mostly of flints and spalls, among them a core and a small leaf-shaped point, found in the field called Dôlmaen (Standing Stone Meadow) on Pentwyn land, and another of 'spalls and fragments', including 'a crude thumb-scraper and three cores', from Nantystalwyn in the Tywi valley. Near the Wolf's Leap, about two miles north of Pentwyn, where the Irfon churns its way through a dramatic miniature ravine, was found a 'perforated pebble mace- head'.

Grimes tells us that 'settled occupation of quite uncertain date is suggested by some Welsh sites', like the turbary in which, on the moorlands beyond Trallwm, a former farmhouse set back from the road to Beulah, were found fragments of sharpened oak and birch stakes or piles, of great antiquity, which have been variously explained as the supporting piles of a bog-dwelling or part of the fencing of stock-raisers, possibly of the Bronze Age. This fascinating find was described at some length in the *Antiquaries' Journal*, vol. XV. The map-reference is SN 8657 5552. The piles were found driven vertically into the peat, the points of some being thrust into the clay below the peat-layers, and the tops of the present remains being at a level nearly that at which a change occurred from wood-yielding peat to pure peat. It has been suggested therefore that the missing upper part of the stakes decayed, above ground, at a time of climatic change from 'conditions favourable to woodland to those favourable to the formation of peat', about 1,000 B.C. The theory that we have here the remains of a woodland settlement have not so far been supported by the discovery of a nearby floor, implements or pottery. The article refers, however, to a local tradition that 'the old site of Tregaron is now under the waters of Llyn Berwyn (O.S. 1 inch 79, D3), a mountain lake about 1,500 feet above the sea, and that the bells of the old town can still be heard ringing in stormy times. This lake is high up on the moorland amid the peat bogs'. The story may indicate local belief, handed down through generation after generation, that settlements on the high moors did exist at some far-distant time.

It is to the Bronze Age, when a drier and warmer climate brought nomadic pastoralists to the hills, that archaeologists attribute many of the cairns and mounds of the North Breconshire hills and some at least of the great standing stones, isolated or in alignment, on the heights or in the valleys. But Abergwesyn and its neighbouring parishes are virtually unexplored country for the archaeologist. Little detailed work has been done. Some of the standing stones are still unmapped.

In a countryside where tales of buried treasure have always had their appeal, it is likely that at some time over the centuries even the remotest cairn has been disturbed by speculative picks and left scattered or untidily repiled. Drygarn (Trigarn on older maps) dominates the plateau, the higher of its cairns (rebuilt for Queen Victoria's jubilee) a landmark for miles. The lower cairn, to the north-east, partly ruinous, still indents the skyline. The recurring glimpse of Drygarn with its cairns from so many distant viewpoints seems a key to this whole landscape. It is in keeping with the many enigmas of these hills that Drygarn itself – not a peak, but a dark rearing-up of the land just a little higher in this one spot – should be something of a mystery. Tri Garn – Three Cairns? But there are only two. Was there a third, perhaps where the triangulation point is now? Or is one of the other versions of the name the right one – Dru Garn or Derwydd Garn (Druid's Cairn)? This is what the county historian, Theophilus Jones, suggested. Writing in the first decade of the nineteenth century, in his entry for Llanwrthwl he refers to *many* cairns on this mountain.

On Drygarn was discovered a Bronze Age rapier which was placed in Brecon Museum. By an old track from Abergwesyn to the Claerwen valley was found in June 1883, near Bwlch y Ddau Faen (Pass of the Two Stones), a Bronze Age dagger, described by Grimes as 'with an ogival blade, much reduced by whetting'. Before Bwlch y Ddau Faen the track passes just to the east of the remaining cairn on Carnau hill. By the pass itself, the 'two stones' form part of a stone circle, whose stones must surely have once stood higher out of the peat than now they do; but from the track approaching the pass from the Carnau direction, it is *two* stones which catch the eye and signal the way. Another cairn lies ahead on a rocky rise to the east of the track as it continues down the valley of Nant Paradwys (Stream of Paradise) to link up with the road by the fifteenth-century longhouse of Llanerchycawr in Llanwrthwl. Yet another cairn is marked by the O.S. just south-south-east of Carnau, on the slopes of Esgair Fraith above the river Cedney; others on the hill above Llednant farm in the Camarch valley: and one on Garn Wen above the oakwoods of Llwynmadog in the Cnyffiad valley.

Abergwesyn's neighbouring parishes have their cairns too. There are some in Llanwrtyd, on the hills to the north-west of the road to Llandovery. A glance at O.S. maps of Llanwrthwl, whose miles of desolate hills march with the wild northern moors of Llanafan fawr, Llanfihangel Bryn Pabuan and the two Abergwesyn parishes, show it as supremely rich in the stone remains of early peoples. Here at Cefn farm in 1954 four spiral torcs were discovered, the work of an Irish goldsmith of the middle Bronze Age. There is an extraordinary concentration of cairns in the north-west of Llanwrthwl parish, particularly on the hills flanking the old track from the border of Llanfihangel Bryn Pabuan to Llanwrthwl village across Rhôs Saith Maen, the Moor of the Seven Stones, an alignment of stones still visible near the track, though now much sunken. An article by D.J. James in *Brycheiniog*, vol. XVIII, numbers the stones as eight. Older maps show another major route (Rhiw Saeson, the English Road) crossing at right angles the track to Llanwrthwl. Cairns mark this cross- route also, seeming to indicate for it a greater antiquity than its name (an echo of the droving days) would suggest.

The word 'cairn' on maps must be treated with caution. At some places so marked it is a round barrow we find, with no trace of a pile of stones. An example is the mound marked as a cairn on Banc Paderau (Hill of Paternosters), a partially afforested hill well to the south of the Abergwesyn-Beulah road. The name may date from pre-Reformation times, when Strata Florida monks on their way to Tirabad grange are reputed to have said their paternosters on the hill. The preliminary drawing of 1820-21 for the first edition of the O.S. map marks, not a cairn, but a 'Mound of Earth', more correctly than the later maps, which have 'Cairn'. Another possible round barrow exists on the hills to the west of the upper waters of the Camarch.

Intriguing is the name Crug, given to a farmhouse now on, and formerly near, a small, steep and at present wooded hill in the Irfon valley about half a mile south of the Pentwyn road junction. The name usually implies a burial mound, but there seems no obvious indication of such burials on Crug hill, which is a considerable landmark in any view down-valley from the hills. However, the tangle of natural woods which share the hill behind the house with a dense plantation of conifers makes it difficult to examine.

Dr Savory tells us that the known sites of burials in the uplands date from the early Bronze Age, or Copper Age, onwards. In Llanfihangel Abergwesyn, on the ridge of Esgair Irfon to the east of the Tregaron road, is a burial cist typical of the middle Bronze Age, when such cists were found under cairns. The cist, which would have contained the ashes of a cremation, is lined with slabs of stone. No mound or cairn now survives. The local name for such cists is 'Druids' Cremation Grounds', possibly a relic of the romantic antiquarianism which saw a druid behind every stone! There are said, on the good authority of older people who have seen them, to be other cists, in poorer condition, one far up the Gwesyn valley and another somewhere on the hillside of Rhiw Garreg Lwyd with its ancient road. The cist on Esgair Irfon is near an old track, too. Known as the 'peat path', from the days when sledges and gambos went that way to collect fuel from turbaries on the hills, it continues along the mountain top, a track wide and clear at times, then obscured again, passing through gaps in old boundary-dikes of uncertain date, some reinforced at intervals by great stones half-embedded in the bank. At the burial cist the path, very faint now, fades finally into the rough mountain grass. Alongside the Tregaron road (SN 8027 5737) is a 'cairn cemetery' on Esgair Gerwyn; there is an article about it on pp. 360 ff. of *Ceredigion* (1978).

Equally mysterious are standing stones. The Welsh word is *maen hir* (menhir, tall stone). The best-known one in this district is probably the one which stands, overlooking a wide expanse of valley land, in a field opposite the Cambrian Woollen Factory just outside Llanwrtyd Wells on the Builth road. John Lloyd in *'Historical Memoranda of Breconshire'* suggests that it and others where guidemarks across a wild and largely uninhabited countryside, or marked roads and driftways. He had noticed, after a snowfall, a track leading due north from the Llanwrtyd stone to Y Foel hill. A lower track winds northwards past Maesygwaelod farm behind the Woollen Factory and makes its way up the Cerdin valley. The upper reaches of the valley have been invaded now by relentless regiments of Forestry conifers. Hidden among the trees in one of the old fields of Nantycerdin farm are two standing stones, side by side, one taller than the other. The Maesygwaelod stone, conspicuous in an open field higher than the countryside it overlooks, is something of a landmark; but the stones at Nantycerdin are hidden from the better-known one by the windings of the valley. Whether they indicated some place of significance for people journeying over the hills and looking down on them in the valley, or whether they had a function totally other than boundary-marking or signposting – religious, astronomical or commemorative, for instance – is unknown.

Another *maen hîr* stands casually in the hedge of one of the roads below Cwm Irfon farm on the road from Abergwesyn to Llanwrtyd. It may be the one noted by Lhuyd in his *'Parochalia'* of 1690 – 'a rude large stone by Nant y Walch [the old name for Cwm Irfon], but unaccountable, only said to be set up in ye time of ye Giants'. There is said to be another in that area, on the hillside, hidden now in conifer plantations. 'Maen' recurs in field-names. Pentwyn, for instance, has Dôlmaen. Mr C. Hope, who used to farm there, remembered helping to lift a great recumbent stone from this field, and finding under it black traces of burning. For a time this stone, he said, did duty as a gatepost, but it seems now to have disappeared. To it was attached the archetypal legend of the 'drinking stone', which at midsummer dawn went down to the Gwesyn to drink.

By one of the reinforced dikes running across the mountain-top near Craig Irfon, to the west of the peat-path, lies a great triangular stone, probably a recumbent standing stone. One of the two conglomerate erratics already referred to, at a crossing of hill-paths in the area between Glangwesyn and Trawsgyrch, seems to have been of some significance. Probably it was the massive one which was named Carreg Lwyd, Grey Rock or Holy Rock, and the name was sufficiently well-known to have survived on maps. 'Maen' is not the term used in this case. Possibly it was the sheer size of the boulder which made it noteworthy, and it may thus have come to serve as a waymark.

Neighbouring parishes, too, have their standing stones. One, nine feet tall, stands by the Chwefru river in Llanafan fawr, just south-east of Dôlfelin. There is another near the Newbridge road, in the Hirnant valley at Llanfihangel Bryn Pabuan. There is a cairn on the hill above Tymawr nearby, and not far away is Carn Pantmaenllwyd, Cairn of the Hollow of the Grey or Holy Stone, on the hills between the Hirnant and the Chwefru. In a marshy area south-east of Fronwen farmhouse, Llanafan fawr, stands a *maen hîr*. D.R. James writes of a recumbent broken stone in the same area. On the hill Fanfed, south-south-east of a cairn on Daren hill, is marked Maen Cam, the Crooked Stone. Sir John Lloyd photographed it fallen in the 1930s. The first O.S. map of 1833 shows both cairn and stone, and a clear trackway branching from Bwlch y Ddau Faen south-south-east and passing west of them on its way to Llanafan fawr near the old farmhouse of Cefnbrân.

Behind Trysgol farmhouse high up the Gwesyn valley is a very steep hill from the rocky summit of which may be had a most beautiful and dramatic view of the landscape for miles around. A triangulation point stands on the hill-top – no cairn. Local tradition has nothing to say about the hill; yet its name, Pen Carreg Dân, Summit of Fire Rock, suggests that it has at some period been used as a beacon hill, for which it is indeed ideally situated. It is not known whether such use and the name to go with it date from historical times or from a lost antiquity when ritual fires were lit here. Jonathan Williams wrote that such ceremonies continued till about the late eighteenth century on the top of Maesmawr above Rhaeadr, not far from Abergwesyn over the hills. There a fire was lit on Midsummer day, perhaps in the early hours, for round it 'the assembled populace, carrying flambeaux in their hands, danced and sang'.

Jonathan Williams recorded also an old Rhaeadr funeral custom. As the bier arrived at the turn of the road to the church, each mourner would throw a small stone onto a heap of stones that had accumulated there, saying 'carn ar dy ben', which Williams translates as 'a stone on thy head'. Could 'carn' be used here half-consciously with a double meaning? Its other significance is 'cairn'.

The O.S. map of Iron Age Britain marks none of that period's characteristic hilltop forts in North Breconshire. 'Defended enclosures' of varying size appear on the western slopes of the central mountains, at the edge of the coastal plain, and on the southern Epynt range. The hills of Abergwesyn in the bleaker weather of the early Iron Age can hardly have been inviting; yet that probably applies to other areas where remains *have* been found. The upland limit of known Iron Age settlement in this area is being pushed a little nearer Abergwesyn by recent discoveries. By 1986 *'Brecknock Hill Forts and Roman Remains'* (RCAHM) recorded three possible defensive enclosures on the North Breconshire hills. One, now in the forests, is at the eastern edge of Cefn Trybedd Gwilym near Llanwrtyd (O.S. SN 8484 4783). In *Brycheiniog*, vol. 14, Dr C.B. Crampton reported on some interesting investigations into soil-use at Aberduhonw, on the hills by the Wye just south and east of Builth. Pollen tests suggested first Neolithic farming in clearings in the primeval forest 4,000 to 5,000 years ago; then 2,500 years ago 'Iron Age Celtic farmers characteristically settled on the local hill-summit', initiating a fresh felling of the woods.

A little-known Abergwesyn hilltop enclosure near Beulah is described later. It is very small and of quite uncertain date.

The place-name 'Dinas' usually suggests a hilltop fortification. In the immediate neighbourhood of Abergwesyn we have Pen-y-ddinas hill and Dinas farmhouse and mill near the old church of St David, Llanwrtyd, and Pengraig Dinas Fach to the west of the present road from Llanwrtyd to Abergwesyn, just north of Penybont uchaf farmhouse. North-west of Cwmdulas, Llanafan fawr, is the hill Allt y Ddinas. There are several 'Dinas' names, too, to the south-west, in the Rhandirmwyn area. It has been suggested that where hilltops are rocky, with shallow soil, ancient fortifications are harder to trace than in areas where earth banks have survived. On the other hand, the apparently total lack of such fortifications on these rocky hilltops, like Dinas, near St Paulinus' church, Ystradffîn, may indicate the name was given centuries later when the romantically citadel-like character of the hill was appreciated.

2. Roman and Dark Age Abergwesyn

Alun Llewelyn writes in the *'Shell Guide to Wales'* of the continuity of history – 'Paths across the moorlands, laid' – or we may think, reinforced – 'in many cases by Roman legionaries supervising the transport of ores, created such places as Abergwesyn, and...the drovers following where they had led, largely founded the modern banking system'. The medicinal springs at Llanwrtyd and Builth are rumoured to have been known to the Romans before Bath (Aquae Sulis) was used.

The O.S. map of Roman Britain has little to tell of this area. It shows the main roads connecting Roman stations such as Bremia (Llanio) fort on the west of the mountains, Y Gaer near modern Brecon (a major station and road junction), Alabum fort at modern Llandovery, well to the south of Llanwrtyd, and the Dolaucothi gold mines near Caio in North Carmarthenshire. But here and there through the inner area of mountain land are further traces of the Roman occupation – cross-country roads, lesser stations, and at Caerau farm, Llangamarch, near Beulah, a fort of some importance. Nash-Williams' *'Roman Frontier in Wales'* (2nd ed., revised by M.G. Jarrett) quotes the 1722 edition of Camden's *'Britannica'* (II.4) – 'It is evident that there hath been a Roman fort at Kaerau; for, besides that the name implies as much...they frequently dig up bricks there, and find other manifest sign of a Roman work'. Caerau was an intermediate station on the Roman road linking the forts at Llandovery and Castell Collen, Llandrindod. It was perched on a small but prominent rounded hill, shared now by a farmhouse, farm buildings and a medieval motte. The outline of the rectangular auxiliary fort encloses the top and sheltered eastern side of the hill. A civil settlement existed where, in fields to the north and east, 'extensive scatters of Roman pottery and building material' have been found. Nash-Williams says it may have continued into the Antonine period. A section taken through the fort in 1965 showed at the lowest level a timber building (possibly the commandant's house) which pottery fragments confirmed as of the Flavian period, that is 'associated with the work of Frontinus in South and Central Wales' (in the 70s A.D.). Over it was revealed a stone granary with floor supported on small stone pillars; this and some reconstructed ramparts were thought to be of the early second century A.D., the time of Trajan and the early reign of Hadrian. *'The Roman Frontier'* lists also, among marching camps recently found, one at Beulah, at map-reference SN 919507.

There is another Caerau not far away at Tirabad; this one used to be thought to be a Roman station of an earlier type, perhaps a campaign station built during the first penetration into the North Breconshire area.

However, this identification is now considered to be unsubstantiated. There is a 'probable practice camp' near Llwyncadwgan farm (O.S. SN 9200 4995), and camp-like enclosures at SN 9209 5017 and SN 0189 5017. An earthwork north east of Builth Castle is now thought to be possibly Roman.

Theophilus Jones refers to the Roman road, 'another branch of the Via Helena or Via Leona...from Caerfyrddin [Carmarthen] to Caerlleon Gawr or Chester' which 'ran through [Tirabad] and over the common called Llwydlo fach. Though no longer visible, tradition...preserved the recollection of it until the beginning of the eighteenth century; or at least several old persons used to assert that they had heard their parents say they had seen it and pointed out its tract'. It passed through the farm Sarnycyrtiau (Causeway of the Assemblies). Jones believed from the appearance of an 'antient road...discovered a few years back in digging turf, resembling in its materials and formation the work of the Romans', that it was a military road connecting Carmarthen with the station of Cwm in Radnorshire. It crossed the Irfon into Llangamarch at Llancamddwr, passing Caerau in that parish, and continuing through Llanafan fawr (in which parish there is a farm called Sarn Helen), Llanfihangel Bryn Pabuan and the present Newbridge-on-Wye to join Sarn Helen at Cwm in Llanyre. Jones suggests that the road passed also through Llanlleonfel and may have accounted for a component in the name of that parish.

The *Transactions of the Radnorshire Society* (1944) contains an article by G. Arbour Stephens on Roman metal-routes, several of which he thinks may have converged on the central garrison-post (and, he suggests, storage-depot) of Castell Collen near Llandrindod. Dr Stephens makes the point that the Romans were not necessarily or even probably the first people to work the silver, lead and gold mines of mid-Wales, and that the roads they used and sometimes improved upon were often 'planned and engineered by the early Celts', and well-marked by them with *carnau*, *meini hirion* and *bylchau* (passes). Waymarks would have been particularly important when the country was more wooded than it is now. The more of these monuments on or near a route, the greater the presumption of its importance. Stephens suggests a route through Caer Cerrig Croes, Newbridge-on-Wye, Llanfihangel Bryn Pabuan, Llanafan fawr and Abergwesyn to Tregaron and the Cardiganshire mines: another from Abergwesyn over to the Tywi valley at Fanog (now drowned by Llyn Brianne) and south via Ystradffîn to the gold mines of Dolaucothi: and a third following the first road to Llanafan, then continuing to Dolaucothi via Llanwrtyd and Cynghordy.

Abergwesyn has local traditions of Roman roads. One of them is said to have been the old track (cut from the rock at one point) up the spine of Cefn Fanog and over the top of that mountain to Fanog – one of those mentioned by Stephens. The last part of this track now enters a Forestry plantation and descends through the trees to the new road round the reservoir, just south of a point above the old site of Fanog.

Just below the grounds of Llwynderw in Llanddewi Abergwesyn, an old 'Roman' road strikes east through Allt y Bryn wood, where it is easier to follow, and breaks off just above a small lay-by at the side of the road from Llwynderw turn to the Pentwyn T-junction. This rarely-walked track, its first part brightened in spring by flanking clumps of daffodils, and its woodland stretch so filled in June by the improbable beauty of massed bluebells as to seem unreal, has an austere charm in winter too, especially when through black trees the red light of late afternoon shines on the dark waters of the sinuous, snowy-banked Irfon below.

If one climbs down the short path to the motor-road and walks towards the village, an old gatepost appears on the right, and through the gap the faint remains of a track making for the river at a point where the road to the village used to ford the Irfon below the confluence of the Gwesyn, continuing for a time on the opposite side of the river from that on which the present road runs. The older road crossed back, this time through the Gwesyn, opposite the churchyard of Llanfihangel. Opposite Pentwyn, a track goes down to ford the Gwesyn and start the long gradual climb up Rhiw Garreg Lwyd. This is the ancient road to Beulah along the crest of the hills. It is the one said locally to have been used by the Strata Florida monks and by the drovers, as well as by countless riders and walkers over the centuries. 'Someone' unidentified, it seems, once cut a section in the track near where it passes over Nant y Rhiw, the little stream which lower down the hill has carved out a deep narrow gully, rich in fruitful mountain-ash trees. The unnamed archaeologist was satisfied that he had found evidence of Roman road-laying in the ancient track. The old road can still be followed through the gate on Pen Rhiw Garreg Lwyd and on obscurely over boggy mountain. Through a belt of conifers Carn Paderau is reached, and the track soon becomes much clearer as it nears Aberanell in Beulah over Cefn Gardys (Cardis) with its wonderful views over wooded hills and up the Cnyffiad valley. Llanwrtyd Wells has its 'Roman road', a track branching left, uphill, from the road to Builth, shortly before the turning to Maesygwaelod farm. As the Pembrokeshire historian E.T. Lewis warns us, traditions of Roman roads do not always imply Roman construction and use. As we have seen, the Romans probably often used older tracks; ridgeways are the oldest of all. Later inhabitants 'could not always distinguish between the old and the ancient'. In the absence of further evidence, one should perhaps be contented to say that it is possible that in the three stretches of old road just described we have three sections of a very old route from the Tywi valley through Abergwesyn and on to Beulah. It is interesting that locally they all have Roman traditions, though caution should remind us that hereabouts whatever antiquities are not attributed to Druids tend to be called 'Roman'!

Both parishes of Abergwesyn have in their remoter valleys many small structures, some of quite uncertain date. Some are marked on large-scale maps as 'old sheepfold' and indeed may occasionally be just that. Some bear the name *magwyr* (walls with no remaining roof – it would have been rush thatch). Others are not marked at all. Many have been swallowed by the forests. Mediaeval summer dairy-houses, or those of later times: little sixteenth and seventeenth century crofts: shepherds' shelters of almost any period: sometimes truly ancient dwellings – probably all these are to be found in the recesses of the Abergwesyn hills. There has been little expert investigation; no-one knows for certain. One type of building may reasonably be dated to the Roman and post-Roman centuries – the circular 'Irishman's hut', the name of which connects it, possibly quite wrongly, with Goidelic inhabitants. In the upper Culent valley, just below Bwlch y Dorfa, the pass over to the Gwrâch valley (a tributary of the Tywi), and near an almost-vanished but once important track up the north-western bank of the Culent and over the pass, a modern fence bisects a faint raised circle in the ground, reputed to be one of these *cytiau Gwyddelod*. Lifting a turf in the centre of the circle revealed fire-blackened stones – a hearth? – and seemed to confirm the local tradition. The people who lived in such huts are thought to have been still mainly pastoralists, but to have practised a little agriculture where possible. How pervasively and how long pastoral tribalism survived, particularly nomadic tribalism, has become a controversial question.

Whether one could expect to find anywhere in this wild area traces of a civilised Romano-British life-style remains a moot point. Once the answer would have been a firm 'no', but positions are less entrenched now. In this district the 'Dark Ages' deserve their name, at least in so far as it implies a hiddenness, an almost total inaccessibility to the questing historian. Through chinks in the cloud a lurid light falls momentarily on two semi-legendary figures, one sinister, one heroic.

We have seen that tradition connects King Vortigern with the area. Expelled from his south British kingdom by the Anglo-Saxon allies he had trusted to help him against the Picts and Scots, and condemned by his ex-subjects for his immorality (his small harem was said to include his own daughter), Vortigern, wrote Nennius, took refuge in the hills toward St Harmon in Radnorshire. Succeeding generations of the family ruled over Gwerthrynion and Buellt. A romantic interpretation of the hoard of gold ornaments found in 1899 hidden among rocks named Cerrig Gwynion on Gwastedin Hill near Rhaeadr suggested that they belonged to one of the wives or concubines of the fugitive Vortigern.

The other figure is that of Arthur. Leland, travelling through the wild region a little to the north of our area, crossed the river Claerddu, and was told that nearby, where it passed between two little hills, 'a gigant striding was wont to wasch his handes'. This 'gigant', said local tradition, was killed by King Arthur. The king swept nearer to Abergwesyn over the hills of Llanwrthwl in pursuit of the Twrch Trwyth, the great boar of the Mabinogion. Arthur's hound Cafall left a paw-mark on a stone. Whoever tried to take the stone found that after a day and a night it returned to a cairn, thence called Carn Cafall, on the hills overlooking the Elan valley.

Did Christianity reach the remote hills of Abergwesyn in Roman times? V. Nash-Williams considers the few seventh to ninth century inscribed stones found in neighbouring parishes and listed in his *Early Christian Monuments* as 'evidence of a feebly-surviving Romanity', though this should not be taken necessarily to imply a surviving Roman Christianity. By the time these stones were carved, the great evangelising movement of the 'Age of the Saints' had taken place. (It is interesting in this context that the modern figure of St David in Llanwrtyd old church brings out the 'Romanity' of the saint.) Nash-Williams lists pillar-stones carved with ring-crosses in Llanwrtyd, Llanafan fawr, Llangamarch and Llandulas (Tirabad). The pillar-stone he describes in Llanlleonfel churchyard now stands in the church. It bears an oddly moving Latin inscription commemorating two unknown men – ''Silent in the shroud Iorwerth and Ruallaun await in peace the dread coming of the judgement''. The carved stone found on Llawdre farm, Llanwrtyd, is now in St David's church. Nash-Williams describes its carved ring-device as ''vaguely reminiscent of a penannular brooch'. Its significance remains, as he deemed it, obscure. The stone squats near the church door, enigmatic and ancient, permitting our guesses.

It was probably to the Age of the Saints that Abergwesyn owed its first church, Llanddewi, one of a group of David foundations on the right bank of the Irfon which are thought to be early 'colonies' of the monastery of St David's and therefore named after that house and its founder – 'given' to St David rather than dedicated to him in the modern sense. E.G. Bowen in *Saints, Seaways and Settlements* quotes G.R. Jones' theory that 'every Celtic church [except the hermitages] appears to have been established in a bond hamlet' – that is, a nucleated settlement of unfree workers, attached to the residence of the local lord, and rendering him dues and services. As we shall see in the next chapter, some kind of early settlement does seem likely to have existed near the church-site here.

Another of this group of churches was founded about four miles to the south-east, Llanddewi-wrth-y-Rhyd (Church of St David by the Ford) or Llanwrtyd, where the carved stone just mentioned is to be found. There are some who posit a primitive saint Gwrthyd to explain the church's name! We shall attempt later to follow the story of the churches; it should perhaps be mentioned here that the original tiny buildings would have been simpler even than those mediaeval Welsh churches which exist on some of the sites today. They would have been little more than four walls, of whatever materials came most readily to hand, a roof and an altar-stone where the Mass was celebrated.

Francis Jones in his *'Holy Wells of Wales'* (1954) lists two St David wells in Breconshire, both in this area – one in Llangamarch, where there was also a Ffynnon Gadferth (Cadferth's Well), and the other near Llanddewi Abergwesyn church. This one is referred to by Lhuyd (*'Parochialia'*, iii, 51). It is not clear where it was. Early wells are sometimes now traceable only to a damp patch in the ground. Old Llanddewi churchyard is in a damp place near the Irfon. Neither is it known how old the well was – whether it was pre- Christian, a pagan healing-well re-named. Francis Jones' list makes it clear that the Welsh David wells were second in number only to the wells of St Mary the Virgin. Did the term 'water-man' applied to St David have a more ancient and profound meaning than just a reference to the austerity of his rule? The Abergwesyn David well, by whatever name it was first known, may have preceded the David church. It could even have been one of the factors influencing the siting of the church, for the missionary monks tried to absorb and transform pagan practices like those of the ancient well-cult. Just across the Irfon was later founded the church of Llanfihangel, in a circular churchyard thought to be typical of sites used for pagan ceremonies – a church significantly named after St Michael, the warrior archangel, triumphant foe of the old gods. Lhuyd does not tell us whether the Abergwesyn David well was a healing well, but, as Francis Jones writes, 'nearly all saints' wells, and those associated with churches or chapels...are also credited with healing powers'.

Not far away, in Llanafan fawr, were Ffynnon Afan and Ffynnon Dduw (Well of God), the latter, Lhuyd writes, 'much resorted unto by the country people for the cure of Divers diseases'. The 6 inch and 25 inch O.S. maps mark 'Ffynnon *Fyw*' (Well of Life – but possibly a corruption of 'Dduw'), not far below the source of Nant Cyfyng, which cascades down behind Cwmdulas farm; the hill itself is called Esgair y Ffynnon (Ridge of the Well). There are two stone basins, about five feet by two foot six, one at the spring itself, one just below. Some of today's Llanafan residents remember being told by older inhabitants that many people used to climb up to the well to bathe there as a cure for rheumatic illnesses. The bleakness and remoteness of the situation, and the icy cold of the water, say much for the faith or desperation of those who sought there for healing; perhaps much too for the real efficacy of the spring.

Ffynnon Oer, also in Llanafan, may have been a butter-cooling well. It is marked on Rees' map of South Wales in the fourteenth century. Lhuyd mentions in Llanwrtyd Ffynnon Dyclid and Ffynnon y drewi. Probably the latter is the Ffynnon Drellwyd (Stinking Well) in whose sulphurous but health-giving waters the spa originated.

It may be that in some of the stream and hill names of Abergwesyn we have other traces of what Charles Squire called 'the oldest, lowest, most primitive religion in the world...which, crouching close to the earth, lets other creeds blow over it without effacing it'. Francis Jones, writing of well-names from animals and birds, warns against too easy an assumption that such names are of pagan religious origin. They may refer literally to the haunts of various living creatures. He does however suggest that in some cases the names may be of birds or animals sacred to the Celts. Local opinion shies away from such an interpretation of the names of natural features, which are more easily thought to commemorate homely incidents of farming life. 'Ffoes y Gaseg' (Mare's Ditch or Bog), for instance – 'No doubt there was an old mare there once that fell in the bog'; and some names were doubtless formed in just such a way. Some, too, may well be a surviving record of the animal life, wild and domestic, of these hills and valleys centuries ago – like Drum Da Gwylltion (Hill of Wild Cattle) near the desolate head-waters of the Irfon. There are certainly many such names, especially in the wild *blaenau* to the north of the present settlement. The upper Irfon has the great Rock of the Birds (Carreg yr Adar), and the mountain ridge Esgair yr Adar. Tributaries include Ffôs Tarw (Bull) and Ffôs y Iâr (Hen). To the north-east are Llyn Carw (Lake of the Stag), with Cors y Hwch (Bog of the Sow) just south of it. Away to the south-east is Carreg yr Ast (Rock of the Bitch). Further south, alongside the drovers' road, the Irfon flows through a ravine one point in which is called called 'The Wolf's Leap'; it is said to have been the spot at which a fleeing wolf bounded across the river. Foxes have done the same.

The name of the Sow recurs. Both the Cnyffiad and the Tywi valleys have a stream called Nant yr Hwch and a farm of the same name. The stream-name is probably much older than that of the homestead. Near the one in the Tywi valley is Nant y Fleiddiast (Wolf-bitch), and higher up Nant y Stalwyn (Stallion). Both these streams give their names to farms.

Other names, too, may reach back to the pagan centuries, or derive from more recent superstitions which themselves have roots in an earlier age. Such are the names containing *gwrâch* (hag). In the upper Gwesyn valley we find Carreg Wrâch, the rocky western valley-side a little above Pwll y March (The Stallion's Pool). One of the tributes of Tywi is Nant Gwrâch. How ancient are these names? One remembers that *gwrâch* was the name given in some parts of Wales to the last sheaf, the focus of many harvest rituals, and that the Hag was one of the three faces of the Earth Goddess. Nant Morwynion (Maidens' Stream) by Llawrdre, Llanwrtyd (just to the east of a hill on which are old walls locally called 'Roman') may commemorate servant-girls who did their washing in the stream of cooled butter there. And yet – another aspect of the Goddess was Y Forwyn, the Maiden. On the hills to the west of Soar y Mynydd chapel in the Camddwr valley, what are we to make of Carn y Saith Wraig, Cairn of the Seven Women?

Certainly if the monks of St David's set up a little cell-like church at what is now Abergwesyn, and another by the ford, now a bridge, at Llanwrtyd, they would have found in these rugged solitudes a stubborn paganism to contend with. A mediaeval church of Llanddewi Abergwesyn is marked on Williams Rees' map of South Wales in the fourteenth century, but no Llanfihangel. We may take it, then, that very early records do not refer to a second church. It is possible though unproven that a first tiny Michael church may have followed not long after that of St David. Willis Bund in *'The Celtic Church'* writes that the earliest known reference to a Welsh Michael church dates from 718 (in the 'Annales Cambriae'). He suggests that most Michael churches are second in antiquity to David churches only, and represent the spread of Christianity beyond lands owned by the evangelising monastery. They are thought to have been dedicated in honour of St Michael because he was traditionally the victor over paganism, and also possibly because he was associated with hills. His churches may therefore mark old places of pagan worship converted into Christian sites. Perhaps this is the reason why Llanfihangel Abergwesyn was built so near to Llanddewi. Miles of moorland and valley stretch to the west of and to the east of the other, yet here they nestled almost side by side, one on each bank of the Irfon, each at the extremity of the territory which, at some time after the Norman organisation, became its parish. In 1861 the Rev Gwesyn Jones wrote of a local tradition that the foundation stone of Llanfihangel was laid some four miles from the eventual site of the church. St Michael, however, disapproved, and every night shifted the day's work of the builders to its present site.

The story is interesting for more than one reason. It is found in many places, told of many churches, and probably indicates some real change of site, some long-forgotten conflict or debate. Perhaps here the wish to provide churches far enough apart to cater each for its own wide area was at war with the necessity to guard, with the help of St Michael, against a resurgence of half-quelled paganism at an ancient and powerful place of worship. Then again, there does seem some faint evidence for the second Abergwesyn church having originally existed, or at least been planned, further away from Llanddewi. It is a story which jumbles up elements from an early period of colonisation with later eras of ecclesiastical organisation. In the upper reaches of the Cnyffiad valley, about two and a half miles from Llanfihangel churchyard, stands Trawsgyrch, once a substantial farmhouse. A former barn there was called Ysgubor y Ddegwm (Tithe Barn). It is so listed in the Tithe Schedule of 1842. (It has no connection with the little nineteenth tithe barns of the two churches, barns which stood near them and still survive.) The track from Trawsgyrch to the ruined farmhouse of Cefngilfach, overlooking the upper Camarch valley, passes near a rock called Craig y Llan. *Llan* was the name given to the original enclosure and burial-ground of the monastic colony, and thereafter to the church which followed. Caution is needed. *Llan* can also mean simply an enclosure, not necessarily ecclesiastical. But the name is suggestive here. A local tradition, very vague, says that Dôlcegyrn, a little ruined farmhouse on the Llanafan fawr bank of the Camarch further downstream, has 'something to do' with Craig y Llan and the tithe barn. As the crow flies, Dôlcegyrn is about four miles (just the distance in the St Michael legend) from the known site of Llanfihangel Abergwesyn, which, incidentally, was for centuries a chapelry of Llanafan fawr.

The nineteenth century Beulah historian D.L. Wooding copied into a notebook an entry he found on the cover of a parish register, or possibly a lost churchwarden's notebook — '1775. 12 Sept. Agreed that the parish church should be rebuilt somewhere towards the lower part of Abergwesyn (at Dôlcegyrn?).' This never happend, but it is interesting to find it being discussed in the late eighteenth century. The local legend, on the other hand, takes us back to the time of the original foundation.

Saint Afan, Bishop Afan or possibly Ieuan of Llanafan fawr, will be discussed in another chapter. He is said to have been murdered by raiding Danes, possibly in the tenth century. Viking raids on Wales occurred between the mid-ninth and late eleventh century, religious houses being a frequent target, but it was the coastlands that were mainly affected. There may however have been some penetration of the heartland, using the main rivers and thence thrusting inland for hit-and-run attacks. W.H. Howse records a Radnorshire tradition of 'Denes' (Danes?) who 'ploughed the hills' and were said to have been 'red men'; but few indeed are such suggestions of Viking settlement in mid-Wales.

3. Abergwesyn in the Lordship of Buellt

No-one writing even in the most general way about any part of southern Wales in the Middle Ages could be other than heavily indebted to the work of Professor William Rees, whose *'South Wales and the March, 1284-1415'*, *'Historical Atlas of Wales'* and *'Map of South Wales in the Fourteenth Century'* are based on a mass of MS evidence on which he worked for many years. Plate 28 of the 'Atlas', *Wales Before the Normans*, shows Buellt as a *cantref* (a major administrative division) of a large mid-Welsh *gwlad*. Buellt was subdivided into the *cymydau* (commotes) of Penbuallt, Treflys, Inan and Irfon, each with its own administrative centre. That for the commote of Irfon is marked fairly high upstream at a spot which the O.S. historical map of Britain from about 850 to about 1050 pinpoints as Abergwesyn. A *maerdref* site is given at map-reference SN 854526, near the church-sites, on flat land near the confluence of the Gwesyn and Irfon, and just downstream from the junction of the road over the mountains from Tregaron and the coastlands. At the *maerdref* site would have been the local courthouse, the *mansio* (a name with a Roman ring), manned by local officials and used as a royal residence when, in the earlier Middle Ages, the local ruler and his court went on their twice-yearly progress round the commotes. They were maintained at each centre by food-and-drink contributions, mainly from freemen, and by fuel and repair-work provided by bondmen. Later, when royal progresses became far less frequent, food dues were replaced by money dues.

In each *cantref* and *cwmwd*, the *maerdref* lands were the 'ancient demesne', the private family lands of the *gwlad*-ruler. Where the lands were suitable, they were brought under cultivation as a home farm and worked in quasi-feudal fashion by bondmen, who lived in the *maerdref* hamlet near the *mansio* or the *llys* (the major royal residence) and were supervised by the *maer y biswail* (dung bailiff) — hence the name *tref* or hamlet of the *maer*. Whether such a hamlet existed at the Abergwesyn site can only be conjectural. Some remote commote centres were little more than posts for the collection of dues. Yet Abergwesyn did have the distinction of being a little trading-centre on the edge of the mountains, on the old road over to the coast. Later, when Anglo-Norman rulers had succeeded Welsh ones, this trading-centre still remained. William Rees' map of the area in the fourteenth century suggests that it was in the area of the *maerdref* site. Apart from Builth itself, Abergwesyn is the only such trading-centre to be marked in the lordship of Buellt (as the old *cantref* had then become). Professor Rees writes that a payment or 'cense' of one shilling a year was exacted for the privilege of making or selling any form of merchandise within the *patria* or Welshry (the upland area of the Anglo-Norman lordship, continuing to a large extent under a Welsh type of administration). In Builth, these small traders or 'chensers' were called 'portmen', and their trading-tax 'portmanrent'. Abergwesyn was allowed a few of these traders.

Theophilus Jones, writing of Builth's position on a main road from Herefordshire through Radnorshire and then across Llwydlo common to Carmarthen, refers to a tax levied at Builth castle in the reigns of Edward I and Edward II for the accommodation and protection of travellers — *porthant berwyn*, a tax on alien merchants or drovers. He calls Builth castle therefore 'the first turnpike house erected in Breconshire', and says the tax survived in his day (the early nineteenth century), having been 'ascertained and limited' in the time of Charles II.

The Welsh word *porthmyn* is often associated specifically with drovers. The Rhiw y Porthmyn, an old track climbing the hill behind Nantystalwyn in the Tywi valley and leading (though now obscured by Forestry plantations) over to the upper Irfon, did form part of a cattle-route from the Strata Florida area, but one cannot discount a possible earlier connection with the mediaeval *porthmyn* of Builth, pedlars rather than cattle-dealers, who carried their packs to the remote homesteads of the upper Irfon and Tywi in the furthest recesses of the Welshry, as later packmen were to do.

To revert to the days of Welsh rule: the *maerdref* in the sense of a bond hamlet, where it occurred, would probably have been the only sort of village to be found at all in these uplands in mediaeval times. A.H. Williams in *'Introduction to the History of Wales'* describes such a *tref* of bondmen (settlers who on their arrival had no right to tribal land) and the *tref* of freemen. The bond hamlet was a close-knit settlement whose members ploughed the available arable communally with a *cyfer* (ploughing team), and were allocated *erwau* (strips of land in an open field). They had a village smithy, village kiln for drying corn, village herd of cattle with its herdsman, even sometimes a village bath-house. But Abergwesyn as it has been for centuries — a countryside of scattered hill farms — is stamped with another pattern, that of the *tref* or township of freemen, native Welsh tribesmen with widely-dispersed holdings. This is the typical pattern of rural Wales.

The way of life among the Abergwesyn hills would not be likely to have suffered much interruption from the various changes between Welsh and Anglo-Norman rule. By 1100 Buellt was a marcher lordship of the powerful de Braoses, lords of Radnor. It returned to Welsh rule when it was ceded to Llwelyn the Great in 1234, but later passed again into Norman hands. At the Treaty of Woodstock in 1247 Buellt became a Crown lordship. Llwelyn the Last regained it, but in 1277 it reverted to the English Crown. In 1282, Llywelyn, on his way to rouse South Wales for his renewed battle against the English, had some success in the lordship, but failed to take Builth castle. Separated from his main force, he was killed at Cilmeri, where a monument to him now stands. His slayer did not at first know who the victim was. By 1284 the Edwardian conquest was complete.

The town of Llanfair-ym-Muellt (Builth) itself, and its immediate environs, experienced at least some of the usual shaping of an Anglo-Norman 'Englishry'. The pattern included castle, Norman church, trading-centre and a degree of manorial cultivation. The story of the castle is told in some detail in Lord Glanusk's notes to Jones' county history (edition of 1911), and by C.J. Spurgeon in *Brycheiniog*, vol XVIII. A survey of 1324 refers to 40 acres of demesne arable at threepence an acre, ten acres of meadow at twelve pence, a ferry, a forest (Talevan), four mills, pannage of hop and various dues. There was at that time 'no villenage here'. The castle was not always occupied; William Rees quotes an example from the year 1343 of the re-sale (at a profit) of an annual tribute of cows which were not at the time needed to stock the larder.

The boundaries of the lordship of Buellt coincided with those of the former *cantref*, the manor and the later hundred. Ministers' accounts for 1344-67, the reign of Edward III, include references to 'Irvon Commote' and 'Aberguessin'. Most of the lordship was wild upland Welshry. In this area the Anglo-Norman overlords, or the Crown, were only too pleased to let well relatively alone, provided that dues were regularly collected and services obediently performed. As Rees writes, it was alien administration, rather than alien rule as such, which was resented. Changes were gradual, but some did come. Over the centuries the tribal life, and the distinction between bond and free, became blurred, as Norman ideas of individual tenure gradually penetrated the remoter areas.

There were other changes, some in church organisation, like the gradual definition of ecclesiastical parishes, and the coming of the Cistercians to Strata Florida. We shall later see how these things were to affect Abergwesyn.

Rees' map of fourteenth century South Wales shows, a few miles to the east of Llanddewi Abergwesyn, stretching over the Cnyffiad and Camarch valleys towards what is now Beulah, the Forest of Talyfan, and at its eastern edge, on a probable route to Llanafan fawr, the lord's demesne of Talyfan. Often such demesnes took over the old *maerdref* sites, where the Welsh chieftain's private lands had once been. Talyfan is not at Treflys commote-centre, however, but at a point where now stands the farmhouse of Dôlyfan, behind which a lane leads to a scatter of farms and into the Camarch valley. The map suggests that this was an established route in the fourteenth century, continuing southwards down the straight Roman road past Caerau and on to Tirabad. The old Cefn Cardis road over the hills from Abergwesyn crossed the Camarch-Caerau-Tirabad route where Beulah is now found. Rees shows also the routes from Abergwesyn over Cefn Fanog into the Tywi valley, and across the mountains to Tregaron, and suggests as a 'probable route' a road up the Irfon valley to Abergwesyn, starting from a junction south-west of the present Llanwrtyd Wells. Another route, he thinks, may have followed the line of the present A483 to Beulah.

A.G. Bradley, who loved this area as he knew it at the beginning of the present century, called Abergwesyn 'a place at the end of all things'. He meant it in no derogatory sense. He was a sensitive and romantic traveller, but he was wrong about Abergwesyn. The place must surely have arisen, grown and survived partly because in mile after mile of 'brown on the map' it was not only the westernmost outpost on this side of the Cambrian mountains, but the gateway to an ancient route across them — probably to more than one, for the continuation of the Cefn Fanog track across the hills and rivers to Llanddewi Brefi is said to be of great antiquity. Abergwesyn's significance was precisely that it was *not* the end, but the way through.

Forests, in the sense of hunting preserves, had been important in early Wales long before the coming of the Normans. On the wastelands of the commotes the *gwlad*-ruler and his court started the hunting season, which afterwards the rest of the community could partake in. The Normans developed the system they found, defining forest boundaries in wide upland areas and establishing forest courts, with sometimes ruthless laws, under the administration of the forester or of the seneschal of the castle. Here, Talyfan forest, as one of those in which Rees calls the 'inner line of lordships', and one which was in some periods a possession of the Crown, would have been one in which the lord had more extensive rights over pasture, wood and beech-mast for pigs than he had, for instance, in those on the Welsh-English border. A vestige of this ancient forest is to be found in Fforest, a wooded hill beside the Camarch near Dôlaeron farm in Beulah. A scramble up through the trees of Fforêst hill leads to an open hilltop on which rises the strange little earthwork of Dôlaeron Twdin. If it was a castle it was certainly a tiny one; Clark's *'Mediaeval Military Architecture'* comments that there was no room in it for anything but a wigwam! Cathcart King says of the ditch outside the little oblong ringwork, 'The labour of cutting this ditch in the hard rock must have been considerable; the castle itself is disproportionately small'. It is, however, perched high, commanding a sweep of countryside; whoever built it must have valued it as a look-out.

The ridge on which Dôlaeron Twdin stands can be clearly seen from another and higher-placed little ringwork (at O.S. 896 521), which stands out after ploughing around it. It is on a hill 1130 feet high, part of Cefn Gardis ridge, and very near the 'ancient road'. In form it is an imperfect circle about seventeen yards in diameter; the centre is slightly raised. The surrounding earthwork is about four feet high; there are faint traces of an external ditch. The date of the structure is unknown.

There are other little fortifications in the area, often referred to as minor castles, but of which little is definitely known. Just outside Builth Wells is Caerberis, where now a hotel stands, on a steep spur of land above the Wye. Llysdinam has a 'weak and small half-ringwork' at Penllys. At Caerau (where the Romans are known to have had a station) is 'a small tall motte' — Cathcart King says that the farm may have destroyed any bailey. All these are sites with other associations than those with the Anglo-Normans. The recurrence of the element *llys* in Llysdinam and Penllys, for instance, stresses the probability of a 'palace' or main court-house having been here. Treflys is the name of another commote and its centre.

The practice of farming out the profitable items in the various lordships, such as mills, fisheries and forests, and even making leases of the entire lordship, gathered force during the fourteenth century. It happened here in Buellt, and was probably accelerated by the series of fourteenth century epidemics collectively called the Black Death. Little detail is known of the course of the plague in this district, but it seems to have passed into the counties to the west by 1349. Theophilus Jones tells a story of one plague which raged in Builth at some unspecified period. At Nant yr Arian (Money Brook) about a mile to the west of the town, 'the country people who supplied the place with provisions put them down here, and were paid for them by money dropped into the water to prevent the spread of infection'.

By the Act of Union in 1536 the Crown and Marcher lordships of Wales were merged with the shire. A new county of 'Brekenock' was formed, including the 'lordships, towns, parishes, commotes and cantreds', of which 'Buelthe' was one. In 1542 the boundaries of hundreds were defined by commission, J.P.s and a Custos Rotulorum for the county appointed, and the stewards of manors empowered to hold courts leet. Builth remained a clear-cut unit. We find it still referred to as a 'lordship' long after the marcher lords had become a memory.

Some of the later story of the Manor of Builth, with Talyfan Forest, may be learned from the transcription of a mass of documents of different periods in John Lloyd's *'Historical Memoranda'*, volume 1 (1899). In 1550 Edward VI granted the lordship of Builth to Sir William Herbert, 'Knight of the Garter and Master of our Horse' — the lands of

'Tallawyn' are mentioned. Not long after, in 1582, Queen Elizabeth I made a lease for twenty-one years at 6s 8d a year of the herbage and pannage of the Forest of Tallavan ('formerly held by Richard Lloyd') with all its rights to David John ap John Lloyd, a distant ancestor of the writer, who thinks the Forest must have been very well known, 'as it was thought unnecessary to give any description of its boundaries'.

The Lloyds we shall hear of later, as one of the old families of Llanwrtyd and Abergwesyn. The David Lloyd here referred to was the eldest son of John Lloyd of Tywi, Abergwesyn, and Porthycrwys, Llanynis, whose effigy is to be seen in the porch of Builth church, with an inscription telling us he was 'squire to the body and servant' to the Queen, whose father he had served in France and Scotland. John Lloyd, who died in 1585, was steward of the manor of Builth under the Earl of Essex, and 'the first Sheriff and first Justice of the Peace that ever dealt in this Lordship after the division of Wales into Shire ground'. His father Thomas Lloyd was Lord Lieutenant of the county for forty years.

Later lessees of the Forest of Talyfan were John Wells, scrivener, of London, and Richard Budd of London, gentleman. In 1593 the lease returned to David Lloyd and his descendants until 1663, but was assigned to others. The last document known to the compiler of the 'Memoranda' was a grant of 1686 from James II to Cristopher Favell and Thomas Young, gentlemen, of the 'lordship and manor of Buelt and all the hamlets, parishes, villages, rents and customs, rent of assize, rent of burgage, demesne land and forest land called Tallavon, and all toll of the vill of Buelt' together with all other tolls and lands except a previously granted 'mill in Southirvon'. The rent of the manor of Builth was about £68 together with £20 for 'a certain Comortha there every second year' — a commuted form of the old tribute of cows. Certain profits and privileges of the manor were reserved to the Crown, including the 'patronage of all rectories, churches, vicarages, chapels' and the royalties of any gold or silver mines.

Theophilus Jones tells us how the manor of Builth came into the possession of the Garth branch of the vast Gwyn(ne) family. One of the grantees in mortgages raised during the seventeenth century was Sir Edmund Sawyer. By his daughter's marriage to Sir Thomas Williams, the mortgage passed into the hands of the Williamses of Llangoed, nearby. The manor of Builth was bought from Sir Thomas Williams, first baronet of Eltham, by the Gwynnes in what Jones euphemistically calls 'a circuitous manner'. Mr Gwyn of Garth was Sir Thomas' estate agent. Acting for his employer, he mortgaged the estate to Mr Gunter of Trefecca. Landowners preferred a docile tenantry who paid up without question, so Rees Gwyn, as foreman of the jury at the court leet, ardently defended the rights of the 'turbulent' tenants of the manor against the claims of the lord, thus depreciating its value as an investment. Discouraged, Sir Thomas sold the equity of redemption of the mortgage to Mr Gunter, who was soon afterwards seen in his true colours as a trustee for Rees Gwyn. When Gwyn had succeeded in becoming the lord of the manor, he stood for no nonsense from the tenants!

Rees Gwyn's son, Judge Marmaduke Gwynne, husband of a £20,000 heiress, came into great possessions in the hundred of Builth and elsewhere. As lords of the manor the Gwynnes did not own all the property within its confines. Over the years farms had been sold to diverse owners. But the Gwynnes had certain rights and privileges in the whole manor, including that of holding the manorial courts. In 1704 'aggrieved tenants and inhabitants of the lordship of Builth' took legal advice on their complaints against the lord of the manor, Marmaduke Gwynne, Esq. (Several members of the family had this name.) John Lloyd reproduced the answer in his *'Memoranda'*. The subjects range from the amount of heriot payable on a death to regulations for street stalls in Builth, and the nuisance of a 'fishpool cross the highway on the hill'. Tenants were to be toll-free in consideration of '£2.13.4 yearly paid to the lord'. They might fish any stream adjoining their own land, make watercourses from the commons to water their lands, and 'dig for stones and tyles in the wastes and mountain for repairing and building their houses' (marks of this quarrying are still to be found near some of Abergwesyn's hill farmhouses). They were to have 'common pasture and turbary', and 'build little houses on the commons according to their ancient custom' — a particularly interesting clause in view of Abergwesyn's many tiny unidentified ruins in the upland wilds. The lord had to get a royal charter if he wanted to make a rabbit warren on a common, and he might not spoil the herbage or prevent tenants killing trespassing rabbits. The 'custom of the gavell kind in Kent' held good — 'the father to the bough and the son to the plough' (meaning the heir of an executed man might inherit). The lord might not hunt nor fowl across a freeholder's land except in pursuit of a 'vermin of prey' such as a fox. Juries at the court baron had to be made up from bystanders. Petty constables were to be chosen by them, and so were keepers of the village pounds, 'the parishioners being at the charge of making and keeping the several pounds in their respective parishes *and this by our custom as well as common law'*. The force of custom is repeatedly emphasized.

On the third and fourth of April 1823 the Gwynne of Garth and Llanelwedd estate, including the lordship of Builth, was put up for auction at the Castle Hotel, Brecon. It had been thrown into Chancery as the result of a legal dispute. It was described as compromising 'the Manor of Builth and about 110,000 acres of waste land and hills, and Freehold Farms containing 4,400 acres of meadow and pasture land, and the Park Wells' (near Builth). The 1,700 acres unsold were auctioned on 15 August 1823. John Lloyd gives the list of property in the Receiver's account for the year ending Lady Day 1823. It was still a substantial estate, but much of the original property had been sold earlier, including, it seems, that in Abergwesyn. Llanddewi Abergwesyn paid 10s 3d and Llanfihangel £1.0.7d as chief rent to the lord. After the Gwynnes, the lordship and manor of Builth became the property of the Bailey family of Glanusk. On 18 December 1984, many acres of wild and beautiful manorial mountain land, now called 'Abergwesyn Common', were sold to the National Trust by the Hon.E.S.J. Legge-Bourke, a contemporary representative of the Glanusk family.

Theophilus Jones says that in this manor there were no copyhold tenures, and that the chief rents were collected in his day by the parish officers. William Rees found that the chief rents had developed from from the *comorth*, which in Buellt was a payment for all annual rents and services, and was 'the only contribution of the freemen' there, who paid no other rent for their lands. Jones' account of 'the payments to the lord and the customs in this manor, which is co-extensive with the hundred' reinforces one's impressions of the separateness of this area. They were, he says, 'some of them singular, and the meaning of *all* of them not clearly comprehensible'. What, for instance, were *Maccwyn* and *Mabryddiaeth*? The former, he thought, must stand for *Tal yn lle magu cwn yr arglwydd* (payment for exemption from rearing and breeding dogs for the lord), a due of 2s 1d at Michaelmas yearly, mysteriously charged on one tenement only, Cefn brith, in Penbuallt township of Llangamarch. As for *Mabryddiaeth*, he thought it might be 'synonymous with *Maboliaeth*, infancy', and be a payment on the heir's coming of age and into possession of his estate. This was charged on the lands south of the Irfon, in the old commote of Treflys, and on Llysdinam in the commote of Inan, but not on certain lands in Llangamarch parish — the township of Brynrhydd, the tenements of Bryncarthog and Cefngast, or the hamlet of Clawddmadog near Llanwrtyd. Evidence for these exemptions he found in 'old presentments' before local courts. In one of 1646 (Rees Gwyn was foreman of the jury on this occasion) it was stated that by custom of the lordship no man's son was to be summoned to do fealty within the court if his father owned lands in the lordship and was still alive. The sons were to be called *Gwrthkinffiaid o Fraint*, a phrase Jones greets with exclamation marks and admits to finding formidable, but finally transforms into *Wrth cyn(t) piaid [piawd] braint* (by primeval possession of the privilege — that is, exempted by prescriptive right).

Perhaps the most interesting of the dues Jones records for this lordship is that of *Tâl diestyn*. Taking possession of an estate involved, under the laws of Hywel Dda, *côf-llys*, the recollection or evidence of the court on matters determined before them, and *ysdyn wialen*, the delivery of a rod to the heir. This practice was still permitted, writes Jones, by some Norman lords, but they 'ingrafted upon it' their tenet of the lord's original ownership of the land, and denied the right of the heir to succeed automatically, some of them levying heavy fines for the investiture by rod. In the hundred of Builth this gave rise to a keen sense of grievance, and 'several of the tenants there compounded with the lords for the exemption from this fine, by payment of an annual sum...known and paid at this day under the term of *Tâl di-estyn*'. Jones points out that where the ancient custom survived, there were no deeds to be found before the establishment of the shire system in Wales. It seems therefore that the elusiveness of early deeds relating to Abergwesyn property may be due in part at least to the late survival of such ancient customs. Jones refers to primitive methods of property-transfer mentioned in the wills of certain inhabitants of Llanwrthwl nearby. One holding for instance, was left 'after the manner accustomed in the said time [1514], in the presence and oversight of four neighbours'. As late as the mid-seventeenth century another Llanwrthwl will refers to the conveyance of lands there without any deed 'according to the ancient manner, in the presence of three or four neighbours'.

4. Churches and Clergy

The *'Taxatio'* of Pope Nicholas IV 'furnishes', as Theophilus Jones writes, 'a true test of antiquity' of the parishes contained in it. Edward I was granted a tithe of church emoluments towards the cost ogf mounting a crusade to the Holy Land, and between 1288 and 1291 a list was made of the parishes at that date and the contribution due from each. From the *'Taxatio'* we find that 'Llanavan', of which Llanfihangel Abergwesyn was a dependent chapel, and 'langamaith' (Llangamarch), of which Llanddewi Abergwesyn and Llanwrtyd were chapels, were aready parishes in the late thirteenth century. Both were assessed at £13.6.8.

Lhuyd's note on Llanafan, at the end of the seventeenth century, derives the name of the parish from 'Hugh ap Avan ap Cedig ap Cyneddau hedig a Penllin ei fam, Bishop of Lincoln in the year 1363 supposed to have founded this church and to be buried here'. (Lhuyd sent a questionnaire to informants in the various parishes, so this represents what was thought locally in the late seventeenth century). Theophilus Jones writes that some pedigrees make Afan the first cousin of St David (so, much earlier than a Welsh-descended Hugh ap Afan of Lincoln). He quotes Giraldus' story of divine vengeance on a profanation of the church of St Afan by one of the lords of Radnor in the time of Henry I. Having slept in the church and quartered his dogs there, he woke up blind and his dogs mad. He redeemed himself in the Holy Wars by rushing to his death in the forefront of battle against the Saracens.

Jones discusses the difficulty of dating this unknown early bishop and martyr, whom he tentatively identifies with the bishop Ieuan listed by Browne Willis. Ieuan was bishop for one day only, and was said to have been 'murdered by the Danes in one of their irruptions into Wales, in a meadow on the Whefri side ... where a maen hir of about six feet was placed' and remains. The saint's undated tombstone in the church bears the deeply incised inscription, 'Hic Jacet Sanctus Avanus Episcopus'. We have seen that a local well bore his name. There is a tradition that he once preached under an oak-tree at Derwen Afan house in the parish. The old rectory was called 'Perth y Sant' (the Saint's Hedge), and a stream and a glen seem also to be called after St Afan — Nant yr Esgob (bishop) and Cwm yr Esgob. Hadden and Stubbs believed that a see did briefly exist here, the bishop's seat having been transferred from Llanbadarn fawr, near Aberystwyth.

The *'Valor Ecclesiasticus'* of Henry VIII lists the Llangamarch prebend of the collegiate church of Abergwili, grouping with it the chapels of 'Llanseynffrede Rayder and Laviched [Llanwrtyd?]'. There is no mention of Llanddewi Abergwesyn. The vicarage was worth £8.14.5

with a tithe of 17s 5d. Dr Leyson, rector of Llanafan fawr, had 'tithes, oblations and other emoluments' to the value of £9.8.7, with a tithe of 18s 10 halfpenny. No reference is made to Llanfihangel Abergwesyn or the other chapels of this huge parish.

The mediaeval churches of Abergwesyn, which may have replaced or extended the even tinier original structures we have already discussed, were of that simplest style, beautifully appropriate to Welsh hill-country, and often slightingly described as 'barn-like'. C.F. Cliffe wrote in his *'Book of South Wales'* (second edition, 1848) of the twin churches 'on opposite knolls' near the confluence of the Gwesyn and Irfon. 'Llanddewi is the very rudest church we have seen in Wales; no better than a cottage thirty feet by fifteen [Dr Radford thought it slightly larger], with three small common shutter windows, and without a belfry. There are only 143 souls in this immense mountain parish. [Llanfihangel] is almost equally primitive'. Llanddewi was said to be the smallest church in the diocese, a distinction now claimed by Alltmawr.

Dr Ralegh Radford thinks the remains of Llanddewi, still to be seen in its ancient churchyard, are those of a small church of possibly the thirteenth century. An old yew and a great crab-apple tree rise amid the lush grass and wild flowers of Llanddewi churchyard. At Llanfihangel no vestige of the mediaeval church is to be found. It was replaced in 1871, as we shall say, by another, now demolished. Scattered Victorian tiles have long disappointed. There are ancient yew-trees here too. Over the Irfon one can see the trees of Llanddewi churchyard, the yew black on shades of green in summer. It is literally only a stone's throw away — a mighty throw, but stories claim it has been done. Between the two churchyards, on the east bank of the Irfon, is the little white Independent chapel, Moriah.

Further down the Irfon valley, the old church of Llanddewi-wrth-y-rhyd still stands, much restored in 1862, but preserving its ancient simplicity. Services are oftener held in the modern church of St James in the present village. The old church of St David used to have more houses near it in earlier centuries. It stands now alone, in its large circular courtyard full of gravestones, some simple, some overpowering, some ugly and some of great charm. One of the most touching inscriptions is that to the 'two Catherine daughters' of Thomas and Elizabeth Thomas. He was the smith of Gorwydd, Llangamarch. The first little Catherine died aged one month in January 1870, the second in March 1871 aged three months. Their Daniel was only nine weeks old when he too died.

The wide south porch of the church has been thought to have been possibly a chantry chapel. Otherwise, the shape of the church is like that of other hill-churches, the simple expression of a simple impulse, with nave and chancel in one, though here the shallow chancel is narrower than the nave and slightly asymmetrical in relation to it. Mrs G.H. Dawson in *'The Churches of Breckonshire'* suggests that the chancel may have been an addition. The pine partition at the west end has been removed, and against the west wall stands a fine life-size figure of St David, carved in oak by Ted Folkard, a sculptor who lives in the district. Through the plain glass of the east window the mountainside makes its own patterns, colours changing with the seasons. A splendid shiny black stove stands midway up the north side of the nave. A portrait and inscription remind us that William Williams, hymn-writer of the Methodist Revival, was once curate here. The adventurous career of one of the Lloyds of nearby Dinas — Captain John Lloyd of the East India Company — is remembered on a wall-tablet. In the south wall, between porch and chancel, a small opening lead to a stone rood-stair in the thickness of the wall. Mrs Dawson comments on the massive ironwork in the hinges of the old church-door — the closed-up west end one — and the blocked or altered windows, including two old ones with round-arched heads. Dr Ralegh Radford suggests that they were originally of about 1500. He notes the moulding of the south door, and the chamfered angles of the outer arch of the south porch. Recently another treasure has been added to the church, an icon of the Trinity, the work of the vicar, Brian Bessant, in memory of a young girl who met with a tragic death.

None of the old churches of the Gwesyn and Irfon valleys was to the taste of the county historian. He saw 'nothing worthy of remark or observation' in Llanddewi Abergwesyn,' said that the mediaeval church of Llanifihangel contained 'nothing interesting', called Llanwrtyd church 'this miserable fabric', and ridiculed what he thought its only interesting feature, an external wall-tablet to the memory of 'an old woman of the name of Jones', a benefactress of the parish.

Theophilus Jones did, however, make an interesting remark about the early history of the Abergwesyn parishes. Writing of the parish of Tirabad (Abbot's Land), he claimed that Rhys ap Griffith, Prince of South Wales, granted Tirabad and all or part of its neighbouring parishes to the Cistercian monastery of Ystrad Fflûr (Strata Florida) in Cardiganshire, which he founded in 1164. Jones' interpretation of the grant, reproduced in Dugdale's *'Monasticon'* with its place-names 'dreadfully mangled and disfigured', is that Strata Florida owned, amongst other lands, 'Llanwrthwl, part of Llanavan Vawr, the whole of Llanvihangel Abergwessin, Llanddewi Abergwessin and Llanwrtyd, part of Llangammarch,... the whole of the present parish of Tyr yr Abad and part of Llandeilo'r Fan'. He goes on to say that much of this territory was lost 'either in consequence of intestine commotion or by exchange', leaving the monastery with a little land 'south of the Irfon and on the borders of Carmarthenshire'. Jones' statements, though confidently made, and worthy of respect as coming from a cautious lawyer and conscientious historian, have not yet been found to be supported by reliable primary sources. Stephen Williams prints an appendix to *'The Cisercian Abbey of Strata Florida'* (1889) a charter of Henry VI in 1426, a transcription of a copy of a copy, confirming earlier grants to Strata Florida of lands including 'the whole land which is between Tywy and Yrfon... also the whole land which is called Elennyth'. Both of these areas are distinguished from 'the pasture also of Comet Deudor' (Cwmdeuddwr in West Radnorshire). The old name Elenydd, revived for the middle mass of the Cambrian mountains, may formerly have referred to the more northerly part of the Elan valley; it is uncertain. The 'land between Tywy and Yrfon' must surely mean Llanddewi Abergwesyn; but so far other evidence of Strata Florida's ownership is lacking.

The Glanusk edition of the county history, in the 'Later Particulars' added by its editor, states that the two mediaeval churches of Abergwesyn were 'served by a monk from the Abbey of Strata Florida', and quotes the local belief that Cae Paderau (Field of Paternosters), now hidden in plantations on Llwynderw Hill, was the spot where the monk on his way over from Strata Florida (about ten miles across the hills) would first catch sight of Abergwesyn, and recite his paternosters. Certainly local place-name traditions support a connection with the monastery. The ancient Cefn Cardis route is sometimes called 'the monk's road', and said to have been the way to Tirabad grange and its now lost chapel of Llanddewi-Llwyn-y-Fynwent. The track goes over Banc Paderau, the Hill of Paternosters, on which is the round barrow called Carn Paderau.

Strata Florida may well have had at one time rights of pasture, if no more, over the wild hills in the north of Abergwesyn, as it did over so much of the hill-country. The monks probably summered their flocks and herds in the Tywi and Irfon *blaenau*, and built little dairy-houses for the making of butter and cheese. It is interesting that the Stedman family, who during the sixteenth century became the owners of Strata Florida itself, and began to build up a considerable estate out of its lands, seem to have had much to do with Abergwesyn. The secular successors to the monks of Strata Florida (the Stedmans, and after them the Powells of Nanteos), as we shall find later in discussing the old estates, owned at least some of the Llanddewi Abergwesyn lands claimed by unproven tradition to have once belonged to the Cistercians. In the Cwmgwili MSS at the National Library of Wales, is an agreement of May 1682 between Thomas William Rees, yeoman, of Llanddewi Abergwesyn, and John Stedman, Esq., of Dôlgaer, Llangammarch (where there lived a branch of the Strata Florida family), relating to tithes of 'cheese, lambs and wool arising and growing on his land for two years, paying to the said John Stedman £3.2s annually'. Perhaps this Stedman was simply the farmer of the tithes.

The earliest known incumbent of Llangamarch with Llanwrtyd and Llanddewi Abergwesyn dates from the first decade of the fifteenth century — Sir John Lewis or Sir John ap Gwilym Lloyd. Of the Llanafan priests-in-charge, who were responsible for Llanfihangel Abergwesyn, the first named by Theophilus Jones is John ap Morgan in 1486. When he resigned in 1491, his successor, Lewis ap Meredith, had to pay him four marks a year out of his emoluments till John could obtain another preferment.

It is doubtful whether the Reformation made much immediate difference to the religious life of thie remote area. The sort of religion held and practised here was probably like that which Professor Glanmor Williams calls 'a mass of traditional assumptions and practices which could be, and were, maintained largely intact notwithstanding official changes in worship and belief which the government of the day might seek to impose'. 'Habit rather than conviction was the mainspring' of this 'dimly apprehended faith'. Perhaps this is part of the explanation for the lack of traces of Catholic recusansy here, in an area which would seem ideal for the survival of pockets of adherents of the old faith. There is an apparent built-in hiding-place in one Llanafan farmhouse (Penybanc), and a suggestion that it is a priest's hole, but few indeed are such traditions in the district. There do not seem to have been any local Catholic gentry to set a lead and give shelter; possibly the nearest known recusant gentry-family in the years of persecution was that of Gunter of Gwenddwr, over the Epynt, on the slopes of the Wye valley.

Among the early post-Reformation clergy responsible for the chapelries of Llanddewi Abergwesyn and Llanwrtyd was the curate from 1576 to 1631, Thomas Howel, father of the celebrated Howel brothers of Cefnbryn, Llangammarch: Thomas, bishop of Bristol, and James, traveller, diplomat, and author of 'Epistolae Hoelianae', Dodona's Grave' and many other works. It was then Thomas Howel senior was presented to a Carmarthenshire living that he married the granddaughter of another local celebrity, Thomas Huet, chantor of St David's cathedral and translator of the Book of Revelations in the Salesbury Testament. Huet built the modest mansion of Tymawr in Llysdinam. In 1578, acting as his brother's administrator, Rees Huet, gentleman, presented to the living of Llanafan fawr (and so to the care of Llanfihangel Abergwesyn) one Richard Meredith, whose daughter married one of the local gentry, Richard Williams of Parc-ar-Irfon near Builth.

At the coming of the Commonwealth, Llanafan and its chapelries passed from the care of a vicar ejected for delinquency into that of Evan Bowen, a mason. Jones makes him sound an ignorant lout, but Pennar Davies in *Brycheiniog*, vol.III, writes that though Bowen had a very limited knowledge of English, he was an experienced itinerant 'who preached fluently and persuasively in Welsh'. A transcript of the old register of Llanafan, quoted by R. Tudur Jones in *Brycheiniog*, vol.VIII, throws some light on the period in this area, as churchmen saw it. After Vicar Williams' ejection, there were at first no baptisms, marriages or burials, and no services except some in private houses, conducted by curates. They 'buried upon their peril'. The register-entry claims that Bowen did not, indeed could not, officiate, so that 'the Church and Chappells belonging of Llanavanfawr were without prayer or preaching or officiating unless in some of them itinerants came once in a month or quarter or year in some not at all during that time or as yet in 1659... some Cried one thing and some an other for the assembly was out of order and the more part knew not wherefore they were come together'. In 1657 Thomas Jones took charge of the parish. From about the end of 1658 Mr Williams 'beganne privately to officiate in Llanafanfawr Ch. to such as came hier', and remained the incumbent till his death in 1670, when his son William succeeded to the living.

Simon Wrench was deprived by the Commonwealth of his Llangamarch living, which with its chapels of Llanwrtyd and Llanddewi Abergwesyn became the charge of 'rector' Samuel Prydderch, of a well-known family of Llandefaelog fach. Another of the family was the Independent leader Rhys Prydderch.

The Restoration can hardly be said to have brought Breconshire an inspiring revival of church life. It was, as R. Tudur Jones writes, a period of 'pluralism, place-hunting and petty squabbling'. A little later, in 1694, Llanfihangel Abergwesyn was in the parish of the Rev. Howel Griffiths, a native of Defynog and a graduate of Jesus College, Oxford. In 1720 he was buried in the chancel 'in the voult where Dr Huet was buried'. Dame Hannah Griffiths presented Llanfihangel Abergwesyn with an inscribed silver chalice and paten cover. The next incumbent was Howel's son Samuel, another Jesus man. J.T. Evans in *'Church Plate of Breconshire'* transcribes a letter from Samuel Griffiths to Bishop Adam Ottley, evidently in answer to a query about Chantor Huet. Samuel 'can only learn [from descendents] that he was buried under a Stone in the Chancel of Llan Avan-Vawr, upon which the Communion Table formerly stood, and where the Vicars of this Church have been buried ever since'. He describes an altar-stone, with a central cross and one at each corner. Griffiths also describes Bishop Afan's stone and sends a copy of the epitaph. At the end of the letter he reaches what may well have been for him the nub of the matter: 'If your Good Lordship will be pleased to promote and hasten at a proper opportunity the Augmentation of the value of some of the many Poor and Far-Distant Chappels annex'd to this scattered and troublesome Vicarage, it will be a very Great Favour...'.

In a presentment at the time of an Episcopal visitation of Llanddewi Abergwesyn in 1694, the churchwardens, Richard David and Morgan Thomas, stated the church to be 'out of repair' but said 'there are workmen at this time repairing it'. It was in need of a large Bible, a book of canons and homilies and a table of degrees of kinship, but it had a small Bible and two common prayer-books. The vicar lived 'within ye parish of ye mother church' (Llangamarch) — he had been the incumbent for eight years. The parish was satisfied with its sexton, who was 'as good and sufficient as such a smale parish can get'. There was no free school, no hospital, almshouse, physician, surgeon or midwife in the parish. No-one took bribes for concealing delinquents, nor were there any corrupt 'aparitours' (ecclesiastical court officers); the number of these was not known.

An early eighteenth century vicar of Llangamarch, Llanwrtyd and Llanddew was Richard Prichard. Theophilus Jones waxes merry over his 'grotesque Bust' in the chancel of Carmarthen church, where he is buried, comparing it to a tradesman leaning over a counter. The inscription below it shows that before being presented to the Breconshire living Prichard had been chaplain to the 'Newcastle' at the bombardment of Calais in 1696, and to the 'Dreadnought' in 1697.

From 1738 to 1763, when he was followed by his son-in-law, the vicar of Llangamarch and its chapels was the historian Theophilus Evans, grandfather of the county historian. Evans had prviously been rector of Llanynis. From 1739 he held also the living at St David's, Llanfaes, in Brecon. It was here he died in 1767, and was buried in Llangamarch. His grandson and great admirer Theophilus Jones asked to be laid in the same grave. The best-known of Evans' books is *'Drych y Prif Oesoedd' (Mirror of Ancient Times)*, which used to be very popular in Wales. At the 1876 National Eisteddfod it was chosen as one of the 'pass' subjects for the bardic degree of 'ovate'.

Theophilus Evans came from Cardiganshire and settled at Llwyneinon, Llangammarch. Among his ecclesiastical offices was that of chaplain to the Gwynnes of Garth House. It is ironical that a clergyman so far to the right in ecclesiastical matters should have been chaplain to a family which was to give shelter and encouragement to revivalists like Howel Harries and to become connected by marriage with the Wesleys. Ironical, too, that Theophilus Evans's curate in Llanwrtyd and Llanddewi Abergwesyn was a man who was to become one of the most celebrated and best-loved of the Methodists, William

Williams of Pantycelyn. Llanfihangel was in his care, too, presumably as it was so far from its mother church of Llanafan. Dr Gomer Roberts tells of story of Williams's Breconshire ministry in his book 'Y Pêr Ganiadur' (The Sweet Singer). Williams did not live in either of the parishes under his care, but at Cefncoed, some ten or twelve miles away, and travelled to and fro over hills and peat-bogs. His vicar was at the time non-resident, for a letter to Howell Harries refers to a Saturday morning sermon (anti-revival) given at Llanwrtyd by 'Mr Evans, from Brecon, who is owner of the Church'. It was on this occasion that Marmaduke Gwynne of Garth took out a book, read ostentatiously, and made audible remarks!

Early in 1742 Harries' diaries have several references to Williams being gravely ill with smallpox. 'O bless dear Brother Williams of Llanwrtyd', cried Harries. 'O my dear Lord give him Strength and Light and Power to help him through'. On 15 February Harries thought Williams was dying. He recovered, but next month fell ill of a fever. This, too, he shook off, and by October Harries could report that Williams 'goes about all ye week and preaches in ye fields... and is much blessed'. But the nineteenth century Congregationalist preacher Kilsby Jones, writes Dr Roberts, asked an old Methodist woman what Williams' preaching had been like, and was told it was sometimes sensible, sometimes rubbish! Thomas Charles thought that Williams during his three years curacy here met with little success from his preaching because of the blind sinfulness of the people of this area! Williams preached not only within the walls of his three little churches in their sparsely populated mountain parishes, but in the open air, wherever people could be induced to gather about him. So it was that in June 1742 the churchwrdens of Llanfihangel Abergwesyn 'presented' their curate in the Archdeacon's Court at Brecon. He was said to have absented himself on several Lord's days and not performed divine service in the parish church. In October he was brought before the General Presentment Court 'for rambling into several other counties to preach and neglecting his duties at home, for not residing in the said parish nor in the county of Brecon... for being absent on the Lord's day lately from the parishes under his care and not performing the divine service either by himself or any other person for him', for not reading the whole of the service, and for not burying the dead.

Daniel Rowland, revivalist curate of Llangeitho, Cardiganshire, commented in the same month on Williams' parishioners' anger with him, but praised him for 'his simple, honest, plain way of dealing with the people... I trust we shall have him out before long'. In June 1743 Williams was formally charged by the bishop of St David's. To the former accusations were added new instances of neglect of duty, including neglect of the sick and weak and of catechising the young, and failure to take a service in Llanddewi Abergwesyn every second Sunday. He denied most of the charges, claiming he read the service in Llanwrtyd every Sunday and in the two Abergwesyn churches alternatively. Abergwesyn registers show that this was still the practise in 1754. They were so near to each other, he said, so small, and the parishes 'Pretty thin of Inhabitants', that one service per Sunday fully met the needs of Abergwesyn; a second one would be unattended. Nor would the inhabitants turn up for any but the greater Holy Days. Williams had tried taking a service on other days, but to no avail. As to catechising the children, those of Llanwrtyd he taught in the church, but though he often asked Abergwesyn people to send their children to church for instruction, there was no response. Indeed he did not think Abergwesyn children were given any education, secular or religious. He could not live in Llanddewi Abergwesyn because there was 'no Parsonage House there', and he could not find 'any proper... place for his habitation... in such a parish, there being not above thirteen houses therein', and not one of them 'commodious' for him. (If his count was correct, Llanddewi was more thinly-populated in the mid-eighteenth century than it had been fifty or so years before, when Lhuyd was told that there were twenty-three houses in Llanddewi, 'besides 4 or 5 small cotts', or than it was to be in the nineteenth century, when the twenty-eight houses of 1841 dwindled to seventeen by 1881).

Williams' application for orders in the Established Church was refused. One Luke Prichard was licensed to serve as curate in Llanafan fechan and Llanfihangel Abergwesyn. From this time on Williams gave up his curacies and threw in his lot with the Methodists. They gained not only a devoted worker but an inspired hymn-writer. One of his most famous hymns is said to have been written after he had walked up the Tywi valley on the rocky path above Fanog gorge on the western boundary of this his most remote parish. Another story has it that the Cothi valley in North Carmarthenshire was his inspiration. The hymn's last verse begins,

> Cul yw'r llwybr i mi gerdded,
> In fy llaw mae dyfnder mawr.
> Ofn sydd arnaf yn fy nghalen
> Rhag i'm troed i eithro i lawr.

> (Narrow is the path I must walk,
> And below me a mighty chasm.
> In my heart I fear
> Lest my foot should slip.)

The Nanteos estate rental-books for 1785 show a clergyman, the Rev. Mr John Jones, as tenant of 'Gallt Rhebog' and Brongynes farms (up the Tregaron road) and of Abergwesyn Mill. 'Late curate of this parish', says his memorial stone; it leans now against one of the huge split yews in Llanfifihangel churchyard. He died aged only thirty-five on 26 September, 1789.

In Llanddewi Abergwesyn churchyard is the grave of a popular curate, John Evans, who served Abergwesyn and Llanwrtyd for forty-five years, dying on 20 March 1841, aged eighty-one. He was called 'the Fighting Parson' ever since the day when as a youth he was the hero of a fight between the young men of Abergwesyn and those of Tregaron, laying about him with the hames of a horse's collar! In gratitude, the people of Abergwesyn raised money to train John for the ministry. His son John married Sarah, the twelfth child of David Jones of Fanog and Llwynderw, local magistrate and wealthy sheep-farmer. Their six year old son, also called John, was buried in Llanddewi churchyard three years before his maternal grandfather. The Rev. John Evans' fighting career did not end with his youth. In a drunken affray after an Abergwesyn funeral in 1809, this time a fight between the Abergwesyn mourners and those Llangamarch, the curate is said to have stripped off his coat and joined in enthusiastically!

Ieuan Gwynedd Jones, writing of a Parliamentary return of 1850 giving the number of services in each Anglican church in Wales at the end of 1848, says that in the area north-west of Brecon 'the great mountain parishes were without exception Welsh... Llangamarch, Llanwrtyd, Llanafan-fawr and its huge chapelries, these all had exclusively Welsh services. The only exceptions in this region were Llanddewi Abergwesyn where the service was in English, and Llanwrthwl where it was mixed'. On 4 May 1876 Kilvert wrote that at Dôldowlod the Archdeacon was told that Llanwrthwl did not need a Welsh service. Llanddewi may seem an extraordinary parish to have needed an English service in 1848. It was surely provided for the benefit of Captain Thomas Turner Roberts of Llwynderw, who with his family and servants often formed the only congregation.

One Morgan Jones — not the vicar, who was the Rev. Edward Jones — replying to the questions of the 'religious census' of 1851, thought Llanddewi church dated from 1400 and Llanfihangel from 1500. There were one hundred and nine free sittings in Llanddewi, one hundred and two in Llanfihangel. The average attendance on Sunday was only nine in Llanddewi (morning service only), and five or six in Llanfihangel (afternoon service only). Neither church had a Sunday school. Little Moriah chapel, in between, could boast of an average morning attendance of thirty-five, with eight in the evening, and twenty-five in morning Sunday school, with another fourteen at the evening class! No wonder that in 1861 the Congregationalist Rev. Rhys Gwesyn Jones wrote that the only use of the churches in his day was to provide a resting-place for a few, and occasionally the scene of a wedding. He said he used to see the clergyman coming to one of the churches many a Sunday morning, and being met only by the bell-ringer. He would go into the church, and quickly come out again, saying 'It's obvious no-one is coming'. After lunch at the nearby inn, he would go back to the other church, walk in and out as he had done before, and then set out cheerfully for home, his duty done. It was Captain Roberts who changed things a little. He and his nine children and maids would attend Llanddewi in the morning, take the vicar or curate home to lunch at Llwynderw, and be at Llanfihangel by three o'clock. One wonders how long the Roberts family kept up their afternoon attendance if the service was in Welsh at Llanfihangel. In 1846 Captain Roberts told the Education Commissioners that Llanfihangel had no service on five out of six Sundays for want of a congregation.

On 21 November 1864 Llanfihangel Abegwesyn was separated from Llanafan fawr, and Llanddewi Abergwesyn from Llangamarch, by Order in Council. In the following March, the two Abergwesyns were united, Llanfihangel being made the parish church. Llanwrtyd became a separate parish in 1871. The first incumbent of the united Abergwesyn parish was the Rev. John Jones, instituted 8 March 1865. The patron was the bishop of St David's. Abergwesyn is now in the diocese of Swansea and Brecon, which was carved out of the huge St David's diocese in 1923.

On 2 February 1865 Miss Clara Thomas of Llwynmadog wrote from London to Mr W.E. Phelps of Nanteos, then 'the principal landowner in Llanddewi Abergwessin', to ask for a subscription towards an Abergwesyn project. Referring to the imminent joining of Llanddewi with Llanfihangel 'under a distinct incumbent', she wrote that it was planned to increase the endowment and build a parsonage and school. At present there were none, and the perpetual curacy of Llanddewi was worth less than £30 a year, and of Llanfihangel less than £60. Both churches were thoroughly dilapidated. The Bishop had promised £100 towards a parsonage, and Mrs Thomas of Llwynmadog £1,500 for increasing the endowment on condition the Ecclesiastical Commissioners provided an equal amount. There was a proposal to rebuild one of the churches. Mrs Thomas promised £50 towards the school, for which Mr Thomas of Welfield had given 'an excellent site of about three quarters of an acre'. He had also presented four acres near the church for a parsonage. The plan's success, wrote Miss Thomas, depended on further subscriptions.

In 1870 the Rev. John Jones applied for a faculty for taking down the old church of Llanfihangel and rebuilding it in accordance with plans laid before a vestry meeting on 7 April of that year. He had to submit the minutes of the meeting, the plans of the church, his name and address and that of the churchwarden of Llanfihangel, Joseph William Stares of Llwynmadog Cottage (the Llwnmadog gardener). The plans show an ambitious cruciform church with a long nave and massive central tower. Reading the correspondence about the project in the Rev. John Jones' bold handwriting, and seeing the detail of R.I. Withers' plans from Doughty Street, London adds poignancy to the emptiness of today's churchyard, where in less than a hundred years the imposing church was to rise and become a landmark, and then, fatally flawed in materials or construction, crumble gradually, and eventually be demolished and carted away.

The vicar's answers to the bishop's questionnaire state that the old church was in ruins and had not been used for some years. The population of the parish in 1861 had been 355. The old church would seat about fifty — perhaps the 102 'sittings' referred to in 1851 really included standing-room? The new one would seat 112 on benches and 50 more on chairs on special occasions. It would be built on the same site as the old one. Today, it is hard to imagine an Abergwesyn which needed a church holding fifty people, let alone one seating over 160! Hard, too, to reconcile John Jones' ideas of the size of church needed with the report of the 'religious census' on attendance a comparatively short time before, and Gwesyn Jones' story of the empty churches.

The estimated cost of the project was £3,250, of which £2,700 had been promised by 'a Lady' and £40 by the Ecclesiastical Commissioners. The vicar made himself responsible for any balance uncollected. The church was to be completed by 24 June 1871.

The minutes of the vestry meeting refer to 'the Temporary Iron Church' in use in 1870. This was a corrugated iron building which long survived, rusty and tumbledown, and was demolished in 1978. It stood at the corner of a field opposite Pentwyn farmhouse, and was built in a sort of corrugated Gothic, and surmounted by little iron crosses. The 'Iron Room' was the first all-year-round village school of Abergwesyn. It once had a porch, virtually a small iron hut, said to have been brought from Llangynllo near Knighton in Radnorshire, once the post-town for Abergwesyn. This was the 'postman's shelter' The original one was even smaller than the one to be seen in later years. It contained a seat and a little stove on which the postman, whom people now living remember coming from Garth, would cook himself a meal during the hours between bringing the morning post up and taking the afternoon one down. It used to get so hot that he had to choose between freezing outside and roasting inside!

The new church of Llanfihangel was, according to some who knew it, dignified and beautiful, ostentatious according to others. Dr Ralegh Radford called it 'an academic exercise in the Romanesque'. It had a very long chancel reached by seven steps. Near the font was a baptistery set in the floor and covered by a removable tiled lid. In the great tower was a peal of six bells inscribed 'Llanvihangel Abergwessin 1871'. One was the funeral bell; the others could play hymn-tunes, it is remembered. Mr and Mrs Evans, the last church cleaners there, were also bell-ringers for over forty years. But the feature of this Victorian church which everyone who knew it remembers is the fine rose window in the west wall. For those coming up the Llanwrtyd road, or down from the hills across the Irfon, it must have been a splendid sight, catching the westering sunlight, or at dusk when lights gleamed from within the church.

A vicarage was built beside the Tregaron road at the expense of the widowed Mrs Thomas of Llwynmadog and Bishop Thirlwall. Four acres of land were set aside for it by Edward David Thomas of Welfield (now Cefndyrys), owner of much of the land in this part of Abergwesyn, and related to the Thomases of Llwynmadog. There are two little tithe-barns, one in a field near the vicarage, one across the Irfon in Llanddewi parish, in each of which the vicar had the right to keep animals and fodder. The one in Llanfihangel looks like a cottage and indeed was once used as a dwelling, when an old woman who had been living at Ty Bwci cottage lost her home in a fire. The Llanddewi barn is said to have been built or rebuilt with stones from Llanddewi church.

Llanfihangel church was ill-starred. Earlier generations would have seen in its story signs of angelic disapproval or mortal hubris. In the 1940s the church roof started leaking into the pulpit and the chancel arch became unstable. By April 1948 S.P.B. Mais found 'the stone of the chancel arch ... falling and the whole East end of the church... marked off as dangerous. The paper of the Visitors' Book was damp to the touch. No visitor had signed his name for over a month'. By this time there was no resident vicar in Abergwesyn, which was served from Llanwrtyd. Attempted repairs proved useless. Two firms were contracted to try and halt the crumbling of the fabric. Both just took down some slates, and gave up. A Cardiff architect estimated that it would cost thousands of pounds to put things right; there seemed no hope of raising such a figure. Later, a lower figure was arrived at, but by this time the church had been abandoned and the work of demolition had begun. The East end had to be blown up. In 1963 the remains of Llanfihangel were carried away by council lorry. In the churchyard, some of them leaning against a yew, are wall-tablets from the earlier church: the Rev. John Jones had to promise to transfer them to his new one. The bells are said to have gone to

Swansea, the rose-window to Staffordshire.

For a time, once a month, the disused schoolroom of Abergwesyn used to blossom into the semblance of a small church, when a village evensong was held there — an oecumenical occasion. The loss of the church is still bewailed, and not only by churchpeople. 'A village is not complete without a church. If only ours could have been saved!' It was a keen Congregationalist who spoke.

On 7 April 1885 John Jones wrote to the Diocesan Registry to announce his intention of applying for a faculty to pull down the more ancient of the mediaeval churches, Llanddewi, at his own expense. He said he did not anticipate any opposition. An article in 'Archaeologia Cambrensis', 1888, however, states that by that time most of Llanddewi church had been 'removed', but 'against the express wish of the parishioners'.

Regular services at Llanddewi ended in 1865, but it was still in use for some time, at least for funerals. The story of the funeral at Llanddewi in January 1876 of Siân, wife of John Jones of Pysgotwr in the mountainous parish of Llanddewi Brefi, and descended from Abergwesyn folk, was told in a Welsh article based on a first hand account. After the long journey carrying the coffin over hills and rivers on the ancient 'Burial Path', the procession reached the old church in its neglected graveyard. Though there were peeling walls and holes in the roof, the vicar took the service devoutly and the mourners attended to his words with all decorum.

John Jones' first attempt to convene a parish meeting and pass a resolution to pull down Llanddewi was unsuccessful. On 4 June 1885 he was the only person to turn up at the church. He took the chair, proposed the resolution, passed it, and sent a copy of the minutes to the Diocesan Registry with an account of the 'meeting' and the remark that there had been no churchwarden of Llanddewi since 1866. On 26 June he held another vestry meeting. This time 'four attended, and it was unanimously resolved that the Vicar should apply for a Faculty'. At that time there was no churchwarden for either parish. 'No-one will act as there are no funds to pay court fees and travelling'.

On 12 August 1885 the vicar wrote for a form of petition, saying 'I am very anxious to remove the old church this autumn'. The preamble to the questionnaire describes the church as 'formerly a chapel of ease'. Llanddewi Abergwesyn had a population of 103 in 1861 and 81 in 1881, when Llanfihangel's had gone up to 328. Llanddewi's burial ground was still open, the vicar stated (it still is today). There were no tombstones or memorials within the church. The churchyard would be 'carefully preserved from desecration' — it had 'a good fence of five wires and quick thorn hedge and an iron entrance gate'. The vicar had burnt the communion table on 4 August 1871 at Bishop Thirlwall's request, and removed the font to Llanfihangel church, whence it later went to Eglwys Oen Duw at Beulah. There was no communion plate belonging to the church. J.T. Evans said it had 'disappeared'. No money and property had been left in trust for maintaining the church.

On 27 November 1885, on the advice of Mr Jeune of the Temple, there was yet another vestry meeting, for the purpose of making clear that Llanfihangel was now to be the parish church of both parishes. Besides the vicar, there were present David, Margaret and Elizabeth Jones. The resolution was once more carried and a copy sent off; and on 18 December the petition followed, expressing the 'unanimous resolve' of the parishioners of the two Abergwesyns that Llanddewi be 'wholly pulled down'. Although four people only 'resolved', one of them the vicar, the bishop 'consented to their prayer' the next day. Notices were affixed on 3 January 1886 to the doors of both churches by William Hopkins of Penyrhyddfa, who had become churchwarden. No-one objected to the proposals during the statutory period of at leat fifteen days before they were taken down, so Mr Hopkins was able to make the requisite declaration before the Rev. Gethin Griffith, J.P., of Aberanell, Beulah, and at last the faculty was granted. No doubt the vicar was not slow in starting demolition work; it is interesting that the church was never wholly destroyed, as the Victorian Llanfihangel, the great pride of John Jones, was later to be. Slight remains of Llanddewi are still to be seen amid the lush grass and tall wildflowers of summer in the old graveyard, or as dark ridges tipped with snow among the white-capped gravestones as one looks down on it from the hills in winter.

In 1875 the church and burial-ground of Eglwys Oen Duw (Church of the Lamb of God), Beulah, were consecrated, the district having been fashioned from part of Llanfihangel (where the church stands), Llangamarch (where the vicarage used to be), Llanlleonfel and Llanafan fawr. The church, given by Miss Clara Thomas, who financed also the building of Cwmbach Llechryd church, near Builth, was for some time rather like a chapel of the 'great house', Llwynmadog. It is a pretty essay in Victorian Early English with a shingled spire (now restored), lancet windows and glazed brick facing on the interior walls. Miss Thomas' great friend Gertrude Lewis Lloyd gave the communion plate. The Census return of 1881 shows the curate of Eglwys Oen Duw living at Trefelen nearby. For some years the vicarage was the old mansion house of Aberanell. The village used to be called Dôlyranell before Beulah Congregationalist chapel was built and gave the place a new name, perhaps indicative of new priorities. Within living memory, the Carpenters' Arms, Beulah, now the Trout Inn, was always referred to by Welsh-speaking inhabtitants of the district as 'Dôlyranell Inn'.

Eglwys Oen Du now comes under the care of the vicar of Llanwrtyd, with Abergwesyn and Tirabad.

Llwynmadog, the church and nearby farms are set in the parklike luxuriance of the lower Cnyffiad valley. By the church are huge Canadian maples, their gold spectacular in autumn. Theophilus Jones, who had no taste for the austere beauties of the lonely uplands, admitted that Llanfihangel Abergwesyn could boast a few 'picturesque vales', and that the country round Llwynmadog was 'remarkably romantic and beautiful'. In 1960 David Verey wrote in the *'Shell Guide to Mid-Wales'* of the Cnyffiad valley as it then was — 'the most lovely valley in north Breconshire' — and mentions 'the pleasant vicarage of Eglwys Oen Duw, and... the charming house Llwyn Madoc,... with lakes, rhododendrons, azaleas, dripping rocks and unusual trees. Further up, the indigenous oak, hanging on the steep slopes of the valley, has little competition except from bracken and bluebells'. It has now. Near Llwynmadog the oakwoods are still glorious, but as one approaches Pantycelyn chapel, the hillsides grow dark with conifers.

The first vicar of the separate parish of Llanwrtyd was Henry Miles. His successor, William Tudor Thomas, was instrumental in providing what Poole calls 'a substantial iron church,... with sittings for 250 persons'. This stood in a field near the late Northampton House, at the upper end of the village. When the present stone church of St James was built in 1897, the iron church (which no longer exists) became a church hall. A collection was made towards the building of a vicarage.

Abergwesyn and its neighbouring parishes have intriguing stories of lost churches in the hills. Chapels high on mountains were not uncommon in the Middle Ages, when unlettered worshippers learnt the lesson of atonement — 'the repentant soul's painful return', as O. Hartwell Jones called it — by acting out the upward struggle out of sin. One such tiny church is locally rumoured to have existed centuries ago in Llanddewi Abergwesyn on a craggy summit above the Tywi, near an outcrop called 'Carreg Clochdy' ('Belfry Rock'). There is more evidence for the little church of St Celynin, not far to the west in the Cardiganshire hills, a chapel of Llanddewi Brefi. From the youth hostel of Ty'nycornel the track downstream passes near the ruins of a farmhouse called Maesybetws (Field of the Chapel). (A *betws*, as distinct from a *capel* — simply a cell for the performance of divine worship — is thought to have implied a resting-place or settlement, an offshoot, as was the *capel*, of the original *llan* or monastic colony.) To the south is a hill named Rhiw Clochdy. An article in *'Cymru'* states that local people had heard of Rhys Pritchard, reforming vicar of Llandovery and author of the well-known collection of moralising poems *'The Welshman's Candle'*, preaching at Betws Celynin. Old Thomas Jones of Draenllwyn Du farm, who died aged 92 in 1830, remembered hearing his mother say that when very young she had been to a service there, and that the church collapsed when she was about thirteen years old. She died in 1799 at the age of 96, so the church must have been ruinous about 1716. The old lady claimed also to have attended a wedding there when the roof had collapsed into the body of the church.

A long hollow on the hillside Llethr Dôliâr in Llanfihangel Abergwesyn is called Pant y Capel. (t is not to be confused with the three acre pasture of Pant y *Cornel* on the nearby slope.) A vague tradition of a church is associated with it. It is thought by some local people that the hollow was a secluded place of nonconformist worship in penal times. Others link it with a mediaeval chapel like the one rumoured on Carreg Clochdy.

Tirabad has not only a lost church but a whole lost grange, said to have belonged to Strata Florida. Local tradition has it that the interesting old gentry-house (now a farmhouse) of Llwynyfynwent was originally enlarged from an ancient church, Llanddewi, probably the chapel of the grange. Though this may not be literally true, the house does indeed stand in a 'churchyard grove' (the meaning of its name). The phrases of old topographers come to life as one goes down the old track. The place is embosomed, embowered in trees — hedge trees, fruit trees, flowering shrubs — and above all, till recent cuttings a solemn rank of huge ancient yews (traditionally associated with churchyards), hiding the house completely from the field below. The stump of another great yew is to be seen in the field, which is said to be protected by a legal stipulation from ever being ploughed up. A farmer who violated the agreement was turned out. The story supports the association with an old burial-ground.

Then there is the old church of Llysdinam. It had been in ruins for a hundred years when Theophilus Jones wrote in the early nineteenth century of the hamlet of Llysdinam, part of Llanafan fawr, yet virtually a separate parish. On the 2.5 inch O.S. map two ancient sites are marked on the ridge above Penllys farm near the mansion of Llysdinam. One, called simply Penllys, is thought to have been, at separate periods, the ringwork fortification earlier referred to, and the court of justice and local royal residence for Inan commote. To the north-east of the ringwork is a hollow, the probable site of the old church — the second point marked on the map. Kilvert, whose vicar owned and rebuilt Llysdinam, talked there on 15 April 1875 to 'a short stout Welshman of 67, a small farmer', named Thomas Gwillim, whose father well remembered 'Baptism and the Communion being administered at a cottage now ruined, near Llysdinam Rhôs. They did commune there in ancient times', he said. Gwillim was not sure whether the worship was

Baptist, or a church service held there after Llysdinam church had collapsed. He said that 'when the Popes came into this county they took the Christian stones [fonts] and turned them into pigs' troughs' — a curious inversion of post-Reformation anti-Popery desecration, or of Cromwellian violations.

A mystery surrounds the lost church of Gelli-Talgarth, which Jones says appeared in ancient surveys of the manor. On the 2.5 inch map its remains are marked as a small rectangle high on the hills overlooking the Chwefru valley. A track runs up the significantly-named Pant y Capel and over to the valley of the Hirnant. The chapel-site is marked to the south-east of the track, on the hill whose south-eastern summit is called Allt y Clych (Bell Hill). Jones' description of the whereabouts of Gelli-Talgarth is confusing. He associated it with the 'boggy common called Rhos y Capel', which is in a different direction — he may have been thinking of Rhôs Saeth Maen at the head of the Chwefru valley. However, the oldest maps, and also Emanuel Bowen's map of South Wales in about 1760, place 'Kethitalgarth' just to the north-east of the Chwefru, where modern maps locate it. The symbol the old maps use is that of a house, not a church. Was Gelli Talgarth a mansion or a chapel attached to a mansion, or, as has been suggested, an enclosure where shepherds gathered to hear mass in the open air? Mounds do mark a small rectangular enclosure of some kind on the hill. The local name for Gelli-Talgarth chapel is Cwmcrogau. Perhaps the best way to get it was from the Hirnant valley up the side valley of the Crogau, past the farmhouse of that name, birthplace in this century of the poet Harri Jones.

Abergwesyn and Llanwrtyd place-names preserve dim memories of the clergy of past centuries. At Cwmirfon farm there is a tradition of a little house that once stood on its land — Llety Witen, home of a lean, dark clergyman, of whom the following rhyme, surely contemptuous in tone, used to be recited —

> Offeiriad du potaten (or, mor du a du potaten)
> Yn byw yn Llety Witen,
> Yngwaelod cwm, ynghysgod graig;
> Yn ddigon llwm ei gefn.
>
> (A priest as black as black potatoes,
> Living in Llety Witen,
> At the bottom of a valley
> In the shelter of a rock;
> His back is bare enough.)

Not far up the road, on the other side, stands the farmhouse of

Penybont uchaf on the brook Nant yr Offeiriad, up whose steep little valley is said to have been Ty'r Offeiriad (the Priest's House); but when, no-one knows. One of the Lloyds of Dinas and Nantyroffeiriad (later Penybont uchaf) is said to have been a curate in the eighteenth century; but the stream-name may date back much further than his day. The dressed stone of a fireplace in Penybont uchaf is said to come from the ruined abbey of Strata Florida, and to have been brought over to the Irfon valley by *elor meirch* (horse-bier).

In the upper reaches of the Gwesyn valley, not far below the summit of Drygarn Fawr, and in surroundings of the utmost desolation, is a little ruin called Magwyr Ficer (Vicar).As to what vicar can conceivably have lived in these solitudes, there is no story to enlighten us. The word is firmly connected with the established church, whereas *offeiriad* could also refer to a Roman Catholic priest. Further to the east, a track described by a local informant as 'the other side of Bwlch y Ddau Faen' — possibly the old path to the Claerwen valley down the Stream of Paradise — is called 'Llwybr Offeiriad' (Priest's Path).

5. Nonconformity

1. Baptists and Congregationalists

a. Baptists

On the left-hand side of the road from Abergwesyn to Beulah stands the Baptist chapel of Pantycelyn, with its long tree-shaded graveyard overlooking the Cnyffiad valley. On the hill-slope across the valley is the solitary farm-house of Llofftybardd. The older road, a green lane now, branches off before the chapel and passes behind it along the hillside towards a point opposite Ty'nycwm farmhouse. From the old road a left-forking track climbs steeply to a pass into the Camarch valley, which has never known a made-up road. Many of the valley's people lie in Pantycelyn graveyard.

The dignified little galleried chapel has a mounting-block outside, reminding us of the days when many of the worshippers would arrive on pony-back from distant farms. It was first built, so its date-stone proclaims, in 1774. But the Baptist cause in Abergwesyn started over forty years before that, in the farmhouse of Trallwm about a mile up the road. In the eighteenth century and for the first few years of the nineteenth it was part of the Baptist community of Pentre, Llysdinam, a house licensed for Baptist worship in 1673 under the Declaration of Indulgence. Thomas Evans of Pentre was a leader of the Particular Baptists, as distinct from the Arminian Baptists of Radnorshire origin.

It was Howell Meredith who, on his move from Llanafan to Trallwm in 1733, gathered about him the original Baptists of Abergwesyn. On his way to preach at Trallwm Caleb Evans of Pentre was taken ill and died in 1739. There was no burial ground at Pentre, so he was buried at the old Baptist chapel of Rock in Llanbadarn fawr, Radnorshire. John Jones in his 'History of the Baptists in Radnorshire' tells a story of a 'pious maid', a Baptist, whose coffin was cast out of the churchyard by the vicar of Llanfihangel Bryn Pabuan, and dragged on a sledge to be buried at Pen y Rhiw crossroads near Pentre at the intersection with a 'wide green road'.

Among the new young ministers who found their vocation under the influence of Howell Meredith of Trallwm were John Evans of Maesygwaelod, Llanwrtyd, and Rhys Jones, who married Meredith's daughter and inherited Trallwm. An external wall-tablet at Pantycelyn remembers this devout man, who died in December 1787 aged 61. His son, the Rev. Isaac Jones, said to have been an eloquent preacher in Welsh and English, and daughter Catharine, are buried at Pantycelyn;

they died at the sadly early ages of 27 and 19, both in 1776. Among the Pantycelyn gravestones are others that tell the same story of early death. The name of Jones of Trallwm recurs. Isaac Jones, who died in 1868 aged 43, was outlived for many years by his widow Margaret; another stone records the prolonged tragedy of their children's untimely endings. 'Three twins (sic) children' were the first to die — Elizabeth and Leah in August 1856, and Jane, aged thirteen months, in June 1857. 'Syble' lived to be twelve, but followed her sisters in August 1863. Eight-year-old 'Christiand' died in October 1868, less than two months after her mother was widowed. John, aged five, was buried in June 1870, and four and a half years later a sister who had survived to womanhood, Margaret, died aged twenty-five. Almost exactly two years after came the death of another Jane, aged eighteen — she must have been the next child born after the 'twin' Jane died. Last of the family here mourned was Thomas, aged twenty-seven, who died in June 1880. Such stories used to be all too common in the days of devastating onslaughts of epidemics, including such scourges as smallpox and cholera, which is mentioned in the church registers.

As well as the ordinary service at Trallwm there were ordinations 'by threes', and, as the membership increased, baptisms were performed there in Cnyffiad, partly for the edification of the inhabitants of the valley who, it was hoped, would profit from the public enactment of adult baptism by immersion. Cwmirfon, on the way to Llanwrtyd, was the scene of Baptist worship and ordination before the building of a chapel in that district.

Rhys Jones of Abergwesyn was one of the trustees of the new Baptist chapel of Pentrenewydd at Newbridge-on-Wye built in 1760. The senior trustee was Caleb Evans of Bristol, grandson of Caleb Evans of Pentre. The name of Evans recurs again and again at Pentre. Between 1741 and 1756 five young men of that name, three of them named John, went from Llanafan fawr to Bristol Baptist College. The first minister at Newbridge was John Evans of Maesygwaelod. By the time he died in 1775, Pantycelyn had just been built; it had about forty members to begin with. Three preachers, ordained together, were made co-pastors of Pentrenewydd and Pantycelyn — Rhys Jones, John Evans and Morgan Evans.

In 1806, when membership had risen to about seventy, Pantycelyn became a separate entity. Its first minister was the septuagenarian Morgan Evans of Tynycwm, a house that kept until recent years its Baptist tradition: a gabled white house in the Cnyffiad valley, set about with streams and flanked by yews, below a wooded bank dropping precipitously to river-level from the present road above. Morgan Evans, brother-in-law of Joshua Thomas, the Baptist historian, had ministered for forty-seven years at Pentre and Pentrenewydd, and preached for years before his ordination. On his mother's side he came of the Jones family of nonconformist gentry in Llanafan fawr. Morgan Evans' altar-tomb at Pantycelyn tells us that he died on 17 August 1822 in his eighty-ninth year, and the sixty-sixth of his ministry. His wife Mary, who was nine years his senior, had died in 1810. Buried beside them are two daughters, Ann, who died aged twenty-five in 1781, and Mary, who was twenty-six when she died in 1785. Two sons lie there also, both Baptist ministers who had assisted at Abergwesyn: the Rev. Josiah Evans, who died in 1792, aged thirty-one, and his younger brother John, who followed him in 1794, aged thirty. Josiah started his preaching career in 1787. He went away to college; it was on a visit to friends in Monmouthshire and Glamorgan in 1788 that he first became ill. He died at Ty'nycwm. John started preaching in 1792, after his brother's death, and in one year obtained his licence to preach. But his health, too, declined, and Ty'nycwm was once more saddened by the death of a promising son

Morgan Evans was followed by George Griffiths, whose brother and assistant David was ordained in 1811 at Cwmirfon. The Rev. George Griffiths left Abergwesyn in 1819 or 1820; in 1821 he was minister of Carmel, Pontypridd, where one account says that he was buried in 1850. He described himself in his Bible as a 'Protestant Dissenting Minister', but in the 1841 Census he is called 'grocer'. It is known that his son kept a grocer's shop in Mill Street, Pontypridd. Next at Pantycelyn came James Davies, who in 1835 moved to Liverpool. He was assisted at various times by David Arthur, Jacob Davies (who later emigrated to America), Samuel Jones (who went to North Wales) and Daniel Jones. In 1835 Richard Hughes came to be minister of Pantycelyn, helped by three deacons, Isaac Jones, Daniel Davies and John Jones. At this time the number of members is said to have been ninety to a hundred, and there was a flourishing Sunday school. A ruined building opposite the chapel door seems to have contained the minister's house at some periods, and also a schoolroom. On the tithe map of 1842 two separate small buildings are marked in Cae Ty Cwidd, the field next to the chapel, on land of Alltfelen farm, and a 'cottage and garden' are listed in the schedule, but not specifically linked with the chapel. However, entries of births at Builth Registry Office include for 1857 Joseph, son of William and Ruth Harries, School House, Abergwesyn, Baptist Minister, and for 1870 Harriet, daughter of Edward Williams and Ellen James, Pantycelyn, Baptist Minister. Edward James' gravestone at Pantycelyn calls him 'minister of this chapel for twenty years'. He died in 1884. With him lie his son Francis, who died aged nine in 1865, and Eliza James, whose death occurred in January 1904.

The Rev. B. Thomas, buried here, was the son of the Rev. Z.

Thomas, minister of the Baptist churches of Aberduan and Bwlch y Rhiw, Carmarthenshire, and 'was admitted into the Academy of Bristol 1780, and afterwards minister of the Baptist Chapel at Prescott, Devonshire for forty-four years. He died triumphantly in the Lord at the residence of his sister Mrs Evans of Builth, 6 January 1835, in his seventy-fourth year'. How often, one notices, did minister sons follow minister fathers, family tradition, desire for education, enjoyment of status and genuine devotion no doubt playing a part in proportions varying with each individual.

The 'religious census' of 1851 tells us that Pantycelyn, a chapel of the Particular Baptists, was used exclusively as a place of worship, except for a Sunday school. There was free seating for thirty and free standing room for one hundred. On the test Sunday, 30 March, general attendance was one hundred and one in the morning, forty-two in the afternoon, with a morning Sunday school of sixty-nine. The minister was Ezekiel Jones, who lived at Pantycelyn; so the house by the chapel seems to have been consistently in use for that purpose. As late as 1900 Mary Evans, who died on 13 September aged sixty-three, was said on her gravestone to be of Pantycelyn.

R. Tudur Jones in his his article *Religion in Post-Restoration Brecknockshire* (*Brycheiniog*, VIII) warns us against imposing 'modern denominational distinctions with their rigid lines of demarcation... on the nonconformity of the age of persecution'. In the early days in Llanafan, from which the Baptist cause here sprang, the Open Communion, Calvinist Baptists met in the barn of Rhydgaled at Pentre, and were led by Thomas Evans, who was ejected at the Restoration from his Commonwealth cure of Maesmynis parish. They were close, literally and spiritually, to those other nonconformists who met at Cefngwaelod and Tanybwlch, and, says Tudur Jones, formed a bridge between Thomas Evans' followers and the Independent (Congregationalist) church of Henry Maurice. A recent study of *The 'Anabaptists' of Llanafan Fawr and Llysdinam* by Owain Jones, appears in *Brycheiniog*, vol. XVIII.

When government persecution was a thing of the past, the Baptists of this district seem to have become more separate from other nonconformist bodies than the latter were from each other; and they still had a measure of persecution to undergo, though no longer an official one. Now it was the rough mockery of uncomprehending neighbours who found their ways, in particular their traditional rite of adult baptism in pools and rivers, distasteful or funny. It is historically doubtful whether the early Anabaptists were at all the same thing as the Baptists whose first church in Britain dates from 1611; but 'Anabaptist' was the term used, as well by the clergyman of 1668 who wrote in Llanafan parish register that Howell Thomas Prosser 'died excommunicate and was buried by the Anabaptists', as by the St David's Diocesan Visitation returns of 1799, which state that in Llanddewi and Llanfihangel Abergwesyn there were 'Anabaptists, Presbyterians and Methodists'.

A satirical ballad by a local bard was sung on 10 November 1822, 'the day the Anabaptists of the Abergwesyn mountains came down to the river Dulas in Llanafan [provocatively close to Troedrhiwdalar Independent chapel] to immerse two men in contempt of their opponents'. These words, and the verse that follows, were quoted by the Welsh writer David Afan Griffiths in 1877.

> Ai swn rhyw udo adgas,
> Sy'n awr ar ddolau Dulas,
> Afleisiol leisiau;
> A fethodd corsydd Teifi,
> Ac aml byllau Tywi,
> Wlychu eu cegau;
> Mae'n rhaid fod Cnyffiad
> Yn llawn llaid,
> Trwy aml olchi
> Eu holl fudreddu;
> Rhaid codi fyny'r haid,
> A dod i ddyffryn Dulas
> A'u hadgas hyllig blaid;
> Ond gwir, ni fydd arosfa hir,
> I'r gwiliaid diffaith
> Yn y gymydogaeth,
> Sy'n gwneud cynheulaeth
> O fewn ein talaeth dir;
> Rhy eglur fod eu trochiad
> Yn gyfeiliornad clir.

> There is the sound of some vile howling
> now on Dulas meadows,
> discordant voices.
> Teifi bogs have failed,
> and often, too, have Tywi pools,
> to wet their mouth;
> the Cnyffiad must be
> full of mud
> from frequent washing
> of all their filth;
> they must have risen in a swarm,
> and come to Dulas valley
> with their hideous faction;
> but indeed, there'll be no long abiding
> for the vicious vagrants
> in this neighbourhood,

making trouble
in our land;
too clear it is that their immersion
is obvious heresy.

Griffiths writes that the well-known Independent minister, the Rev. David Williams of Troedrhiwdalar, once preached at Cribarth, Llanafan, in the time of a much-respected widow, Mrs Griffiths. This is the Griffiths family we have already come across, that gave Pantycelyn more than one of its ministers. John Griffiths and his wife Margaret were buried there, she in 1816, he in 1849. David Williams seems to have been nervous of the occasion, which brought together a mixed congregation of Baptists and Independents, and with his customary tact he avoided controversial points in his sermon. He had a more difficult time at a similar service in an unnamed farmhouse near Pantycelyn. It was announced at the meeting that a baptism would follow. An outcry went up, and it seemed likely that a fight would develop (it often did, at baptisms), especially as some of the congregation were armed with staves, the favourite local weapon! Somehow, the worthy minister managed to keep the peace; but after that, old Morgan Evans, minister of Pantycelyn and a great friend of David Williams, agreed with him that public joint services were not advisable. A great gulf between ways of life and thought then and now opens up in the naively partisan remark of an old Baptist woman known to David Williams, that the words of the Bible should be changed to make it clear that baptism was to be 'in the water', not merely 'with water'. Another zealous old woman exclaimed, 'Good gracious, don't deceive people! You know better from best!'

During the 1840s there was something of a Baptist exodus from Abergwesyn. In 1844 John Prothero of Alltfelen, a descendent of the Rev. George Griffiths, left for South Wales and found work in Aberaman. In 1846 his mother Margaret and her second husband John Davies, together with other Baptist families, left Abergwesyn for work in Aberaman, where in due course Capel Gwawr was built.

By 1884 Pantycelyn had fifty-six members, four Sunday school teachers and twenty-four scholars. It is still in use, but services are held less often now. Crowds come only for special events, like a big funeral. Many of the Camarch valley farmhouses from which people used to come to worship here no longer exist, or are holiday homes.

Zion Baptist chapel in Llanwrtyd had a comparatively brief life. Founded in 1863, it had in 1884 fifty-nine members, six Sunday school teachers and thirty-six scholars. It is now demolished, after a period of disuse. The congregation had so shrunk that winter services were held in the vestry. According to Poole, the most flourishing Baptist chapels in the area in 1884 were Ebenezer, in Builth, built in 1787, and Pisgah, Llanfihangel Bryn Pabuan, dating from 1827. In 1851 Pisgah's minister, the Rev. David Jarman, had claimed that its afternoon congregation was 275, which must have crowded its free standing-room for eighty-eight and its 'five seats and thirteen long benches for siting (sic)'. This is the chapel the poet Harri Jones, born at Cwmcrogau, remembered in Australia, where he died in 1964 — the kinsfolk and neighbours of his youth 'all suddenly startled into song' in 'the ugliest building I have ever seen — / Pisgah I shall never see again'.

Like all the churches, the Baptist church played its part in education in this area. We have already found a nineteenth century Baptist minister whose address was School House, Abergwesyn. Ten years earlier, according to the *'Atlas Brycheiniog'*, a Baptist school was functioning at Tymawr, a farmhouse on the hill behind the former Abergwesyn Post Office. At the time, the Prothero family were at Tymawr. William Prothero is said to have held a daily morning service in his house. He was particularly noted for his skill at weaving into extempore prayer any complaints against members of the household. A maid tactless enough to mend the fire during the service would find her ineptitude being 'brought before the Lord' by her eloquent master.

(b) Congregationalists (Independents)

The little whitewashed Independent chapel of Moriah, on the bank of the Irfon near the bridge, was first built in 1828-29. It was rebuilt in 1867 and again in 1907. But long before the nineteenth century, Independent dissenters were meeting for worship in Llanafan fawr and Llanwrtyd, which bordered on the strongholds of Dissent in Llanfair-ar-y-Bryn, Carmarthenshire. Pennar Davies in *Brycheiniog* vol. III casts doubt on the local tradition that the sixteenth century Puritan martyr John Penry of Cefnbrith, Llangammarch, or possibly some followers of his, worked as evangelists in this area towards the end of that century. There is clearer evidence for Dissenting preachers and congregations in the seventeenth century. Leaders famous throughout Wales inspired the earliest members — leaders including Henry Maurice, the 'Apostle of Brecknockshire', and Rhys Prydderch of Ystradwallter in North Carmarthenshire, related to the old Prydderch family of Llandefaelog fach on Mynydd Epynt. These and others upheld amongst the North Breconshire hills 'the Independent voluntarist principle of the gathered church'.

Both Llanafan and Llanwrtyd had little thatched chapels by the late seventeenth century, precursors of the later more stoutly-built places of worship. Services were held in farmhouses in the days of persecution, and in later times as well. Tanybwlch in Llanafan, near the present chapel of Troedrhiwdalar, was one of the early meeting-places; there are said to have been burials in a field near it. David Williams of Cefnygwaelod was fined £5 in the time of Charles II for holding religious services in his farmhouse. Later, at the time of the ninteenth century revivals, there were services in many houses nearby, Cwmdulas, Dôlyfelin and the ancient longhouse of Cwmchwefru among them.

The first Independent chapel at Llanafan fawr is usually said to have been built about 1689 on a field of the farm Llwynllwyd, on land belonging to Cribarth, where lived that Jones family which was to give leaders of considerable local distinction to more than one nonconformist body. There is another tradition, however, which places the site of the first chapel at Llety'refail. Troedrhiwdalar chapel as it is today, a pleasant colour-washed building at the roadside on the way to Newbridge, with a house adjoining and a graveyard stretching up the hill into the woods, is the result of several rebuildings over the years.

The earliest traditions of Independent worship in Llanwrtyd are of little groups of men and women going secretly by night to services shared with people of Llanfair-ar-y-Bryn at Castell Craigywyddon. Gradually the Llanwrtyd cause, from which Abergwesyn's Congregationalists sprang, was to become linked with that of Troedrhiwdalar. Rees and Thomas wrote in their Welsh history of Congregationalism, published in 1875, that in 1715 Troedrhiwdalar and Llanwrtyd jointly had eight hundred in the congregations, thirty of them landowners. The traditional link between land-owning families and the Established Church seems in this district to have been a weak one in the seventeenth and eighteenth centuries and the beginning of the nineteenth. Not till after that time did families like the Thomases of Llwynmadog conform to the church-going and almost wholly English-speaking pattern usually thought of now as typical of the gentry. Rhys Gwesyn Jones's accounts of life at Llwynderw, Abergwesyn, in the early nineteenth century, as a poor relation of the Jones family, suggest a transitional period in the use of Welsh by the wealthier families, when it was well understood still, but had declined into a language used mainly to servants and work people — though very importantly, it would also have been the language of the chapels to which many of the local gentry still at that time belonged.

Early Independent meetings and communion services were held at Maesygwaelod farmhouse. At some date unknown, but before 1693 (when a deed refers to the chapel, already in existence), Gelynos chapel was built on a field called Clos Rhedynog (Ferny Close), near the present road from Abergwesyn to Llanwrtyd, some distance past the old church and bridge. A small graveyard still exists, the one attached to a later rebuilding of the chapel; but there is no longer a building to be seen. The land for the first chapel was given by Rees Jones of Dôlycoed, just below, a gentry-house which for long was a hotel. Rees Jones was the brother (such are the idiosyncrasies of Welsh nomenclature) of another local gentleman, John Lloyd of Dinas, whose wife Ruhamah must have been brought up a devout Dissenter; her father was John Jones of Cwmcamarch, who was a preacher at Llanwrtyd. The land was granted on a thousand year lease for the rent of one penny a year if asked, to five Llanwrtyd trustees. This chapel, like the first one at Llanafan, was roughly built and rush-thatched, with a door of woven twigs. It is said to have lasted — no doubt patched from time to time — till 1758, when it was burnt down. The builders of the new chapel were just about to start on the roof, which again was to be of humble rush or straw thatch, when Squire Gwynne of Garth (a Methodist sympathiser) passed by, and was saddened to see a house of God about to be so unworthily roofed. His offer to pay for a stone-tiled roof was gratefully accepted. In 1837 the chapel was once more in need of rebuilding. It had to remain on the same plot of land, as none was forthcoming in the village. Not till 1868, when the coming of the railway had greatly accelerated the development of Llanwrtyd Wells as a spa, was an Independent chapel finally built there. Gelynos, too, was still standing for many years after this.

Whether there were Abergwesyn people amongst the earliest Llanafan and Llanwrtyd Independents is not known; but certainly well before the building of Moriah, meetings were being held and a Sunday school established at the cottage Dôliâr, on a field of that name to the east of the old track to Pentwyn ford. The cottage disintegrated long ago. Its stones were drowned by the Gwesyn during one of its changes of course, and the site is now only roughly known. It was there in the late eighteenth century, possibly much earlier. In Llanfihangel churchyard lies 'John Thomas, late of Doleyiar in this parish, who died Oct. 2nd 1787 aged 71 years'. In 1816 it became the home of Isaac Williams, whose example in throwing open his house for worshippers and Sunday scholars was followed by other householders, like two devout old women who then lived at Ty Isaf, over the track by the ford. For twelve years the Rev. David Williams (Isaac's brother), one of the most worthy, popular, energetic and long-lived local ministers, and one of the chief fashioners and supports of the Llanafan and Llanwrtyd Congregationalist churches, came up the valley to minister to the worshippers meeting in the scattered homesteads of Abergwesyn. Others, too, came to give help and encouragement. One old deacon invariably started the meeting with his favourite hymn.

In 1828, Peter Jones, Esq. of Llwynderw, great-grandson of the Independent preacher David Jones, Gentleman, of Cribarth, granted for a chapel a piece of land on a 999 year lease at a rent of one shilling a year.

The chapel, Moriah, was opened in 1829. Gwesyn Jones wrote that it had cost £60 to build and that not enough lime had been used in the mortar, but hastily added that nevertheless it had been a blessing for the place. Peter Jones seems to have had no particular religious convictions, but his wife Elizabeth, who had been a Miss Lewis of Nantgwyllt in Radnorshire, and whose brother, Thomas Lewis Lloyd, Esq. was staunchly church, was swept into a lasting religious fervour by David Williams's preaching at Llanwrtyd, and became a devout Independent shortly before the building of the chapel. By 1842 Moriah had ninety members.

An Independent Sunday school is said to have met at Pwllybô, home of Evan Jones and his wife Elizabeth, in Llanddewi Abergwesyn near the Llanwrtyd border. Then there was the Sunday school in the chapel itself and, as we shall find later, a day-school during the winter months. The 1851 religious census shows that the day-school was functioning at that date. Free sittings in Moriah were one hundred and there were eighteen other places.

Beulah Independent chapel was built in 1822 and extended and raised and a gallery added in 1841. From the first it was closely connected with Troedrhiwdalar. Beulah chapel had, as we have seen, the distinction of giving its name to the village. At the time of the religious census, it was still in Llanlleonfel. Interestingly, we are told that the chapel was erected first as a schoolroom, by public subscription. In 1851 the Rev. David Williams stated that average Sunday attendance was about two hundred at Beulah, four hundred at Troedrhiwdalar and one hundred and fifty at Olewydd in Llanafan fechan. The interest of such numbers comes partly from comparison; in Llanafan fechan church, for instance, the average attendance at that time was four, in a church which had seats for a hundred and six. Beulah chapel had the good fortune to have as precentors for many years two fine local musicians, Daniel Jones of Llwyncûs and his son D.B. Jones ('Alaw Buellt').

One of the earliest and most sweet-natured of local Congregationalist clergy was Isaac Price (1735-1805), said to have been handsome, neat in dress and of a truly saintly disposition. It was he who first persuaded David Williams to preach. David was born in 1779 in the now-vanished farmhouse of Nantydderwen in the Cerdin valley, Llanwrtyd, of a long line of sheep-farmers and weavers. On his mother's side he could boast of a left-handed descent from the gentry family of Price of Maesyron in Llangamarch. David chose shoe-making rather than weaving as his trade. He served an apprenticeship with one Rhys Jones, first at Nantycrâf in the Culent valley, then at Blaengwenol in a fold of the hills above the east bank of the Irfon on the way to Llanwrtyd. After a period in Merthyr and Cardiff, he set up a workshop at

Maesygwaelod Mill by the Cerdin, where his old master joined him. Williams was ordained in 1803, and became a phenomenally active minister, travelling all over Wales and outside it. Poole says of him that 'if he was one day in the saddle he was in it ten years of his life... he would go thirty-five miles with two pennyworth of hard gingerbread in his pocket'.

A devoted husband and father, Williams eked out his modest salary (£15 a year at first and never more than £40) by farming, having like others to struggle through the hard seasons at the end of the Napoleonic wars. Of strong physique though nervous temperament, he could still, at ninety-five, amaze his juniors by the stamina which, just a few months before his death, permitted him to leave his Llanafan home on Saturday, preach in London three times on Sunday, again twice on Monday, and be in Llanwrtyd on Tuesday! For seventy years the 'Patriarch of Wales' was pastor of the local Independent cause, including for part of that time Abergwesyn.

'Tal-a-Hen' in his article on David Williams in *The Red Dragon* of November 1882 wrote that Williams's predecessor at Nantydderwen was known as 'the dog deacon'. Abergwesyn congregations consisted mainly of sheep-farmers, their families and their dogs. In the time of the Rev. John Griffiths, a dog-hater, who found these noisy and insanitary members of the congregation very trying, Prydderch's job was to weed them out, and admit only 'well-conducted, seriously-disposed dogs' to the service. Others were hit on the nose with his shepherd's staff.

A later Independent minister well-known in Llanwrtyd and Abergwesyn and beyond, and a very different man from the Patriarch, was the Rev. James Rhys Kilsby Jones. Just after passing old Llanwrtyd church on the way to Abergwesyn, one sees a modern house, 'Kilsby', among the trees on the hillside across the Irfon. This is a recent remodelling of what was once a tall, damp, derelict double-fronted villa, an unexpected flowering of Victorian pretentiousness in a country of unostentatious functional farmhouses — Glenview, or as one North Wales owner re-christened it, Genau Cwm Irfon — the dream-house and much-loved home of 'Kilsby'.

A stately man, six feet tall, with 'flowing locks, massive forehead, large and brilliant eyes'; an eccentric feared for his sharp wit and loved for his warmth: a 'born Radical' and a lover of nature: a dreamer and a reformer — Kilsby was all these, and inspired every feeling except indifference. His fellow-minister, Gwesyn Jones, born at Abergwesyn, thought Kilsby highly talented, but of more promise than performance — not 'serious' enough. One is reminded of Kilsby's retort to a Calvinistic Methodist who accused him of being 'very light' — 'Don't you think that the Almighty was fearfully light in making me and the monkey so much alike?'. Kilsby's rough jokes long raised a laugh by the firesides of the district whose beauty he loved with a love 'second only to that of women, and with a passion which sober men pronounce madness'.

Kilsby, born in 1813, son of a farmer-minister, dearly loved his mother, who died when he was seventeen; he later bought Gellifelen farm, where she was born, and built Glenview on its land. Dismissed from college for his 'dangerous' wit, Kilsby took refuge with David Williams at Llanafan. The good old man is said to have feared for Kilsby's sanity when the latter asked if God would judge the people of his native Ffald-y-Brenin one by one, or in large lots like the old sheep at Llanybydder fair, to avoid 'losing time' over such fools!

Shortly after ordination (in 1840) Kilsby married. When he lived at Glenview he would ride over the hills to Rhaeadr and Llandrindod, where he organised the building of Christchurch chapel. His pastorate was not without problems, over the administration of the church, over his many absences, and his intolerance of lay attempts at public prayer by 'a sinful and ignorant brother'. He was a brilliant preacher, but not in the heart-rending revivalist style. His was a lively, cerebral type of sermon, with no ranting, and no harping on the 'horrors of the pit'. He said that Christianity was happy — 'It is music. It is love. So, you young people, be joyful — for the darkness will come into your hearts soon enough'.

Kilsby was a well-known *eisteddfodwr* and a writer in Welsh and English. He was joint author with Dr Richardson of Rhaeadr of a pamphlet on Brecon and Radnor mineral springs. He edited the works of William Williams, Pantycelyn and a Welsh version of *Pilgrim's Progress*, and brought out a new edition of Peter Williams's Welsh family Bible. He worked for education in Wales; he was a supporter of the foundation of the university college at Aberystwyth. Unlike many nonconformists, he was in favour of state aid to schools, seeing it as a means of escape from a time when, as Vyrnwy Morgan writes, 'anyone in the shape of a man was deemed fit to teach children'. On another controversial point, too, he made enemies — he was heartily in favour of every Welsh child learning English, as a language of international culture. He wrote a Welsh aid to English idiom. As we shall see, he kept a school of his own for a time at Glenview.

Kilsby was an enthusiastic Liberal, campaigning for Mr Maitland of Garth House against the elderly Howel Gwyn. He was anti-teetotalism, recommending a thin teetotal minister to have four or five glasses of stout poured down his throat every day. In dress he was sometimes so unlike the conventional cleric as to have been once as a visiting preacher mistaken for a manservant and made to wash at the pump! He specialised in arrogant and humorous rudeness, usually directed at fashionable visitors to the Wells, some of whom deserved the treatment. Quizzed through an eyeglass, Kilsby, on pony back, responded by quizzing back through his stirrup-iron.

Kilsby hoped that if he was buried in Glenview garden his son would refrain from selling the house and land. But his wishes were disregarded, and when he died in 1889 after a week's illness, the religious iconoclast' was buried 'by the Church, in the soil of the Church', just across the valley. Kilsby's son would not even let local nonconformist ministers say prayers at the house before the funeral, although the vicar joined Congregationalists in trying to persuade him. Mr Maitland refused to subscribe to the memorial, as a protest against the lack of regard paid to the wishes of his old ally. Perhaps because of this uneasy feeling that a dying man's request had been ignored, a rumour soon spread through the valley that a ghost was to be seen on his grave at night, like a shifting light on the tall stone. People watched for it, and some swore that indeed a light was to be seen. Eventually they decided it was just the light shining across the Irfon from an upper window of Kilsby's old home on the opposite hillside, straight on to the obelisk that marked his grave.

The story of the Congregational cause in the Gwesyn and other nearby valleys is in part the story of nineteenth century revivalism. As this was triggered off by the Methodist Revival of the eighteenth century, we shall discuss it in the next chapter.

6. Nonconformity

2. The Methodist Revival and the Revivalism of the Nineteenth Century

There has never been a Methodist chapel in Abergwesyn itself, but it produced a somewhat ambiguous revivalist preacher, John Powell, helper or thorn in the flesh of Howell Harries; and numbers of Abergwesyn people were caught up in the tides of 'enthusiasm' which in the eighteenth century and later swept through the Tywi valley on the one hand, and along the hillsides of Epynt on the other. In both the Abergwesyn parishes, and in others nearby, these people included some of the local gentry.

Both Calvinistic and Wesleyan Methodists evangelized in this district, but Welsh Methodism was predominantly Calvinist. In spite of the Wesley brothers' close association with Garth, and their preaching in the neighbourhood, it is Howell Harries (1714-1773), William Williams (1716-1791) and Daniel Rowland (1713-1790) who immediately come to mind as the Methodist reformers *par excellence* in the hills and valleys around Abergwesyn. Methodism started as a movement of reform and revival within the established church. Rowland and Williams were clergyman. We have seen William Williams, as curate here, in trouble for his field-preaching. Daniel Rowland was for most of his life the curate of Llangeitho, Cardiganshire, assisting first his brother then his son. Howell Harries had at first intended to enter the ministry of the Church, which he never actually left. All three were influenced by the reformer and educationalist Griffith Jones, vicar of Llanddowror, who was no separatist. Nevertheless, as early as 1747 a Methodist chapel was built in Builth — Alpha, which got its name from the fact of being among the first in Wales. Though such chapels were meant to be additional to the parish church, rather than replacements for it, their building was in effect a step away. They were eventually licensed, like other dissenting meeting-houses, and by 1811 Thomas Charles was ordaining Calvinistic Methodist ministers. John Wesley had done so as early as 1788.

Even before the chapels were built, of course, Harries and his followers had been setting up what David Williams calls 'the characteristic Welsh Methodist organisation, the *seiat*, a group meeting for devotional purposes at a fixed centre', and though, as the historian continues, 'there was no intention of forming a separate denomination,... since a new organisation was being set up, parallel with the church, it is difficult to avoid the conclusion that the seeds of disruption were there from the start'.

There is a tradition that Howell Harries visited the Hundred of Builth early in his preaching career, which began in 1736. He is said to have started a 'society' at Glanyrafon, Llangamarch, about 1742. From this beginning grew the Methodist community of Gorwydd, where a chapel was built in 1778. One of the early 'advisers' of this group was Rhys Morgan of Glancledan fawr, of whom Poole writes 'His talents were few but his piety was undoubted'. A reminder of the wild and lonely surroundings in which these little religious groups developed is given us by the circumstances of Rhys' death aged eighty, in a snowstorm, on his way home from visiting his married daughter at Panteulu, not far away. Services were held in the house of another adviser, Rhydderch Price. A more formidable man was 'Siams Ffôsyrhebog', Thomas James, who lived to be a hundred. He is said not only to have struck out a member's name for marrying a non-Methodist wife, but to have refused six times his application for re-admission. The seventh appeal succeeded. The marriage plans of members were very much the business of the *seiat* — mixed marriages were frowned upon.

Gorwydd chapel absorbed the small Methodist communities of Llanafan and at first Llangamarch. It was rebuilt in 1795. In 1799 'the estate of the late Mrs Catherine Powell of Castle Madoc', a mansion on the Epynt, was sold by auction under the terms of her will. Among the properties bought by Penry Price of Rhayader we find 'Gorwydd meeting-house and stable', then in the holding of the Rev. Daniel Rowland and others under a 199-year lease from Michaelmas 1781 at an annual rent of five shillings. This was a chapel which benefited also from legacies from Edward Thomas of Llwynmadog, Abergwesyn and from his 'worthy friend' the Rev. Evan Evans of Ffôsyrhendre, Llanwrtyd. It was endowed, too, with a small farm, Penllêchbach, by Mrs Pugh and Mr Bevan of Aberanell, near Llwynmadog.

New members were brought in by 'waves of revival' in 1777, 1790 and 1812, while in 1828 one hundred and sixty people joined Gorwydd. A Sunday school was started there in 1802. Members included inhabitants of Tirabad and other parishes. In 1851, when Gorwydd was flourishing, and Nazareth in nearby Penbuallt, built in 1818, also had a large membership from several parishes, only twenty people were attending the one service in the ancient parish church of Llangamarch.

Before Nazareth was built (one of its deacons being John Bevan of Aberanell) mansions and farmhouses in and near Llangamarch continued the tradition of housing Methodist meetings, as they had done from the early days. Such houses were Llwynmadog, home of the Thomas family of Abergwesyn, and Dôlgaer in Llangamarch, the old mansion of the Stedmans, which became the home of Edward Thomas' daughter Anne on her marriage to David Pritchard. Here Methodist ministers were often given hospitality. Others included Coryn, Aberbudran, Llwyneinon, Dôlyfelin and Parc.

A few miles from Gorwydd was the little village of Pontrhydyfere, later to develop into Llanwrtyd Wells. According to the Rev. John Hughes' Welsh history of Calvinistic Methodism, it was a light-hearted young daughter of Nantycae farm here who, about the 1740s, became, improbably, almost accidentally, a leader of Methodism in Llanwrtyd. She sounds by our standards a very normal girl, fond of dancing and the harp and the company of other young people, and full of curiosity about the news of the district. It was this curiosity which led her, while still only fifteen, to go with friends on the eight-mile walk to Cilycwm in North Carmarthenshire, where, they had all heard, marvels were happening at the meetings of the new preachers. The girl's parents were no strangers to Dissent. They were Independents, and had housed preaching-meetings themselves; but their daughter was not interested in religion. At Cilycwm the revivalist Peter Williams was preaching (he was later to be cast out for heretical views on the Trinity). Every word of his hell-fire sermon on the dreadful fate awaiting those of light and idle life struck home to the girl from Nantycae. We are told that thenceforward her life was transformed. She became an earnest and devout Methodist.

It is hard for us to rejoice, thinking of the extinction of all that youthful exuberance, or to feel other than regretful about the old harper of Abergwesyn who, repenting, flung his harp under the bed, never to play it again. Perhaps the exuberance found a new channel, and the harper knew songs unheard even sweeter. After all, of two old Abergwesyn women it was said 'The Revival was a banquet to them'. As for the emphasis on sin and guilt, the vivid, almost mediaeval picturing of the pains of Hell, this was something people came to demand of their preachers, this hot, heady, purging draught that induced the flowing tears, the protestations, the leaping and the shouts. Not only the Methodists were called 'Jumpers'. During the nineteenth century revivals which swept through other dissenting churches as well, the Llanafan Independents came to be called 'the Jumpers of Troedrhiwdalar'. Hell gaped, but the blood of Christ streamed in the firmament, and one drop only, one moment's total conviction, would save the soul; and then, after life's bitterness, hardship and sorrow, unutterable bliss waited. 'Gogoniant!' they shouted, 'Glory!'

In January 1744 Llanwrtyd had a Methodist society of thirty members under the care of Brother Thomas James, who supervised also those of Builth, Llanafan and Llangamarch. Rhys Morgan was the 'private exhorter' of Llangamarch and Llanwrtyd. Howell Harries said of Llanwrtyd, 'This Society is as a water'd Garden, most of them walk with

God! it would rejoice your heart to see their love, zeal, meekness and order; their peace, unity etc. — they [meet] almost every night, tho they live at a Great Distance from Each other, and perhaps part not till near day, the Lord coming so amongst 'em — Most of them are in Great Liberty, and ye rest pressing after it, I believe, with their whole Hearts'. By the following June they were 'growing up in one body in the Lord, walking very humble and full of Zeal, adorning the Gospel in their Lives'.

The young Methodist of Nantycae married another early adherent of Methodism, William Jones, who with his brother Edward had previously been an Independent of Gelynos. John Hughes points out how little difference there was between the work of the two denominations at that time, and how little bitterness was caused by members attending both services. William Jones and his wife went to live at Abernant on the outskirts of the present village. In about 1770 a few Methodists would meet for worship at Llofftwen (up the track opposite the side of Dôlycoed), an old farmhouse where a room is still said to be the meeting-room, with a niche for a light to be set for Bible-reading. The meeting became known as 'Seiat William Siôn Abernant'; 'Wil o'r Nant' was clearly the leader. No sinecure, this — for some time he entertained visiting preachers out of his own inadequately-filled pocket. Every month the little group, like the one at Gorwydd, would go on the long and arduous walk over rivers and mountains to Llangeitho, to receive communion at the hands of Daniel Rowland. They were still technically members of the Church and could have gone to communion at their local church, but they wished to take communion from hands they considered worthy. The trek to Llangeitho became something of a pilgrimage; again we find an echo of the pre-Reformation Church, whose rituals, however dimly understood, must have deeply satisfied something in the nature of the Welsh people. Communion at Llangeitho was a spiritual experience not to be conferred, it was felt, by clergy outside the Revival.

Wil o'r Nant is said to have started building with his own hands a rough chapel on Nantycae land, but for some reason it was given up, and a straw-thatched house was rented in the village instead. Wil's financial difficulties were relived by generous gifts to the cause from prosperous local families — Evans of Ffôsyrhendre again, and Winstone of Esgairmoel (owners of the local woollen factory) among them. In 1799 the Visitation Returns of St David's diocese stated that at Llanwrtyd 'David Parry and Evan Evans are the Teachers of the Methodists'. David Parry of Gilfach was a shoemaker and a well-known preacher. He and Evan Evans were ordained at Llandeilo in 1811. To them and to David Jones as trustees Edward Thomas of Llwynmadog by codicil of 1808 to his will of 1805 left £25 for the local Methodist congregation. He left a similar sum to the Baptists of Pantycelyn and the Independents of Troedrhiwdalar.

The western part at least of Llanddewi Abergwesyn derived its Methodism from revivalism rolling up the Tywi from Ystradffîn, where Daniel Rowland often came to the old church of St Paulinus, and where a little Methodist group grew amongst the 'Mountains of Dewi' there and in the parish of Llanddewi Brefi. Here in the wilds of the Camddwr valley the isolated chapel of Soar y Mynydd, Soar of the Mountain (Capel Saron as the early O.S. map marks it), was built in 1822. But for eighty years before that services were held in farmhouses on either bank of the Tywi and in the fastnesses of the hills. John Hughes wrote of the change the Revival brought to the remote and bleak countryside of scattered and isolated sheep-farms. As early as 1740 Howell Harries preached in Rhiwhalog, a Camddwr valley farmhouse, where the wife, a convert, prevailed on her husband to go to the then great expense of buying a Bible. Later came William Williams to preach in the area; but it was through the poetry of his hymns that he spoke to the hearts of all, not only of Methodists. It will be remembered that the Baptist chapel at Abergwesyn bears the name by which he was known. Sir Thomas Phillips in 'Wales' (1849) laments the lack of use made by the Church of his day of the power of 'psalmody' over a nation which loved religious song, and contrasts this failure of the Church to make full use of the beauty of music and liturgy with the greatly-loved and powerful hymns of Williams and Wesley.

Dôlgoch, now a Tywi valley youth hostel, gave hospitality to Howell Harries and doubtless to other revivalists. Just downstream are the ruins of Cwmdu, where the first society meeting was held in 1747; near it on the hill, by the new road over to the Camddwr, is Bronyrhelem, and nearer the river was Hafdre. All these held services visited by the leaders of the movement, and continued to house society meetings year after year.

It was at a Tywi valley service in 1779 that one of those sudden ebullitions of enthusiasm broke out which spread wider and wider through the district and beyond — 'tân grug', as Daniel Rowland called it, 'a fire in the heather', burning through the hills, and unextinguished in the Tywi valley itself for four years. In 1812 came another, and a greater one in 1819, which began in Nantllwyd, still a working farm, on the hills south of Soar y Mynydd, and now just out of reach of a long tongue of Llyn Brianne. Each revival brought an increase in membership, but so sparse was the population of these mountains that huge congregations were not to be expected. Hughes estimated the communicating membership of Soar y Mynydd in his time (about 1854) as forty, with seventy in the Sunday school and a hundred 'hearers'.

Roy Saunders wrote in the *Western Mail* of 30 January 1935 of his recent visit to Soar y Mynydd. Coming upstream and missing the bridge to Soar, he forded the Tywi opposite Bronyrhelem (no longer a farmhouse), and on over the hill by a 'muddy track' to the Camddwr valley and the chapel amid its pine-trees. He met two shepherds riding up the track after service, and saw the road to Llanddewi Brefi winding up the steep hillside opposite, 'dotted with riders... [like] flies on a window-pane'. Twenty-five farmers and shepherds had been at the service, one from seven miles away. The caretaker (monoglot Welsh) lived alone in the chapel house. A family of five children would walk over the mountains each morning to school at Soar. The teacher stayed there during the week and rode home to Llanddewi Brefi at the weekend. An old lady remembered an eisteddfod at Soar in 1930, when 'the hearty excited clapping of the Cardiganshire farmers frightened their shy mountain ponies so much that they broke loose and scampered away'. Occasional services are still held at Soar, though today's worshippers come by car along made-up roads. The visitors' book brims with names from all over Britain and from many countries overseas.

From the Tywi valley Howell Harries sometimes travelled on to Garth House, where he would stay with the sympathetic Squire Gwynne, whose original antagonism had been overcome by a 'truly evangelical' sermon of Harries and by his 'zealous and affectionate manner' — like one of the Apostles, Mr Gwynne thought. Mrs Gwynne took longer to persuade. She was not pleased to find her husband bringing back to dinner with them an man whom on religious, political and social grounds she totally distrusted. So appalled was Mrs Gwynne at hearing the Squire apologise to Harries before the family, and observing the deference he accorded the low-born evangelist, that she left the room, and 'passed much of her time in tears at the supposed infatuation of her family'; for her daughter Sarah, too, was deeply influenced by Methodist teaching. Slowly Mrs Gwynne was won over; she was eventually to become the mother-in-law of Charles Wesley, who married Sarah at little Llanlleonfel church opposite.

Other houses, on the Abergwesyn bank of the Tywi, had Methodist occupiers. Fanog, now under the waters of Llyn Brianne, was rebuilt about 1778 by David Jones, the wealthy gentleman sheep-farmer who was later to make his home at Llwynderw. David had spent much of his childhood at Dygoedy(dd), Llanfair-ar-y-Bryn, of which his father took a lease. It was the house where the first Methodist Association in Wales, even earlier than the better-known Watford Association, had been held in 1742. Perhaps it was in his Carmarthenshire home that David became a Methodist. Certainly when he came to live in Abergwesyn he was one of the foremost of the wealthy nonconformist gentlemen who seem to have been characteristic of this area in the eighteenth and early nineteenth centuries. His uncle John Jones, Esq., of Cribarth, son of the Independent preacher David Jones of Cribarth, gentleman, was sympathetic to the Methodists, and protected Howell Harries from the violence of some of his Radnorshire opponents. David Jones of Llwynderw's second wife, Lettice Williams, shared his Methodism and his mystical experiences — they are said to have heard heavenly choirs. Lettice came of a Boughrood branch of the Williams family of The Screen (Ynis Grin), in Llandeilo Graban in South Radnorshire, from which family Howell Harries himself took his wife Anne (not without considerable opposition from her relatives). In a diary entry, Harries thanks God for 'opening the door' for him at 'Skreen, Gilwern and Garth'. Gilwern, in the Camarch valley near Beulah, was at one time the home of a locally prominent Bowen family. It is interesting that Harries groups it with the better-known, and clearly 'gentry', houses of Screen and Garth.

Later, a quite different Jones family lived at Fanog. Miss Jane Jones, who died in 1916 aged seventy-two, was the great-niece of Thomas Jones of Fanog, Esq. She was a devout adherent of Soar y Mynydd, and an open-handed friend to the needy young theological students who came to preach there, giving them not only food but money. The lonely homesteads of the Soar members took turns at entertaining the young preachers, who were met at Llanwrtyd, Tregaron or Pontllanio on Saturday, and rode (some of them for the first time) on local ponies to their weekend destination. Most of the farms entertained a preacher every eight weekends, but Nantystalwyn and Fanog took one every five weeks. One visitor, making his way alone to Fanog, missed his path and from Llanerch-yrfa, high in the Irfon valley, was taken by Mr Edwards of Nantystalwyn over the mountain to that farm, where Mr Edwards' sister was startled at being woken at midnight to make supper for the unexpected guest.

When the minister was staying at Fanog (one, twenty-seven year old Evan Jones, was there on Census Day in 1881), the morning service at Soar was supplemented by one at Fanog at three in the afternoon. There is said to have been a stone pulpit in the main ground floor room at one time. A Sunday school, for adults, in the Welsh manner, not only for children, would then be held in one of the tributary valleys. When it fell to the Tywi valley to provide the Sunday school, the venue was often Pantyclwydiau, about two miles upstream from Fanog.

During the eighteenth century Abergwesyn produced its own itinerant revivalist, the complicated and stormy John Powell. Howell Harries' diaries have a number of references to him, though we are never told exactly where in Abergwesyn was his home. Richard Bennett in

'*The Early Life of Howell Harries*' wrote that about 1736 Powell was 'apprehended through Harries' ministry', but before long joined the Baptists, and that he was an unstable man, though exceptionally gifted as a preacher. At first Harries' references to him are full of praise. In 1737 he wrote 'I had much gladness from John Powell from beyond Builth. I saw in him great signs of God's spirit, great humility, wisdom and love to Christ'. Powell's opposition to infant baptism, and his preaching of 'an experimental assurance of forgiveness and salvation' were controversial points which caused Harries much worry; but on the latter question Harries later agreed with Powell — 'Oh! how dear John Powell of Abergwesyn is now, who was so despised by everybody because he had experienced things that none other of us had known'. The two men were close enough for Harries to advise Powell against a hasty marriage, and for Powell to confide his wish to marry a 'godly and prudence [sic] woman'.

Throughout 1740 Harries was recurrently troubled about John Powell. Harries prayed for him 'and all Baptists'. In March he saw 'plainly now that the spirit that leads John Powell is not of God'. In August he wrote Powell 'a living letter full of sweetness', and prayed for him to be purified. But in December Powell was stirring up trouble in Haverfordwest over the baptism question. On 9 December Harries was staggered to hear of Powell's drinking four or five pints of beer before a revival meeting: giving way to fits of anger; being self-centred: 'reviling with bitter language': being a bigot: 'having no concern in seeing a whole country set by the ears, and many poor people set to expense about him': temporising in his preaching: boasting about his gift of language and his number of converts ('far more than Harries's, he claimed): lack of 'unity of spirit' with good men: and lack of growth in humility.

Next day Harries wrote that the Abergwesyn evangelist had 'done great mischief' in Pembrokeshire, 'incensed poor people vastly, and brought poor children over to them, that were very raw'. He had also listed six errors of Harries's, who in his turn criticised Powell for yet more faults, including 'pride in clothes... stirring up animosities...: lightness and rashness, and seeming want of awe and sight of God in his works'. 'I dread John Powell', wrote Harries. 'He comes after me to draw down [my] good work... I feel no bitterness... but... am stirred by a sense of my duty... to expose him, the flesh is against it as I know he is a bitter enemy far more knowing than me, and has vast many followers'.

At Rhostrywarch, Pembrokeshire, Powell 'convinced' many, but 'was drunk, poor man, the Lord pity him, at Newport in preaching, and drank four pints afterwards'. Compassion now overcame Harries's censoriousness, even when he heard of Powell's sewing seven guineas of collection-money into his coat! Next February Powell, who was still drinking and giving way to avarice, had added an addiction to tobacco to his other shortcomings. 'Yet he has amazing gifts and great experience'. The two evangelists continued to work together, and Powell continued to be a nagging worry to Harries, who in July 1743 dreamt that he was fleeing from a murderous Powell! By December Powell's sins had all come to light and he had been 'cast out'. Harries felt he himself was 'much blacker [and] was broken and humbled'. Soon after, a letter from Powell, said Harries, broke his heart.

Though Howell Harries and the other Welsh revivalist leaders followed the Calvinist Whitfield, between whom and the Wesleys a rift opened in 1741, relations between Harries and Wesley, as David Williams writes, did not cease. They were, after all, both members of the established Church. Wesley visited Wales forty-six times, though he found his lack of Welsh a difficulty, and he and Harries 'preached by invitation to each other's followers', but did not proselytise 'each other's people'. We do not know of a visit of Wesley to Abergwesyn, where he would certainly have been much handicapped by his inability to speak Welsh; but he preached at Builth, Maesmynis and Garth. The nearest Wesleyan chapel was opened at Builth in 1806, and re-opened in 1866. Wesley more than once visited Strata Florida, preaching at the Abbey House in 1768 and 1769, and starting a Wesleyan society at Tregaron, which met at an inn for many years.

The Methodist Revival not only created, eventually, and against the will of the first leaders, a separate religious denomination, but had the effect they did desire — of waking new life in some of the existing churches. Amongst the Independents of this district there were recurrent revivals well into the nineteenth century. For us to understand something of what they were like, we have to recreate imaginatively the tremendous feeling of urgency in saving souls which was the dynamic of the Methodists' precursor Griffith Jones, of the revivalist leaders and the most obscure 'exhorters', of each 'saved' member of a household longing for the salvation of the rest.

Howell Harries wrote from London in 1742 of how Welsh people could 'grow' spiritually faster than any Londoners, yet on a far more meagre diet of 'one sermon a month'. 'Some nights... all night on the hill, under the tree, singing, praying, and consulting together. Many of them could not make ten shillings among them, living, too, on bread and water and lying on beds of straw, the wind and cold coming through the paper walls'.

Rhys Gwesyn Jones said that in the early nineteenth century Abergwesyn was still a rough, wild little community. There were three taverns, at one of which met a drinking club, that had most of the young people in its clutches. Drunkenness led to fierce fighting, and occasionally to an ineffectual morning-after remorse. Moriah chapel was an agent of reform, and the personal influence of the newly-converted lady of Llwynderw, Elizabeth Jones, was very strong.

Of the revivals at Troedrhiwdalar chapel, D.A. Griffiths mentions in particular those of 1812, 1821, 1828 and 1840. That of 1828 started amongst the Llanwrtyd Methodists. The 1840 one was the greatest of all. On one communion Sunday in Troedrhiwdalar over sixty boys and girls of all ages were baptised. Crowds, unable to get into the packed chapel, gathered in the open air around it, about three thousand in all, with hundreds of horses. The liveliest manifestations of enthusiasm took place at the public meetings rather than the Sunday services. One of a crowd of harvest-workers in a field would start a prayer, others would join in, and continue for an hour or more, afterwards going on all the more heartily with their work. On a clear calm night, anyone walking the hills near Troedrhiwdalar would have heard singing that might well be thought heavenly.

Gwesyn Jones has left an interesting description of how Abergwesyn 'caught' the 1840 revival. He was fourteen at the time, so would have heard of the incident and remembered it. One night, after the prayer-meeting, five members of Moriah were sitting by the fire — Rhys and Isaac Jenkins, Roderick Williams of Abergwesyn Mill, Thomas Price, who farmed Llwynderw, and Dafydd Morgan of Penywern, the house where Gwesyn Jones was born (now faint mounds in the depths of a Forestry plantation on the hill opposite the chapel). One man asked why Moriah had been untouched by the revival that was in full swing in other parts of the area. The five decided to pray together, but felt no 'spirit of revival' descend on them. They prayed again, and were this time more hopeful. Their third attempt was completely successful. They were 'new men', full of inspiration, and began to speak with tongues. They were away from home so long that their families grew anxious, and on coming to look for the missing men at about one o'clock in the morning caught their enthusiasm. The next Sunday the revival 'broke out in tears and praise'. One or two Sundays after, some Abergwesyn worshippers, and many irreligious folk with them, wrote Gwesyn Jones, went to Beulah to see if the revival had reached it. Finding a great crowd weeping and singing there, the godless shed tears with the godly. They walked home over the mountain. Somewhere on Banc Paderau, where the monks of old were said to have prayed, two or three men stopped and began a prayer. For half the night, then, they all stayed there, praying and singing out on the hill, just as Howell Harries had described people doing in the previous century.

That revival was powerfully felt for three months. People would often go to a prayer-meeting at Penybont farmhouse on the way from Llanwrtyd, then on to Pwllybô, then to the old farmhouse of Nantybrain near Llwynderw, and so till about two or three in the morning, a few perhaps dropping off at each house to go their own way home, singing hymns as they went. They seemed to be invigorated rather than worn out by these nights of prayer, getting up for work as early and as energetically as if they had been asleep for hours. Sometimes they would go well into Cardiganshire, over the Tywi, six or eight miles over rough tracks. Sometimes it was the Llanwrtyd and Abergwesyn bank of the Tywi they visited, going north from Trawsnant, calling at Fanog, Nantyrhwch and Nantstalwyn, and coming back south again to walk up the Gwrâch and over to the Culent valley, where they would hold a meeting at Nantycrâf. Or they might cross the hill from Nantystalwyn and come down the lonely upper Irfon, to pray and sing at Llanerch-yrfa near the Devil's Staircase.

Gwesyn Jones vouches for this constant journeying, night after night, meeting after meeting, endless prayer, endless singing, and says he cannot account for people's total lack of weariness or reaction. Old and young alike, they thrived on the revival. No wonder the five worshippers had deliberately set about inducing the fire to descend.

Pegi Jones and Gweni Dwm of Abergwesyn were two old Methodist women who had in years gone by been brought into the fold by Daniel Rowland. They were *aficionadas* of revivalist meetings, who leapt in the *hwyl* (untranslatable, but roughly 'enthusiasm') at every meeting, says Gwesyn Jones, and loved to sing the hymns of Williams, Pantycelyn 'until the eternal fire kindled a second time' and the jumping and the shouts started anew. Mrs Jones of Llwynderw once asked Gweni why she said 'Amen' so inappropriately, for instance adding a resounding 'Amen' to the preacher's account of the torments of the damned. 'Dear Mrs Jones!' replied Gweni, 'you are learned, and able to follow the preacher, but I have to think about what I hear, and by the time I have understood, and can say "Amen", he is talking about something else!'

Someone who sounds like an early atheist lived in the second half of the eighteenth century at Llanerch-yrfa, the scene of nineteenth century nocturnal prayer-meetings. An article in *'Cymru'* speaks of this 'remarkable man', who attended neither chapel nor church, stayed away from all religious services, did not hear the gospel, and though he went to funerals, would not attend the prayers in the house or enter the churchyard. His reckoning would be all the less when he appeared before the Judge, severely commented the author of the article. Possibly this obdurate non-joiner was Morgan Williams of Llanerch-yrfa, born 1753. According to the tombstone in Llanfihangel churchyard (obviously he did not escape from being buried in consecrated ground!) he died in March 1840 aged ninety-three, followed by his eighty-five year old sister Leah in the following month. Perhaps it was he, as an eccentric of some notoriety and a nonagenarian, who gave his name to a path over Bryn Mawr, near Drygarn, known as 'Llwybr Morgan Williams'.

INTRODUCTION

1. *Abergwesyn, July 1972. One of the nodal points of Abergwesyn village, showing Tŷmawr, Post Office, Gwesyn Cottages (now Tŷ Gwesyn), Tŷ Gof, Glangwesyn, Trysgol.*

2. *Abergwesyn from Forestry Road, January 1979, showing Tŷ'nllan, Irfon Cottage, two churchyards, Pentwyn Farm.*

3. Maesgwaelod Standing Stone, Llanwrtyd.

4. Standing Stone by Nantcerdin, Llanwrtyd.

5. Standing Stones in dyke between Gwesyn and Irfon.

I EARLY MAN

6. *Cerrig Pictaniaid*

7. *Burial Cist above Craig Irfon*

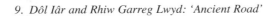

8. *Old track above Cefn Fanog (looking towards Abergwesyn)*

9. *Dôl Iâr and Rhiw Garreg Lwyd: 'Ancient Road'*

III THE LORDSHIP OF BUILTH

10. *Rhiw y Porthmyn, Nantystalwyn*

11. *Mound at Caerau, Llangamarch: probably motte.*

IV CHURCHES

12. *Old church of Llanfihangel Abergwesyn*

13. *Llanddewi Abergwesyn church*

IV CHURCHES

14. *Llanwrtyd Old Church (St. David's)*

15. *Eglwys Oen Duw, Beulah*

IV CHURCHES

16. *Old Vicarage (Delfryn), Abergwesyn*

17. *The Victorian church of Llangfihangel Abergwesyn*

AWN.7   THE CHURCH, ABERGWESYN

18. *Pantycelyn Baptist Chapel*

19. *Mounting block steps, Pantycelyn*

V NONCONFORMITY

20. *Moriah Independent Chapel, Abergwesyn, after flood, August 1973.*

21. *Kilsby Jones's tomb and Glenview (now 'Kilsby') 1070.*

VI NONCONFORMITY: Methodists

22. *Soar y Mynydd, Camddwr Valley*

23. *Dôlgoch, Tywi Valley*

24. Cwmdu and debatable land, Easter 1969

25. Abergwesyn School (now Village Hall)

26. Iron Room, August 1967

27. School group at Tŷhaearn (when the school was at the Iron Room)

28. *Llwynmadog*

29. *Trallwm (1976)*

30. *Celsau*

31. *Cefn Morarth*

32. Cwm Irfon, Llandwryd

33. Dinas, Llanwrtyd

7. Education

1. Early Schools

We do not know what schools there were in the Abergwesyn district before the eighteenth century, but it seems that some form of education existed for at least some of the inhabitants. Early wills show that of the minority who made a will many could at least sign their names, as did some of the witnesses and appraisers; and the totting-up of items valued in the inventory is usually correct.

In pre-Reformation days, the monasteries were a source of education for some. How far Strata Florida was able to cast its benevolent net is uncertain, especially in view of the wildness of the country and the badness of the roads, which remained, particularly in bad weather, a nightmare to would-be travellers till comparatively recent times. Remembering the tradition that a Strata Florida monk cared for the Abergwesyn churches, one wonders if he made some teaching of the children one of his responsibilities, and if so whether it extended beyond basic instruction in the Faith.

Post-Reformation clergy, or some of them, took on the role of teachers. For centuries, here and there were to be found parsons and curates, some learned men with private libraries, some with a minimum of education themselves, who kept little schools in their houses, or acted as tutors to the children of the local gentry, who in their wills frequently left money or property for the education and maintenance of their children. Younger sons or the sons of impecunious gentlemen might be 'settled' as apprentices, like Rees, second son of David Prees of Llanfihangel Abergwesyn, gentleman, in 1728. The executors were to choose 'some honest calling such as he shall best like, and in the meantime to expend [some money] to teach him to write'. Though in the sixteenth century Wales blossomed into a fine show of grammar schools, many country-dwellers, as G. Dyfnallt Owen remarks in *'Elizabethan Wales'*, were restricted by money and distance in getting to such schools, and those many who shared the widespread longing for literacy at that time often 'had to rely on more local institutions'. It was not only the clergy who taught — Owen cites an example of a North Welsh stocking-knitter who taught in two rooms of her shop.

A.H. Dodd writes in *'Studies in Stuart Wales'* of the 'obscurer private academies' of the seventeenth century with their smattering of a classical education for the sons of the more prosperous, and 'a host of unremembered "country schools"'. He suggests that the large output of Welsh printed books aimed at people familiar only with colloquial

83

Welsh implies a 'humbler but quite extensive reading public' at that time. On the other hand, he points out, the reforming Vicar Prichard painted gloomy pictures of the 'abysmal ignorance' of 'sheer illiterates'. One suspects that in a poor and remote district like this, such illiterates must have abounded, and remembers Williams Williams's remarks in the following century about the failure of Abergwesyn parents to procure any kind of teaching for their children.

None of the seventeenth century charity schools was very near to Abergwesyn. In 1694, at the time of an episcopal visitation of Llanddewi Abergwesyn, there was 'no free school'. There was a Welsh Trust school in Brecon in 1674, and by 1699 one of the S.P.C.K.'s schools was functioning in Llandeilo'r Fan on the Epynt. But it was the circulating schools of the Rev. Gruffydd Jones, working well with Methodist sympathisers, which first made real inroads here. Gruffydd Jones' schools, which began in the 1730s, and those of Madame Bevan which continued their work, were frankly religious in their purpose. They taught through the medium of Welsh wherever that was the language of the the people, and they were itinerant. The Rev. Tom Beynon has described their method of procedure. On the setting-up of a circulating school in a parish, the favour and help of the clergyman would be sought. Often the use of the parish church would be granted. The parson was expected to report on scholars and schoolmaster, to catechize and examine. The Bible and the Church Catechism were the textbooks.

In many schools two thirds of the pupils were adult. A report of 1744 on the progress of the schools tells how a bribe of bread-dole in church lured those 'old in ignorance' to submit to gentle questioning, 'not to puzzle or give them cause to blush'. If all went well, they would eventually come willingly to be instructed. Many masters taught for several hours in the evening people who had to be at work by day. Subjects were limited. The 'poor ignorant people and their children' were taught to read the Bible in Welsh, and by talks on Christian duty and the dangers of worldly vice were prepared to receive religious instruction from their parish clergyman. They learnt the Catechism, and to sing a psalm, and make the responses correctly in church.

Llanwrtyd had a circulating school in 1738-39, with seventy-four pupils: 1739-40, with sixty-eight: and 1741-42, with thirty-four. Edward Phillips, vicar of Maesynis from 1740 and a friend of Daniel Rowland, is said to have been instrumental in getting a circulating school to Pontrhydyfere, the lower village, where it was opened in part of Abernant farmhouse. Then there were a number of years without such a school, and when one visited Llanwrtyd again in 1753-54 it had only eleven pupils. There was a slight increase of interest in 1767-68, when thirty-eight people attended a circulating school there, at Ty Newydd.

Abergwesyn had a school in 1741-42, with thirty-eight pupils, quite a good attendance for such a tiny scattered place, and again in 1742-43, with twenty-seven pupils. Then after a few years' gap we find in Llanddewi Abergwesyn (perhaps the earlier school was in Llanfihangel) a circulating school with thirty-eight pupils in 1746-47.

William Williams of Pantycelyn was much much interested in education in this district. As we have seen, he regularly gave religious instruction to those children sent to him in Llanwrtyd church. He testified to the value of the work of 'R.M.' in the Llanwrtyd circulating school. The master of the school near Pentretywyn, he said, was good 'without taking it upon him to be an Exhorter'.

Circulating schools opened from time to time in Llanwrthwl, Llanafan fawr, Llanfihangel Bryn Pabuan, Llanganten, Llanlleonfel, Llangamarch and other nearby parishes, occupying for a period of months in each session churches, chapels, vicarages, farmhouses or outbuildings. Of course the curriculum was narrow. It was meant to be. The urgent need was seen to be that of saving souls. In the process people learnt to read, and read in their native language.

Sunday schools (never in Wales, started just for children) played a large part in local education. The Rev. William Williams (another of that name), influenced by Mr Raikes of Gloucester, the pioneer of the movement, opened the first in Wales at Cilycwm, just to the south of this area, and before the end of the eighteenth century established one in 'Bont' (Pontrhydyfere). The Calvinistic Methodist historian, John Hughes, describes the scene on a fine Sunday in what was to become the village of Llanwrtyd Wells, with people sitting out of doors, Bibles open before them or loose pages held in their hands, learning to read the Bible. We have already seen how the Sunday schools proliferated in the district, the best-attended being usually those of the nonconformist churches. It may come as a shock to read what a later Methodist leader, Thomas Charles of Bala, gave as his reason for using Welsh to teach his child pupils in Sunday school — that English, the language of social advantage, was for that very reason irrelevant to the needs of children most of whom would die young! We recall the tombstones at Pantycelyn, and the many-branched pedigrees of the gentry, with the repeated legend 'died in infancy'.

What other schools were there in this area to supplement the circulating schools and to follow them when in 1785 they ceased to function? Llanwrtyd and Llangamarch benefited from a bequest in 1783 by Mrs Margaret Jones of Great Queen Street, London, a native of Llangamarch. Part of the charity supported small free schools in the two parishes, superintended by trustees including the vicar. John Lloyd, the historian, of the Dinas, Brecon family whose ancestral home had been

Dinas, Llanwrtyd, tells us in his *'Historical Memoranda'*, vol. II, that such small schools were the only ones in Llanwrtyd and Llangamarch till 1860, when the building of parish schools got into its swing.

This John Lloyd's ancestor Captain John Lloyd of the E.I.C. attended some years before 1764 (when, aged sixteen, he went to sea) a school said to have been at Abergwesyn church, probably Llanfihangel, as family tradition says that he used to sleep at Rhiwddalfa, a remote farmhouse up the side-valley of Nant y Fedw, which debouches by Llanerch-yrfa. It seems strange that he did not just come up the Irfon valley from Dinas each day, if his parents were living there. A conflicting local tradition says that the school itself was at Rhiwddalfa. There does not seem to have been a circulating school at Abergwesyn at the time; if the school *was* at the church, probably a local clergyman instructed the children. John Lloyd later moved to a 'better school' at Merthyr Cynog. Lastly, he was sent to St Harmon, Radnorshire, to learn navigation from the vicar, the Rev. Llewelyn Davies, a very good mathematician and clock-maker, whose sons Joel and James both became clergymen.

At the end of the eighteenth century, David Williams, later to be the well-known Independent minister, went to a day-school in Llanwrtyd church. His biographer tells us it was kept by the vicar of Llanwrtyd and Abergwesyn, the Rev. Morgan Jones, who lived at Nantyrhebog (possibly Nantywalch — it means the same, 'Stream of the hawk', and is now called Cwmirfon). In Theophilus Jones's list of incumbents no Morgan Jones appears for the relevant parish. Perhaps he was a curate. The one in question is said to have had a wife who was a member of Gelynos chapel. D.A. Griffiths says he taught his pupils to read audibly and interpret punctuation marks, helping them by a rough-and-ready comparison of commas, semi-colons and so on to pauses of varying length along a road.

Theophilus Jones refers in about 1800 to 'a good Latin grammar school' formerly kept at Llanafan fawr, but discontinued in his day because of the vicar's poor health. Captain Frederick Jones of Llwynbarried, Nantmel, noted in his diary (ed. R.C.B. Oliver, *Radnorshire Society Transactions* LIV) in September 1804 that on Tuesday 15th he he and his wife returned from a visit to Llwynmadog, Abergwesyn 'by Perthsaint', Llanafan Fawr, which Mr Oliver explains was the vicarage house of the Rev. Henry Beynon, M.A., 'who had earlier kept a good country grammar school there'. In the nineteenth century we find a variety of little schools functioning from time to time in the district. We have come across the early Independent Sunday schools at Dôliâr near the River Gwesyn, on Pentwyn land, and later at Moriah chapel: the Baptist schools at Pantycelyn and, in the mid-nineteenth century, at Tymawr farmhouse: and the Sunday schools of the Calvinistic Methodists at Llanwrtyd, and, well into the twentieth century, in the farmhouses of the Tywi valley. Moriah chapel had a winter day-school, too. Rhys Gwesyn Jones attended it; for two quarters he was taught by 'Tomos y Twrne' ('the Attorney'), of whom he remembered little, finding he learnt much more by playing with the Jones children of the local mansion, Llwynderw, his rich relations, who spoke English with their playmates. Then came a Morgan Jones, who kept school each winter for some years. What was learnt in the winter was forgotten in the summer, said Rhys, who seems to have taken the Sunday school more seriously, being helped by reading in the Welsh Bible at home with his mother the chapters he was studying in English at school. By eight years old, he remembered, he could write and count, but had to get help with his sums from young Frederick Jones at Llwynderw.

Morgan Jones was a 'character', an excellent scholar who had been destined for the Church, but took to drink and 'missed his vocation' — one of the many *manqués* in the teaching profession at that time. Rhys says he boasted of being a wizard at Greek and Latin, but taught only the three Rs, reading being from the New Testament. There were no grammar or geography lessons and no stories. Morgan made full use of the cane, and if it was not to hand drew blood with a ruler across the pate. He kept school, said his ex-pupil, for a living, not from love of the work. Morgan Jones is said to have lived first at Nantyneuadd, up the Gwesyn valley below Trysgol. Its small ruins are still to be found in a most beautiful spot at the lower edge of the woods on the eastern side of the valley. Later, Morgan and his wife Bridget lived at Ty'nyddôl (Ty isaf) near Pentwyn ford. By 1851 they had two sons and two daughters. Morgan died in 1860.

In 1846 the Education Commissioners who toured Wales painted such a gloomy picture of life and education in that country that their reports, and the alleged unfairness of some of the questioning (in English) on which those reports are partly based, were to win lasting notoriety as 'The Treachery of the Blue Books'. Sir Thomas Phillips in 'Wales' (1849) expresses his distrust of some of the commissioners' opinions on Welsh morals and social conditions, and condemns their over-idealistic notions of what to expect from schools for the poor.

Indeed, the Commissioners' denigration of the Welsh character was met throughout Wales with justifiable outrage, so much so that as Gwynfor Evans points out in 'Land of my Fathers' it masked 'the real treachery — the betrayal of the language and the civilisation of Wales'. The commissioners attacked the Welsh language itself as 'a vast drawback to Wales and a manifold barrier to the moral progress and commercial prosperity of the people', and their report did much to further the institution of state education in English for all Welsh children, though it was not till 1870 that this became compulsory.

But the Blue Books did amass facts which were to say the least disturbing, pointing not to any inherent inferiority in the pupils, but to the unworthiness of their accommodation, equipment and books, and the inadequate training and poor pay of their teachers. Breconshire teachers had the third lowest average pay in the thirteen counties, earning an average of £23.15.2 per year. School buildings often wretched, lack of sanitation, inadequate furniture, no Welsh books — indeed, often a shortage of books of any kind — teachers usually untrained and often uneducated, 'desultory' attendance, poor discipline and a very early leaving age, all combined to ensure an all too frequently abysmal leaving standard. Girls fared even worse than boys.

Commissioner Henry Penry came to Abergwesyn on 4 November 1846. At Llanfihangel he examined Mary and Thomas Davies, thirteen and ten, 'living opposite the church'. Mary had spent a little while at Sunday school, Thomas had never been to school. 'Neither could read. They could not tell me how many halfpence there are in a shilling: how many pence in half a crown or five shillings. Neither knew what the name of the present month is, how many there are in the year... Did not know the Ten Commandments, and could not repeat the the Lord's Prayer. The girl knew who Jesus Christ was... but the boy did not answer a single question correctly on any subject'. Abysmal ignorance? Or the confusion of Welsh-speaking country children addressed in English by an alarming stranger? Possibly both.

The two Abergwesyn churches shared a curate and a parish clerk. The latter told Henry Penry that he was going to open a school on the following Monday. About twenty was the usual number of children one could expect here, he said. 'The amount obtained by fees from these is too little to support a proper teacher, and he is only doing it that he may educate his own children'.

At Llanddewi Abergwesyn Penry examined ten-year-old Mary Jones, living at Pwllybô. 'She could not read. She was able to answer scarcely any questions put to her upon general knowledge, but the questions I asked her upon Scriptural subjects were answered very well, as she had been taught these things by the daughters of the farmer whom she is living with'. They were members of Moriah Congregationalist Sunday school. On this, the Inspector obtained information from its patroness, Mrs Jones of Irfon Cottage, formerly of Llwynderw, who took an active part in its running.

The same day, on the road to Llanwrtyd (Penry keeps referring to 'Llanelwedd', but the context shows this to be a slip) the commissioner pounced on John Jenkins, aged sixteen, and his brother Thomas, aged fourteen, of Penybont farm. They attended Llanwrtyd school and Moriah Sunday school and answered all Penry's questions 'very correctly, more so than any I had before examined in Wales'.

In the vestry of St David's church, Llanwrtyd, the commissioner visited the Margaret Jones charity school, and met the schoolmaster, 'a very well educated man, one who received a classical education to prepare them for the church'. His own four children attended the school; the eldest boy had made 'considerable progress in arithmetic; and... also answered me very well the questions I put to him on the rudiments of English grammar and a few of the leading events in English history'. (It was to be a long time before any idea that a Welsh child might reasonably be expected to know 'a few of the leading events' of *Welsh* history was to gain currency!) The report on this vestry-school was quite favourable. As the endowment had been suspended for three years to pay a legacy-duty, pupils were having to pay — one reason, Penry thought, for the poor attendance. On 4 November the school had only just recommenced after the 'summer recess'. The vestry was 'more comfortable for a schoolroom than any similar' Penry had seen, with its relatively good lighting and raised floor which made it dry and warm. However, the roof wanted mending and the inside cleaning.

Far worse was the situation at nearby Tirabad, where another commissioner found the little church-cum-school 'with large holes in the roof and evincing every symptom of neglect and discomfort'. On the floor beside one of the pews at the back of the smoke-filled church was a peat fire, around which huddled twenty children, reading aloud in turn 'out of dilapidated primers or dog-eared Testaments; all except two were reading English. The master sat among them with his hat on', never questioning his pupils. They were surprisingly good at English spelling considering their ignorance of the words' meaning. 'These children were evidently very shrewd and quick', able despite their conditions to answer many of the visitor's questions. Their writing was very bad — hardly surprising, this, as they had to write standing up, and on a desk improvised on the pews. They were probably coughing, too, in the all-pervading peat-smoke.

A day-school was kept from time to time in Beulah chapel, which is said to have been first built for a school. The masters varied considerably in quality. John Jones, who taught there in the 1830s, was described by David Lewis Wooding, a former pupil, as 'of the old school, and of a most inferior class therein'. He was, in fact, a pig-killer, and was often late for school because of the exigencies of his craft. A far better Beulah schoolmaster was David Davies of Penycrug, Llanafan fawr, who at various times kept school in other parishes too, including, Wooding says, at Pantycelyn in Abergwesyn. He was a man respected in the area, a

'Guardian of the Poor' in Llanafan, Registrar for Abergwesyn district, and something of a poet.

Kilsby Jones, the Independent minister, kept a school at Glenview from about 1856, employing as schoolmistress, so Vyrnwy Morgan writes, a Miss Gibbon from Rugby. The subjects taught included grammar, arithmetic, sewing, knitting, music, painting (oil and watercolour). The fee was 12s a quarter. After Kilsby himself moved to Glenview, boys were admitted; he taught them himself. Thomas Powel, later to be Professor of Celtic Studies at the University College, Cardiff, was among Kilsby's pupils. Vyrnwy Morgan mentions, too, 'Bridgend School, Llanwrtyd', home of Mrs Barker, another ex-pupil of Glenview. Later private schools have included, in this century, one at The Grange, just to the Abergwesyn side of Llanwrtyd Wells.

At the remote farmhouse of Cefngilfach, to the ruins of which an old track still leads high above the upper Camarch, a night-school is locally said to have been kept in the latter part of the nineteenth century by one of the Herbert family, brother of little Catherine Herbert the dwarf, of Fedw, lower down the valley.

Some 'born teachers' worked through the Sunday schools. Rhys Gwesyn Jones, in his article on Abergwesyn (1861) in *'Y Diwigiwr'*, wrote of Charles Jenkins, the eldest son of a large family from Penybont bach, which once stood on the roadside near the present farmhouse of Penybont uchaf. Jenkins was a deacon of Moriah chapel and related to a vicar of Gwenddwr who gave Penybont bach to the Church. Charles Jenkins once 'borrowed' the vicar's sermon notes to prove that Anglicans could not preach without them! He was a Sunday school teacher in Llanwrtyd, where he worked wonders with one Beni Ty Cwrdd, an inattentive youth, by bribing him with pennies to attend to his book. Beni profited in all senses from this treatment, for in six weeks he could read, and in after-years was recommended for the ministry.

Local marriage registers suggest that for a long time women lagged behind men in, at least, the ability to write. The surviving marriage registers of the Abergwesyn parishes, and those of Llanwrtyd too, show in the eighteenth century and the first part of the nineteenth century a high though diminishing illiteracy for both sexes (the emphasis in the circulating schools was on *reading*); but the number of marriages where the bride could write her name and the groom could not are few indeed compared with the many where the groom signed and the bride made her mark. Between 1813 and 1837 Llanddewi Abergwesyn had an unusually high proportions of literate couples; at ten marriages both bride and groom could write, compared with eleven at which neither could write, and eight at which only the groom signed. What this seems to indicate, however, is a higher than usual marriage-rate, between those years, of the more prosperous parishioners, such as the Jones family of Llwynderw and their connections, rather than any general improvement so long before compulsory education.

8. Education

(ii) The 'Iron Room' and the 'Stone School'

The first school in Abergwesyn to be housed in a building of its own and conducted on a full-time basis was established some time between 1865 and 1870 in a corrugated iron structure near the Grouse Inn (Pentwyn). A modern bungalow has now been built on the site of the old Iron Room, whose rusty and unbeautiful bulk loomed for many years in a corner of a field by the road-junction, and with its ecclesiastical air was often an object of curiosity to visitors. Services were held there while the Victorian church was being built; indeed, as we have seen, in 1870 it was called the 'temporary Iron Church'. The Glanusk edition of Jones' county history tells us that the school was maintained partly by the Thomas family of Llwynmadog, near Beulah, and we have noted that in 1865 Miss Clara Thomas was seeking subscriptions for it as well as for the church.

Mr and Mrs Henry Thomas had earlier been the chief subscribers to the 'first elementary school under Government inspection in the district lying between Llandovery and Builth'. 'Neighbouring landowners and farmers' had also contributed. This school, at Beulah, was built about 1850; its foundation stone was laid by the young heir of Llwynmadog, Evan Llewelyn Thomas, who was to die in 1864 aged twenty-five. According to the records of the National Society for Promoting Religious Education, the school was first called 'Llanafan Abergwessin School'; it was then in Llanfihangel Abergwesyn, still part of Llanafan parish. Later the school was to be called 'Llwynmadoc British School'. A school at Llanafan fawr was also generously helped by the Thomas family.

Herbert Vaughan, for fourteen years a friend of Miss Clara Thomas, daughter of Henry Thomas, writes in *'The South Wales Squires'* of the Thomases' work for and with the children of the neighbourhood. Eglwys Oen Duw, the church built and endowed by Miss Thomas, was at Beulah, and the nearby school to which her parents had been the major subscribers 'took up much time and attention from the lady of the house and her lifelong friend, Miss Gertrude Lewis Lloyd of Nantgwyllt. On Sunday afternoons the two ladies always taught their classes of boys and girls at Llwyn Madoc House'. After the widowed Mrs Thomas died in 1877, Miss Thomas continued her mother's help with Abergwesyn education too.

By 1870 the Rev John Jones, vicar of Abergwesyn, was trying to raise funds to build a National schoolroom and teacher's residence.

Apparently the school in the Iron Room was already functioning, but the building was regarded as temporary. The correspondence in Society for Promoting Religious Education records shows that the population of the united parish in 1870 was about 470; the proposed schoolroom was to accommodate about eighty children. 'A site had been obtained [presumably the one given by Mr Thomas of Welfield in 1865] and the cost of the project was estimated at £450. Towards this sum £80 had been raised locally; the Government had granted £125; the Diocesan Board had promised £60 and £20 was expected from other sources. Towards the upkeep about £30 had been promised in annual subscriptions and a Government capitation grant would be available but it was expected that it would be necessary to charge from 1d to 6d a week according to the means of the parents in order to maintain the school. The Society offered to contribute £50, but this was not taken up, nor was the Government grant ever paid. No further correspondence exists, but the school did continue, the Iron Room being used for many years to come. The school held in it is listed in official reports from 1872, from which date it received annual Government aid. In 1871 'number One, School Cottage' appears in the Census return, occupied by John Thomas, a thirty-eight year old Glamorganshire man, who, with his Cardiganshire wife, taught in the 'National School'. They had six children and two lodgers. Number Two was well-filled, too, by a widower stone-mason, his sister-in-law and his four children. The divided 'School Cottage' is thought to have been the present corrugated-iron bungalow of Tyhaearn, which stands next to the field where the old school was built. It may well have been erected at the same time as the Iron Room; the late Mr J.R. Hope of Pentwyn believed Tyhaearn to date from about 1865. It appears as 'One and Two Iron House' in the Census of 1881. Number Two was occupied by the twenty-two year old schoolmaster, Edward Thomas. In 1891 the teacher living there was nineteen-year-old Florrie Thomas, born in Australia.

The Iron Room was built to accommodate seventy-two children; in 1872 the average attendance was thirty-one. This number slowly dwindled over the years until 1892-93, when there were only eleven children. The school evidently closed soon after this, as no further grants were made.

An old photograph of unknown date, but thought to be of about the 1880s, shows a school group on the verandah at Tyhaearn, at the end (now a garage) opposite the old Iron School. Eighteen serious boys of assorted ages, most of them in high-buttoned jackets, stand astare, presided over by a handsome dark-haired young woman and another (a visitor?), looking slightly apprehensive, in a hat with a striped scarf wound round it. In the front row two girls, booted and white-aproned, their shoulders draped in plaid shawls (products of the local woollen industry?), flank three round-faced, thoughtful smaller girls with boyish haircuts. One wonders if the preponderance of boys is anything more than an accident of that day's attendance, or whether there really were more boy-pupils than girls at that time.

On Saturday 17 July 1880 Miss Clara Thomas invited superintendents and teachers of thirteen schools to a celebration at Cwmbach Llechryd, near Builth, for the centenary of the establishment of Sunday schools by Robert Raikes. Everyone met at Pencerrig School by noon for light refreshments. (Pencerrig was Miss Thomas' other house in the area.) Over a hundred clergy and teachers arrived by train at Builth Road Station, and progressed to the schoolroom, headed by Llanwrtyd Brass Band. An assembly in the 'little iron church' (how this material seems to haunt the period!) was addressed by Canon Bevan of Hay, familiar now to readers of Kilvert. Then the congregation marched to Pencerrig, and enjoyed a 'sumptuous luncheon' for about 120, in a room decorated with evergreens and exotics. The Rev A.T. Coore of Builth headed the tables; Miss Thomas herself, to whom a toast was drunk, sat at the head of her own Sunday school staff. The Beulah Glee Club sang Welsh and English part-songs. Mr Roberts of Builth, Queen Victoria's Harpist, played Welsh music on the national triple harp. Llanwrtyd Band performed. The *Hereford Times* article praised Miss Thomas' interest in the 'moral and spiritual life of the neighbourhood', her mother's and her own building and maintaining of churches and schools, and her many charitable works.

When the Iron Room school closed, a so-called 'British School' opened in its place in a new stone building. Unlike most British Schools, however, it seems not to have been managed by the British and Foreign School Society, which has no record of it. Such management would have implied undenominational education, and the school at Abergwesyn could hardly have been more 'Church', with its regular Diocesan inspections and Scripture examinations. In its earlier days, at least, it lived under the wing of the vicar and the local Church gentry, who were regular visitors. Not long after it opened, a small boy was punished in school for talking in church the previous Sunday — he had to write 'talking' fifty times! A list of equipment and textbooks received by the schoolmistress in September 1895 shows that the school used the National Society's history readers — another pointer to its Church affiliation. In February 1898 £10 was granted, £5 to increase the teacher's salary, £5 for equipment, 'under the Voluntary Schools Act of 1897 under a scheme submitted by the South Wales and Monmouthshire *British Association* and approved by the Education Department'. Here may be the origin of the term 'British' in this area. Abergwessin School is called a 'British School' in *Kelly's Directory* for 1895. In January 1900 'Abergwessin British School' received a grant of £12, £6 to increase the teacher's salary, £6 for the monitress. Later, a departing teacher referred, in 1919, to 'Abergwesyn Non-Provided [i.e. Voluntary] School'.

The new stone school was given the same official number as that in the Iron Room, 5148, and kept it till 2 May 1906, when it was changed to 34. The new building had in mind a possible total attendance of forty — half the number which it had been hoped might be housed in the schoolroom proposed in 1865 — and in its first year, 1894-95, the schoolroom was well-filled, even more than the forty officially catered for being present on good days in its best years, then once more dwindled till in spite of temporary recoveries the number went down again to about eleven children, and the school finally closed in 1927. The school had to prove its worth before it got any grant, and in later years capitation was an obvious preoccupation, teachers seeking excuses not to mark the registers when the numbers were poor enough to make a drastic difference to the average.

The first teacher, Margaret Jones, who took charge on 2 April 1894, when thirty-one 'neat, clean and punctual' pupils turned up, stayed only just over a year. Already what were to prove perennial problems were making themselves felt — isolation: the devastating effect of bad weather on attendance in a district of scattered mountain homesteads: coughs, colds, epidemics: and the fact that parents and pupils put farm and home before school. Among reasons for absence over the years we find peat-cutting, turf-cutting and stacking, potato-setting, potato-lifting, shearing (this above all, for it had a social side as well), lamb-marking, haymaking, corn-harvesting, nursing the baby, caring for sick relatives, and boiling the kettle for dinner. The boys occasionally acted as beaters. There is no doubt that the children were often genuinely needed at home. The work there and on the land always had priority. It is sad, though, to read occasionally in the log-books of bright children removed willy-nilly as soon as they reached fourteen. They did not always want to leave school; they had no choice. Sometimes parents tried to remove them too young, and even entered into premature contracts with employers.

Pouring rain, thunderstorms, gales, sleet and heavy snow all took their toll of attendance. In November 1894 we find the first of a number of references to Llanddewi Abergwesyn children being unable to get to school owing to the flooding of the Irfon, which they had to ford or cross by a foot-bridge. In a flood of 1897 the foot-bridge collapsed. It was not till the advent of the present road that a more substantial bridge was built, further downstream, itself to be replaced by a larger one in 1969. Even today flooding can cut off Llanddewi from Llanfihangel.

Then there were the local festivities, for which in the early days children were often kept at home by their parents. Later, the school authorities admitted defeat, and gave holidays for some of them. The School Treats, of course, were permitted holidays, with their games, racing and tobogganing and their lavish feasting. Pupils often competed in local *eisteddfodau*, and in Beulah in 1905 the Abergwesyn headmaster adjudicated in the Literature section. The schoolchildren took part in many a *Cymanfa Ganu* (chapel Singing Festival) and went to church and chapel teas, Sports at Llanwrtyd, Beulah and Abergwesyn, Empire Day festivities in Llanwrtyd, a Sunday school fete at Gwernyfed Park near Glasbury, and missionary exhibitions at Llanwrtyd and Brecon. And whether or not they were officially allowed to go, how could they be indifferent to a local hare-coursing match, or sheep dog trials, especially a yearly one in Abergwesyn itself, held in the field opposite the school? Weddings and funerals could affect school attendance, and so could farm sales, to which children were sometimes taken by their parents.

In May 1895 Miss Esther Morgan (Certificated First Class) was appointed headmistress: she was to stay for nine of the school's best years, and to return for a further six and a half years. A comparison of the Government reports on the school in these two periods shows a change in attitudes to education. Miss Morgan seems to have been a dedicated and conscientious teacher of the old style, a disciplinarian, though one who tried persuasion before resorting to the cane. Though she had 'kept her Welsh', she seems to have had no conception of the school as a Welsh one for Welsh-speaking children. When she mentions patriotism, she means loyalty to the English Crown and the English flag; one of her proudest moments was when the school was at last given a Union Jack of its own. Her predecessor had taught the children to sing 'Hurrah! Hurrah for England!' Miss Morgan introduced some Welsh songs, but went no further. During her first nine years there, the school flourished; reports were glowing. When she came back, she did succeed in improving it when standards had slipped; but this time the inspectors criticized her methods, the rigidity of her discipline, and the exclusive use of English in such an area.

When Miss Morgan first took over the school, the visiting H.M.I. reported the school in good order, but the children very backward in the three Rs, needlework and drawing, which was a subject for boys only, and continued to be so. Gradually things improved. By 1898 the school was 'extremely well taught'. Miss Morgan was well supported by the school managers, who visited regularly — in particular members of the Thomas family of Cefndyrys, Llanelwedd, then called Welfield, and of Glangwesyn, Abergwesyn, who had given the plot for the building of the school. They owned most of the land in this part of Abergwesyn, as the related Thomases of Llwynmadog did at the Beulah end.

Clean faces, clean hands, tidy hair, clean and well-mended clothes and well-scraped boots were insisted on, and neatness in sewing and writing much approved of. The visitors seem to have enjoyed their encounters with the hard-working teacher and docile pupils, and there is no reason to think that Colonel Thomas of Glangwesyn imagined the children's 'happy faces' which he noticed with pleasure in July 1900. Attendance was excellent at this time in the school's history. If the children had been unhappy or bored, or if their parents disapproved of the education they were getting, many of them would have made use of some of the classic country excuses and stayed at home, as indeed they did at some other times.

Nor did the visiting gentry appear briefly, smile at the smiling faces and make an exit. They stayed, and took more than a superficial interest. Mrs Thomas of Welfield was for some time the school correspondent. Calling at the school in May 1902, she came one Tuesday afternoon and again on Thursday, staying two hours each time, inspecting needlework, drawing and handwork and hearing the singing. Her husband was at one time chairman of the foundation managers; he was followed by his son Mr (later Captain) Aubrey Thomas. All of them regularly visited, and gave presents and prizes. Mr and Mrs Aubrey Thomas gave a school treat at Glangwesyn for a number of years. Other managers too took an interest in the school. Mr Rhys Llywelyn Williams brought visitors in September 1902, who not only listened to the children singing, but sang to them in return. In 1905 Miss Clara Thomas of Llwynmadog, an occasional visitor to the school, and one of its managers as she had been of its predecessor, brought her friend Miss Lloyd of Nantgwyllt, questioned the children on geography and gave them a talk on her travels.

Other visitors to the school in this its blossom time included, as well as the Vicarage families, managers Mr Rhys Morgan Hope of the Grouse Inn and Mr Davies of Tymawr farm, whose young son Hugh died tragically in 1895 of 'inflammation of the spinal cord'. Sadly recording his fatal illness, Miss Morgan wrote how all would miss this 'bright, intelligent lad', now, in May, 'lying helpless'. Mrs Roberts of Llwynderw sometimes visited the school; in September 1901 the Misses Roberts called to invite the pupils to a treat at their Llanddewi mansion.

In later years successive teachers were to complain of the then managers' indifference and neglect, and their timidity over tackling such problems as refractory cleaners! But in the 1890s and early 1900s all went merrily as the school bell. Problems existed, of course, the chief enemy being 'winter and rough weather', when even if the children came, their hands were too numb to write, and the little ones cried with cold. (Miss Morgan tried to interest the older ones in a lesson on 'Fuel'!) When easterly gales blew, the fire smoked, causing sore throats and smarting eyes, and dirtying pictures and walls. Then there were the ailments and epidemics — coughs, swollen throats, colds, sickness, mumps, measles, German measles, whooping cough, chicken pox, scarlet fever — some of them causing school closures or extensions of holidays, after which lost and forgotten work had to be made up, with no help for the hard-pressed teacher except that of an untrained monitress. At times she too was ill, and the head teacher was left battling alone.

By January 1902 the strain was telling on Miss Morgan. The winter had been bad, November rains being followed by heavy December snow. The school closed for two days, 'for the first time in [Miss Morgan's] six and a half years'. Now in January half the children were away with 'flu, and she herself was struggling against a cold, headache, loss of voice and general weakness, but 'tried hard to keep on the school for the few who were able to come'. It was not the first time she had had trouble with her throat and chest. The wretched east wind blew smoke down the chimney again. Temperatures sank to many degrees of frost.

With spring, life and work improved, and the school was back in the round of managers' visits, occasional holidays (two days in June for the Coronation of Edward VII), inspections and examinations. These had always been big days. In 1896 there was a half-holiday after the Government examinations; walls had been swept, pictures and maps cleaned, and the room scrubbed for the occasion, and Mrs Thomas of Welfield, who visited three times that week (once on the same morning as Mr Williams and Mr Hope) brought 'choice flowers' for the schoolroom. The visits of the Diocesan Inspector and the annual Scripture examination were important too, and were almost invariably followed by a good report and the presentation of certificates for religious knowledge.

In late June, 1902, a severe measles epidemic caused the school to close early for a six-week holiday. Soon after it re-opened, Miss Morgan recorded with satisfaction the installation of a new water supply. But December brought renewed strain — the dreaded east wind returned, to be followed by incessant rain and floods. The school was closed from 20 January to 23 February for scarlet fever; when it restarted a few were still absent with fever. Then wet weather and influenza came together. In late March Miss Morgan succumbed to bronchitis. The monitress carried on, doing her best to follow a scheme of work the head-teacher worked out. Miss Morgan tottered into school again at the beginning of April, but was weak and ill for some time.

Summer, and good reports from both the Diocesan Inspector and H.M.I., worked their usual cure; but winter brought another problem. In the stormy January of 1904, Miss Price, the monitress became ill with pleurisy and was away for some months. In February Miss Morgan herself had a bronchial cold, and found teaching 'the two divisions of Infants and the six divisions of older scholars' at the time, particularly in arithmetic, 'especially difficult'. About the 19th there were three days of heavy snow; Miss Morgan gave a lesson on 'The Snowflake'. By the 26th she was still hoarse, and to add to her miseries sprained her right thumb. In March, sleet and snow continued. Towards the end of the month a helper was at last sent from Builth, but was useless with the older girls' needlework, and incapable of coping with a class of infants.

After the Easter holidays, the doctor said that Miss Morgan's ill-health was serious. The school closed till the 25th to allow her to rest. As soon as she came back she complained of 'mental strain'. The monitress was still away, and in May there was an average attendance of over forty. Poor Miss Morgan, struggling to teach the Infants a new song, 'The Duck', and cope with the older children's work as well, found it 'increasingly difficult to carry on...owing to [her] Mental state'. On 20 May, 'with intense regret', she gave up the school, suffering from a 'breakdown of health'.

Abergwesyn children had an unusually long summer holiday. In September there arrived a headmaster, Thomas Griffiths, certificated but untrained. With him came his wife Sarah as assistant teacher. Mr Griffiths plumed himself on his good order, enforced at first by frequent 'strokes', though by March 1905 he could write that corporal punishment was now at a minimum. He also congratulated himself on an excellent attendance record. In October 1904 Abergwesyn School was the best-attended in Breconshire, and next month in appalling weather 'some of the children heroically faced the tempest, and came from long distances'. Mr Griffiths praised the parents. The school was so well-attended, in fact, that one of its problems was overcrowding! Some of these children had to walk three miles to school, up hill, down dale and across river. Sometimes they were wet through when they got to school, and had to dry out their clothes and take turns by the fire. No wonder Mr Griffiths thought the schoolroom fire ought to be 'brilliant'! Then at the end of the day those miles had to be trudged again, and more thawing-out was to be done at the home hearth. It is hardly surprising that their parents occasionally kept the children at home.

Like most teachers who came to Abergwesyn, Thomas Griffiths criticised the state of the school when he took over. He admitted that there was some excuse for backwardness, as owing to Miss Morgan's illness there had been no school for three months, and the children had forgotten their tables and spelling. They read without understanding or 'modulation'; indeed, their first examination results showed weakness in all three Rs. Their dictation was 'degrading'!

The managers continued to be exemplary visitors. Mr Griffiths' second day was enlivened (or harassed) by the appearance of Mrs Thomas of Welfield, Mrs Aubrey Thomas of Glangwesyn, Mr Rhys Llywelyn Williams and Mr Davies. The vicar, the Rev A.T. Jones, followed on the next day. On 21 November 1904 Mrs C.L. Thomas promised attendance prizes. A new cloakroom was added to the school, and Mrs Aubrey Thomas and Mr Thomas of Welfield came to admire it on 30 November. Next day came gifts from Welfield — a garment for each child, and the promise of book-prizes. A 'remarkable interest', thought Mr Griffiths.

Nature and nature-drawing, especially in colour, interested the children. Mr Griffiths complained of the parsimony of the Local Education Authority (established in 1902) over materials. A little girl brought a hedgehog to school, and a lesson was given on it. Tadpoles, minnows and a bat followed. Over the years many living creatures were brought, including a fox-cub. Some teachers took the children for walks, and gave open-air lessons.

By the end of the year work was improving. The standard of English was 'very satisfactory in a country place like this', though marred by 'provincialisms' like 'drownded'. In May 1905 Mrs Griffiths became ill and had to stop work. She had previously had sick headaches and was sometimes 'nervous'. Now the headmaster was up at night, losing sleep, and feeling strained, giddy and lacking in enthusiasm. Next month a new monitress was appointed, as Mrs Griffiths had resigned, though she still helped with the needlework. There was the usual summer trouble of absences for the many shearings, which, however, Mr Griffiths called 'a most attractive feature in this neighbourhood. The parents invariably take their children to regale on the good things provided'. The opportunity for feasting was not to be foregone in a hard countryside. One remembers how the bards praised the generous feasts at their patrons' tables.

After the summer holidays there was a success to announce. Two pupils were awarded exhibitions for farmers' sons to Builth Intermediate School. J.R. Hope was second on the list, Roderick Davies fourth.

By December the worst attendance for years resulted from epidemics of scabs and whooping-cough. The monitress' scabby face was 'sickening'. The Griffiths' baby sometimes ailed. Soon, Mr Griffiths resigned. One parent removed his son and sent him to Llanwrtyd school, 'being that there are so many changes at Abergwessin'. A plan to keep the school open under the care of two monitresses, Miss Price and Miss Watkins, was abandoned. It closed on 28 January 1906 and did not re-open till 17 April, when Miss Dora Palmer, taking charge, found twenty-five well-behaved but backward pupils awaiting her. The sing-song recitation she tried to cure with an infusion of 'Curfew must not ring tonight'!

Miss Palmer stayed just over a year. She was followed on 2 September 1907 by Miss Ruth Rees, who was soon reporting arithmetic backward and multiplication tables unknown to some of the older children. Soon she had the help of Miss Ann Davies, monitress. Miss Rees' 'scheme of work' for 1907-08 refers to 'British' history. Wales and the Welsh made no appearance; even the songs were all English. H.M.I.'s report in November 1908 regretted the fall in the standard of work, but hoped for an improvement. Attendance had been declining for some time. By Miss Rees' departure on 24 July 1908, the weather, shearings, all the standard reasons and excuses were markedly affecting attendance. There seems to have been a lack of *hwyl* about the school at that period.

At this juncture, Miss Morgan returned. She was highly critical of the teaching methods used since she was last in command, and thought that the three Rs had been much neglected in favour of drawing and singing. There were now twenty-eight children at the school. Miss Morgan thought some of the excuses for absence inadequate, and reported a couple of parents who kept five children home to attend an auction at Trallwm farm. Soon she was able to write of improved attendance and work. There were a few mild discipline problems, especially with the older boys, one of whom stamped with unnecessary force while marching in from play, and muttered insolently when reproved. The headmistress eventually had to resort to 'a few stripes' of the cane.

The Iron Room was still in occasional use; on 10 March 1909 it was the scene of Abergwesyn Eisteddfod, at which one of Miss Morgan's pupils won the first prize for reciting the poem 'Disenthralled'. Gradually, under Miss Morgan's rule, attendance crept up — the total was thirty in March 1909, thirty-seven in June 1910. The Vicarage families visited, Mr Aubrey Thomas, now of The Skreen, Erwood, called and signed the register, and Mrs Thomas sent presents for the school, among them four pairs of scissors and a needle case. She offered prizes for attendance and sewing. She was pleased with the needlework examination — 'they are all so good'. The School Treat was still held at Glangwesyn. It was at the one in 1911 that Mr Thomas delighted Miss Morgan by a gift of a Union Jack for the school. She had 'wished for it greatly'.

In May 1910 Miss Morgan decided to devote a few minutes daily to speaking on the late king and his successor, 'to inculcate a feeling of Loyalty and Patriotism'. She saved royal portraits for the school, and descriptions from London papers. She got the children to sing 'God Save the King' several times. On 24 May, Empire Day was an occasion for saluting the Union Jack, marching along the road for five minutes, and (once more) singing 'God Save the King'.

The following autumn was to see a decline in attendance. There was a good deal of illness, and also of absence for local events such as fairs. All this interfered very much with school work. H.M.I. had reported a few months after Miss Morgan's return that much had to be done to restore the school's standard, and that good progress was expected. But by 1911 the then Inspector, Mr Price, found the instruction 'only fairly satisfactory'. He advised the cultivation of intelligence and self-reliance in the children, who were reluctant to answer when questioned. In 1913, the H.M.I., Mr Abel, while praising the 'solid effort' of the headmistress, working under difficulties in a school where attendance was irregular and the only help that of a monitress, young and unqualified, thought Miss Morgan's discipline (formerly much praised) 'excessively rigid', the children's essays stereotyped, reading monotonous and arithmetic weak, and considered that attendance would improve if school work were made more interesting. Above all, he criticised the 'unsatisfactory place given to the Welsh language' — the home language of nearly all the children. It should be 'largely the language of instruction' throughout the school, and certainly used for the Infants' work. Yet it was 'restricted to a few Welsh recitations and songs and a little reading in the lower classes', with the result that the pupils had no real command of either language, so could hardly seem other than unresponsive.

Perhaps the report upset Miss Morgan; in the following year she started having nervous troubles again. Dr Tarbutt of Llanwrtyd listened to her symptoms — severe pains in the head, and a film rising and falling before one eye — and prescribed rest and a strong nerve-tonic. One day, when in spite of great pain in her head and eye (it sounds like migraine) Miss Morgan was struggling to cope with her charges, an unknown gentleman came by, and questioned the children in their own language. He spoke courteously to the ailing headmistress, praising the way she had 'kept her Welsh', and pronouncing the children intelligent, though a little shy. He was none other than Owen M. Edwards, perhaps Wales' best-known Chief Inspector of Education.

Two years before, in 1911, we find the first reference in the log-books to the observance of St David's Day, in compliance with instructions from the Education Committee, Brecon. One hour in the morning was devoted to the singing of Welsh songs; there were addresses on 'St David', 'Eminent Welshmen' and 'Patriotism'. A similar programme characterised later St David's Days; Empire Day continued to be observed as well. The children sat or marched as instructed, but a later teacher commented despairingly on their total lack of patriotism (either Welsh or 'British', presumably!).

There were fewer visitors now than in the old days. When on 19 July Miss Morgan wrote 'With great regret and deep sorrow I record the death of Miss Clara Thomas of Llwynmadoc', she was recording the end of a whole era in the valley's life, and that of the school. Then came the war. Miss Morgan made no direct reference to its outbreak, though on 1 September 1914 she gave a singing lesson on 'Flag of Britain', and got the children to salute the Union Jack in the chorus.

Regular health inspections by Medical Officers and school nurses had been the practice for some time. On 12 November 1914 a lecturer from the National Memorial Association spoke for an hour on 'The Prevention of Consumption'. November and December were months of high winds and sweeping rainstorms. There was much sickness, and the monitress became ill. Miss Morgan battled on, feeling ill, and much troubled by the shifting film before her bad eye. For a week she succumbed and the school had to close. Then she tried for two more days to carry on, but this time hopelessly. On 14 December the school closed early for the Christmas holiday. When it re-opened, it was under a new head-master. Miss Morgan never returned.

On 18 January 1915 a temporary headmaster, Mr E. Davies, took charge, when 'the ground around [was] covered with a mantle of snow'. He stayed till mid-June. The winter months were hard, with snow, heavy rain, and a 'strong wind driving up the valley'. In March Mr Davies wrote 'This is the coldest district I have ever visited'. He had the help of his wife with the sewing and knitting, and grown-up children, themselves teachers with experience of the work of 'a large and well-conducted school' occasionally assisted. Mr Davies' son taught the Welsh National Anthem and 'God Bless the Prince of Wales'.

Next came as headmistress Miss S.V. Jones. She was soon working particularly hard at arithmetic and English, in which she sometimes gave extra tuition instead of sewing and drawing. Soon after she arrived, her monitress, Miss Evans, spent a week at Llanwrtyd studying Infant teaching. The total number on the Abergwesyn books was quite high again — on 7 July there were thirty-nine on the register but only fifteen were present, because of shearings at Llwynderw and Alltfelen. Trawsgyrch shearing followed a week later — the usual summer pattern.

In January 1916 Miss Annie Winstone Jenkins started as supplementary teacher, soon encountering the familiar 'thick snow' varied by 'very rough weather'. There were St David's Day talks on 'The Origin of the Leak[sic]' and 'True Patriotism'. The Roll of Honour was read. 'A few facts about the war was [sic] told the children by the head teacher'. March 28 was marked by the 'heaviest and worst snow this year', with very high drifts. Only three children turned up. Roads were blocked. The teachers' report on the spring examinations was good. Arithmetic was still weak, but for Scripture most children got nearly full marks, and writing was much better now that they were no longer using the side of their pens. 'Most of the children find great difficulty in expressing themselves, but their grammar is not at all bad, considering they are country children and nearly always speaking the Welsh language'. By June the Diocesan Inspector was reporting an improvement — more thorough work, and a 'good tone'. Next month both teachers left, and the school was closed for two months.

On 2 October 1916 Mrs M.J. Johnston started duties. Soon stormy weather had reduced the number of pupils present to twelve, and she reported 'not much progress'. There was no supplementary teacher, and she felt the disadvantage of her own lack of Welsh, which made working with Infants particularly difficult. There was little kindergarten equipment. Miss M.E. Lewis' arrival as assistant on 30 October must have been welcome. Next month there was an echo of the old days — a visit by Mr and Mrs Aubrey Thomas. Winter again provided a crop of difficulties — ailments, snow, rain, sleet, roads blocked with half-thawed snow, bitter cold — no wonder Miss Lewis fell ill! But she was soon back, taking Welsh recitation and songs — 'They seem to enjoy Welsh lessons very much' — though only till the end of January 1917, when she left for another post. Mrs Johnston was alone again. In February she wrote that making comforts for soldiers had given the girls a fresh interest in knitting. Her St David's Day talks included some reference to Welsh music.

April tests were 'very disappointing', and she was pleased when the arrival in May of a Miss Jones as supplementary teacher gave the neglected Infants a chance of some attention. This year the Welsh national anthem was sung on Empire Day as well as 'God Save the King'.

An extension of the summer holidays was granted to allow the children to help with the harvest. When school re-opened on 10 September only nineteen were present, as a wet summer had made the hay and corn harvests late. Some children had left the district; one was going to school at Swansea; another was over age. There were now only twenty-seven on the register. Another hard winter lay ahead, of extreme cold and drifting snow. On 18 January 1918 not one child came to school. The thaw, with pouring rain, had made roads impassable with water and slush. The children's feet were soaked after a few yards' walking. In 1918 there was no St David's Day half-holiday, because of previous closures, and no Empire Day, as minimum attendances had to be kept up.

Miss Jones left on 26 April 1918, to be followed as assistant by

Miss Daniel. Mrs Johnston herself left at the end of May, and Miss Daniel was joined by a supply teacher, Miss Mary Davies. H.M.I.'s report spoke of promising work despite the obvious disadvantage of Mrs Johnston's lack of Welsh. Miss Daniel was able to get into much closer touch with the Infants, as she shared their home language.

After the summer holiday Miss Davies was away ill. At the end of September she resigned. In January 1919 Miss Annie James, 'new Supply Teacher for Breconshire', took temporary charge, Miss Daniel remaining as her assistant. Of all the teachers who came to this little school, Miss James seems on the evidence of her log-book to have been the least perceptive of its virtues, the least sympathetic to its difficulties, and the least capable of achieving any kind of rapport with children or parents. Her first entry pronounces (possibly not without cause) that the school is 'in a deplorable condition both in discipline and work.... They seem to have been allowed to go their own way for years'. Weak arithmetic and monotonous reading were criticised by several teachers, but Miss James was also perturbed by the children's failure to pronounce 's' or 'th'; she thought this was the result of having too many English-speaking teachers (someone has queried this with blue pencil in the margin). She was to return to this charge later and more strongly — it was 'cruel and negligent of the managers to have appointed English teachers', as the children could only learn English through the medium of Welsh, and therefore they were now very backward in both. These sentiments, which now seem unexceptionable, may lead us to suppose that Miss James felt considerable tenderness for children she considered educationally deprived. Other entries may disabuse us of the notion. On St David's Day she gave a short lecture on the saint, and set an 'appropriate recitation', but wrote 'They are so unpatriotic in this part, and I cannot find out whether they are English or Welsh'! She thought them too lethargic to be Welsh — where was the fiery spirit of the Celt? (Destroyed by English teachers, she suggested.) One naughty boy was 'fit only for the Reformatory School'. Later she wrote that it was time he and his whole family went to one! A number of 'thrashings' were given. A brother and sister, punished for 'idiotic mistakes' in reading, stayed home for over a week. 'They must have queer parents', commented the enraged Miss James. One suspects that her chivvied pupils reacted with stubborn unresponsiveness, They had never heard of arithmetical tables before her time there, wrote Miss James, and resented having to learn them. Their reading was 'daunting' (a favourite word) and their attendance deplorable. It was the most backward school she had ever seen.

Giving in her notice on 16 May 1919, Miss James complained of three months' lack of progress, and blamed the weather and the parents' negligence. Miss Daniel was leaving too. 'Although the present teachers [had] spent many weary hours trying to improve the ennunciation [sic] and expression' and taken endless pains, it had been 'all in vain'. Miss Daniel, wrote Miss James, was leaving because of her class's 'stupidity...knowing that she would lose her reputation as a good teacher if she stayed with this lazy, lethargic lot'!

Not only children and previous teachers suffered Miss James' verbal thrashings in the log-book. There is no doubt that her problems were real, but her nature was obviously intransigent. The school was the filthiest she had ever been in. The school managers were afraid, she said, to stand up to the cleaner! (Her successor agreed.) And the Education Committee were 'deaf to [her] continual reports' that one little boy had long been away from school. 'He lives so far away no-one can find out anything'.

On 18 July the school closed for six weeks, an extra week having been allowed 'to celebrate Peace after the terrible and devastating War''. In September there was a muddle, and school opened with no children. Gradually they returned, some having been corn-harvesting. Miss A.M. Williams took charge. She stayed only one term, but was sympathetic. She saw that irregular attendance had caused backwardness, and agreed that the school needed a good cleaning; the managers ought to have seen to this, and to having her own lodgings put ready. In fifteen years she had never met with such conditions. 'Where to begin?' she wondered, with such neglected children? She was fond of them, though, and they responded. Soon she was able to report improved attendance, even of those living far away from the school. By late October the children were 'getting more interested', but she could get no response from the Committee to her appeals for an assistant. Giving up the school in December, Miss Williams wrote 'I feel quite sorry to leave the children, whom I found very easy to get on with. The parents have also been most nice and considerate'. The managers 'could help a lot to make the teachers happy here'. One remembers the much-visited, much-supported school of the 1890s.

Miss E.O. Rowland came briefly as supply teacher in January 1920, and found thirteen children present. They dwindled to seven in the snows of March. Miss Jane Powell came in May, and stayed till the Christmas holidays. She was soon finding the lack of an Infant teacher a problem, and kindergarten materials non-existent. In June she admitted a twelve year old girl who had never been to school before. There are occasional references in the log-book, to such late arrivals, and also to children who would later have been in an E.S.N. school; then, they vegetated for years in the Infants' class. In October 1920 there were fifteen pupils on the register, two of whom hardly ever came — they lived three miles away.

The teacher makes several references to the non-arrival of expected equipment, one of the school's persistent problems.

Miss Powell's successor was Mr John H. Allsopp, who became headmaster on 11 January 1921, with thirteen children present. He was to stay for five years, restoring to the school some continuity of teaching. He is remembered in Abergwesyn as an amiable academic Englishman, no disciplinarian — he used to call in the help of the District Nurse to get the children down from the trees by the school-room!

H.M.I., visiting in June 1921, was dissatisfied. 'Every one of the children in this school comes from a Welsh hearth and speaks Welsh freely...so it is unfortunate that a monoglot English teacher has to contend with the difficulties of instruction in a school of this type'. Arithmetic was too mechanical. There was too much transcribing of names of counties and county towns of Scotland and Ireland. New songs were needed.

'Full knee-deep lies the winter snow', wrote Mr Allsopp in January. A February of storms and sickness ended with a holiday in honour of Princess Mary's wedding. Then St David's Day was 'celebrated as far as numbers would permit'. Mr Allsopp's log-book entries are on the whole perfunctory, briefly recording the usual round of local and school events, the weather, epidemics, occasionally his own absence through illness. On 11 December 1925 he was pleased to record a modest success — 100% attendance for the week despite bad weather. He resigned at the end of the following March. In Llanfihangel churchyard his tombstone records the death of John Henry Allsopp on his birthday, 22 November 1930, aged sixty-six.

The school had now only a year to live. Mr Esiah Jones, a supply teacher, came from 13 April 1926 to 28 June, when he left for Abercraf. Last of all came a temporary headmistress, Miss C.S. Felix. There was no material for special lessons, she complained — no raffia or clay, for example. After the summer holidays there was the usual failure by Brecon to notify parents of the beginning of term; only two children came, and Miss Felix had to call at the other homes herself. The December examination was 'fairly good'; dictation and spelling had improved, and she was reasonably satisfied with what proved to be the school's last examination, in March. On 5 April 1927 the Director of Education visited Abergwesyn School; on 14 April it closed for the last time. Since then Abergwesyn children have attended Llanwrtyd or (till it closed) Beulah primary school. The Iron Room no longer exists, but the Stone School is kept in repair by voluntary effort, and serves as village hall.

9. Estates and Gentry

(i) Llanfihangel Abergwesyn

County historians have been castigated for undue concentration on gentry families. Admittedly there is plenty of genealogical material in Theophilus Jones's Breconshire history. Very much a man of his era, he obviously enjoyed it, thought it important, and expected his readers to do so. They probably did — many of them could study their own family trees in his pages. To go to the other extreme, and allot the land-owning families of such a district as this no more than a brief notice, would be for more than one reason unrealistic. Sometimes the land-owning families are the only ones whose story it is possible to trace, from sources such as wills, deeds and family papers; though Alan Macfarlane has shown in *'Reconstructing Historical Communities'* what can be done to piece together the 'annals of the poor'. The very word 'landowner' carries within it the implication of power over the lives of the tenant farmers and labourers who did the actual herding and tilling, and lived by the land they worked and which they held from the Thomases, Lloyds, Joneses and other lesser-known local gentry who have slipped into the shadows. They, too, were sometimes leaseholders only, the ultimate owners of the land being more substantial families from further away, like the Powells of Nanteos, and before them the Stedmans of Strata Florida.

As we enter Llanfihangel Abergwesyn from the Beulah end of the Cnyffiad valley, we pass through land which once formed the estate of Aberanell, the mansion (just over the Llangamarch border) which later became the vicarage of Eglwys Oen Duw. The Lloyds of Aberanell and of Rhosferig, near Builth, claimed descent from the eleventh century prince Elystan Glodrydd, as did most of the old families in the Hundred of Builth. The entangled branches of this vast tree provide genealogists with an unending feast of work and conjecture. Welsh-style nomenclature meant that some generations of the Lloyd family bore the surnames Prees (Price) and Williams.

When Theophilus Jones was writing his history about 1800, Aberanell was the home of John Lloyd, Esq., 'the last lineal descendent of the oldest line of Elystan'. Jones thought Aberanell a strange choice of mansion — distant from market and 'wanting in wood' except by the house itself. John Lloyd was High Sheriff of Breconshire in 1793. He died in 1812 aged ninety-one, and was buried in Llanganten near the church door, leaving all his landed property in the Hundred of Builth to his nephew George Pryse Watkins.

Amongst Llwynmadog records is a copy of a survey of Aberanell estate made in 1815; the properties are grouped as follows:

(1). Aberanell demesne in Llangamarch and Llanfihangel Abergwesyn. Llwynowen and Cefngardys, Llanfihangel Abergwesyn.

(2). Bryngwyn, Llangamarch. Cefncendu, Llofftybardd and Cefnmorarth, Llanfihangel Abergwesyn.

(3). Penceulan, Llanfihangel Abergwesyn. Llednant and Dôlcegyrn, Llanfihangel Abergwesyn (the houses are on the Llanafan bank of the Camarch).

(4). Clyn Farm (now Glangwesyn) and a house and garden, Llanfihangel Abergwesyn.

(5). Esgairlys, Llanfihangel Abergwesyn.

(6). Penybont, Merthyr Cynog.

(7). Bryn Banneth, Maesmynis. Two cottages(?) and yards in Builth.

(8). Erwhelem, Maesmynis.

(9). Ty'nyrheol, Maesmynis.

By the time of the Tithe Schedule of 1842 George Pryse Watkins was still the owner of the now-vanished farm of Erwcleisied, near Aberanell. The overall ownership of Aberanell itself remained with another branch of the family. William Williams of Aberanell had died in 1760, leaving his real estate to John Lloyd of Brecon, his nephew, for life, and the reversion to another nephew, David Williams Hopkins of Pantyfedwen, near Strata Florida, father of William Lewis Hopkins. The latter was pricked High Sheriff of Breconshire in 1830. That same year he died childless aged sixty-five at Aberanell. A local story said that it was from the after-effects of a three-day, three-night drinking-bout with two other gentlemen, who, also, died soon after.

Hopkins' widow Anne Elizabeth then married Charles White, Esq., of Lincoln, said by D.L. Wooding to have been 'a widower with many children' and the tenant of Llwynmadog nearby. Whether the beauty of the Anell and Cnyffiad valleys or their profitability held the greatest charm for this Lincolnshire gentleman is not known; but he settled on his wife's estate, and it was at Aberanell that he died in 1845. The Llanfihangel Tithe Schedule shows him owning in 1842 considerable property in Abergwesyn — the lands of Penybanc near the Aberanell end of the 'Hen Rhiw' (Old Driftway): Llwyn Owen (for some time the home farm of Llwynmadog) and some cottages which then belonged to it: Ty Coch, another nearby cottage: Llofftybardd and Cefncendu isaf, the former still farmed, the latter, now demolished, on the side of the forest-ridden Peisoden valley: and near the head of that valley, the sixty acre farm of Esgairlas, long gone: the larger farm of Penceulan, in the lower Camarch valley, near the slate quarry (the pretty gabled cottage is now a holiday house): and some of the pasture land of Llednant, a still-occupied house on the Llanafan bank of the Camarch. Up in Abergwesyn itself, White owned the 134-acre farm of Clyn, later to be rechristened Glangwesyn: nearby, the 'house, smithy, shop and garden' called Troedyrhiwafallen: and the house, reputedly haunted, Ty'nyddôl, later Ty isaf, by Pentwyn ford.

Anne Elizabeth White, who died in Bath in 1847, was buried near her first and second husbands next to the front wall of the old church of Llanfihangel Abergwesyn. When the Victorian church was to be built, an altar stone to their memory is said to have been removed and laid flat on the earth a few yards from its former site; but a search of the old churchyard has not revealed it. It may be buried. Charles White's property was later bought by the Thomas families of Llwynmadog and Welfield (Cefndyrys), who by purchase from this and other sources, added to their already substantial holdings shown in 1842, came to own most of Llanfihangel Abergwesyn. Some of their possessions have since been sold to the Forestry Commission and the Economic Forestry Group and to private purchasers, but the two families remain the major landowners of the parish.

While the Thomases bought parts of the Aberanell estate from Mrs White's trustees after her death, Aberanell itself (according to Wooding) was sold for £3,250, and its timber for £1,100 to a Scots surgeon named Bellamy. When local gossips gleefully discovered that he had been acquitted of poisoning his late wife, they so effectively destroyed the peace he had come to seek that he soon sold Aberanell to Thomas Thomas of Pencerrig in Llanelwedd. On 28 May 1853 this Thomas Thomas is on record (in one of the Pencerrig Deeds) as paying David Thomas (presumably of Welfield), acting as a trustee, '£1,100 more on account of the Aberanell purchase money', and by 1855 the timber on 'Llangwy and Aberanallt' had been sold to one Mr Daniel Evans.

The Stedman family of Strata Florida, Cardiganshire, of Dôlgaer, Llangamarch, and elsewhere, was linked by marriage to the Cardiganshire Lloyds of Maesfelin, with a branch at Crucadarn, a Wyeside parish bordering on the Hundred of Builth. The network had marriage-connections with the Lloyd-Prees-Williams family of Rhosferig and Aberanell; so it is perhaps not surprising that we find in the seventeenth century the Stedmans and the Cardiganshire Lloyds involved with property in Llanfihangel Abergwesyn, not far from Aberanell. Almost certainly the Stedmans had an earlier involvement by virtue of their acquisition of the lands of Strata Florida Abbey.

In January 1663 Dame Mary Lloyd of Llansawel, daughter of John Stedman and widow of Sir Marmaduke Lloyd of Maesfelin, a judge on the Brecon circuit, left her grandchild Mary Lloyd 'lands and tenements bought of [Dame Mary's] nephew John Stedman in the parish of Llangamarch', together with lands 'purchased in the name of [the grandchild's] father Marmaduke Lloyd' — Tir y Cwm, Tir y Garreg Wen and Melin y Cwm (near Llwynmadog). At eighteen, Mary was to receive the deeds of Cribyn and Cwmbys in the Gwrâch valley, Llanddewi Abergwesyn, lands bought of Dame Mary's nephew William Vaughan. In 1712, the marriage settlement of Dame Mary's great-granddaughter Frances and her bridegroom Thomas Williams of Talley referred also to other Abergwesyn farms — Fron fawr and Fron fach, and Dôlberthog (in the hinterland of Llwynmadog) and Cluniau bach (high up the Camarch valley).

James Stedman of Strata Florida, Esq., in 1762 left to his eldest son John 'all the houses and lands purchased by me of David Lloyd of Kelsey, co. Brecon'. Celsau is a farm which has for some time formed part of the Llwynmadog estate. The present house stands less than half a mile from Aberanell. A deed of 1726 in the Cwrt Mawr collection at N.L.W. shows Stedman property in Abergwesyn in the late seventeenth and the eighteenth centuries to have been extensive. In Llanfihangel it included Pentwyn: the nearby Alltyrhebog, of which now only the barn remains, by the road to Tregaron: Brongwesyn (where, too, there is now only a barn to be seen, on the hillside beyond Tymawr, at the opening of the upper Gwesyn valley), 'with the water corn grist mill thereunto belonging called Gwessynne Mill': Nantygarreg, a roadside cottage in the Cnyffiad valley, Fronfelen, possibly Fron, near Llwynmadog: and other houses and lands less easy to identify. Much of the ancient Stedman land was in Llanddewi, as we shall see.

By the marriage of Anne Powell of Nanteos, Cardiganshire, to the last Richard Stedman of Strata Florida, who died childless and intestate, Richard's property passed to the Powells. This included property in both Abergwesyn parishes. In Nanteos rental-books for 1776 (in which year they first appear) the estate's Llanfihangel Abergwesyn holdings are listed as Alltyrhebog and Brongynes, Pentwyn and Perthybi, Llanerch-yrfa and Caellwyd, Tymawr and Brongwesyn, Fron and Brynbach, Nantygarreg and Penybanc. The rents were then received by 'Dr Powell' — the Rev William Powell, Ll.B. In 1788 these farms were sold to the Thomas family of Llwynmadog, but the Llanddewi property was retained by Nanteos.

The Gwynnes of Garth and Llanelwedd had a little Abergwesyn property in the eighteenth century. Howell Gwynne's marriage settlement of 1742 mentions some Abergwesyn 'messuages' unnamed, and refers also to others in Sarah Gwynne's jointure in 1718, among them 'Troed Rhiw y Ddalfa' (up the now afforested valley of Nant y

Fedw behind Llanerch-yrfa near the Devil's Staircase), Cefncendu, and a 'dwelling-house in the village of Abergwesyn'. By 1785 an abstract of deeds lists among Gwynne properties 'Lletty hirwin' — Lle'rtaihirion, a ruin in recent years in the Camarch valley, in a glade of the forests, and now levelled to extinction by a forestry road: and 'Esker fraith' — Pencae Esgairfraith or Pencae mawr by the Cedni, a tributary of the Camarch. This very isolated farmhouse has not long been unoccupied. These farms were in 1785 'in the holding of Edward Thomas, Gentleman' of Llwynmadog. 'Errwdalva' (Rhiwddalfa) is again mentioned.

The break-up of the old estates, the making of marriage-contracts, sometimes across county boundaries, the vagaries of testators — there are many possible reasons for the puzzles of land-ownership and tenure in these lonely valleys. Trawsgyrch, near the headwaters of the Cnyffiad: even more remote Cefngilfach: Cenfaes, on a hillside within sight of Trawsgyrch: Trefal Gwyn, unknown now, which once stood on Trallwm land not far away: and Ffoesygaseg, perhaps the long-ago Gwesyn valley farm between Pentwyn and Tymawr — all these appear mysteriously as far back as January 1651 in the post-nuptial settlement of one Jenkin Morgan of Caron, a parish on the Cardiganshire side of the Tywi, and of his bride Margaret, née Williams, who also seems to have been of a Cardiganshire family. Cefngardis, the ruins of which remain near the old drovers' road above the oakwoods opposite Llwynmadog, forms part of a marriage-settlement of two other minor gentry families of Gwnws and Caron parishes.

Who was Lewis Jones, Gentleman, of Llanfihangel Abergwesyn, who in February 1747, 'very sick and weak in body', made his will, leaving Penyrerw and its garden to his daughter Catherine Price, a few very modest legacies of money and stock, and all his 'lands, messuages and tenements' to his beloved son John Jones? Penyrerw vanished long ago; it stood on the land of Nantyrhwch in the Cnyffiad valley, where Lewis Jones may have lived. His apparel, 'old household stuff' (worth ten shillings) and stock — six cows, two old mares, two fillies, one colt, two small oxen, two bullocks, twenty sheep and five small heifers — totalled £17.10.0.

David Prees of Llanfihangel, whose will of 1728 was not proved till 1741, was also styled 'gentleman'. He made no reference to property, but owned ninety pounds' worth of goods, money and stock. There is no lindication in the will as to where in the parish he lived with his wife Sarah and their four sons and three daughters, but it may well have been Bwlchygorllwyn uchaf, as his son William is probably to be identified with William Price, gentleman, of that house, who in 1741 (when David's will was proved) sold a number of farms to the Thomas family of Llwynmadog. Some of David's seven score sheep were in the care of Thomas Rowland of Nantyrhiw. Even the site of this old farmhouse cannot now be traced with certainty. It stood in the Gwesyn valley, somewhere on the lower slopes of Rhiw Garreg Lwyd, near the stream whose name it bore, and below the ancient road. Carn Rhys Rowland, an outcrop on the hill above, took its name from one of the family, said to have been a drover who would sit on the outcrop while his beasts fed on the grass nearby.

For centuries, wrote Theophilus Jones, the mansion of Llwynmadog in its 'remarkably romantic and beautiful' Cnyffiad valley parkland, had been the seat of the Thomas family, descendants of Prince Elystan Glodrydd. Llwynmadog might possibly have been the mansion or temporary residence of Madog ap [Maredudd ap] Bleddin ap Cynfyn, Prince of Powys. The arms granted in 1797 to David Thomas of Welfield, second son of Edward Thomas of Llwynmadog, and thenceforward borne by both branches of the Thomas family, are those of William Thomas of Llanthomas in Llanigon, Breconshire, who was executed by order of Queen Mary in 1554. David claimed that these were the arms 'constantly used by his family', and pleaded lost documents to account for his inability to provide proof of descent. The arms have no connection with Elystan Glodrydd, while the device on a seal used by Edward Thomas in 1701, and also by his bride's uncle Oliver Oliver of Llanwrthwl, is 'a fess between three wolves' heads, crest a wolf's head' — totally unlike the gryphons and sea-horse adopted by David Thomas or the 'lion rampant reguardant' of Elystan Glodrydd.

Whatever the early history of the Thomas family may have been, the first member of it now traceable is Evan Thomas ap Meredith of Abergwesyn, a modest enough farmer who died in 1676, leaving sons Meredith, Thomas and Rees. He owned some horses, cattle, sheep and corn, but no property; his eldest son was the householder and 'leased' him his household stuff. Jones is not correct in his statement that this son, Meredith, sold Llwynmadog to his younger brother Thomas Be(a)van (or ap Evan). The few family papers which survived a fire at Llwynmadog during the Second World War show that Thomas bought Llwynmadog and nearby lands from his wife's uncle, David Arthur of Llwynmadog, Gentleman, in 1676.

Captain Christopher Pearce, acting agent to the Llwynmadog estate in the 1930s, collected a mass of information about Llwynmadog history based on letters, deeds and a journal kept by Evan Thomas (died 1790). His notes (which include transcripts of now perished manuscripts) supplement the evidence of those original documents which still exist. In 1933 he wrote to Mr Thomas of Pencerrig, Llanelwedd, about some 'very old deeds of Llwynmadog' in a tin box then in possession of Mr

Algernon Evan Thomas of Llwynmadog. From these deeds it can be shown that in September 1568 one Thomas ap Gwilym sold Llwynmadog and the Erw to Rees Riccard ap Jennet, who was thenceforward called 'of Llwyn Madoc, Gentleman'. A deed of 1594, a copy of which hangs today in Llwynmadog, shows that in that year Griffin ap Rees ap Riccard of Llanlleonfel, Gentleman, Rees' son, sold the 'land of lloynmadock and land of erowe vawr in Abergwessin' to David ap Rees of Llangamarch, Gentleman, his brother. David's son Arthur David ap Rees added Y Wenallt and Cefn Morarth to the property in 1619; then in 1676 Arthur's son David Arthur sold it all to Thomas ap Evan, who had married Ann, one of the four daughters of David's sister Elizabeth by her husband Edward Meredith of Trallwm, Gentleman.

In his will of 1694 Thomas ap Evan left Llwynmadog and other property to his wife for five years, then to their eldest son Edward Thomas. Tyr Goddrevan (the nearby farm of Coedtrefan) was similarly left, and Tyr ddryscoll (Trysgol in the upper Gwesyn valley) was left to Edward's sister Mauld for life, then to their brother William. Captain Pearce surmised that Trysgol was the original home of the family in Abergwesyn before the acquisition of Llwynmadog. William and Mauld were very young when their father died, and their mother was again pregnant at the will-making. Edward, though an executor, was still a minor. Their mother Ann took as her second husband Lewis James, Gentleman.

Overseers of Thomas ap Evan's will were his 'trusty and well-beloved friends' William Williams of Aberanell and William Thomas of Llanfihangel Abergwesyn. The latter is probably William Thomas of Cenfaes above Trallwm, who by his will of 1709 left Cenfaes to the parish in order to raise a yearly sum for the 'poor parishioners and alms-receivers' of Llanfihangel Abergwesyn. The charity still exists, though the poor alms-receivers are now harder to find. Edwin Davies in his additions to the county history says that the charity was 'by some confusion described in the 1869 Commissioners' Report as the "Ricketts Charity" '. There was no confusion other than a mis-spelling, for it was as 'William Thomas [ap] Rickart' of Llanfihangel, Gentleman, that this benefactor was named a Chief Constable of the Hundred of Builth in the Quarter Sessions records for 1685 to 1714. Perhaps Thomas ap Evan's second son William was named after his father's friend. Theophilus Jones' pedigree shows him as of Trysgol, married, with a son William who died without issue. Captain Pearce, in a draft letter about the connection of the Thomas family of Llwynmadog with that of the old house of Talwrnmaenog in Llanwrthwl, identifies William and his son (the son and grandson of Thomas ap Evan) with William Thomas of Abergwesyn and Llanwrthwl (died 1761) and William Thomas of

Llansantffraed Cwmdauddwr, Radnorshire, near Llanwrthwl (died 1798), who moved to Talwrnmaenog on the death of his brother Evan in 1790. The connection between the two Thomas families is proved by a letter of 1790 in which the third Edward Thomas of Llwynmadog refers to the death of 'our relation Evan Thomas of Talwrnmaenog'.

It is possible that the first Edward Thomas of Llwynmadog, eldest son of Thomas ap Evan, lived for a time at Talwrnmaenog. In 1697 one of the trustees of the will of Jeremiah Powell, a Cwmdauddwr gentleman, was Edward Thomas of Talwrnmaenog, Gentleman. Edward Thomas of Llwynmadog took a Llanwrthwl bride, Winifred or Gwen, daughter of David Evans of Blaenycwm, who linked the Thomases with an enormous network of kinship involving gentry families — Evans, Oliver, Powell, Lewis, Stephens — throughout the wild marches of North Breconshire, West Radnorshire and Cardiganshire. In his marriage-settlement of 1701 Edward is described as ''late of Llanfihangel Abergwesyn''. Edward and Winifred made their home at Llwynmadog. They had two sons, Evan and Edward, and two daughters, Mary and Ann. Winifred was much lamented when she died in 1728. 'There was more people in her burial than ever I saw in any other', wrote Edward to his son Evan in London. Winifred had 'lost her speech' from 4 November until her death on 15 November. 'She suffered very hard'. Edward dreaded his elder daughter Mary's impending marriage. 'The Lord knoweth how I should live, but as long as we shall be together I may live as well as I did before when grief is over'. Mary did marry before long; her husband was Evan Lloyd of Cwmemliw, Disserth. Among her visitors there were her uncle Morgan Evans of Llwynbarried, Nantmel, who kept in frequent and friendly touch with the Llwynmadog family. (On at least one occasion Mary sent a Christmas goose to London for Evan; perhaps he shared it with their uncle Oliver Evans, whom — as well as another uncle — he sometimes met there. Probably he was at this Oliver's wedding in 1739 at St George's, Hanover Square, to the widow Mary Killmain of Knightsbridge.)

Mary Lloyd's husband died aged only thirty-seven, in 1736, and his father the following year. Mary was left with two young children, Evan and Jane, and a farm to run. In 1740 she wrote to her brother Evan that she had now been farming Cwmemliw for three years, and though she had no one large debt was worried by many small ones. She asked for a loan of £20; three years earlier, her father had been urging Evan to lend her a similar sum! Mary's son Evan, who later moved to Weobley, had a very large family, but seemed well able to provide for them; his son of the same name became General Sir Evan Lloyd of Ferney Hall, Shropshire.

In January 1737 Ann married John Price of Castell-bach, Nantmel.

'The land lieth on a bank', wrote her father to Evan. 'There is a good ground there for corn and sheep and good quantity of hay.... His grandfather gave [John] all his stock — cattle, sheep, corn, cheese, household stuff and implements of husbandry, and he tells me that he hath enough of money to [pay] his charges. They are to maintain the old man during his lifetime; [he] is four score years of age but is still at something or other [while] he hath his health'. Edward's only complaint was of the 'want of a wife to your brother' (Edward). He 'is so full of business' (running the home estate) 'that [I do] not know when he will spare time to look about for one'. Edward senior was having to make do with the help of 'a maid that is but 19 years of age to manage the old [house]', with the result that 'Llwyn Madock is poorer at [present than] ever I saw it'. Still, apart from gout, Edward was well, and 'as well contented as ever I was since I buried my dear wife'. Deeds of 1732, shortly after Evan's marriage, had assured Edward of 'the chamber called the new chamber over against the staircase in Llwyn Madoc dwelling house' with a four-poster bed, featherbed, bolster, blankets and rug. He was also to have a horse, forty sheep, his fuel and £5 a year. Edward died in 1742. The tablet Evan raised in the old church to the memory of his parents now leans against a yew-tree.

Very different was the life-style of Evan Thomas, the first of the family to be styled 'Esquire'. Two portraits of this plumpish, prudent-looking man hang at Llwynmadog. He it was who built the family fortunes, not only, Jones tells us, by his two marriages to wealthy women, but by 'industry and application to business'. Evan started his London career at fifteen. He was 'intended to be placed to the Law, instead was placed in the counting-house of Rawlins and Co., merchants', where he paid for three days a week of instruction in accounts and book-keeping. In 1722 Lord Carlton gave the youth a recommendation to the Earl of Rochester (later Earl of Clarendon), in whose household he became Clerk of the Kitchen and house steward, earning his employer's trust and regard. To the Earl's eldest surviving son, Henry Hyde, Viscount Cornbury, Evan felt a particular obligation. Lord Cornbury taught the young man his job, and was 'an indulgent master' in whom Evan found much of 'the Father and the Friend'. At the christening in 1732 of Evan's son Henry the godparents, who attended personally, were the Earl of Clarendon, William Shaw Esq., and Lady Charlotte Hyde. Lord Cornbury died in 1753 after a fall from a horse. Evan lamented the loss of his 'best friend'. Recently he had come back from 'attending Lord Hyde at Paris' about the business of selling an Oxfordshire estate to the Duke of Marlborough; now he had to go to Paris again for the sadder task of settling Lord Hyde's affairs. In his will Henry Hyde left Evan Thomas £500 and an annuity of £100 p.a.

In 1756 Evan was appointed by the Earl of Granville and Thomas Villiers (who in 1782 was created Earl of Clarendon) to be auditor and receiver of the estates in 'England and Ireland' of Henry Thynne, Lord Weymouth, later first Marquis of Bath, who had just come of age. Two years later, at Lord Weymouth's request, Evan Thomas became a J.P. of Herefordshire, as well as of Breconshire, and in 1762 of Radnorshire, of which county he was Deputy Lieutenant. He was president of the Brecknock Agricultural Society in 1761 and 1789, and a commissioner of the Brecknock Turnpike Trust, a post which after his death aged eighty-six in 1790 was filled by his nephew David Thomas. Evan's son Henry succeeded him in 1786 as agent to the Marquis of Bath.

During Evan Thomas' lifetime the Llwynmadog estate was greatly enlarged by purchase. A schedule in the writing of Edward Thomas the second and endorsed on the outside by Henry Evan's son lists his main acquisitions. To the paternal estate, consisting of Llwynmadog, Coedtrefan, Perthybi (Llanafan) and Trallwm with Trafelgwyn, were added in the 1740s a number of Abergwesyn farms bought from William Price of Bwlchygorllwyn uchaf, Gentleman — Caegwyn, Cwmnewydd (or Cwmcywydd), Fronserth, Brynynis, Bwlchygorllwyn isaf, Cae'rgof and Ffoesygaseg, the latter exchanged later with his nephew Edward for Brynbach and Fronfelen, which had formed part of the Nanteos estate. From Owen Evans, Esq., of Pennant, to whom had come the lands of the Maesyfelin Lloyds, were bought in 1755 Ty'nycwm and the nearby mill, Dôlberthog and Bronydd, Cluniau Bach and Gribin Rudd, which last went to Evan's nephew Edward in 1759. 'Mr Jones of Cribbart' sold more Abergwesyn farms to Evan — Trawsgyrch and Cernygilfach, which he exchanged with his nephew for Penrhiwtrefan in Llanafan. Much property in Crucadarn (including the capital mansion of the Llawrllan estate) and in many parishes of the Hundred of Builth was bought in 1768 from Owen Evans' son Thomas. There were purchases from other people, including Mr Stedman Davies of Dôlgaer. The Cribarth estate came in in 1788, bought from Thomas Jones, Esq. of Pencerrig; and in that year Edward acquired the Abergwesyn farms of the Nanteos estate. Mr Penry Price sold Evan three Llanafan farms in 1789. Evan Lloyd of Weobley, son of Evan's sister Mary, sold him two Radnorshire farms.

The other group of farms in the schedule are Radnorshire and Montgomeryshire properties which came to Evan from the Rev. Thomas Wa(l)ters, father of his first wife. Elizabeth was the only child of this wealthy Congregational minister, a gentleman of Cardiganshire origin, whose seat was at Glyn, Rhaeadr. Her portrait at Llwynmadog shows a formidable-looking lady; she was much sought-after, a great 'catch' as an heiress with some pretensions to beauty. The Pearce transcripts include a love-letter from William Williams of Aberanell to 'Lovely Miss Waters at Glyn', written not long before her marriage to Evan Thomas. Other letters suggest that it was almost an elopement, and one much desired by Evan's family. In August 1731 Edward wrote to his son in London advising him to 'marry Miss Waters without delay' even if the marriage settlement is not completed. Morgan Evans of Llwynbarried (Edward's brother-in-law) thought that 'if Miss Walters could have been got to marry' Evan as soon as she came to London 'the talk would have been all over by now'. Betty Walters' friend Mrs Postuma Lewis of Nantgwyllt (who called Mary Lloyd, née Thomas, her 'dear cousin', and was delighted with the prospect of Betty's marrying someone so nearly related to 'Molly') wrote that for weeks people at home had talked of nothing but Miss Walters and her 'amour'. Mr Walters wrote to a cousin that he had sent Betty a tender letter; she 'owned the conditions to be very fair upon which I would have her return, but answered she could not comply with them.... It seems...they have real affection for each other.... If she returns with you at full liberty, she'll be heartily welcome... I wish from my heart that in words and actions they utterly abhor all manner of vice'. Betty assured him that she would act honourably, and he must leave the decision to her. Evan versified this letter from his father-in-law, which later came into his possession —

> The last Lord's Day your letter came to hand —
> good cousin, what to do I'm at a stand.
> You know my arguments were fair and strong.
> Judge then the case! Who think you in the wrong?

— and so on, in couplets of tolerable polish.

Evan and Betty were married (as 'of St George's, Bloomsbury') on 21 December 1731 in the Rolls Chapel, Chancery Lane, after banns had been duly called. A witness to the marriage was Oliver Evans, Evan's maternal uncle. Morgan Evans wrote to Evan that there was no need to spread the news of the marriage locally, as his uncle William Thomas had waited outside Llanwrthwl church after service last Sunday to tell everyone about it as the congregation emerged! The following October, Henry was born. Friendly letters from Postuma Lewis congratulate Betty on her marriage and the birth of her first son. A baby Elizabeth, born in 1734, died soon after her fifth birthday, and Walter, born in 1736, lived only four months. Thomas was born in 1739; his life can be traced up to the age of forty, when he was appointed a Clerk of Introitus at a salary (with fees) of £350. After starting as a solicitor's clerk and becoming Clerk of the Vestry of St James' he had got into debt, thrown up his job and sold some property to his father. There is no record of a marriage.

Elizabeth died soon after Thomas' birth. Evan wrote that he had lost his greatest happiness. Mr Walters was inconsolable, but, said Postuma Lewis, nothing would 'relent' Mrs Walters, 'no, not her own flesh and blood'. Thomas was 'sent to nurse Needham's'. Mr Walters wanted to have him at Glyn "as he thinks the town will not agree with him''. He had decided to alter his will and make his two grandsons joint executors. In May 1741 Thomas went to Rhaeadr to live with his grandfather. Evan remained a widower for over twenty years. When he was nearly sixty he married Ann, the forty-year-old eldest daughter of Cribarth, Llanafan. Her father, John Jones, Esq., a lawyer who had been under-sheriff of Radnorshire, had died in 1745 (it is said that he collapsed and died after losing a case at the Town Hall, Brecon). Signatories to the marriage-settlement of 29 April 1762 were Mary Jones, the bride's mother, 'sister and heir of John Hope of Lincoln's Inn, Esq.' and Ann's brother the Rev. Middleton Jones of Tarporley, Cheshire. Ann was said to be now 'of St George's Hanover Square'. The money settled included £3000 South Sea Annuities and mortgage-money on Cribarth, Llandrindod Hall and a long list of farms in Llandrindod and Disserth. Evan was exempted from making any similar settlement, 'since he has as yet made no proper provision for his sons' Henry and Thomas. Ann's portrait at Llwynmadog shows a plump, dark, prim, reserved-looking woman. She outlived her husband by twelve years. In her will, legacies include, besides those to her husband's family and connections, some to members of the Jones family from which she came.

Certainly his marriages and his business acumen made Evan a rich man, and one whose life-style was wildly different from that of his father in the increasingly neglected old house of the 1730s. Was Edward senior ever invited to visit his successful London-Welsh son? The evidence is lacking. Soon after the older Edward's death, repairs were put in hand at Llwynmadog; those in 1774 were preparatory to the 'great repairs' which took place during the next few years. A datestone at the present house has the legend 'E.T. 1747'. London, however, remained a major sphere of activity for Evan. His will made in 1787 shows him to have a rented house in Parliament Street, Westminster, where his furniture included a 'walnut tree commode', and his wife owned, as well as 'clothes, jewels and personal ornaments' some of the books and pictures. Silver plate is also mentioned. Henry is requested not to remove his father's pictures while his stepmother still lives in the house, 'as removal will cause expense and will require painting'. Ann was left for life the part of the Llwynmadog house and offices which Evan reserved for his own use when he was there. Ann received also a life-interest in the nearby mill, liberty of cutting peat for fuel on Caegwyn (the house there is now a ruin in Forestry plantations), and the benefits Evan was entitled to by virtue of his agreements with his 'tenants of the Hundred of Builth for their carrying coals from Brecknock to... Lloynmadock'. She was given Evan's postchaise, and money for travelling. To Henry was left another Westminster house, a cheesemonger's premises. Property in many parishes of the Hundred of Builth, and the Llawrllan estate, were left to trustees, three 'very good friends', including Evan's cousin Morgan Evans of Llwynbarried, Radnorshire, to provide Ann with an annuity. Eventually the property was to go to Henry. Evan died and was buried in Llanfihangel Abergwesyn. His will had stipulated that if he died in London he was to be buried 'in a private and devout but very frugal manner in the forenoon in a vault in the parish church of St James, Westminster'.

Evan's younger brother Edward had died many years previously, in 1751. He married Catherine Davies of Sarn-y-geifr in North Carmarthenshire, who survived him by forty years. They had three children, Edward, David and Evan (Evan died young). Edward (Catherine's husband) seems always to have been mainly concerned with the practical day-to-day running of the estate. In February 1736 his father wrote to Evan, 'Edward has set 60 perches of woods, and doubled the ditch about them on Kaenewidd on Kevenmorarth. He will make a way to carry a sledful through the wood from Kaenewidd to Llwyn Madock'. He it was who dealt with tenants' rents, reporting, for instance, in 1739 that 'Trusgerch tenants are too poor to pay anything'. He lies buried at Abergwesyn — he was only forty-two when he died — with him are his widow Catherine, their baby son Morgan and a six-month-old granddaughter.

Edward's son of the same name continued his work on the estate, acting as land-steward and agent for his cousin Henry, Evan's son. In 1781 Evan had granted this Edward a lease of Llwynmadog for three stated lives (it ended in 1841). The second life was that of Edward the third's son Rees Evan, who died in 1800 aged twenty-seven, and the third that of Rees Jones, stated to be about thirty years of age in 1808. Edward was active in local public life. In 1802 he was a nominee for the High Sheriffric of Breconshire, though he was not pricked. He was a trustee of the Turnpike Trust, and between 1793 and 1797 served as an inspector of the road over the new Irfon Bridge just outside Builth. Application for land needed for 'the diversion of the road at Irfon Bridge Steep' had to be made to John Lloyd of Aberanell, who also was active in the Turnpike Trust over a number of years.

Edward's first wife Letitia, 'daughter of Roger Price of Maes-yr-On, Gentleman' is buried at Abergwesyn. She died less than two years after her baby Anne. Her son Evan (named as Rees Evan in the 1781 lease referred to) matriculated at Oriel College, Oxford, aged nineteen. He, too, is said to have been buried at Abergwesyn. Edward Thomas, who died in 1808 aged sixty-nine, shares the tomb of his second wife, Ann, who died in 1798. With them lies their son Edward, aged six months, born when his mother was forty-five. Ann, daughter of Peter Jones of Dugoedy (Dygoedydd), North Carmarthenshire, and Nantybrain, Llanddewi Abergwesyn, by his second wife, Mary Williams of Ystradffîn, was, as we have seen, a widow when Edward married her. Her first husband, Evan Evans of Bwlchciliau, Llanafan, is said to have been a Builth surgeon, but no record of his work there has been traced. He had a brother Thomas who became Thomas Evans, Gentleman, of the ancient house of Llanddewi Hall in Radnorshire. Ann's brother was the wealthy David Jones for whom Llwynderw, Llanddewi Abergwesyn, was built or rebuilt in the 1790s. The family network was close and complicated; Ann's father had as first wife Elizabeth Evans, a niece of the Winifred Evans of Llanwrthwl who married the first Edward Thomas of Llwynmadog!

From the marriage of Edward and Ann sprang the Thomas family of Welfield, Llanelwedd, which takes its present name of Cefndyrys from the old farmhouse nearby, a house which was there before the mansion was built. Edward and Ann's surviving son David inherited that estate with its imposing Palladian mansion, a landmark on the hillside above the present Royal Welsh showground, from his bachelor uncle David Thomas, who had it built. Both of the Thomas mansions are to this day owned and occupied by members of the respective branches of the family. (At Talwrnmaenog, too, today's Thomas family is directly descended from the shadowy local gentlemen of the seventeenth and eighteenth centuries, whom we have attempted to place.) An article in *Old Wales* sketches the successful career of David Thomas (senior), who from near bottom of the list of eight clerks in the Army Pay Office in 1762 rose by 1804 to be head of the permanent staff as Accomptant General at the then massive salary of £1,200 p.a. He had held also lucrative appointments abroad, being Deputy Paymaster of the Forces at Rhode Island from 1778 to 1779, and Paymaster at New York from 1780 to 1781. David Thomas was also agent for the regiments of militia raised by the counties of Cardigan, Carmarthen and Radnor. He retired in 1813 and died in the following year. He was unmarried but had a dearly-loved illegitimate daughter Catherine, who in 1796 married Captain Townsend. Their baby son Samuel Thomas Townsend of Welfield was christened at Llanelwedd on 15 August 1797; Edwin Davies' edition of Jonathan Williams' *History of Radnorshire* prints in Appendix 16 'Lines written in 1800, on Welfield House' by the Rev Charles Price of Ty'nygraig, near Builth. The writer sings the praises of the 'lofty building' with its plantations of 'infant trees' outside and 'tap'stry rooms within', and describes the portrait of the 'great Proprietary' with his beloved daughter as a child, before 'a martial hero saw her charms, and lov'd'. Partially blind, Captain Townsend still mingled 'in the toils of fight', at the moment in his native Ireland.

Both Evan Thomas of Llwynmadog and his nephew Edward took their wives from families of strongly nonconformist sympathies. Evan's first wife was an Independent minister's daughter. His second wife's father, John Jones, Esq., of Cribarth, had in his time befriended Howel Harries, the Methodist reformer, and was himself the son and nephew of distinguished local preachers. Edward's will leaves legacies to the local Methodists, Baptists and Congregationalists; the 'worthy friend Mr Evan Evans' he refers to was a prominent Methodist minister of Ffosyrhendref in Llanwrtyd. Edward was said to have been once a tower of strength to the established Church; later he was a dedicated member of the Calvinistic Methodist chapel of Gorwydd. Some of the services were held at Llwynmadog before the building of the chapel. Edward's brother-in-law David Jones of Llwynderw and his second wife Lettice were devout Methodists, so perhaps it was Ann's influence that brought her husband into the Methodist fold. Later generations of both Thomas families became as firmly Church as Edward was nonconformist; but his daughter Anne Pritchard of Dôlgaer followed her parents as a Methodist and a helpful hostess to nonconformist clergy.

Evan's son Henry, and in fact the senior line of Llwynmadog in general, do not seem to have shared the nonconformist connection, despite the marriages made by Evan himself. Family letters and Evan's journal show that Henry attended Fulham School and Mr Watt's Academy in Poland Street. In 1749, having 'finished his classical learning and his studies', he was admitted clerk in the Exchequer by Lord Cornbury's interest; he was then seventeen. For the next nine years his salary was £50 p.a. In 1765 he was promoted Clerk of Patents, and two years later Clerk of Exitus, at a salary of £150 p.a. The summit of his climb through the Exchequer sinecures was in 1784, Clerk of Introitus, at £420 p.a. He was now a married man; in 1777, aged forty-five, he married a Pembrokeshire lady, Martha Gwynne of Brynaeron, who died in 1785, leaving him with a son Evan and daughters Mary and Jane. In 1786 he took his father's place in the 'honourable trust' of agent to the Marquis of Bath, and Henry died in Streatham in 1809.

Portraits of Henry and Martha are amongst the most attractive of the family likenesses at Llwynmadog. Their daughters remained spinsters, amply provided for by their grandfather's will. Henry and Martha's son Evan was High Sheriff of Breconshire in 1813, and Chairman of Glamorgan Quarter Sessions from 1823 to 1832. He owned in that county the estate of Sully, on the coast, where he carried out various agricultural experiments. An unpublished history of Sully describes Evan as a bountiful owner, resident at Sully House. Two of his daughters lie in the churchyard at Sully, and are commemorated by a tablet in the church. He started an estate school for which he provided the teachers, and paid for medical care for his workers. To implement his plans for farming the estate, he imported a number of Scots and their families. Lewis' *Topographical Dictionary* calls Mr Thomas of Sully 'one of the best agriculturalists in South Wales' and says that his 'Scottish system' succeeded well. It cannot have continued to do so, for Evan Thomas was eventually impoverished by his ventures and the Sully lands passed to the Guest family. The wall-tablet in the church there celebrates Mr Thomas of Sully and Llwynmadog rather as 'resident proprietor' and Chairman of the Quarter Sessions than as agriculturalist. 'The cause that he knew not, he searched out.... Through much tribulation He entered into rest at Bathsford On the 4th July 1832 aged 54 years'. It may have been first in Evan Thomas of Sully's time that Llwynmadog was let to Charles White, who later married Elizabeth Hopkins of Aberanell. Evan had married in 1807 Alicia Rankin of Belfast, whose mother was from Pembrokeshire; forty years later Alicia was buried at Llanfihangel Abergwesyn aged eighty-five.

The division of Llwynmadog into mansion and farm continued. David Thomas of Welfield (1783-1830) was steward of the Llwynmadog estate for his kinsman Evan Thomas of Sully. By 1842 the mansion was owned and occupied by Henry, son of Evan and Alicia Thomas, and the farm owned by Henry but occupied by David Thomas's eldest son Edward David Thomas. The term 'occupied' does not necessarily imply that the occupier lived there full-time; the Census returns show that in 1841 one house at Llwynmadog was lived in by a gamekeeper and a female servant, and the other by an agricultural labourer and his family. David Morris, the labourer, was still there in 1851 — so was a miller — while the main house was now being run by a range of domestics including a butler, a Scottish gamekeeper forming part of the household. By 1861 this Lachlan Mackinnon with his Breconshire-born wife and their children had moved to the 'cottage' and was now termed 'bailiff'. The mansion was being run by a housekeeper and domestic staff. It is not until 1871 that we find the widowed Mrs Clara Thomas, her daughter and other relatives, with a full range of servants, living at Llwynmadog itself, and at the 'Lodge' the gardener and his family, the Stares. Their house is called 'Ty Lwyd' by 1881, when on Census Day Llwynmadog itself was being looked after by the groom, John Evans, and his housekeeper wife, with the help of an under-housemaid. The gamekeeper lived at Coedmawr. Another gardener (whether of Llwynmadog is unknown) lived at Bwlchygorllwyn isaf.

Henry Thomas (1808-1863), J.P., D.L. Co.Brecon, was the eldest of a large family. He and his brother Charles Evan had six sisters. Charles later took the surname of Evan Thomas, and was of The Gnoll, Neath, Glamorgan. He served as High Sheriff for Breconshire in 1885. Henry Thomas married Clara, daughter of Thomas Thomas of Pencerrig by his second wife Bridget, née Gwynne. There were great local festivities on this occasion; on Y Garn Wen behind the house an ox was roasted on a bonfire, and drink flowed freely for all who climbed the hill to share in the banquet.

Henry was nominated for the Sheriffric of Breconshire in 1838, 1844 and 1842, but never pricked. At his request his name was struck from the roll in 1852, when his brother Charles pleaded that Henry was Chairman of the Glamorganshire Quarter Sessions, and also held adjourned sessions shortly before the Assizes to lighten the Judges' labours. Sixty-three prisoners had been tried at the last one. Nine times a year he travelled ninety miles for each attendance in Glamorgan.

No doubt as generation succeeded generation the process of anglicisation separated this family, as it did the vast majority of Welsh gentry, from the ordinary life of *y werin*, the people of these valleys. But the Thomases were esteemed for their honourable and humane dealings with their tenants. D. Avan Griffiths tells how the Rev David Williams was at first dubious about moving in 1825 from the Welfield estate and a landlord he knew, David Thomas, to the Llwynmadog estate. But his new landlord, Evan Thomas of Sully and Llwynmadog, won his confidence by a verbal promise of security of tenure, a promise which was honoured by Evan, by Henry, Henry's widow Clara and doomed son Evan Llewelyn, all of whom David Williams was to outlive, and finally by Miss Clara Thomas. At the time of the 1837 election the Llwynmadog agent was Thomas Price of Pendref, Builth, who tried to coerce David Williams into voting Tory with his landlord. Mr Williams would not give in completely, but, no doubt having in mind some incidents of tenants dispossessed for voting against their landlord's party, decided to abstain. Later, in conversation with Mr Thomas, he found that the latter would have had no objection to his voting as he wanted. Williams seems to have been pleasantly surprised.

The building up of the Llwynmadog estate in Henry Thomas' time included the purchase of parts of the Aberanell estate that came on the market at Mrs White's death. The buying and occasional selling of farms, houses, pieces of land, continued over the years, as though each landowner had in his mind a great jigsaw picture which, fitting in a piece here, rejecting a piece there, he was slowly realising in the landscape about him.

Henry Thomas died at Dover in December 1863, it is thought on his way to see his son in Paris. Money raised by public subscription was used to raise his tomb in Llandâf Cathedral. His memorial in Llanfihangel Abergwesyn churchyard is a tall Celtic cross of pinkish-grey Radyr stone. He shares it with his son Evan Llewelyn Thomas, the young heir who died in Paris at the age of twenty-five, less than three months after his father. Four years back, Evan's majority had been celebrated at Llwynmadog with a great dinner for the tenants, not only of his father's estate, but of other estates over which the Thomases had shooting rights.

Thomas Jenkins of Llandeilo, who in January 1864 stayed at the Carpenters' Arms, Beulah, to make an inventory and valuation of Henry Thomas' effects (his estimate was £1,533.1.0), wrote in his diary that Mrs Thomas, Mr Charles Llewelyn Thomas (Henry's brother, Charles, later Charles Evan Thomas, is perhaps meant) and Miss Thomas had left for Paris. Estate business was being handled by the then agent, Mr David Davies of Blaencamddwr, Llangamarch. At the house were housekeeper, butler, under-steward, two gardeners, two coachmen, two gamekeepers and servant-maids. Jenkins had wet weather for his walk to and from Llwynmadog each day, and for his journey over Cefn Gardys to value two boats on the 'mountain lake, constructed by Mr Thomas'. Jenkins noted that Henry Thomas' library contained 1,780 volumes; he valued them at £232.0.0.

Now there were left of the senior branch of Llwynmadog only Henry's widow and their daughter Clara, who, a beautiful girl of twenty-one, became the wealthy heiress to Llwynmadog and lands in several counties. To the revenues of the mid-Welsh lands had been added, by the Pencerrig connection, rich profits from the coal of South Wales. Clara became a benevolent autocrat, called in her home district the 'Queen of the Valley'. We have already met with her as church-builder and fosterer of local education. The widowed Mrs Thomas, while her health allowed, joined her daughter in helping the churches and the developing schools. After her mother's death in 1877 and her burial at Llanelwedd, in which parish Pencerrig stood, Miss Clara shouldered the many works of charity and the responsibilities of the head of a large estate. It was the church, educational and charitable work which was her forté — a survey of the estate in 1873 does not show it to have been particularly well run at that time. Some houses were in a wretched state, and one of the pressing problems was an infestation of rabbits! In her own chosen work Clara had the help for many years of her friend Miss Gertrude Lewis Lloyd of Nantgwyllt, Radnorshire, a home itself the centre of a paternalistic estate of 30,000 acres. A room at Llwynmadog was kept for Miss Lewis Lloyd, who is said to have brought there a now-lost relic of Shelley — 'a small pane of glass from a window at Nantgwyllt, whereon Shelley had cut his name and a date with a diamond ring'. From Nantgwyllt Miss Lewis Lloyd would ride over the wild moors and through the desolate Pass of the Two Stones. Victorian ladies were not necessarily shrinking and over-protected. Gertrude's sister Emmeline was once attacked on the moors 'in pouring rain and driving mist', with night drawing on, by a couple of hen-harriers whose nest she had accidentally disturbed, and had to stumble home through wet heather, just managing to protect her eyes from the angry birds. Emmeline was a well-known Alpine mountaineer, the first woman to climb some of the Swiss peaks.

Gertrude helped Clara Thomas with her Sunday school, and took her turn at saying morning and evening prayers for the household. The wrought-iron gates of the porch at St John's church, Llechryd, built by Miss Thomas in memory of her mother, were Clara's memorial to Gertrude Lewis Lloyd.

Herbert Vaughan called his chapter on Clara Thomas in *The South Wales Squires* (1926) 'The Lady of Llwyn Madoc'. His treatment of the subject has just the mixture of respect and romanticism that the title implies. He may be a little adulatory for our more astringent taste; but it is an affectionate portrait he gives of 'the highest example...of the Welsh squires', and a nostalgic account of life at Llwynmadog in 'pre-motor days, [when it] might be termed a self-contained community' with 'some two dozen souls sleeping beneath that roof. The life lived was easy, useful, unselfish and spontaneous...never a day passed without some act of kindness or help to poorer neighbours'.

Llwynmadog itself Vaughan thought a 'human oasis amidst the solemn woods and moors and swelling hills. Nasturtiums trained on long cords swathed the low-gabled front from base to roof. During the summer months an endless succession of visitors filled the house, so that two carriages-and-pairs were regularly employed to drive the guests to and from between Llwyn Madoc and Garth station, some five miles distant'. They enjoyed tennis, croquet, billiards, fishing and shooting, and above all 'lovely walks' with Miss Thomas or Miss Lewis Lloyd 'over the slopes of Carnwen and Cefn Gardys, whence you looked down on the buzzards hovering below in the valley' — walks that can still be enjoyed. Picnic parties set out in brakes and on ponyback 'often so far afield as the Wolf's Leap on the Tregaron road'. It is said that Miss Thomas organised treasure-hunts, and that some uncovered 'treasures' may still lie among the rocks and tussocks by the Irfon. 'Idyllic', Vaughan called it all, complaining only of the weather. 'Often for days the mist would come rolling down from the bleak hills: "the grey mare whisking her tail down the valleys", as the country-folk around would describe it'. He had reservations about at least one of the home industries approved of by his hostess, who once took him 'to a distant farmhouse in order to see the housewife dyeing her cloth with a preparation made from the yellow-flowering genista known as "dyer's green". I must confess that the tint produced, which was a dingy yellow, was not very attractive. But the operation was interesting to witness as a survival of a once-common but now almost extinct practice', which by the first decade of the twentieth century could only be seen in a 'primitive' district like this.

In winter Miss Thomas moved to Pencerrig, where, 'surrounded by neighbouring houses', she entertained freely, and gave a New Year dance, in part for children, who came in fancy dress. In spring she went to Italy. Clara Thomas was in late middle age when Herbert Vaughan first met her — 'stately and handsome', he wrote, with a kind face and a sweet smile. He remembered her at the Pencerrig parties, 'truly...the grande dame...with that sweet face framed in its aureole of soft grey hair' and wearing inherited diamonds. She bought no new finery of any value, said Vaughan, regarding herself as merely he 'steward for life' of her riches. Kilvert met her at a dinner-party when she was much younger, in February 1870, and thought her 'very pretty and nice in blue silk high dress', and very kind and cordial too. She talked to the young clergyman about her boy-cousins at Cranmers, near Mitcham in Surrey, whom he had tutored — Llewelyn, Owen and Hugh, three of the children of her father's brother, Charles Evan Thomas, later of the Gnoll, Neath. Kilvert's diary has several references to these boys and to visits to them, their parents, and their mother's family, the Pearsons.

Portraits of Clara Thomas as a young girl which hang at Llwynmadog show that she was indeed beautiful. Why did she never marry? Some said she was afraid of fortune-hunters, some that her mother's protracted illness had given Clara an obsession with the possibility of handing down an inheritable disease. Herbert Vaughan 'never met any man worthy of her', but said that in any case she was clearly satisfied with her own happy and useful life. Even the admiring Vaughan recognised more than a hint of the autocrat in Miss Thomas, who 'could on occasion say No with emphasis'. Though allowing Vaughan free access to a MS diary of Thomas Jones of Pencerrig, describing the artistic society of Rome in about 1870, she unexpectedly and firmly refused him permission to publish it. The occult was taboo, as young Oliver Valpy found to his cost when he tried to tell a house-party at Llwynmadog of his encounter with the house ghost, 'a servant-maid wearing an antique print dress', who haunted the 'curious attic' where Valpy was sleeping. Local stories bear out the legend of a beautiful, benevolent but despotic ruler. One thing particularly remembered is her love of trees, which no-one was allowed to damage with impunity; still, today, the loveliness of the oakwoods around Llwynmadog, and the varied beauties of the trees in the grounds, charm everyone who comes into the Cnyffiad valley.

Miss Thomas died shortly before the outbreak of the First World War, and was buried 'on a glorious afternoon in mid-June'. Her coffin was borne down the larch-bordered drive and past oak woods to Eglwys Oen Duw, in the churchyard of which Gertrude Lewis Lloyd already lay, and, too, was to be buried a suitor and devoted friend of Miss Thomas, the Ven. Henry William Harper, Archdeacon of Timaru and Westland in the diocese of Christchurch, New Zealand, who presented Eglwys Oen Duw with a private communion service in memory of Clara. The vicar of Llandefalle, formerly of Eglwys Oen Duw, wrote an elegy —

> Be this thy monument — no worthier one than this,
> A people's grateful heart, a people's farewell kiss.

After Miss Thomas' death, Llwynmadog passed to the family of Charles Evan Thomas. Mr Algernon Evan Thomas, who died in 1939, was followed by his younger brother Charles. While this Charles Evan Thomas was away in the Navy during World War II, Llwynmadog was for a time a school for the handicapped. Today's resident owner, Mr Mervyn Bourdillon, is a grandson of Mr Algernon Evan Thomas, eldest son of Charles Evan Thomas of Neath.

10. Estates and Gentry

(ii) Llanddewi Abergwesyn

One of the earliest Llanddewi Abergwesyn gentlemen whom it is still possible to trace is that John Lloyd of Tywi mentioned earlier, whose story is told on his effigy in Builth church. His mansion in Llanddewi is described by Theophilus Jones simply as 'on the western boundary' of the parish. Lloyd was called 'of Blaentywi'; we may imagine a very simple house near the 'blaen' (source) of the river, in the bleakest and most desolate of countrysides, perhaps near the present derelict farmhouse of Moelprysgau, whose land was for many years a sheepwalk of the Nanteos estate. It existed in some form as a gentry-house many centuries ago, if, that is, we may identify it with the 'Moel-y-prisc' of Jones' pedigrees. Could this earlier version have been John Lloyd's first Welsh mansion? 'Very sensibly', thinks the comfort-loving Jones, he 'changed his residence and removed to a more sheltered spot', Porthycrwys in Llanynis, of which house 'no vestige now remains'.

From John Lloyd's half-brother Rees, by his first marriage to Jane Herbert of Colbrook, descended the Lloyds of Dinas, Llanwrtyd (still a substantial farmhouse beside the track up the Henog valley behind the old church), of Nantyroffeiriad (on the land of Penybont uchaf further up the Irfon), and of Cwmirfon (also still an inhabited farmhouse). It is said that the Lloyds owned Llanddewi Abergwesyn property too, other, that is, than Blaentywi. Possibly this included the site now called Old Alltyrhebog, that little-known spot on the hill above the present Alltyrhebog barn (by which a farmhouse once stood) beside the Tregaron road. Jones' references are confused, for Cwmirfon was earlier known as 'Nantywalch' or 'Nantyhebog' (both meaning 'Hawk Stream'), and at one point he mentions also an Abergwesyn 'Llwynyrhebog' ('Hawk Grove').

The story of the ancient family of Lloyd, which claimed descent ultimately from Cunedda the Great through the line of Elystan Glodrydd and his grandson Llewelyn, Lord of Builth, is told in a Brecon Museum booklet by the Rev Canon J. Jones-Davies, writing on the history of a later Lloyd mansion, Abercynrig. John ap Rees David Lloyd of Dinas had two sons, John (who took the surname Lloyd, and married Ruhamah Jones of Cwmcamarch, Abergwesyn) and Rees (who under the surname Jones was the ancestor of the Jones family of Dôlycoed, Llanwrtyd). When they were first married, John and Ruhamah lived at Nantyroffeiriad, where they won a local reputation for hard work and thrift. According to a Welsh account, one early member of the Lloyd family at Nantyroffeiriad was the Rev John Lloyd, curate of Llanwrtyd. We have earlier suggested that this may be the origin of the local tradition that a 'vicarage' once stood high up the Offeiriad stream. Perhaps the ruins of the old Lloyd farmhouse itself are the remains of the 'vicarage', or rather the curate's family home.

John and Ruhamah would have moved to Dinas when he came into the property, for their son was Rees Lloyd of Dinas, probably the one who served as a Chief Constable of the Hundred of Builth. He and his wife Elizabeth had a large family and were soon sunk in debt. Their son John is the man celebrated on a tablet in Llanwrtyd old church, the one who, after starting his education at Abergwesyn, learnt navigation and joined the East India Company about the time, as the Rev. Canon Jones-Davies points out, that Clive returned to India for the third time to 'purify' the service of corruption. John made a dozen voyages to India, was shipwrecked twice, and became captain of the 'Manship', conducting himself with gallantry and efficiency when the East India fleet was attacked at Porto Praya. Later he was captured by 'Tippoo, Sultan of Mysore', and suffered two years' imprisonment. 'By good conduct and perseverance', John Lloyd made enough money to retrieve the failing fortunes of Dinas, Llanwrtyd and to embark on building a new mansion of the same name near Brecon, which became the seat of future generations of the family. Contact with the Irfon valley was not lost. Captain Lloyd's son John (High Sheriff of Breconshire in 1839) was a considerable classical scholar and a poet who in his volume published in 1847 wrote of the old Llanwrtyd Dinas,

> Home of my fathers, thy oak-circled hill,
> Abrupt on every side, and towering high,
> A mountain fortress formed by nature's skill,
> Might well the foreman's fiercest shock defy:
> But tranquil now beneath the summer ray,
> In heightened contrast either shore is seen,
> Here purple heath, with rock of time-worn grey,
> There the dark fir, and oakwood forest green:
> While Irvon, ever as it circles near
> Thy sheltered churchyard, and romantic hill,
> Its voice is speaking more than to the ear,
> And long-forgotten dreams awakening still.

Cwmirfon Lodge became the Lloyd's holiday home. In the late nineteenth century the poet's second son, Penry Lloyd of Glanhenwye, returned to his beloved Llanwrtyd and opened the Victoria Wells there.

Almost as forgotten as the Lloyds are remembered here is the old family of Prees or Price of Abergwesyn and of Rhosforlô, Llan(afan) fechan. Theophilus Jones writes that some eighteenth century tombs in the churchyard of Llanfechan by the present main road from Beulah to Builth are of a family who once lived in Abergwesyn, and were of an unidentified branch of the 'tribe of Elystan Glodrydd'; Richard Price of Rhosforlô, Gentleman, who died in 1770 aged fifty-nine, his widow (d. 1787) and his sister-in-law Beatrice, widow of Joshua Price of Alltmawr, Gentleman, are grouped with with Samuel Evans of Gwarafog, Esq. (Richard's brother-in-law), who died in 1779. This Price family were once in possession of the little estate of Digiff in Llanddewi Abergwesyn. Their property included farms in the valley of the Gwrâch, a tributary of Tywi, now a fjord-like arm of Llyn Brianne, overlooked by the ruins of Clynglas, one of the farmhouses of the Prees estate. The first of the family to emerge from the mists at all clearly is one Richard (a)Prees ap Jenkin, whose will proved in 1655 at the Prerogative Court of Canterbury shows him to have had a wife Margaret daughter of Morgan, to whom he left a hundred sheep, assorted cattle and a horse or mare: a son and heir Rees ap Richard (Prichard) who received lands, stock, 'household stuff' and profits: a younger son John ap Richard who was left some stock and £40 'on a tenement of lands y Klyne Glass and Maes Gwrach', property we find referred to earlier in a deed of 1632, when it was granted to Howell Thomas ap Richard of Llanddewi Abergwesyn. 'Richard' and 'Rees' recur, producing Welsh-style surnames Prichard and Prees or Price in the same family.

Richard ap Rees ap Jenkin had two grandchildren, Richard ap Rees and Richard David. One Richard Prees of Llanddewi Abergwesyn was a Chief Constable of the Hundred of Builth towards the end of the seventeenth century. The marriage settlement of Richard Prees, made on 16 December 1685, when he was about to marry Joan Prees of Llanlleonfel, includes Digiff (his father's farm), Hennant nearby, Pwllybô on the way to Llanwrtyd, Ty'nygraig in the Tywi valley, Clynglas and Maesgwrâch, and Crug and Gyrdda Mawr, just over the border of Llanfihangel parish, in the Irfon valley. The ruins of Digiff, at any rate of the most recent house on the site, can be seen across the Irfon from the Tregaron road to Tregaron. It stands in a spectacularly beautiful position on a natural mound in a riverside clearing. Above rise the lovely oakwoods of the Nature Reserve on the craggy hillside. Hennant is a tiny hidden ruin by a stream. Pwllybô is a holiday house, Clynglas a ruin, Maesgwrâch unknown. Crug is inhabited. Gyrdda Mawr is a rumour in a forest.

The word 'estate' can all too misleadingly conjure up a picture of parkland and a great house inhabited by 'carriage folk'. Nothing could be less like the simple farmhouse and modest acreage of such an 'estate' as Digiff (about 600 acres in the eighteenth century); and as for carriage folk, Abergwesyn was well into the nineteenth century just what Theophilus Jones called it about 1800, one of 'the wildest, most uncultivated, and uninhabitable parts of Breconshire... where no carriage, unless it be a small wheel cart and sledge, [could] pass with safety'.

In 1699 'Richard Price of Llanvechan, Gent.' is the grantee in a deed concerning the Gwrâch valley property; a later deed, mentioning this Richard's wife Joan, and involving amongst others Samuel Evans of Llanlleonfel, a trustee in the marriage settlement, makes it clear that this gentleman of Llanfechan is indeed Richard Prees ap Jenkin's grandson. The move to Rhosforlô seems to have marked an upward turn in the family fortunes. A later Richard Price married Rachel Evans of Gwarafog, Llanlleonfel; their son Thomas was left much property by his mother's unmarried kinswoman Sarah Prydderch. Thomas, a lawyer, became Thomas Price Esq. of Gwarafog, Llanlleonfel and The Strand House, Builth. He married a Radnorshire heiress, Mary Davies. Later, Thomas bought Cilmeri Park, Llanganten, which had been the seat of a different Price family, and was to become that of Thomas Price's collateral descendants, the Blighs. It was as Thomas Price of Cilmeri that he became High Sheriff of Breconshire in 1820. The sheriffric was an expensive distinction; he was indeed a gentleman of means. Less happy in his family life, Thomas had to endure the loss of all four of his children at ages ranging from fifteen to thirty-two. One at least, probably all, died of consumption. They are remembered on tablets at Builth parish church.

One Richard Price was of an Alltmawr family, a little further down the Wye. Was he kin to the Rhosforlô Prices? Certainly there came to be a marriage connection. Beatrice, widow of Joshua Price, who lies buried with her Llanfechan relatives, was sister to Samuel Evans and Rachel Price. Perched high in a remote spot above the Wye valley is the interesting tall-porched old farmhouse of Alltmawr isaf, near Builth. It is called in a *Brycheiniog* article 'the equal of most of the gentry-houses' of this district. Probably it *was* a gentry-house. Its imposing malthouse, barns and granary add to its distinction. The granary used to bear a cartouche telling all who found their way to this hidden place that 'this Pile was built by Richard Price Esq. 1716'.

A junior branch of the Rhosforlô family lived at Maesllêch, Garth, and has descendants to this day. Some of these Prices moved to Llanelieu and Talgarth; from them David Jones of Llwynderw, Abergwesyn, is said to have bought Digiff near the end of the eighteenth century.

The Powells of Nanteos, who as we have seen acquired by an eighteenth century marriage the Stedman lands, remained for well over a century the overlords of much of Llanddewi Abergwesyn. The Rev.

William Powell was followed by his son Thomas Powel Esq., and he by *his* son William Edward Powel, Lord Lieutenant and M.P. for Cardiganshire (d. 1854), whose first wife was Laura Edwina Phelp(s) of Corston House, Leicestershire. In 1865 we find Miss Clara Thomas of Llwynmadog writing to W.E. Phelps, Esq., at Nanteos, as 'the principal landowner in Llanddewi Abergwesyn'. The son of W.E. Powel, Esq. and his wife Edwina nee Phelps was Col. William Thomas Rowland Powell. Poole's *'History of Brecknockshire'* shows the Powell family as still owning in 1878 well over 8,500 acres of Brecknockshire land; and *Kelly's Directory* of 1895 gives Cornelius Powell, Esq. (younger brother of the Colonel) as the principal landowner of Llanddewi Abergwesyn. However, the Llanddewi Abergwesyn lands of the Nanteos estate, the Tywi and Culent valley farms listed in 1776 (mistakenly as in 'Llanvihangel'), 'Moelprysce, Nantystalwyn and Nantyrach, Nantyrhwch and Nantgwyn, Nantyflaiddast, Pantyclwydiau, Tynygraig, Vanog and Abergrach, Nantycrave, Nantysinglas and Caregyfran, Brongilent', disappear from the rental-books in 1882. Perhaps this apparent discrepancy is connected with the fact that when shortly before 1925 they were purchased by Sir Courtney Mansel they had for some prolonged period been in Chancery. The Mansel family eventually sold some of the property to Mr Glyn Hope, and the rest to the Forestry Commission.

The chief Llanddewi tenants of the Powells in the late eighteenth and early nineteenth centuries, and owners of other property there in their own right, were the Jones family of Fanog and Llwynderw.

What were the origins of the man who among the wild hills of Llanddewi Abergwesyn built the tall, grey, oddly urban-looking Georgian mansion of Llwynderw? An article in *Brycheiniog* on the houses of this district (vol. IX 1963) postulates an 'affluent Mr Jones' of obscure ancestry, with a fortune made elsewhere. Kilsby Jones called David Jones an 'energetic, self-made sheep-farmer'. In fact, the David Jones who built or re-built Llwynderw at the end of eighteenth century was the grandson of David Jones of Cribarth, Llanafan fawr, through his youngest son, Peter Jones of Dygoedy(dd) in Llanfair-ar-y-Bryn and Nantybrain, Abergwesyn. Theophilus Jones wrote sadly about 1800 of the dilapidated mansions of Llanafan parish, including Cribarth with its decaying buildings, neglected gardens and courts, and windows stopped up to avoid window-tax — a sure sign of 'fallen opulence'. About 1700, said Jones, Cribarth was 'inhabited by a family of some note, of the name of Jones'. According to *Brycheiniog*, Cribarth was at that time, the turn of the seventeenth-eighteenth centuries, a fairly new house, and for that period in that district 'a striking innovation in plan and appearance', with its 'lofty hipped roof, coved eaves and tall windows', its combination of 'native ruggedness' and 'lowland sophistication'. Who was its builder, and what sort of people were the Joneses? The same questions are asked about that other strangely sophisticated house of a hundred years later, Llwynderw, which after Cribarth had passed out of the hands of the Jones family and fallen into decay was raised among even wilder hills for a younger generation of the same name and blood.

David ap John ap Morgan of Cribarth is referred to in Rees and Thomas's Welsh history of the Independent Church of Wales (1875) as one of the local gentry, and also a devout Congregationalist, in fact a regular preacher at Troedrhiwdalar. The first chapel there was on Cribarth land. His brother John Jones was of Cwmcamarch or Blaencwm(camarch), Llanfihangel Abergwesyn. Not many years ago a nineteenth century house on the site was blown up by the Forestry Commission, owners of much of the Camarch valley. John, too, was an Independent preacher, at Llanwrtyd. His will of 1735, proved in 1736, refers to his wife Ann, fourth son David, fifth son Peter, two other sons Benjamin and Joshua, and granddaughters Theodosia and Ruhamah Jones. David was left Nantyneuadd, probably where the little ruin of that name stands in the upper Gwesyn valley: Benjamin and David (the executors) jointly received Cwmcamarch itself (a holding then called Erwriffith) and other Camarch valley property: Peter was left £30: Penrhiwtrefan, further downstream in Llanafan, was to supply £40 for Theodosia and Ruhamah, and thereafter to pay the debts of Joshua, possibly the black sheep. Ruhamah was probably named after her aunt, John and Ann's daughter who had married John Lloyd of Nantyroffeiriad; if she was a little girl at the time of John's will-making she may have been the Ruhamah Jones left an annuity by Edward Thomas of Llwynmadog in his will made in 1805 — she would have been his wife Ann's kinswoman. It is typical of the close-woven net of kinship in these valleys that she should have been remembered in this way.

David and John Jones are said to have had a third brother, Rhys, of Simddelwyd, Llanafan. Family tradition says he had twin children, and through the marriage of a daughter was the grandfather of the well-known minister of Pantycelyn, the Rev. Morgan Evans. David Jones's will made in December 1711 when he was 'sick of body', and proved in London in January 1713, leaves £100 and a £40 bond to his son David in London, a seemingly untraceable member of the family, who according to a family story eloped with a maidservant, became a surgeon, and fathered three sons, all of whom went abroad. David Jones senior's Llanddewi estate, which seems to have come into the family some time in the late seventeenth century by purchase, consisted of Nantybrain, the 'capital mansion' (still farmed and inhabited),

Ffoesboidi, which was once to be found in a field on the Llwynderw bank of the river Culent, and Gwegilhindda, the ruins of which can be seen further up the Culent. The profits of these houses and lands were left for four years each to David's daughters Sarah, Mary, Gwen and Susannah. Hannah, who was not mentioned in her father's will, was probably already married. After the sixteen years were up, the property and profits were to go to David's son Peter. David's wife Ann (said to have been born a Hope) was to accept as dower for life the rents of three Llanafan and Llanfihangel Bryn Pabuan farms and half of David's stock and household goods. Residuary legatee was their son John, who was charged with making a few payments, including a 'pair of clothes' to David's cousin Philip, and twopence to every poor man who came to the funeral — David obviously wanted it to make a fine show! Cribarth and the Wenallt are described as 'the lands I live in'.

John Jones of Cribarth, Esq., was a lawyer, under-sheriff of Radnorshire in 1718. His wife was Mary, daughter of Middleton Hope of Llandrindod Hall. Their son Middleton, baptised in 1717, died a year later, but a later son of the same name became a clergyman, survived three brothers and died unmarried at Chester in October 1775. He bequeathed £1000, then a substantial sum, to his cousin David Jones of Fanog (later of Llwynderw), and his estates in Breconshire and Radnorshire and elsewhere, for her lifetime, to his mother, who also received his postchaise. After her death the property was to go first to his maternal cousin Hannah Jones of Pencerrig and her husband Thomas Jones, then to their son (Major) John Jones. After the latter's death, Cribarth, with other property, was put up for sale by his brother Thomas Jones the artist, and as we have seen was bought by the Thomases of Llwynmadog. Middleton Jones's elder sister Ann had married Evan Thomas in 1763. (She too, we may remember, was left a postchaise in her husband's will. It seems that light carriages were usable in the 'lower part' of Llanfihangel and Llanafan, even if not on the rougher tracks of Llanddewi.)

With the Cribarth line extinct and Cribarth itself gone out of the family, the scene shifts to Llanddewi Abergwesyn. David Jones' youngest son Peter took a lease on Dygoedydd, a substantial North Carmarthenshire farm, the house having, as we have seen, a strong Methodist tradition. Peter's father's Llanddewi Abergwesyn estate, too, came to him. He married first a daughter of David Evans, junior of Blaencwm, Llanwrthwl — Elizabeth, niece of the Winifred who married the first Edward Thomas of Llwynmadog — yet another link with the Thomas and Jones families. Peter's wife seems likely to have died in childbirth, for the burial of an Elizabeth Jones in Llanfihangel Abergwesyn on 15 August 1738 was followed by the baptism at

Llanddewi Abergwesyn (where Nantybrain stands) of a baby Elizabeth Jones on 24 August. Her mother may have been buried at Llanfihangel because of her Thomas connections, though her aunt Winifred was long dead. In 1752 Morgan Evans of Llwynbarried, Nantmel (and of the Blaencwm family), in a codicil to his will, added £50 to a legacy of £15 for Elizabeth, daughter of his 'kinswoman Elizabeth Jones deceased'. In 1758 Elizabeth died aged twenty and was buried at Llanfair-ar-y-Bryn with a half-sister, Sarah.

Very soon — in 1739 — Peter remarried. His second wife was Mary, eldest daughter of Rhys Williams of Ystradffîn, an ancient and distinguished house still standing in the Tywi valley near Rhandirmwyn. Rhys' brother William Williams of Dôlgoch was High Sheriff of Cardiganshire in 1725. Mary is buried with her son Rhys in Llanfair-ar-y-Bryn churchyard. She 'delectably ended her life Sept. 27th 1781 aged 68'. On the stone she is called 'the wife of Peter Jones of Digoedydd'; the church register names her 'wife of Peter Jones of Bailey Glas'. The widower evidently moved to Abergwesyn, for he died at his son David's Tywi valley house of Fanog, and is buried in Llanddewi churchyard, where his neglected tombstone tells us that Peter Jones of Nantybrain, Gentleman, died 22 May 1782 aged seventy-three. With him are buried two infant grandchildren, the first two children of David Jones of Fanog by his second wife.

Peter and Mary had four children. Their elder daughter, Anne, was the one who married first her kinsman Evan Evans of Llanafan fawr, and secondly Edward Thomas of Llwynmadog, by whom she had a daughter Anne who became Mrs Pritchard of Dôlgaer, Llangamarch, an active Methodist, and a son David, who by his marriage to a distant relative, Catherine Jones of Ystradwallter, became the progenitor of the line of Thomas of Welfield (now Cefndyrys). A younger son of David and Catherine was the Rev. William Jones Thomas, vicar of Llanigon, who did not consider the diarist Kilvert, a hard-up curate, a fitting suitor for one of his large brood, Fanny.

Peter Jones's younger daughter, Mary, married David Watkins of Aberllêch, Llandeilo'r Fan, on the Epynt. There were no children of the marriage. Mary's crumbling tomb is in Llanddewi churchyard. It is said that the coffin was borne home, eleven years after her husband's death, to be buried near the grave of her much-loved brother David. Mary's husband was High Sheriff of Breconshire in 1786. His was an old and distinguished family, some of whom took the name of Lloyd. Sir Watkin Lloyd was knighted for valour by Henry V at Agincourt, at the same time as Sir Dafydd Gam and Sir Roger Vaughan of Bredwardine.

Mary and her husband seem to have kept in close touch with her brother David and sister Anne. David Watkins was bondsman in Edward

Thomas' application for a marriage licence. There is a family story that David Jones and his first wife Mary once rode with Mary and David Watkins to Tregaron Fair. A fight broke out between the men of Abergwesyn and the 'Cardis', in the course of which David Watkins' tethered horse was struck, and, plunging violently, broke its bridle. Mary Jones lashed out at the Tregaron men with her whip until she was struck from her horse by a staff (a favourite weapon in such affrays), and her husband received a deep cut which left a permanent scar on his head. Whether or not the story is true in every detail, the fact that it was handed down through the generations, and believed, is some evidence for the wildness and roughness of the lives of even the gentry of the eighteenth and early nineteenth centuries in this remote area.

By her will of 1812, proved in 1814, Mary Watkins left £300 apiece to her brother David's children David and Lettice (there were many others, so perhaps these were her favourites) and £500 to her sister's daughter, Ann Pritchard. Her nieces Lettice and Ann were to divide her clothes between them. The residuary legatee was 'David Thomas of Welfield House, Radnorshire', the executor.

Peter Jones's eldest son, Rhys, is thought to have carried on the Cribarth tradition of nonconformist preaching. His tombstone at Llanfair-ar-y-Bryn calls him 'of Ystradffin in this parish, Gent.' Rhys died on 31 May 1779 aged only thirty-four. His wife was Catherine Williams of Llwynberllan, sister of the wealthy Colonel David Williams of Henllys. She not only survived Rhys, but lived to extreme old age. The daughter of her second marriage married Rhys' nephew David Thomas. Rhys' connection with Ystradffin came through his mother, daughter of Rhys Williams of that house. Catherine was descended from the other brother, William Williams. Rhys Jones died at a now-forgotten house in Cilycwm — Penybryn. His will of 1779, proved in 1780, left to his wife a life-interest in Neuadd, Maesmynis, not far from Builth: Gilfach in the Cerdin valley, Llanwrtyd: and Llwyncôl in Llandeilo'r Fan. She was to take over the rented farm, Penbryn, where they were living, to have the furniture and implements there, 'such part of the furniture at Nantybrain [Abergwesyn] as she was possessed of at the time of our marriage', and some cattle and horses. The reference to her possession of Nantybrain furniture is interesting; perhaps it was her first married home. After her death, Rhys' brother David was to get Neuadd, Maesmynis and Gilfach, and their sister Mary Llwyncôl for life; then as she had no children it would pass to Anne's daughter by her first husband, Mary Evans. The will gives us the whereabouts of Rhys's Abergwesyn flocks. He left to Catherine for life the profits of those on Pantyclwydiau in the Tywi valley. In the same valley he had sheep on Nantyfleiddiast, which were left to Anne's son Evan Evans by her first marriage. Those on Ty'nygraig and Fanog, also in the Tywi valley, he had sold to David, who was discharged from payment for them, and was left also those on Nantycraf in the Culent valley. (These Tywi and Culent valley farms were held by David Jones from the Powells of Nanteos.) There are small bequests, but of most interest to us is the destiny of the Abergwesyn property. Nantybrain, Gwegilhindda and Ffoesyboidi must have come to Rhys in his marriage settlement, for in his will he had the disposal of them, and left them for life to his father and mother, and afterwards to his brother David, then in trust for David's children. Also left to Rhys' parents for life were the new Abergwesyn properties, now mentioned for the first time — Llwynderw, Tyr y Llan and Troedyresgair. On this last, Peter Jones was enjoined to build a dwelling house as soon as possible after Rhys' death. Was this simply an injunction to equip a piece of land with a farmhouse, so that it could be let? Or did Rhys envisage a new family 'mansion' rising on the low ground by the Culent, where small mounds are now to be seen with difficulty — all that remains of the little house of Troedyresgair? Did Peter delay, and did his son David decide to build instead at Llwynderw? Troedyresgair was the very last piece of the Abergwesyn estate to pass out of the hands of the second Peter Jones, David's son. And what did Rhys Gwesyn Jones (distantly related to the Llwynderw family, as we have noticed) mean by writing that the position of Llwynderw was 'unfortunate'? It is not so in any obvious sense. Could there have been in some people's minds a feeling that Rhys's dying wish had been flouted or misinterpreted, and that the new mansion of David Jones would bring his family no luck? And did a later generation of wiseacres say 'I told you so'?

The Nanteos estate rental-books show the gradual increase in the amount of Llanddewi lands held under the Powells by David Jones. From 1776 he was tenant of Moelprysgau, and from 1777 is called 'Gentleman'. Fanog he acquired in 1778, Ty'nygraig in 1779, and the Culent/Rhyd Goch farms — Nantycrâf, Nantsinglas, Carregyfrân and Brongilent — in 1785. Llwynderw had already become David's dream. His first wife was Mary Price of Rhôsybedw, Llanycrwys, probably the Mary baptised at Cilycwm on 13 July 1750, daughter of John Price, Gentleman and his wife Mary, of Cwmcroyddir. David and Mary were joined at Fanog after September 1781 by his widower father, who died the following May. Mary Jones died in 1787. One wonders if the blow she received at Tregaron Fair only two years before damaged her health. Her grave in Llanddewi churchyard she shares with two grandchildren of her husband and his second wife.

David did not remain long a widower. Family tradition has it that Lettice (Letitia) Williams of Rhydnes, Radnorshire was brought to work at Fanog as housekeeper for David Jones by her aunt, and that as was hoped David soon married this pretty, smart, spirited young woman. The wedding took place at Llanddewi in November 1788. Letitia brought no great fortune. The will of her father, John Williams of Rhydnes uchaf, Llanstephan, Gentleman, shows him to have died one month before Letitia's marriage. He had three sons and six daughters, a formidable number for a gentleman of modest means to provide for. Letitia shared with Sarah and Elizabeth £200 charged on Cefn Perthi. Letitia's mother Ann appears to have been unable to write; she made her mark as signature on the permission for her under-age daughter's marriage. David's writing is clear if laborious.

After his first, childless marriage David Jones could now hope for an heir. The deaths of little Mary Anne in 1791 aged one year and three months, and Peter, who died a year later aged ten months, must have been a great grief and disappointment. But two months after the baby boy died, another son was born, and named Peter after his dead brother, according to the custom of the time. He was to be followed by Marianne, Lettice, David, Elizabeth, John, Fortune and Rhys (who both died young), another Rhys, Sarah, William and Caroline (born in April 1810, two months after her father's death).

Abergwesyn has a legend about the source of David Jones' wealth. It exists in more than one version. The best-known runs as follows. In the latter part of the eighteenth century, Sackville Gwynne of Glanbrân near Llandovery (for long a tall ruin on low-lying ground below the main road from Llanwrtyd, but now demolished) eloped with Catherine Prydderch ('Catti Clynsaer'), the daughter of one of his father's tenants. Having sent her ahead to Liverpool, whence they were to take ship for Ireland, Sackville packed a bag with gold sovereigns and set off across the mountains. Not far from the spot where Llwynderw now stands, the gold proved too heavy, and the young man buried some of it on the hill, meaning to come back for it. It was found by David Davies, shepherd for David Jones of Fanog. Davies brought it back to his employer, who used it towards building his mansion of Llwynderw. The shepherd was often asked about the affair, but would never say 'yes' or 'no'. (A local tradition says that Llwynderw cost as many pounds as there are stones in the facade.)

David's mansion was not the first house at Llwynderw. One local tradition says that the oldest house there was on the present stable-yard, and was followed by a small farmhouse on the site of the present house. The eighteenth century registers of Llanddewi have references to a Llwynderw from 1756 on (it may have been there long before that.) An Evans and ap Rees (Price) family lived there then. David Jones is said to have started building in 1794 and finished in 1796, a date carved on the king-pin still to be seen in the rafters, together with the inscription 'J.T. Bilder' (sic). Yet as late as March-April 1796, banns were being called in Llanddewi for the marriage of John Jones of Dôlgoch over the Tywi and Madalene Evans of Llwynderw. The house may have been divided when it was completed — an accepted arrangement here, where a 'Gentleman's House' and 'Farmer's House' sometimes refer to two parts of such a building, whether it was divided endways, like Glangwesyn in recent memory, or front from back, like Llwynderw. Mid-nineteenth century Census returns have 'Llwynderw Hall' and 'Llwynderw Farm' —two houses, perhaps?

'A handsome house', wrote the county historian between 1800 and 1809 of the new mansion of the 'gentleman by the name of Jones'. The *Brycheiniog* article of 1963 thinks Llwynderw as it now stands ascribable to the late eighteenth century 'on stylistic grounds'. 'Inside and outside it has the excellent proportions of late Georgian architecture, with moulded ceiling cornices, wooden door-cases and... other details'. Once L-shaped, Llwynderw has undergone numerous alterations over the years, including extensions during its recent incarnation as an hotel. Architecturally, it is full of unsolved problems. The back of the house seems older, more primitive in construction. Was it perhaps the former farmhouse, aligned at right-angles to the present house? There is a blocked-up, north-facing door in the present dining-room which bears out this suggestion. Richard Haslam's *'Powys'* (erroneously listing Llwynderw under Llanfihangel Abergwesyn) refers to its 'modillion cornice and ... Tuscan porch ... pilasters supporting arches in the stairwell, and door and fireplace details'. The dining-room's 'big fireplace with stone voussoirs' is perhaps of the seventeenth century. If Haslem is right, the new house included parts of the old one.

Why did a sale-notice of 1831 refer to the house as 'built within twenty years'? This suggests that after David died in 1810 his heir Peter did so much new building as to make this description plausible. An old inhabitant of Abergwesyn, now dead, said that the mid-nineteenth century owners, the Roberts family, took out some fine heart-of-oak window-frames (why?) bearing the date 1812, and so of Peter's day. A descendant of Captain Thomas Turner Roberts wrote that there 'used to be no communication between front and back on the upper floors of the house except by going down the front stairs and up the back stairs from the (then) kitchen — now the dining-room. The top floor can still be reached only by the back stairs, a fine flying staircase, though at first-floor level a door and passage now connect it with the front landing. The Robertses or some later owner solved the problem by driving two oblique passages through from front to back of the first floor; these no longer exist.

Where did David Jones or his builder 'J.T.' get the idea for his sophisticated house, if it was in 1794-96 that Llwynderw took its classical shape? David may have been influenced by his sister Mary's tall L-shaped mansion of Aberllêch at Llandeilo'r Fan. An article in *Brycheiniog* (1968-69) dates Aberllêch from 'probably not long before 1786'. Mary's family, certainly a brother as close to her as David, would have been keenly interested in this house, whether it was built just before or just after her marriage to its owner. *Brycheiniog* speaks of 'the more or less complete separation of the best rooms from the workaday part' of Aberllêch, but says its weakness was the lack of a secondary staircase. This weakness was overcome at Llwynderw. Aberllêch has points of similarity with Llwynderw inside, ceiling mouldings, simple cut-out patterns in the wooden sides of the staircase below the banisters, a lofty white mantel and flower-carved fireplace, now unfortunately removed, but originally gracing the drawing-room. Outside, the pillared front door has no projecting front porch, as Llwynderw has, and its tall front ground-floor windows are Venetian in style, but in general shape and classical air are reminiscent of the younger house.

Letitia Jones, who was remembered in the family as loving finery, may well have been eager for a fashionable establishment. Such stories about her as linger in the district are significant. There is the anecdote (poking fun at Letitia's fashionable English words) about a servant sent by his mistress to buy 'veal' at Llandovery, who, looking at his purchase on the way home, exclaimed (in Welsh, of course) 'God knows if this is veal — it looks to me very like *gig llô* [calf meat]'! Perhaps it was Letitia who urged David to secure a builder capable of planning and realising what was for these parts an avant-garde mansion. But we must remember that, as long as a hundred years before, it was David's ancestors who had launched the building of another house, Cribarth, unusual for its time and place.

Rhys Gwesyn Jones, that poor relation who as a barefoot boy enjoyed much hospitality at Llwynderw in the time of David's son Peter and his wife, wrote in his article of 1861 that the workmen who built the house worked in all weathers for sixpence a day and their food. A sure way to get invited in on a rainy day to chat by the fire was to flatter David's skill as a sportsman. Apart from this harmless weakness, David Jones was thought an estimable man, strong, reliable, just and kindly. He was a devout Methodist who often gave hospitality to the preachers on their way to and from Cardiganshire over the mountain tracks.

Most of David's and Letitia's huge family were born at Llwynderw. The church registers later record the marriages of some of them, and the baptisms of another generation, till the last of the young families had left. Peter's charming younger brother David, for instance, married Jane

Lawrence of Llanelwedd Hall (on the present Royal Welsh Agriculture showground). He is said to have eloped with her. David followed his father as tenant of Fanog and other farms of the Nanteos estate. Nineteen-year-old Charles Jones and his sister Rosa, aged seventeen, were to perish at Dôlfach with their Lawrence grandmother and maiden aunt Matilda in the great Duhonw river flood near Builth in 1853. Edward Williams told Kilvert of the furniture swept down to Hay, and the one-armed body of Mrs Lawrence taken out of the river. Peter's sister Marianne married her maternal cousin Thomas Prosser, surgeon to the 35th Regiment of Foot; they both died in St Lucia in 1827, she, it is said, of grief at his death. Her brother Rhys Jones, a clergyman who took his degree at Jesus College, Oxford, married a daughter of Francis Henry Thomas, Esq., of Bewell House, Hereford, and died there in 1867. Young Lettice married Llanwrtyd born Rev. David Evans; her sister Sarah became the wife of an Abergwesyn curate's son who came of the eighteenth century Evans of Llwynderw family. A child of the marriage lies in Llanddewi Abergwesyn churchyard. Others survived, and left the area.

The 'Hereford Journal' of 27 March 1799 lists 'David Jones of Vaynog, Esq.' as one of the jurors to meet to appoint income tax commissioners. His fellow jurors were John Lloyd of Brecon, Esq. and David Thomas of 'Llwyn Madock', Esq. David Jones was a subscriber to the first edition of Theophilus Jones's 'History of Brecknockshire'. The 'Hereford Journal' carried an obituary notice on 7 March 1810 – 'On Monday se'nnight died, aged 62, David Jones of Llwynderw, one of his Majesty's Justices of the Peace for the County of Brecon'.

When David Jones died in 1810, his heir was only seventeen. He came into a very substantial estate — not all of it freehold, for as we have seen part of the property was held from the Cardiganshire land-owners, the Powells of Nanteos — thousands upon thousands of sheep on the great sheepwalks of the surrounding hills. 'Woe to Abergwesyn', men had been wont to say with a rueful smile, 'that ever Deio Dygoedydd crossed the Tywi river!' Yet they seem to have liked the giant who had swallowed the lands of Llanddewi. In David's will, some of his property was left to younger sones. David junior was left Pwll Gwyn and Gwernllinog in Llanddewi'r Cwm. From the stock on Moelprysgau (another sheepwalk which his father held from Nanteos) he was to make £500 for his mother to give any of the sisters, who were also to receive £500 each. Rhys came into Maesycwm, Llanddewi'r Cwm; William was left Neuadd, Maesmynis. The young people's trustees and guardians were to be David Thomas of Welfield, Esq. and John Lloyd of Dinas, Esq.

Peter and his mother were appointed joint executors, and seem to have clashed from the start. Letitia was left for life a half-share of the rents of David's Abergwesyn estate, and a half-share of all the stock till Peter married. He was made responsible for providing a house for her at Nantybrain or elsewhere. She chose Nantybrain, and was exigent in her demands for alterations and improvements there — the whole south-facing wing may date from this time — and a constant source of trouble and expense to her son. Rhys Gwesyn Jones wrote that the resulting litigation helped ruin Peter Jones. Gwesyn Jones was obviously unsympathetic to Letitia, whom he painted as a possessive and feckless woman, incapable of caring for her children, yet unwilling to accept help. A note on a list of the Nanteos farms in Abergwesyn in April 1812 seems to bear out the view of Letitia as a demanding and contentious woman. Of the holding of Nantsinglas, Carregyfrân and Brongilent, W.E. Powell's agent James Hughes wrote 'The widow of Mr Jones claims about two hundred acres of this as her own property, but it can be clearly proved it is not so. She holds there at will' (that is, by short renewable leases).

Peter's romantic marriage while still a minor to the sixteen-year-old Elizabeth Lewis of Nantgwyllt, Radnorshire, took place in Cwmdauddwr church on 26 January 1813. Elizabeth came of a very old and highly respected family of Radnorshire gentry, of which Clara Thomas' friend Gertrude Lewis Lloyd was a later member. Nantgwyllt was set in surroundings of great grandeur and beauty. Elizabeth's mother had made a runaway match with John Lewis the Huntsman, who is said to have been a descendant of one of the daughters of David Jones of Cribarth. Elizabeth was not driven to the lengths of elopement; her mother was dead, and Rhys Gwesyn Jones says that the young girl was used to getting her own way. Handsome and wealthy, the newly married pair were the romantic ideal of the countryside. Gwesyn Jones remembered thinking as a child that the Jones family of Llwynderw were the richest people in the world, and that the gracious Elizabeth was the loveliest and most saintly person one could ever meet.

The young couple started their married life at Nantybrain, where the first of their eleven children was born — David John, named for both his grandfathers; he was to die at the age of eight. By 1816, when Elizabeth Mary was born, her parents had moved to Llwynderw. Caroline, their seventh child, was the last to be baptised in church; after that, Mrs Jones became an ardent Congregationalist, so the other four children were baptised in chapel. The stock seems to have weakened since David and Letitia reared ten children out of fourteen. Many of Peter's children were to die young. Besides David, there were Peter and Jane who died in infancy, and Margaretta, who was seven when she died. Frederick and Harriet, full of charm and promise, died of consumption in their twenties.

143

Caroline lived to be fifty-five, but was mentally abnormal — it was thought, as a result of a terrifying childhood episode when she was left out in the fields during a thunderstorm.

Unfairly, perhaps, Peter Jones is remembered — in so far as any member of this now little-known county family is remembered — as the man who lost the wealth his forebears had amassed. Gwesyn Jones presents an unflattering portrait of his quondam host, stressing his addiction to solitary drinking, and his protracted and money-consuming lawsuits against his mother, and painting him as a man physically run to seed (he became hugely fat) and morally incapable of resisting adversity. It is a biased portrait. Gwesyn Jones himself (whose critics called him a man of marble!) had for his 'second mother' Elizabeth Jones a veneration so great as to leave little room for a sympathetic view of her husband. Peter does indeed seem to have lacked the business acumen and farming expertise which had enabled his ancestors to add lands to lands and build up those vast flocks which grazed on the hills around. By a twist of fate, it was he who had to face one problem and disaster after another, while no doubt trying to keep up his position among the local gentry, such as the more secure Thomases of Llwynmadog and Welfield, or the Aberanell family. In August 1810, for instance, the three families put a joint notice in the *'Hereford Journal'* stating that permission for grouse-shooting on their lands was to be obtained from Llwynderw or Welfield. The Peter Jones who in 1812 witnessed the will of John Lloyd of Aberanell may well have been the owner of Llwynderw.

Peter, as a very young heir and bridegroom, must have found dealing with his mother's demands a great harassment. The period was one of hard winters, which brought massive losses of stock. It is said that crows gathered thickly about Llwynderw to glut themselves on the carcases. After Waterloo there was a sharp drop in the prices for animals and produce. At Llwynderw there were more and more mouths to feed. Gradually over the years property was let, mortgaged (some to Elizabeth's brother, Thomas Lewis, who had taken the final surname Lloyd), sold. Llwynderw itself was up for sale in 1831, and finally sold in 1833 to Captain Thomas Turner Roberts. Peter and Elizabeth moved to Nantybrain, then to Irfon Cottage, on the Llanddewi bank of the river, where they stayed until Elizabeth's death in 1860, living on an annuity generous to his nephews too, and probably to his nieces, for they are said to have been well educated. But both Thomas Lloyd Jones and his doomed to be well educated. But both Thomas Lloyd Jones and his doomed younger brother Frederick, staunch Dissenters like their mother, feared there might be strings attached to largess from their Anglican uncle; they rejected his offer of training for one of the professions, and turned, Thomas to farming, and Frederick to carpentry. It was at Thomas' farmhouse, Fronddorddu, at the northern edge of Llanwrthwl, that Peter Jones died in 1872, a sad old man of eighty. Those other of Peter's children who survived to adult life had long left home. Eliza Mary and Emmeline Lewisa had married and left the district. Marianne, who was to die some years before her father, had married David Lewis Wooding, a Beulah shopkeeper whose family had held the Dôlaeron Woollen Factory, today a holiday house, by the bridge (now a footbridge) over the Camarch near the present road to Newbridge. Marianne's husband was a keen local and family historian, with an excellent habit of recording events and traditions in the neighbourhood. He was especially interested in the many-branched family into which he had married, with its fascinating aura of departing grandeur.

Miss Sanders, a great-great-granddaughter of Thomas Lloyd Jones of Frondorddu, says that through her grandmother Florence Eliza Jones there came into her family's possession a sampler of 1866 bearing the picture of a house, stylised devices of trees and birds, and the legend 'Caroline Davies, Rhymney, aged 14 years'. The house this unknown Caroline embroidered is recognisably the Jones family's lost mansion of Llwynderw, sold thirty-three years before.

Captain Thomas Turner Roberts, who bought the Llwynderw estate in 1833, was the son of William Hancock Roberts, D.D. (a clerical headmaster and a J.P. of the county of Worcester), by Sarah, daughter of Richard Turner, LL.D. (vicar of Elmley Castle), who was the son of Thomas Turner of Weobley, founder of the Caughley porcelain works. Thomas Turner Roberts took his degree at Oxford when he was twenty. He became a captain in the 6th Bombay Native Infantry, and spent some time in the East India Company. He married in 1819 Jane, daughter of a Worcester solicitor, Charles Cameron. A descendant writes that Captain Roberts is said to have been something of a martinet, and extremely hasty-tempered. He was an excellent oriental scholar, but when someone suggested that he might use his linguistic talent and give lessons, he was so offended that he hurled his oriental books into the fire! Captain Roberts was also a keen amateur scientist and had a fine collection of British shells and insects.

Llwynderw seems for much of its life to have been the home of large families. Thomas Turner Roberts and his wife had ten children. Two, Jane Sarah and Amelia Jemima, died young, and another, Lucy Barbara, lived only to twenty-three — she is buried by her father in Llanddewi churchyard. The other daughters were Mary Anne, Frances Elizabeth and Anastasia Sophia, and the sons Thomas Archibald, Richard Willett, Charles Ingram and William Henry Sherwood. Even if, as we are told, the congregation in the Abergwesyn churches at one time consisted almost entirely of Captain Roberts' family and servants, they alone must have made a not unimpressive show, filing in under his command!

Captain Roberts, who served as a J.P. for Breconshire, was on the roll for the sheriffric in 1844, together with Henry Thomas of Llwynmadog; however, the gentleman chosen to serve was Howel Gwyn of Abercrâf. Though the Census of 1841 makes no mention of Captain Roberts (Llwynderw being then farmed by Thomas Price), the Tithe Schedule of 1848 shows Roberts as owner-occupier of Llwynderw itself, with an old farmhouse on its land, Penybryn: Foesyboidi, which was just pasture: the Llanddewi part of Nantybrain land — not the house, which, with Gwegilhindda, now belonged to the solicitor Philip Vaughan, and was occupied by Peter Jones' son Thomas: Hennant, a little farm on the west side of Irfon, and Digiff, the old Prichard-Prees farm further up the Irfon. He owned also Penyrhyddfa, at the northern limit of Llwynderw's Irfon valley lands — this was farmed by William Jones: and Ty'nyllan, whose tenant was John Price. Twenty-one acres of land north of the old track to the Tywi valley through the Rhyd Goch bog (now drained by the Forestry) were in dispute between Captain Roberts and the Powells of Nanteos, whose Abergwesyn lands formed their 'Breconshire Estate'. Peter Jones was living then at Irfon Cottage, and still owned Troedyresgair, whose occupier was David Edwards. The tenancy of Fanog and the other houses and lands in the Tywi and Culent valleys had now passed out of the Llwynderw estate.

In 1851 Captain Roberts with his wife and two daughters were at 'Llwynderw Hall', and Thomas Price at 'Llwynderw Farm'. Captain Roberts died at Llwynderw aged seventy-six in 1855 and was buried at Llanddewi. His widow died in 1857 at Bath. Their eldest son Thomas Archibald Roberts, a barrister, inherited Llwynderw. He makes an enigmatic appearance as a name inscribed in the inside of a cupboard door at Coedymynach, an old farmhouse near Rhaeadr, on the road to the Elan valley. Major-General R. Stedman-Lewis, a descendant of the Lewis Lloyds, writes in the *Transactions of the Radnorshire Society* (1965) that Hubert Smith, a Bridgnorth solicitor, during the second half of the nineteenth century took rooms at the farmhouse on several occasions, and made the cupboard door his 'visitors' book'. One entry reads 'Thomas Archibald Roberts, Avocet Llwyndderw (sic): 1864 29 Augt.' Thomas Archibald probably rode there over the mountains from Abergwesyn. An interesting coincidence is that the house belonged to the Lewis Lloyds, and had been the home of Elizabeth Jones's widower father. Or perhaps it is not a coincidence. Perhaps Mr Roberts had become interested in the story of his family's precursors at Llwynderw — we may be sure that they were still a talking-point in Abergwesyn — and went to Coedymynach of set purpose.

Thomas Archibald Roberts married Myra Elizabeth Tweedie; they had five daughters and three sons. In 1953, Major Chester L. Roberts, son of Captain Roberts' second son Richard Willett Roberts, wrote to a niece about his happy memories of youthful visits to Llwynderw. Major Roberts' parents had spent their honeymoon at Llanwrtyd, and the family had great affection for the district.

Captain Roberts had farmed the Llwynderw lands, which in the mid-nineteenth century carried about two thousand sheep and a few cows and ponies. During the latter part of the nineteenth century, at a period when the Robertses were not living at Llwynderw, the Abergwesyn registers record births and deaths in various families at Llwynderw, and mention a 'Llwynderw Cottage' which then existed. According to Major Chester Roberts, Llwynderw passed out of his family's hands for a time.

In 1859 Mrs Elizabeth Williams died at Llwynderw. She was the widow of the Rev. Rhys Williams of Merthyr Cynog and Tirabad, who lived at Henfron, Llanwrtyd, and travelled his parishes on horseback. Their son Rhys Williams (1810-80) was 'of Llwynderw' (a descendant, Mrs Evered, has some of his visiting cards). He and his wife Ann spent some years in London, and then returned to Wales. Their London circle included the novelist Anthony Trollope, whom Rhys met probably through their work as Post Office officials. After leaving Ireland in December 1859 Trollope became Chairman of Surveyors, with a home at Waltham Cross and later Montagu Square. An oak table in Mrs Evered's possession is said to be the one at which Trollope wrote during a visit to Llwynderw. Rhys Williams built Brynderw in Llanwrtyd and went to live there. In 1861, John Lewis and his family were at Llwynderw Farm; Rhys Williams's sisters Margaret and Ann and his nineteen-year-old son Rhys Llewelyn Williams lived at Llwynderw Hall. Later, all three moved to Irfon Cottage.

By 1871 the Breconshire Electoral Roll shows the 'freehold lands of Llwynderw' owned by two of the Roberts family (Richard Willett Roberts and the Rev. Charles Ingram Roberts) and by David Pritchard of Glanyrafon. According to the Census, the house (one only) was occupied by a Shropshire-born farm bailiff, John Wild, and his family. From about 1879 Elizabeth Ann, daughter of Rhys Williams of Brynderw, and her husband William Jones from Nantyrhwch in the Tywi valley, brought up a large family at Llwynderw. Their third child, Evan, was the first of them to be christened at Llanddewi. The 1881 Census shows eight children, a servant and a nurse.

During the Boer War, Llwynderw returned to the possession of the Roberts family, when the widowed Mrs Myra Roberts went to live there. An attempt to breed polo ponies having failed, Mrs Roberts reluctantly sold Llwynderw. The farming tenants, the Hopes, old inhabitants of the district, eventually bought it. John Jones Hope, eldest son of Pentwyn, made a success of the farm, and was followed there by his brother Rhys Hope, then in 1946 by the latter's son, Mr Glyn Hope. At one time house and lands were sold to the E.F.G., but later an enclosed area near the house belonged once more to Mr Hope. The house and grounds were sold by the E.F.G. to Mr Hutton, who regained a little of the land; then they passed to Mr Pruden, who opened a small hotel there, and eventually, in 1968, sold it to Mr J.M.L. Yates, who, as a Welsh inscription over the great dining-room fireplace proclaims, 'enlarged and adorned it', 'adorned' being an appropriate word for an elegance which gained in savour from the wildness of the now almost deserted hills around.

Major Roberts, visiting Llwynderw in 1935, during Rhys Hope's time there, found the house 'finely furnished' and 'well-kept, with new stabling'. The present stable used to be a barn; the former stable stood by a flight of steps up to a lean-to cottage on the south-west side wall of Llwynderw, a cottage enlarged by Rhys Hope. Here all the household used to eat — Rhys, his wife, their three daughters and the servants. Visitors were entertained in the big kitchen (the present dining-room), and singing practices were held there.

Llwynderw has its ghost-stories. The stable-yard is said to be haunted, and a woman in vaguely-described 'old-fashioned clothes' has been seen in the house itself. The Roberts family believed that the haunted room was at the front of the first floor.

A railed tomb in Llanddewi churchyard commemorates a Jones of a different family from the Llwynderw one — Thomas Jones, Esq., of Fanog, 'a fervent Christian, a kind husband, an affectionate parent, a truthful and an honest man', who died in 1847 aged seventy-four, followed two years later by his 'relict' Charlotte, aged fifty-nine. Nearby is a row of tombstones of members of the same Jones family. Thomas Jones was the son of Evan Jones, the Powells' tenant at Pantyclwydiau in the Tywi valley. With the inevitable half-crown in his pocket, Thomas left home to make his fortune in trade in London (as a milkman, it is said) and returned to Abergwesyn, where he took the tenancy of Fanog, and built up a leasehold estate, mainly on the Cardiganshire bank further downriver. Most of this estate he left, subject to a number of charges for the benefit of his wife, sister and nephew, to his 'reputed daughter' Hannah, wife of the Rev. James William Morris, and after her to her children. His leasehold farms are interestingly called in the will 'the four forests of Llanddewi Brefi'. There was indeed a great forest on the 'Mountains of Dewi' in mediaeval times — Fforest yr Esgob is said to be the remnant of it. Thomas Jones's 'four forests' were Henfaes,

Dalarwen, Troedyrhiwcnwceithinog and Troedyrhiwcymer. Charlotte received the furniture, plate, linen, china and farm implements at Fanog, with three cows and two horses of her choice, and Thomas' moiety of the sheep there. His nephew Thomas Jones, then at Pantyclwydiau, was to have the sheep on Charlotte's death. Thomas junior later became the farmer of Fanog. When his wife Anne died, Thomas, then aged seventy-five, was fined £5 for getting his workmen to dig her grave at Abergwesyn without asking the vicar's permission. He was followed at Fanog by his daughter, Miss Jane Jones. But the Cardiganshire estate, after the death of the first Thomas Jones, was no longer any concern of the Fanog family.

11. Farms and Farming

1. From Early Times to the mid-Nineteenth Century

In 1794 John Clark of Builth, steward to Viscount Hereford, made a report to the new Board of Agriculture on the state of farming in Breconshire and Radnorshire. His strictures have been described as 'vitriolic'. 'The natural poverty of the soil' of north-west Breconshire, he wrote, 'is rendered still more unproductive from the uncommon indolence of the inhabitants'. Peaty water 'oozing' from the hillsides was not drained. 'Rushy wastes' abounded. Cornfields seemed to have been ploughed only 'to produce a most luxuriant crop of weeds'. The soil was further impoverished by an 'exhausting rotation' of grain-crops not varied by green ones — a rotation typical of upland Wales. Farmers contented themselves with depasturing small sheep and cattle on the moors and commons. Roads were hopeless, and the primitive sledge usually the only possible mode of transport.

The county historian, Theophilus Jones, writing at the beginning of the nineteenth century, was hardly less critical of methods or lack of method, but was fair enough to add that highland farmers, living from hand to mouth, were usually too poor to attempt improvement. Grazing their animals, tilling their difficult fields to produce a few acres of oats or barley, they were contented, said Jones, if they could pay their rent and carry on. Walter Davies in his *'General View of the Agriculture... of South Wales'* (1815), while he had no illusions about the backwardness of the area from the point of view of resolute improvers, found 'intelligent and discerning men' among the upland farmers, good calculators of expense and profit. To try to enclose and improve the high mountain wastes, he thought, would be to declare war on Nature. Even at lower altitudes, poor soil far from lime-supplies meant that the attached sheep-walk was often worth more than the farm. Rich men had beggared themselves trying to 'improve' such a farm; it was mad to load a poor farmer with 'opprobrious epithets, for not manuring and improving his almost Siberian desert'.

In the uplands of the Hundred of Builth we have a countryside stamped with an ancient pattern of settlement. What seems indolence to one seems passive endurance to another, and is not without that heroism which invests the figure of man mutely and endlessly struggling with his storm-swept mountain land. The struggle is centuries-old. After the warmer climate thought to have prevailed during the Bronze Age, and which permitted the movement of pastoralists on the high plateaux, and possibly the beginning of a little cultivation there, came sterner weather when the drift was downward from the now unfriendly hilltops, thenceforth to be used, as they were in Abergwesyn, for their acres of common rough grazing-land and their fuel-providing peat-pits.

The pattern of farming settlement laid down in the early centuries was to remain characteristic of the North Breconshire hills and valleys to the present day: small widely separated *tyddynod* (farmhouses), each with its fields, often small, around the house, enclosed pasture on the slopes, and right of common on the high moors. We remember that when the manor of Builth took shape, its tenants had 'common of pasture' and other rights. The basic requirements governing the choice of site were the need for water, shelter, access to the fields, and if possible, a sunny slope. A glance at the six-inch O.S. map of 1890 shows 'spring', 'pistyll', 'spout' again and again by the scattered homesteads, tucked in as they usually are to a sheltering slope, or screened by a windbreak of trees. Some springs are praised by natives of Abergwesyn for their bountiful yield of water through the sternest season of drought. (Droughts do occur, even in a high-rainfall area like this, the hard ground and yellowed grass seeming malevolent in their startling difference from the norm). Such an unfailing spring is the one at Carregyfrân, a ruin for many years now on the hillside near the Rhyd Goch rocks in Llanddewi.

Dorothy Sylvester in *'Landscape of the Welsh Borderland'* writes of the difficulty of deciding 'how, when and in what density' the dispersed farmhouses and cottages of the uplands came into being, a difficulty increased by the near-impossibility of dating simple stone-built houses. Though it is not possible to prove continuous occupation of some of the Abergwesyn farm-sites from the earliest time of settlement onwards, such continuity may with fair probability be conjectured — from the basic needs of the hill farmer, from the persistence of ancient patterns, and from such documentary evidence as we have of the antiquity of holdings and the practice of rebuilding, sometimes over and over, on or near the same site.

Stock-rearing seems always, from the earliest settlement here, to have been the characteristic type of farming, with the ratio of cattle and horses to sheep varying somewhat, as we shall see, over the centuries. But some corn was grown, indeed continued to be grown till very recently, and at some periods seems to have been produced on unexpectedly high ground. The Napoleonic wars were no doubt such a period, here as elsewhere. The marks of old ploughing at a date unknown are pointed out at about 1,200 feet on the hill opposite Carregyfrân Rocks.

We would expect to have found here, in the days of Welsh rule, a pattern of land-use based on common ownership of the patrimony by the extended family unit, the *gwely*. More than a hint of tribal attitudes is even now to be detected, as we shall later see. Much 'compacting' has taken place — the tendency of larger farms to swallow smaller ones, leaving now disused farmhouses to become barns, holiday houses, ruins, or a memory lingering by a few indeterminate mounds in an empty valley, a scatter of stones in a Forestry plantation. Yet it is basically the old pattern still that we find, of 'non-nucleated settlement'. There are intriguing clues to be found, possibly pointing back to very old days indeed. The Llanfihangel Tithe Schedule of 1842, for instance, shows Edward David Thomas of Welfield and Henry Thomas of Llwynmadog as joint owners of a certain eighteen acres or so of *tir cyd* (common land) — a rough triangle to the left of the ancient road where, coming from Pentwyn ford, it reaches the top of Rhiw Garreg Lwyd above Carn Rhys Rowland. May this possibly be a relic of that open pasture which, as Dorothy Sylvester writes, once divided family groups of farmsteads from each other? It differs in being privately owned from the true commons of Llanfihangel Abergwesyn. Or have we faint evidence here for gavelkind, surviving its banning at the Act of Union? Edward and Henry were the great-grandsons of two brothers.

There are interesting differences between the tithe maps and schedules of the two Abergwesyn parishes. Both give the characteristic picture of dispersed settlement, but whereas the Llanfihangel ones (1842) show a parish of mainly small farms with extensive commons, the Llanddewi ones (1848) list units on the whole larger, some very large, because here the grazing-ground forms parts of the farm lands. It seems that the two parishes show traces of that clash of 'pastoral' and 'feudal' concepts of grazing rights noted by T.P. Ellis, and discussed by R.H. Sayce in *The Old Summer Pastures* (*Montgomeryshire Collections*, Vol. 54). Llanfihangel may be an example of a parish showing the survival of a pastoral or clansmen's concept of 'general right of occupation' of grazing territory, which could include the use of small areas for growing crops. Llanddewi at some date unknown seems to have changed over to the feudal idea of the 'exclusive allocation of definite areas... to units or individuals', an interesting development in view of this parish's even greater inaccessibility, and, one would think, imperviousness to change. The changeover may have been comparatively recent, for Breconshire Quarter Sessions records at N.L.W. contain applications for commons depasturing licences from Llanddewi farmers. In 1674, for instance, John Rees William paid £10, Thomas Powell £5, and Thomas Prees £5. We are not told, however, the whereabouts of the commons they used, so there is no certainty as to the system.

The field-names of Llanfihangel farms answer in the main to the description given by E.J. Howell in the *Land Use Survey* of 1943, vol.

III, being convenient for the individual farming family's own use, related to the house and to other fields, illustrating 'smallness and irregularity', and showing little or no trace of community planning. For instance, we have *cae cornel* (corner field): *cae cam* (crooked field): *cae dan y ty* (field below the house) and so on. There are a number of such names in the Llanddewi schedule too, but also more unnamed, and ones labelled simply 'pasture', 'meadow', in the field-name column as well as the land-use one. Whether this is just evidence of a less rigorous research into local names, or represents a genuine difference, is uncertain. In both lists, and in present-day use, the name *erw* is that of the old Welsh acre, but is unrelated to the extent of the field. Theophilus Jones thought that in Breconshire an *erw* was always in his day equal to an English statute acre. *Yr Erw* on Pwllybô in 1848 was a five-acre meadow: *Erw Pentwyn* in 1842 a seven-acre pasture: *Erw* on Crug a four-acre arable field. *Cyfairestr* on Pwllybô, a four-acre pasture, also bore a measurement-name, the ancient *cyfer* (two thirds of the English acre) being still in the early nineteenth century the usual Breconshire unit of land-measurement. Walter Davies said that the Breconshire cyfer was three yards and a quarter long, and that in his time farmers were gradually taking to the *cyfer y brenin* (King's or statute acre). On Penceulan, near the slate-quarry in the Camarch valley, we find *Cyfermawr* (Great acre, a two-acre meadow), and *Cyferbach* (Little acre, an acre or so of arable land). Theophilus Jones reminds us that the word *cyfar* meant 'ploughing together' — co-aration — and derives from the ancient custom of sharing oxen and implements for the ploughing, an acre being set aside as payment for the expense, and another, the *erw'r ych du* (acre of the black or dead ox) to recompense any man who lost an ox during the communal ploughing.

The ancient practice of transhumance was still alive as late as the turn of the nineteenth to twentieth centuries in parts of Abergwesyn. In its purest form this was the movement of upland herdsmen on *Calan Mai*, the beginning of summer, with their families, their flocks and herds, from the *hendref* (the old homestead, the winter dwelling) to the *hafod* or summer dwelling, a rough hut high on the moors. The animals were turned out on to the upland pasture for the summer months; butter and cheese were made at the *hafod*. Before *Dydd Calan Gaeaf*, the beginning of winter, the return journey was made. The Camarch valley is one where transhumance is said to have been practised till recent times. And on Trawsnant mountain, in the midst now of bogland drained by the Forestry, rises the outcrop Cnapau Hafod Llewelyn. This ancient *hafod* is thought by some to have been the refuge of Prince Llewelyn while his enemies sank in the encircling peat-bog, and by others to commemorate some unknown herdsman of that name. One might think that the animals would have been at as much risk as the prince's enemies in such a situation. The desolate reaches of the northern Irfon hold a number of tiny ruins, some just to the north and south of Carreg yr Adar; these may well be the remains of summer dairies, some possibly very old. Tradition says that nineteen once existed near the upper Irfon, the furthest into the wilds being Aberceinciau, where the remains of two little buildings are still clearly to be seen, one by Nant y Gorlan (Sheepfold Stream), the other opposite. These little huts belonged to Abergwesyn farmers, who would trek north in May. Those northern wilds may also have held *hafotai* of Strata Florida in the days of monastic farming.

R.H. Sayce's article (referred to above) gives an account of transhumance in Wales up to the eighteenth century, when in most parts it came to an end. Sayce admits that Wales possesses few records of the life of the *hafotai*. He draws analogies from the practices in Scotland, Scandinavia and other countries in an attempt to construct a picture of the great spring migration in early Wales, the summer life in the wilds, and the return to the homestead for autumn harvesting and the 'vacant' but safer winter life at the *hendref*, less exposed than the *hafod* to danger from wolves, eagles, kites, storms, precipices, bogs, robbers, outlaws and cattle-raiding neighbours. He suggests that in early Wales, and in other Celtic lands, cattle-raiding forays were probably a test of manhood.

A spot on the Tregaron road, about three hundred yards higher up than Alltyrhebog barn, is locally called 'Twll John Bevan' after a mid-nineteenth century farmer of Erwgleisied, a former farm at the Beulah end of Abergwesyn. John's pony stumbled and threw him there one evening on the way home from Esgair Adar, where his sheep were grazed in summer. This seems to have been a modified late form of transhumance, the flocks being taken to summer pasture on the high commons, and visited there without the family actually moving to a *hafod*.

Upland areas like this one were the parts of Wales whose life and institutions were least affected by the Norman Conquest. The spirit of tribalism long survived its forms. The practice of farming here has changed more drastically during the present century, especially since the Second World War, than for countless generations before that. We know little in detail about medieval farms and farming in the area. Giraldus wrote in the twelfth century of the rural Welsh as living in wooden houses on the edge of woods. The hills of mid-Wales were then more widely covered with deciduous forests than they are today, when many of them are bare or, too often, densely afforested with conifers. Abergwesyn still has hillsides rich in the sessile oak — the Gwesyn valley upstream from the old Post Office, parts of the Irfon valley, and the Llwynmadog area. Hilllsides like Rhiw Garreg Lwyd, bearing stumpy hawthorns and, by the streams mountain ash, were probably once wooded. The intense violet-blue of the bluebells on this and other open hillsides in late spring and early summer is said to be an indication of former oakwoods. If this is so, the now bleak valley of the Culent opposite the south side of Llwynderw must once have been wooded, for in a luxuriant year walkers looking for the old track to the lead mine find themselves treading on a profusion of bluebells. Walter Davies pointed out that the irregularity of old enclosures, as distinct from the straight-line boundaries of modern ones, came about because they were originally, at the very beginning of agriculture, hacked out from woodland. The component *llanerch* in the name Llanerch-yrfa, given to the farm near the Devil's Staircase on the Tregaron road, suggests the possibility of its being such an ancient enclosure — the word means 'glade' or 'clearing'.

Giraldus wrote of three spring and summer ploughings for oats. 'Almost all the people live upon the produce of their herds, with oats, milk, cheese and butter; eating flesh in larger proportions than bread' — the reverse of the diet of such an area in later centuries. Walter Davies, for instance, commented in 1815 upon the 'Braminical' quasi-vegetarianism of the rural population. He wrote not long after Malkin had remarked on the extraordinary frequency, for that period, with which meat was offered for sale in Builth shops. It was probably being sold from necessity, instead of being eaten by the farm family.

It is possible that the climate in this area was at one time such as to permit grape-growing out of doors, and the making of wine of a sort. R. Green-Price wrote in the *Red Dragon* (1882) that 'as late as the eighteenth century the grape was freely cultivated out of doors, and wine made in abundance'. G. Dyfnallt Owen reminds us of Dinely's remarks about the West Carmarthenshire gentry in the seventeenth century 'supplementing French wines with choice wines of their own growth off the mountains'. Perhaps we have an echo of former viniculture, mediaeval or later, in the field-name *Erw win* (Wine acre) in 1842 on Dôlberthog in the Camarch valley, and *Dol winllan* and *Cae winllan* (Vineyard meadow and Vineyard field) on Penceulan nearby, at a spot where in February 1813 the *'Hereford Journal'* had advertised three hundred and eight oak trees for sale, 'standing on *Wynllan* farm adjoining Penceulan.

R.H. Sayce emphasizes the high proportion of cattle to other stock in the Middle Ages and later. Tudor surveys showed that goats outnumbered sheep (Leland wrote later of their depredations on the woodlands near Strata Florida), and cattle-numbers surpassed those of goats and sheep together. There were a number of swine, too, depastured on the waste.

The Middle Ages saw the development of the Welsh droving trade, which until the coming of railways in the mid-nineteenth century was to channel thousands on thousands of Welsh cattle, as well as sheep, pigs and even geese from some places, towards England over a growing network of drovers' roads. The impact of the drovers on Abergwesyn we shall discuss later. Most of the cattle on their way through Abergwesyn on their way to the Midlands for fattening, or to the great English fairs, would have been bought on the western side of the mountains, so though the settlement grew in importance as a shoeing centre and one providing food and drink for the drovers, farmers here would be immediately affected mainly by the need to keep local beasts clear of the surging tides of cattle passing through. There were, early and late, small and local movements of cattle too. The will (1575) of John ap Thomas of Llanyre, Radnorshire, names as a debtor Lewys ap Llello of Llanfihangel Abergwessin for four young steers (£6). (Jevan Waith of Llanavan Vawre owed money for cheese and wool.)

Leland's account of his Welsh travels in the sixteenth century has little detail about the Hundred of Builth, but he does tell us that it had 'good plenti of woode', and that Builth itself was a good market town with a 'fair castel of the kings'. About the county in general he says that 'Walschmen yn times past, as they do almost yet, did study more to pasturage than tylling, as favorers of their consuete idilness' — a foretaste of Clark's acid observations!

From the sixteenth or seventeenth century, it is thought, may date the *magwyrydd* of the upper Gwesyn valley — small roofless ruins, once rush-thatched, under the looming bulk of Drygarn. Magwyr Ficer and Magwyr Ffoes y Tir Las (Ditch of the Green Land) are perched on platforms of the high moor, looking downstream. A generation less tolerant of isolation and hard-living finds it difficult to imagine life in these 'post-mediaeval crofts', as they have been tentatively diagnosed. They were probably encroachments on the waste, and look incredibly small and rough in a forbidding landscape. There are others in the wild *blaenau* of the rivers of the Hundred of Builth. Two puzzling sites in rather different situations are hard to date. There is Old Alltyrhebog (O.S. 147/851.533), of which mounds only remain, on a shelf of the hill high above the oakwoods of the Tregaron road. (By the roadside below is Alltyrhebog barn, and behind it the slight traces of a farmhouse.) On Glangwesyn land, again above a wooded slope, is another possible platform site (O.S. 147/861.541)

So far no documentary evidence has come to light for the Abergwesyn farms before the seventeenth century, but there are late sixteenth century deeds referring to Llanwrtyd holdings, some of which are still identifiable. We have already noted early seventeenth century references to the farms of the Gwrâch valley in Llanddewi Abergwesyn, and to Trawsgyrch and Cenfaes (Cefnymaes) by the upper Cnyffiad. There are others traceable in seventeenth century deeds — Tir or Ty'nycwm, and Melinycwm, near Llwynmadog, for instance, Pwllybô in the Irfon valley (the old house, which stood much closer to the hill than the present one), and Crug (again, the old now-vanished longhouse, the outline of which can be seen in the ground on a shelf of land across the Irfon from Nantybrain). It was replaced by the present Crug, on the northern slope of the round hill, sometime between the tithe map of 1842 and the O.S. map of 1890. Brongilent, above the confluence of the Culent and the Rhyd Goch, was rebuilt just below the site of an older house. The recently-demolished house of Blaencwm-(camarch) was built about 1890, but the site had probably been used again and again, as the holding was an ancient one.

The Hearth Tax assessment of Llanddewi Abergwesyn on Lady Day, 1664 shows a pattern of small one-hearth houses scattered over its mountainous acres. Lhuyd estimated it, nearly thirty years later, as fourteen square miles in extent. There were twenty-one houses in 1664, if the list is accurate, two with *dau pen* (two ends), so with a hearth in each part, and one in which Rhytherch Thomas and David Gwillim shared one hearth. (Lhuyd's estimate was 'twenty-three houses besides four or five small cotts' — they must indeed have been small, as the *houses* were not very big!) In 1664 Llanfihangel had one three-hearth house, David Lloyd's, one two-hearth house occupied by Thomas Pugh, and fifty-three single-hearth houses. If the enumerators were correct, even the early gentry-houses of these parishes must have been very humble.

A few traditions handed down in Abergwesyn's neighbouring parish of Llanafan fawr give us a glimpse of seventeenth century farming there. The first potatoes, it is said, were brought to Cefnygwaelod by some of the family of that David William Howel Watkin whom we have found being fined £5 in Charles II's time for holding preaching-meetings at his house. By the nineteenth century potatoes were to become a staple food, though never to the same extent that they did in Ireland. Another piece of information handed down through the generations was that only two farms in Llanafan were shoeing their horses by the mid-seventeenth century; the only saddle then used in that parish was the *panel croen*, the pack-saddle used in Breconshire for transporting peat, dung and lime. Lhuyd in his 'Parochialia' found that in 1690 Llanafan fawr had 'more pasture than corn, indifferent fertil; partly champion [open country], partly mountainious, ground pretty well wooded'. Rye, oats and barley were sewn. An eighteenth century Llanafan farmer named Neuadd Wen Owen, Llanfihangel Bryn Pabuan, as the first farm in the district to sow rye.

Llanddewi Abergwesyn was, according to Lhuyd, 'for the most part pasture, mountainious, heathy, rocky, barren, but breeds plenty of good sheep, and keeps a good stock of black cattle for ye summer'. Some of the surplus cattle were probably sold to English drovers at the autumn fairs. Others were slaughtered for salting; the Welsh name for November is 'Mis Tachwedd', the 'Month of Slaughter'. (Clark in the following century was to write of the mowing of short bog-hay in the late summer for feeding cattle during the winter, 'though they shunned it in summer'. Jones said it was short enough to be carried home in a sheet or thrown into a basket on a sledge.) Lhuyd recorded that in seventeenth century Abergwesyn very little grain was sold 'besides small oates, which ye ground bears not without some manure and that is either done by tyeing their cattle to stakes upon it at nights or at noone in summer or by penning up their sheep in foulds or hurdles'. (The name 'Pantyclwydiau' given to one of the Abergwesyn farms in the Tywi valley means 'Hollow of the Hurdles'.) Abergwesyn had the distinction of breeding 'ye best and largest sheepe this side ye county'. Llangamarch grew 'all sorts of grain but most oates and Rye', fertilised by the same methods as the Abergwesyn oats and by 'fallowing and carrying of muck'; and also by 'pareing ye surface of ye earth and burning it' — a practice in Llanfihangel Abergwesyn too, as we shall see.

From the seventeenth century a few Abergwesyn wills have survived and tell us a little of the farms and stock of that time. Morgan John of Llanddewi, for instance, whose will was proved in 1666, owned a number of sheep and horses, seven bullocks, two heifers, a drake and two ducks. Elizabeth Williams, who died in 1677, had a little farm in Llanfihangel where she grew oats and barley and kept three ewes and three lambs, four cows, one two year old heifer, three yearling bullocks, one horse and one mare. She left to her only daughter Margaret the reversion of a holding called 'Tir-y-Graig and Tir Ffos-y-Gaseg'; perhaps this is where she lived. In the same year died John Prees of Llanfihangel, who owned seven cows, one calf, sixty sheep of all sorts, one old horse and one old mare.

Abergwesyn wills of the eighteenth century reveal the same sort of small-scale mixed farming. The usual estimate for goods and chattels in the inventories is about £10-£20, and stock consists of a few cattle, a modest number of sheep, and perhaps a mare and a colt. David Prees, Gentleman, whose will of 1728 was proved in 1741, had 'seven score sheep', twelve cattle including two calves, four oxen and three horses. At his December will-making he referred to 'flesh' in the house (presumably salted carcases) as well as cheeses and butter. We have already noticed the will of William Thomas of Cenfaes, who in 1709 founded the Cenfaes charity. He was for his day and place more than usually prosperous, owning on his own property and in the care of others sixteen cows and a bull, four oxen, nine bullocks, seven heifers, four calves, a horse, three old mares, two hundred and fifty two sheep and fifteen lambs, one pig, geese and poultry, hay and oats 'standing and growing', butter and cheese, oatmeal, wool, bedclothes and the usual household goods and implements of husbandry. At the other end of the scale would have been the crofters we found referred to in a document of 1704, with their 'little houses on the commons' and right of turbary and of digging for stones 'according to their ancient usage'. An inventory of the goods of a small farmer of Llanafan fawr, whose will was proved in Brecon in December 1748, gives some idea of the sort of household possessions one might have expected to find in a little thatched farmhouse of the Hundred of Builth at that period. His total personal estate, including fifteen sheep and any other stock, was valued at £21.16.6; he owned two old coffers, a 'bedstick', an old feather bed and two 'cushings', an old box, a bakestone, an old 'baril' and old churn, two iron pots, two old blankets and a rug.

As we should expect of times when more cattle figured in Abergwesyn farming than they do now, dairy produce was part of the farmer's livelihood. It supplied his own needs, and surplus butter and cheese were sold at nearby markets and taken on foot and pony-back sometimes considerable distances to the Border counties and the ironworks area of the South. The more local selling of butter in particular was to continue with some fluctuations well into the present century; not only the farmers, but cottagers owning a cow, would make enough butter to take to Llanwrtyd, for instance, and sell at the house doors, each supplier having regular customers. Self-sufficiency long remained the characteristic of the remoter Abergwesyn farms, as once it had been of all. The two Davies brothers, of whom the survivor died in 1968, lived for many years at secluded Cefncendu uchaf, far in the hills behind Llofftybardd, at first with their mother, who lived to be over a hundred and for many years never left the farm, and after her death on their own. They made their own butter, bread and cheese, very skilfully, and were talented at all kinds of woodwork.

An article on the Rev. David Williams of Troedrhiwdalar in *The Red Dragon*, November 1882, decribes with some nostalgia the life of the hill-farms in and around Llanwrtyd in the late eighteenth century, when David Williams was born. Plain nourishing food, including plenty of creamy milk, available because with butter just then at threepence a pound this point in the century was experiencing one of the 'fluctuations' referred to, when it was hardly worth saving the cream and making much butter for sale. There was plenty of 'sweet crisp oatcake', too. The diet was healthy, judging by the number of octogenarians who are recorded, says Tal-a-Hen, the author of the article. Infant mortality statistics might be used to prove the opposite, were it not for the fact that the children of the rich died also.

Potatoes were still a far more exotic food than they were later to become. A local man, Tomos Dafi Tomos, 'never would say "grace" over "taters"'. Tea was an expensive luxury at twenty shillings a pound; teapots and cups were dear too, so perhaps it is no wonder that the men of the house claimed to despise the brew, or that the women indulged in it furtively, setting out an improvised tea-tray in the open drawer of a chest, and hastily concealing the evidence when the 'master' was heard coming. One Rhys, a travelling tailor of the Llanwrtyd area, was 'head detective for ferreting out secret tea-drinkers'.

Williams' biographer D.A. Griffiths describes farmhouse food in the nineteenth century, when David was a grown man; it does not seem to have changed very much, though a little salt pork and beef are now included, and very occasional fresh meat, to vary the 'Braminical' fare of oat and barley bread, *uwd* ('hasty pudding'), milk, butter and cheese. White bread was rare, but not apparently non-existent. Not much coal was burnt; wood and peat were the fuels used. Tea-kettles and tea-pots were still rarities — David Williams brought his parents one each from Merthyr; they were treasured as heirlooms while the old people lived, and later kept at David's home, Tanyrallt, Llanafan fawr. Several Abergwesyn stories concern teapots. Morgan Williams at Llanerch-yrfa in the mid-nineteenth century, is remembered partly for making a wooden bottom for the holey teapot of an old lady at Rhiwddalfa! And Thomas Davies of Penybryn, an excellent though bibulous shepherd, who died in 1937, was often teased for having concealed from his wife the breakage of a new teapot he had bought for her, only to be detected by her discovery of the lid in his shopping-bag. Obviously kettles and teapots were still newsworthy, probably because of their past rarity; though Morgan Davies' day was a far cry from the turn of the eighteenth-nineteenth centuries, when the only two tea-kettles in Abergwesyn were at Llwynderw and Llwynmadog, and there were only three in the parish of Llanwrtyd! Other exotic items in those days were clocks. It is said that in 1779 the only Llanwrtyd people to own a clock were Rhys James of Dôldymer, a churchwarden: Thomas Winstone of Esgairmoel isaf, a woollen manufacturer: Mr Courtney of Dôlycoed: and Captain John Lloyd of Dinas. The average farmer would not possess such a luxury.

Tal-a-Hen writes that in the late eighteenth century clothes were warm and serviceable. Farms were largely self-sufficient, as we have found. Town shops were little needed when food, clothes and even saddlery were made at home, either by the family or by visiting craftsmen. The use of sledges rather than carts meant that blacksmiths' bills were light. Harness was improvised from hemp and horsehair. The article-writer's all too idyllic account is of a primitive but contented people, owning little but wanting little, dwelling 'securely under the shelter of their hills and under cover of the old Welsh language'. The concept of the language as something which protects, 'covers' a way of life, almost hides it from a potentially dangerous outer world, is interesting, in view of the determined assault made on that language over the centuries by those who extolled the benefits to the Welsh people of freeing them from Welsh! Preservers and destroyers shared a belief, more or less explicit, in the importance of the language.

The eighteenth century seems to have been a time here of a shift in the balance of stock-farming in favour of sheep. David Williams, author of *'Modern Wales'*, points out that sheep were then reared particularly for their wool, which 'was made up into cloth for the farmers' own families, and was also sold for use in the army, as well as for export to European countries, to Africa, the West Indies and the American colonies... Welsh cloth was used extensively on the slave plantations'. An article on the houses of this area (*Brycheiniog*, vol. IX) suggests that by the time the present, now deserted, farmhouse of Nantystalwyn was built in the Tywi valley, probably in the early nineteenth century, there had been 'a change in the nature of the stock' from predominantly cattle-farming (requiring the byre, at the lower end of the longhouse, to drain downhill, and therefore causing farmhouses to be sited at right-angles to the main slope of the hill), to mainly sheep-farming, which made no such demand. Nantystalwyn 'makes a complete break with longhouse siting and planning' by lying, 'uncharacteristically for the district ... parallel with the valley'. Other Abergwesyn farmhouses as they now stand do the same; but in most cases there is reason to suppose they too were rebuilt at no very distant date, so the *Brycheiniog* thesis is not disproved, though perhaps not proven either. Certainly Nantystalwyn is now remembered as one of the leading sheep-farms of the district, with a field that used to be crammed with neighbour's ponies on shearing days.

The Tywi valley, with Llanddewi Abergwesyn on the river's east bank and Caron and Llanddewi Brefi, Cardiganshire, on its west, is one which offers a certain amount of information about stock-variation and land-use. Not far downstream from Nantystalwyn, but on the Cardiganshire bank, stands Dôlgoch, now a Youth Hostel. Here lived William Williams, Gentleman, High Sheriff of Cardiganshire in 1725, and father of two more Cardiganshire High Sheriffs — William Williams of Pantseiri, near Tregaron, the great sheep-farmer called the King of the Mountains (High Sheriff in 1751) and Nathaniel Williams of

Fynachlog fawr (High Sheriff in 1776). Of the elder William the story is told of his encounter with a clever sheep thief, a master of camouflage, who would lie down in the pasture at dusk, covered with a white cloak. When darkness fell, he would find it easy to catch the unsuspecting sheep! Mr Williams warned him that he would be hanged one day. 'And you will be High Sheriff when that happens!' cheekily replied the thief. His words came true, for both of them, in 1725.

In the second half of the nineteenth century, if not earlier, Dôlgoch became a cattle-farm for summer grazing. For this purpose Hugh Jones took it about 1863. Many Cardiganshire farmers at that time would send their cattle up for the summer to the Twyi valley; ponies, too, were seen in great numbers on the hills. After Hugh Jones' death in 1897, aged eighty-nine, Dôlgoch swung back to sheep-farming. It is said locally that labour problems were the main reason for the change. Hugh's youngest son John, his white-headed boy, followed him at the farm, but as a sheep-farmer. He bought Dôlgoch from Lord Lisburne's Trawsgoed (Crosswood) estate, and about 1948 sold it to the Forestry Commission, remaining as their tenant till 1967. Dôlgoch appears on Emanuel Bowen's map of South Wales in 1760 — one of the few local houses to do so. An interesting early map is a field-plan of Dôlgoch and part of neighbouring Cwmdu in 1781. The accompanying schedule, among those of the Lisburne estate's Tywi valley farms, is in elegant copperplate and headed 'Dôl Goch' within a scrolled cartouche bearing devices of crossed spade and fork, rake and hoe, hook and scythe. It enables us to identify the fields and their uses in the late eighteenth century — 'some good meadow, part turbary' in the upper and lower dôl (water meadow), the calves' field, short hay 'between the hill and the river', 'sideland arable', nine acres of it, above the house and garden, and rising above all the then wooded slope, 'Yr Allt', and the bare ridge of Cefn Dôlgoch. Beyond that, to the north and west, Dôlgoch sheepwalks stretched away, and over the brook on the south-west boundary extended those of Cwmdu. The present century has seen the hills planted with conifers, and eventually the reservoir Llyn Brianne reach thirstily upstream.

The latter half of the eighteenth century saw the development of agricultural societies for the encouragement of better farming. Breconshire's was the first, established in 1755. It was, as Walter Davies wrote, a combination of charity and academy, disseminating new ideas and upholding standards in farming, and doing this partly through the medium of mild bribery — 'premiums' offered, rather like the prizes at a show, for good seed, good crops, draining, improved stock, 'top-dressing' with peat-ashes and so on. The Hundred of Builth, as one of the 'least improved' parts of the country, was, with the Hundreds of

Merthyr (Cynog) and Defynog, offered a premium of its own, for the best quality of clover-seed raised. Till more modern methods filtered in, whether or not through these societies, Welsh agriculture remained, as Sir Leonard Davies wrote, 'medieval in simplicity'. Probably the Brecknock Agricultural Society had little influence on this area. Well into the nineteenth century new ideas had hardly reached remote districts like this. If any changes were made in Abergwesyn (like the introduction of green crops to improve the monotonous grain crop rotation) they may have come through the involvement of a few local gentry in the new Agricultural Society. Its first president in April and May 1755 was Charles Powell of Castlemadog, by the road over the Epynt to Brecon. Marmaduke Gwynne of Garth served in September 1755 and April 1758, John Lloyd of Aberanell in February 1756, Evan Thomas of Llwynmadog in April 1761, and George Pryse Watkins of Rhosferig, near Builth, in October 1790. Changes if any could hardly have been on a large scale in an area so remote from great markets and so lacking in passable roads. Clark pointed out that for small hill-farmers it was not easy to provide the horses needed for bringing in lime for dressing fallow. The road were too narrow and rutted for yoked oxen (which long remained the usual working beasts of the farms) to be used with carts. The first person, it is said, to have brought a wheeled cart up to Abergwesyn was Lewis Evans of Nantyrhwch — perhaps about the same date (1820) when one Rhys Price took the first one to Tirabad.

Eighteenth century improvers, and those of the next century, had not only poor soil and climate, remoteness and bad roads to contend with, but a stubborn resistance to change in the people themselves. Walter Davies, though more sympathetic than Clark, wrote of the effect of open wastes (like those of the Abergwesyn moors), 'They encourage a kind of independence ... too commonly the parent of indolence, in the lower class, who dwell on their borders, or have erected cottages, and made encroachments upon them'. 'Vulgar errors, local prejudices, bigotry [as] to system [that is, rotation] and contempt of innovation' Davies thought among the main 'obstacles to improvement' in an area such as this. Labourers manifested their disapproval and distrust of new machinery by pretending not to understand it; really, they feared loss of wages and jobs. Farmers clung to the old ways. R.J. Moore-Colyer suggests the possibility of this entrenched conservatism having been, in some areas, a reaction to uncontrollable anglicisation and the accompanying attack on the Welsh culture and life-style. Certainly, as he further points out, farmers were not prepared to accept improvements they feared might bring an increase in rent, preferring a low income and standard of living provided the rent was kept low. This, as D.W. Howell writes, was the attitude of a countryside of peasant farmers, who 'equated "successful" farming with low expenditure', and , lacking capital, had no wish to borrow money for improvements which in any case they considered a most dubious investment. There were great strengths to balance the weaknesses of this small mixed hill-farming, with its stubborn adherence to traditional ways. In times of depression, the small farmers survived. They were used to hard times. Abergwesyn's best-known story of farming failure is that of Peter Jones of Llwynderw, one of the few large-scale local farmers, and one of the gentry. And, too, Abergwesyn seems to have shared the comparative immunity from nineteenth century agricultural labour unrest which D.W. Howells notes as a characteristic of rural Wales, where, in his opinion, among the factors making for good relations between farmer and labourer were the lack of class difference between them, and the patriarchal atmosphere of the farmhouse with its shared meals. We remember the 'cottage' meals for family and servants alike at Llwynderw in the days of Rhys Hope — evidence again for the late survival of traditional ways of life in Abergwesyn. D.W. Howells' view is not shared by all authorities, and local opinion tends to be on the side of the objectors to it. Here, it is considered, there *was* for generations a feeling of class distinction. It was rare for the farmer and his family to actually sit as the same table as the work people. The more prosperous farmers were considered 'higher class'. Labourers resented the precarious nature of their employment, which could cease at any moment if, for instance, a farm changed hands. Men who in slack winters sought temporary work in industrial south Wales often ended by leaving this area for good.

As for the indolence which troubled Clark and other commentors, no country and no century, surely, is without lazy farmers. In general, Howell is probably nearer the truth when he says that where incomers often failed, the small Welsh farmers managed to keep going, and that become of their 'willingness to work relentlessly and to live frugally'. They even saved money, and might with greater accuracy be accused of parsimony than indolence.

By the early nineteenth century the Nanteos estate, which in the previous century had included farms in both Abergwesyn parishes, now owned land only in Llanddewi. Estate maps of the year 1819 survive for some of these farms. Not all of the Tywi valley farms are shown as having arable at that date; Nantyfleiddast, Nantyrhwch and Ty'nygraig had none, but the tithe schedule of 1848 shows some arable on each of them. Nantyfleiddast had over ten acres, and others had some enclosures of arable and meadow or arable and pasture. Nantystalwyn, Pantyclwydiau and Fanog all had arable fields in 1819 — about fifteen acres on Pantyclwydiau and sixteen acres on Fanog — and still had some in 1848. The farms owned by the Powells of Nanteos in the Rhyd Goch valley near Llwynderw — Carregyfrân, Nantsinglas and Brongilent —had quite a stretch of arable land, the twenty-one acres at Carregyfrân leaving a tradition locally of being particularly productive, and noted especially for fine oats, some of the seed from which was taken down to Garth for sewing there. In 1848 Nantsinglas and Carregyfrân had become part of Brongilent farm. All were still growing some crops.

Despite the predominance of pastoral farming, farm gardens of the district did have their special glories, remembered even now when so many of the farmhouses have long been ruins. Nantserwydd, even the site of which is hard to trace in the Irfon valley near the Tregaron road, was very proud of its splendid carrots; while Gwegilhindda, by the Culent, had a much-admired potato-field, still traceable in some lights.

Theophilus Jones, writing of the Hundred of Builth in the early nineteenth century, said that most of its small farms were let on annual leases ('leases at will') beginning on 25 March. The outgoing tenant kept the outhouses till May for foddering his cattle on hay and straw, and had access to water. Rentals for the sort of land one would find in Abergwesyn ranged from three to seven shillings an acre. Very little wheat was grown, except near Builth. (In and near Llanafan fawr, a local tradition says, wheat was first grown at Erwddôl farm in 1735.) Farmers continued to rely on the sale of sheep, cattle and dairy produce. These annual tenancies had the disadvantage of uncertainty about being allowed to renew the lease, or about renewing it at the same rent; but some farmers preferred such leases, under which they were not responsible for building improvements. Then, too, tenants were sometimes afraid that an appearance of greater prosperity might tempt the landlord to raise the rent. Landlords had their own problems. Mr Thomas of Llwynmadog, when he guaranteed David Williams security of tenure and a fixed rent for life at Tanyrallt, told him he did not wish to make any new leases on his estate, as he had lost so much money on existing ones. In the late eighteenth century 'leases for lives' had still been a common practice; the Jones family of Fanog and Llwynderw, in their days of increasing prosperity, held such leases on some of their lands. Walter Davies thought that this type of lease led to over-much security and lack of effort. Twenty-one-year leases, like Peter Jones the elder's lease of Dygoedydd, were another well-known mode of letting.

Theophilus Jones wrote that a ploughing team consisted of four or five horses, or six oxen, or four oxen and one horse. Probably some of the small farmers of Abergwesyn would have had to pool their resources to make up a team — a form of *cymorth* (mutual help) which echoes mediaeval co-aration. Ploughs were clumsy; some Breconshire ones can be seen at Brecknock Museum, where there are also peat-cutting tools from Abergwesyn. Despite the deficiencies of the implements,

Breconshire ploughing with its straight-line expertise earned a high reputation. Late in the nineteenth century a Llanwrtyd craftsman was still making wooden ploughs; the last one made by John Williams of Glancledan fach is said to date from 1880. The corn-harvest was late — from August till mid-October in Jones' day. The sickle was then being superseded by the scythe, with which a good workman could earn fifteen to eighteen pence a day with food and drink, or two to three shillings without. Threshing was done by hand with a flail. Walter Davies said that by 1815 threshing machines were common in some parts, but we may be reasonably sure that Abergwesyn was not one of them. Winnowing on small hill farms was done in the open air, or on a threshing-floor, using the through draught from the open doors, or by the sheet-and-sieve method. A boy or girl would fill a sieve with corn and chaff, which a grown-up helper would feed into the airstream created by two others wielding a sheet. In an area such as this a typical crop might be as low as nine bushels an acre; thirteen bushels was considered a fair crop.

The mills of the district, like the Gwesyn Mill and Melinycwm, if their procedure was the same as that Davies describes as typical, would at that time have ground the farmers' corn for a 'toll' of the grain, or for money per measure. Mills also bought corn and sold meal and flour by weight. There were 'two capital mills in Builth' to which much wheat was brought from the uplands of Breconshire and Radnorshire in Davies' time. At some mills and farmhouses in the western counties, he says — and we find it true of some Abergwesyn farms too — corn was dried, before grinding, in open kilns. The 1842 tithe schedule of Llanfihangel has a *Cae cylyn* (kiln field) on Pentwyn, and *Dol y cylyn* on Tymawr. *Cylyn* is an obsolete word; *Nantyrodyn* farm in the Cerdin valley, Llanwrtyd, used the now-surviving word *odyn*.

The two tithe schedules are in many ways an interesting sources of information about Abergwesyn farms and farming methods. The Llanfihangel one shows a dozen or so farms of under 100 acres, sixteen of 100 to 200, three of 200 to 300, and two of 300 to 400. In 1848, Llanddewi, where we noted the absence of common land and greater extent of enclosed pasture, had two farms of 100 to 200 acres, two of 200 to 300, three of 300 to 400, one of 400 to 500, one of 500 to 600, one of 600 to 700, one of 700 to 800, one of 800 to 900, two of 1000 to 2000, and one holding of sheepwalk only, at Moelprysgau, over 2000 acres. The farmhouse here was beyond the parish boundary, in Cardiganshire. The acreages of some of the farms as given in the Census returns of 1851, 1861 and 1871 differ markedly from one decade to the next. Frequently that given in 1871 is the same as, or similar to, that recorded in the tithe schedules, a fact which suggests that an apparently marked fluctuation in farm-size may sometimes be due to a different method of estimating its acreage, certain pastures being sometimes included with the farm and sometimes not.

We have already ventured *à propos* of early farming patterns into the hazardous area of field-name interpretations. Certainly some of the less dubious and corrupted names can give miscellaneous information about the countryside as it used to be. Many of the field-names in the tithe schedule describe their position; as we have noted, this is chiefly in relation to the farmhouse or to other pieces of land known to the farmer. Such are *cae flaen drws* (field before the door), *cae dan y ty* (below the house), *cae bryn canol* (middle hill). Others describe shape: *y ddôl gron* (the round meadow), use: *cae lloi* (calves' field), distinguishing features: *gwaun y pistyll* (meadow of the spring), or type and quality of land: *rhôs* (moorland), *gwern* (alder grove), *cae garw* (rough field), *cae glas* (green field). There are also the measurement names already noted, such as *yr erw*, *cae pedwar cyfer*, and others measuring a unit of work, like *task nau ceiniog* (task worth ninepence) on Bwlchygorllwyn uchaf. One haymaker could cut with the scythe one acre a day; hence *gwaith y pedwar gwr* (work of the four men) on Llwyn Owen, and *cae gwas du* (field of the dark manservant) — two of these on Clyn (now Glangwesyn).

Some names tell us about woods and trees — the little orchard at Celsau, the plantation at Bwlchygorllwyn uchaf and nursery at Trysgol. Walter Davies had advocated the planting and protection of trees in the Wye and Irfon valleys, both for beauty and for their value as saleable timber. A marginal note to Clark's report of 1794 said 'There is no timber left in the county; and the tenants lop and top what is left, and no care is taken of the young timber'. Davies wrote that eight years later Mr Gwynne of Garth and Mr Thomas Price of Builth had 'detached woodlands from various farms and put them in the care of woodmen'. By the time Davies was writing his book, there was already a wonderful difference — the woods were growing luxuriantly. The tithe schedule shows birch-trees on Trallwm, holly on Llofftybardd, oaks on Erwgleisied. A few fields here and there named 'field without trees' suggest that this was worthy of comment — that in some parts of Abergwesyn fields *with* trees were the norm. A 'field without trees' on Celsau in 1764 had in 1842 become one of the farm's two 'bietting' fields, that is one where turf-paring and burning for fertiliser was carried on. There was another on Llofftybardd.

Cae hysfa on Ty'nycwm used a word, found elsewhere as *rhesfa*, which refers to hill common traditionally attached to a certain farm without being actually owned by it. *Cae'r ychain* on Llwyn Owen land near Cefn Gardys may refer to the farm's own oxen, but in view of its proximity to the *hen rhiw* probably indicated a drovers' stopping place. *Ffos yr hyddod* on Trallwm must surely be an ancient name (boggy place, or ditch, of the red deer), dating perhaps from the time of great deer-filled forests on these hills. *Cae banadl* (broom field) on Llwynmadog reminds us of Miss Clara Thomas' fostering of the old craft of dyeing with broom flower extract.

In the first part of the nineteenth century, bad winters and poor harvests, and a period of depression after the Napoleonic Wars, made for lean living. Rents, now much higher, were hard to pay. In 1812, the Nanteos estate agent wrote 'The distresses of the lower order of people are indeed truly deplorable'. Holdings were abandoned and in some areas whole families migrated to Glamorganshire and Monmouthshire. However, though the population of Llanddewi Abergwesyn decreased from one hundred and ninety in 1841 to eighty-seven in 1881, that of Llanfihangel increased from two hundred and sixty-four in 1841 to three hundred and sixty-eight in 1871, reducing to three hundred and twenty-eight in 1881. Such pre-Census references as we have (and they are to the number of houses, not a count of individuals) do not suggest that the 1841 figures represent any great decline from earlier times; certain little houses had vanished, but others had taken the place of some of them. Something that happened in many areas was that two or three farms were grouped together by landlords as an inducement to tenants to put what capital they had into a larger farm. The resultant limiting of available houses and employment was then a further cause of migration. The Abergwesyn tithe schedules, particularly that of Llanfihangel (1842) give some evidence of the running together of holdings. In many districts acres of roughly-cultivated oats and barley were converted into rough pasture, though, as we have seen, there was still arable on the majority of Abergwesyn farms. Tal-a-Hen, writing in 1882 of the dwindling-down of old field boundaries, suggested that marks of old ploughing on the hills indicated not only this change of land-use, but also that the climate in the eighteenth century had been more 'genial' and had made possible the cultivation of corn at heights which would not have supported it later.

Among farms which had already 'gone down' by the mid nineteenth century were Nantyrhiw, on Tymawr land, whose 'little gardens of Garreg Lwyd' can still be seen in outline on the hill of that name, and Y Guidfa, on Crug land, whose ruins can be traced in the depths of a Forestry plantation. Some have claimed to see its ghostly lights, shining through the trees into the black night of the Irfon valley. Many old houses, some confirmed by fleeting appearances in old wills and deeds, were already a memory by the time of the tithe schedules and Census returns of the nineteenth century.

The Rev. David Williams' biographer tells us something of the hard times local farmers lived through when his subject was a young married man farming Tynewydd on Bryngwyn hill in Llangamarch, then a wild common from which Williams hedged in a few fields. In 1811 he returned from a fund-collecting tour for his chapel to find all his cattle had died of the dreaded *hen glefyd* (old sickness). Gifts of in-calf heifers from his father-in-law and a wealthy neighbour gave him a fresh start. Three bad years then came, when wheat was costly to buy. In 1813 frost held the land for thirteen weeks. Every mill stopped, so corn could not be ground. Snow was hedge-high. Sheep died by the hundred; farmers lost two-thirds of their flocks. In one snow-bound winter about this time so many sheep died that Peter Jones of Llwynderw sold, it is said, two and a half thousand fleeces for £150, and one day killed with a single burst of shot twenty-eight crows feasting on carcases near the mansion! In 1814 David Williams' brother Isaac had bought some cows for £10 a head and another for £13. After Waterloo, he got only £4 (in Kent) for the £13 one, and £2.10s. for one of the others. Farmers were often driven to pay their rent in kind.

Walter Davies complained that the uplands of Breconshire had 'too many very inferior cottages' and other buildings. Certainly the smaller farmhouses were rough and ready. At Nantydderwen in the Cerdin valley, David Williams' birthplace, the children's bedroom ('the hiding-place of mice and rats') had a floor of loose, unplaned boards, one of which the six foot Rhys Prydderch used to lift with his head when standing to be measured for a suit of clothes by Elias Elias, a local Methodist tailor. Rough though the house and the life may have been, there were many who survived it and even thrived. 'A hardy race,' Tal-a-Hen called them. When the Williams family moved from Dinas Mill to Maesygwaelod, behind today's woollen factory, 'an additional room was thrown up', earth-floored, with mud walls thatched with rushes, and a cockloft over it, approached by a 'ladder or rough ricketty staircase' — like the loft-bedroom of little Brongilent, near Llwynderw, where slept the children of the last family to occupy it, earlier this century. Houses like these in Abergwesyn and the country round are shown in the watercolours of Mrs Trahaerne, in a book of Welsh views (1833-59) now at the National Library. Those of the Irfon valley show little whitewashed thatched houses, Henfron and Dôldymer in old Llanwrtyd, among them. They have extraordinary crooked thatched chimneys blossoming out of a stone foundation. One of Dôldymer's chimneys has vertical frame-poles projecting at the top. No wonder there were a great many fires, especially in parts where inflammable straw bedding was an additional hazard. There were other accidents, too. The original farmhouse of Gwybedog, on the Epynt, was thatched with rushes cut in autumn with a scythe, and carried by gambo and *car llusg* (sledge). It had one downstairs room, from which a door led straight into the cowshed. One great beam supported the upper floor. Shortly before 1890 it collapsed with the wall while the children were in bed, and landed on the table. No-one was hurt. A new house, with three rooms downstairs, was built with stones carried from a nearby river by the children; it was roofed with North Welsh slates. At the site of Gwybedog one can see today the shape of the old 'horse-round', where a pony walking round a raised circular bank would work simple farm machinery.

34. Aberllêch, Llandeilo'r Fan

35. Clibarth, Llanafan Fawr

36. *Nantybrain (older wing)*

37. *Llwynderw*

38. Lle'r taihirion (now demolished)

39. Llofft y Bardd

40. *At Tŷmawr, August 1970*

41. *Abergwesyn from Cefn Fanog, 1972 (Fern stacks)*

XI & XII FARMS & FARMING

42. *At Pentwyn shearing, 1972*

43. *Scyth-sharpening (Mr. David Jones) 1970*

XI & XII FARMS & FARMING

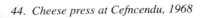
44. Cheese press at Cefncendu, 1968

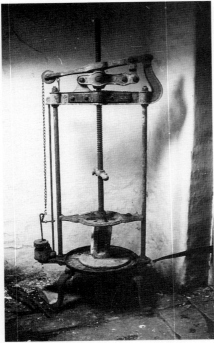

45. The late Mr. E. Lewis, Pencae Mawr, August 1967

12. Farms and Farming

2. The Later Nineteenth Century to the Present Day

Sir Leonard Davies wrote in 1939 that much of the life of mid- and west Wales then would have been quite familiar to a Georgian or even Elizabethan ancestor. Indeed, despite a degree of mechanisation, this seems to have been a district where there was remarkable continuity of life-style and type of farming well into the present century. The Second World War was a watershed of change here, though late as the 1960s one could still find a farm or two with scythed hay gathered into heaps, and one where an old lady would emerge at tea-time and milk her cow straight into a jug.

It is the continuity that strikes us; but the Glanusk edition which brought Jones' county history up to date in the first decade of this century stressed the changes that had come about in Breconshire since the 1850s, and some of which would have affected Abergwesyn. The introduction of farm machinery, writes the editor, had contributed to the drift to industrial areas by causing confusion among farm labourers. By 1880, the scarcity of labour led to a rise in farm wages; much land was going out of cultivation, and farmers were concentrating more and more on stock-raising. The farmer's wife and daughters still made butter and cheese, and reared poultry, selling the surplus at the nearest market, or to 'hucksters' who took it to Glamorganshire. In Abergwesyn between the wars women were still taking butter for sale to Llanwrtyd. For some time now there has been no butter- or cheesemaking on the farms, and cheese-presses and butter churns like those which in the 1960s still stood in the then derelict farmhouse of Cefncendu uchaf (later restored) have disappeared, having acquired antiquarian value.

Lord Glanusk write that many of the sons and daughters of Breconshire farms had left the land for banks, post offices and shops, but one son at least was brought up to succeed to the farm. Often, at that date, farms were still occupied by families who had been there for generations. (Even when tenancies were ostensibly on a yearly basis, most people could rely on security of tenure, and the son's understood right to take over the farm on his father's death.) In Abergwesyn, Pentwyn was a farm which had remained in the Hope family for generations. When the Hopes left in 1973 for Cae Pandy, near Builth, they ended a chapter of Pentwyn's history that stretched back over a hundred years.

The process of absorption of smaller farms by larger ones began long ago In the first decade of the nineteenth century Jonathan Williams, the historian of Radnorshire, lamented the 'too prevalent practice of uniting many small farms into one, and suffering the buildings to fall into decay', but pointed out that any loss of population was balanced, in his county, by the growth in the number of cottages on the wastes. 'The race of little farmers,' he wrote, 'who in former times supported themselves and families with credit, has... become extinct, while the rapid and overwhelming spread of pauperism excites universal alarm.' Among the old houses and cottages, some of which we have seen had disappeared by the time of the mid-nineteenth century Tithe schedules and Census returns, were probably a number inhabited by crofters whose rights of common enabled them to live at subsistence level. Possibly the 'cottagers' of the 1881 Census, such as thirty-eight year old Margaret Davies of Nantygarreg, were survivors of this way of life in an area which, though most farms remained fairly small, had like other districts experienced a degree of 'compacting' over the decades.

Some pauperism, perhaps not enough to excite 'universal alarm', is shown in the Census returns. In 1841 Anne Thomas lived with her five-month baby Elizabeth and her sixty-five year old pauper mother in one of the Dôliâr cottages by the Gwesyn. In 1851 Anne and Elizabeth were lodging at Crug, and their former cottage was empty. In 1861 they were back at Dôliâr, both working as stocking-knitters. Evidently by 1871 they had failed to make a living, for Anne Thomas is now described as a pauper, and her daughter as 'unemployed'. There do not appear to have been in Abergwesyn many able-bodied paupers receiving assistance at home, though in Builth Union District as a whole Poole's statistics show the 1850 numbers for 'outdoor relief', 849, to be second only to those of Brecon Union. The Builth figure decreased till in 1874 we find only 524. In 1881 the thirty parishes of the Builth Union had seventy-three indoor paupers (that is, those housed in a workhouse) and two hundred sixty-six receiving relief at home. Most mid-nineteenth century Abergwesyn paupers were elderly, most female, and we find them scattered one here, one there, in the farmhouses of the two parishes, or occupying cottages. At Lle'rtaihirion in the Camarch valley in 1841, for instance, was Gwen Morgan, the oldest of them, aged between ninety-five and a hundred. 1851 was the Census year when most paupers were to be found here. In some cases we are told what their work used to be. Sixty-seven year old David Davies at Troedyresgair, and Moses Jones at Cefncendu uchaf, were formerly agricultural labourers. Gwen Jones, aged seventy-four, at Digiff, used to be a servant. The two old women at Nantyneuadd were 'pauper hose-knitters'. In 1861 there was only one house whose inhabitants were called paupers — Cenfaes, where the widow Charlotte Davies, aged fifty-eight, had three daughters and a grandson living with her. A number of houses in 1871 contained paupers; two of them were 'idiots'. The 1881 Census, too, shows six paupers in Llanfihangel and two in Llanddewi. All were women, one aged ninety-four and three over eighty. In 1891, John Edwards (sixty seven) of Clynglas was a pauper.

In 1861 'almswomen' make an appearance at several houses. There were seven of them, their ages ranging from eighty-three to forty-six. There were a number of child paupers in the returns, and in 1861 two 'motherless children'. In 1881 there were a number of child 'boarders' in Abergwesyn — three, for instance, all at school, and of ages eight, ten and fifteen, at Penybont Cottage in what is now Beulah. The eldest, William Williams, was local-born, the others natives of Aberystwyth and of Disserth, Radnorshire. It is interesting that William had not been compelled by necessity to leave school by the age of fifteen.

The latter part of the nineteenth century was in general a time of agricultural decline, when the industry of south Wales took over the role of Wales' chief occupation. The desertion of rural holdings for industrial towns continued. More food came to be imported, and the new railways made possible a wider distribution in hitherto remote areas. Some bad harvests, such as that of 1879, deepened depression. Labourers showed a growing 'independence' (always a two-edged and dubious quality, if one listens to nineteenth century commentators on the rural scene!), as in some parts of Wales, workman and farmer alike gradually broke the quasi-family bond of the past. Here and there rural risings imitated the style of Rebecca. Abergwesyn has few traditions or records of violent affrays of this kind. There are isolated examples, among them the poaching affrays of the 1850s to 1870s on local rivers, following the formation of the Wye Preservation Society at Builth in 1856. Before that, local people had taken salmon from the rivers in winter almost as though by right. The stringent tightening-up of the laws affected farmer and labourer too, and both were involved in such affairs as that of the massive Rebecca-type armed gang which very ostentatiously went poaching near Rhaeadr in 1856, and the similar gangs which, as D.W. Howells writes, 'burned' the Camarch, the Irfon and the south Radnorshire Edw. A differently-motivated act of reprisal was a Llanwrthwl arson-case of 1868, the story of which we shall tell later; this was a protest against commons-enclosure by a large landlord, and was an uprising of local farmers.

In an area like this,the essentially mixed nature of the farming was some protection against major disaster, as no doubt were the relatively low expectations of a district of hard, penurious living. There were instances of failure, but not general ruin. In fact the number of specialised farm servants employed on Abergwesyn farms at the time of the 1881 Census do not suggest drastic decline here at that time. A handful of farms in 1871 and 1881 had enough cattle to warrant employing a cowman, and in 1881 fifteen farms had a waggoner. As we have seen, the population of Llanddewi did dwindle, but not so that of Llanfihangel.

Again the gulf between landlord and tenant (in religion and language as well as education and class), often exaggerated as a source of trouble and misunderstanding in the Welsh countryside, was only just widening by the mid-nineteenth century in this neighbourhood, which, as we have seen, had at least some nonconformist gentry, attending Welsh-language chapels, till well into the century. Even when the gentry families did become markedly anglicised, the fact that here they seem to have been benevolent paternalists mitigated the evil. So did the fact that in the later nineteenth century they were mainly resident. Poole's *'History'* (quoting from the government Domesday Book) shows that in 1878 the Nanteos estate still owned 8116 acres in Breconshire. Here, then, was a non-resident landlord, but one not far removed. However, the 8910 Breconshire acres of the Llwynmadog estate, the 4635 acres owned by the related Welfield Thomases, and the 3841 belonging to Mr Fuller-Maitland of Garth House were not too often afflicted by absenteeism. Numbers of local farmers owned over a hundred acres, as did a few clergy and tradesmen. Some, such as the Williams family of Glangwesyn, owned considerably more. Rentals they could charge varied, of course, with the position and quality of the land. In 1896 Sir Joseph Bailey (the Lord of the Manor) said in evidence to the Royal Commission on Land in Wales and Monmouthshire that the best farms of the area could command a rental of eighteen shillings per acre; even very poor land was improved in value by the proximity of the spas.

Many of the 'old ways' that reach back far into the last century, and beyond that too, can be remembered by people now living, whose minds lovingly hold a great store of particularities of time and place. There is a flat stone, for instance, by the runs of Nantycrâf in the Culent valley. It was used for threshing by hand with a flail. There was art in fitting one rod-like stick into the other at an angle sufficient to give a good swing. An expert could calculate just where the grain would fall, and direct it to the right spot.

Peat was in past centuries the main fuel of Abergwesyn farms and cottages. Sir Joseph Bailey stated that before the coming of the Mid-Wales Railway coal had to be hauled twenty miles to the Builth area, and so 'the price of comfort was then very great'. Peat continued to be used well into the present century; in fact, its use has never entirely stopped, and in recent times has sometimes been revived by people moving into the district, trying out old methods or bent on using all available natural resources. Nantyrhôs farm, Llanwrtyd, which uses peat from Waun Rydd, and Hirnant farm at the top of the Elan valley, Radnorshire, are examples of farms which still cut peat in the ancient manner. In Abergwesyn one main turbary, on the hills between Gwesyn and Irfon, was reached by the 'peat path' from the lower Gwesyn valley. The light gambo or the sledge was used to carry the peat down. The gambo had two high wheels set in the middle of a long body with two shafts. This vehicle was also used for carrying hay. When the fields were very steep, it was the *car llusg* that was employed — a wheelless sledge drawn by chains and a lantry, and a sometimes steered from behind with lines, like a plough. Another horse-drawn vehicle was the *car gwair*, which had shafts, and an upright rack at the back to support the hay. The back of this cart dragged on the ground. Worn-out pieces could be replaced. There were no nails in its construction, only wooden pegs. Some farmers used very small wheels under it, to make it easier for the horse to pull.

Mountain hay, *gwair cwta*, was hard to cut, even with the sharpest of scythes (Walter Davies was saying this too, in 1815!). The *rhip*, for scythe-sharpening, was fastened to the scythe by a nail and a wooden peg which fitted into a hole in the *rhip*. In one pocket the scytheman carried a horn of pig-fat (goose-grease was here considered less effective), attached to which was a cord with at its other end (in the opposite pocket) the bag of sand or girt used for sharpening blades on the greased *rhip*. The grit preferred was bought by the hundredweight from the Black Mountain in Carmarthenshire, and sold at about a halfpenny per pound. Men cutting mountain hay were away from the farmhouse all day if the hay was to be stacked up in the hills. Food was carried up to them by the farmer's wife, her maid or a young boy. A favourite refreshing drink before cider became popular in Abergwesyn was *dwr a blawd* (water and oatmeal).

Abergwesyn used to have a fern-harvest (of bracken from the hill slopes) for litter for cattle during the winter. It continued till the late sixties at least.The hay-harvest, which some people thought unlucky to start on a Saturday, used to be later than it is now, for sheep-shearing once began later, and here it is the needs of the flocks that determine the rhythm of the farming year. Harvest and shearing, in particular, are still, in Abergwesyn as elsewhere in rural Wales, times of neighbourly co-operation, albeit somewhat diminished as festivities. Shearings used to follow each other at time-honoured dates on the various farms, and combined hard communal work with the fun of a big social event. In the nineteenth century there was a great shearing-feast in Abergwesyn; it is mentioned in Kilvert's diary. Pentwyn's, in the days of the Hope family there, and probably much earlier, was a particularly big shearing; and to Glangwesyn, too, came farmers on foot driving sheep from as far afield as the Epynt — driving them back, too, in the evening. As we have seen, one has only to turn the pages of the school log-books to see what an important feature of the Abergwesyn summer was the regular routine of shearing-time, and how all the stages of the farming year were occasions for co-operation.

It is said, for instance, that the farmer of Trawsnant in the Tywi valley, a house which remains today, empty and derelict, on a hillside above Llyn Brianne, could stand on a hilly point near Cae Gwartheg (Cattle Field), near the track up-valley to Fanog, shout aloud for help with his haymaking, and be sure of a good response to his call. Ffynnon Wen (White Well) near the brack was his weather-glass; when it was full, he would arrange his haymaking. Trawsnant, with its huge hearth across which an enormous log would be wedged and lit at both ends, is one of the houses about which farming stories accumulate — like that of John Jones, who a year before his unwilling departure (at a change of owner) in 1861, sold off all the 2550 sheep on the farm, in order to prevent the incoming tenant from having them, and to give him the formidable task of settling a completely new flock of sheep on the open mountain, with no old wethers left which knew the boundaries.

Among the practices which continue here is one not unlike transhumance — the 'tack' system, the sending of animals to winter pasture in milder areas, such as the Cardiganshire coast. Until a few years ago, the last weekend of October or the first of November would see the rounding-up of the hill ponies, which would be driven into Pentwyn yard for the night, and next day would journey in a long, stamping, mane-tossing procession over the Tregaron road to the coastlands till spring. In former days, it is said, they used to files along, the halter of one tied to the tail of the one in front. Sheep, too, are sent to tack. Within living memory, they used to be taken on long journeys on foot over the hills, sometimes in bitter weather, to and from winter pasture — a sort of transhumance in reverse, leaving the home base for winter, not summer. The late Mr Evan Lewis of Penycae near the upper Camarch used to take sheep to Llanilar, near Aberystwyth, stopping one night at Pentwyn, and another at Tregaron. He remembered sometimes struggling along the drovers' road in snow so blinding and cold so bitter that each step was an effort. In recent times the east-west journey was made on 10 October, and the return one on 10 April. It was considered worth the trouble and expense for the improvement both in flesh and wool. Nowadays sheep are sent to Carmarthenshire and Pembrokeshire rather than to Cardiganshire, returning in spring, as they left, in stock-lorries.

Mr Evan Lewis continued a book of sheep's earmarks compiled by his father. It has been said that between Penycae and Plynlumon there is not a single fence, and that in the whole of that huge mountain area there was not a stray whose owner the Lewises could not discover from their encyclopaedic knowledge of sheepmarks. Evan Lewis and his brother John, who in 1982 lived alone at Penycae, the last left there out of eleven children of the farm, were renowned for their strength. At the big Pentwyn shearings they were the champion catchers, effortlessly lifting sheep all day.

Ewe-milking is still remembered by older people of the district. Very little ewes' milk was required to enrich cheese. One method of milking was to get the ewes into the compartments of a spoked frame, with their heads inwards, and to milk them from behind. Each ewe would recognise her own compartment and walk into it at milking time.

With the coming of tractors, working horses gradually followed the oxen of bygone years into the shadows. There were still some in use up to the mid-1950s: it was not till about two years after the end of World War Two that the first tractors arrived on the farms. Not many years ago, in the old stables of vanished Hafdre on the further bank of the Tywi, one could see hanging from pegs the tack of the horses once used at Bronyrhelem on the slope above.

The hiring-fair, once such a familiar feature of rural life, seems remote to us now; yet a little hiring was still being carried on in Builth as late as the 1940s, and at some of the Radnorshire market towns. In the earlier decades of this century such fairs were the recognised agricultural 'labour exchange', though as time went on hiring at home gradually replaced hiring at fairs. Farm servants were hired by the year, and casual labour by the day or week. Older people well remember standing for hire at Garth Fair, for instance. They say that often the farmers came to find workmen they already knew, or who had been recommended to them; the catchment area of the fair was not great, and everyone knew everyone else. The words of 'Sweet Emma Griffiths' to Kilvert — 'I never liked to break my time' — are echoed today by Abergwesyn people who took equally seriously the obligation of keeping their contract.

When we look back at the nineteenth century Census returns, we cannot but be struck by the youth of some farm servants, and of children of the farm who were employed at home. At Blaennant, for example, in 1841, an eight year old boy was the male servant. At Penceulan in 1851 the eldest son, aged ten, worked on the farm. This was not so in every case, however: at Llanerch-yrfa twelve- and eight-year old sons Morgan and Rees Williams are described as 'scholars', though they were probably kept home from time to time to help with some of the farm work. At Cluniau Siân near the Camarch, David Hughes's thirteen-year-old sister-in-law was a 'hose knitter'. Not far away, at

Penycae, the male servant was twelve and the female one thirteen. Mrs M. Jones, an octogenarian who died in January 1958, mother of Mr David Jones of Abergwesyn Post Office, went at the age of eight to work for her aunt, none too easy a taskmistress, at the lonely farm of Llethr in the hills of Llanddewi Brefi, a farm that still looks like a green oasis across a formidable expanse of peat-bog. By the time she was ten, she was driving a flock of sheep several miles over the hills to meet with others for the sheep-washing at Ffrwd-ar-Gamddwr, the ruins of which can be seen by the Tregaron road near the turn for the Camddwr valley. Mr Jones himself remembers very young farm servants in his own time; and Abergwesyn school log-books show what a temptation, sometimes necessity, it remained for parents to remove their children from school prematurely, or at the earliest legal moment, to swell the labour-force at home. Probably some of these young farm-servants of more recent years were as competent as the little herd-girl of Walter Davies's story, who, when her employer was attacked and gored by a bull, advanced menacingly upon the savage animal with only her hat for weapon, and in no time had it retreating meekly before her!

One of the great changes this century has brought has been the loss of the young from the farms — not only the many children who brought life and noise and energy to houses now quiet, but a whole now-missing class of farm-workers. People who remember growing up in valleys which to us may seem bleak and lonely recall a youth in the main very sociable, full of movement, when the scattered houses were full of young people, and the miles between cheerfully travelled on foot or pony-back.

The later Census returns are more specific than were the earlier ones about the work of the farm-servants, or perhaps that work became more differentiated. By 1861 we find not only shepherds but carters and dairymaids, while the 1871 and even more the 1881 returns show, as we have seen, waggoners and cowmen. Shepherds were sometimes themselves the occupiers of farmhouses, as was the case in 1881 at Llanerch-yrfa, Cefnymaes (Cenfaes), Lle'rtaihirion, Cluniau Sian, Pencae esgairfraith (Pencaemawr), Nantyrhwch (Cwm Tywi), Nantystalwyn, Penrhyddfa, Nantybrain and Brongilent (further evidence of the diminution in number of small independent farms), and recently at Nantybrain, where Mr S. Jones was the shepherd employed by Mr G. Hope of Llanwrtyd.

In Canon D. Parry-Jones's *'Welsh Country Upbringing'* there is a good photograph by the late Miss Wright showing the Tywi valley farm of Fanog, Abergwesyn. Here in its heyday is one of the best-known sheep-farms of the area, house and outbuildings sparkling with whitewash, gardens trimly laid out, sycamores in full leaf, three-bay peat-house in good repair, potato-field proudly-ridged on the hillside

XIII JOBS: FARM & HOME

46. *The shoeing enclosure, Pentwyn*

47. *Rhiwgam Drovers' Road, near Llanerchyrfa*

48. *Melin y Cwm (now demolished)*

Above: *49. Former Dôlaeron woollen factory, Beulah (now private house)*

Left: *Cambrian woollen factory, Llanwrtyd Wells, 1972*

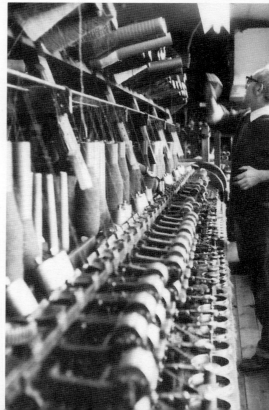

XIV JOBS: LOCAL INDUSTRIES

51. *Part of old lead-mine workings, Cilent Valley, Llanddewi*

52. *Adit, waterfall in Nant Byr*

53. *Dôlycoed Hotel, 1972; meadows where Sunday games were played and people went after chapel*

54. *Penry Lloyd's Memorial, Victoria Wells, Llanwrtyd*

55. *Dôlycoed Wells, Llanwrtyd (pump room), 1967*

6. *Dôlycoed Wells (pump room), 1967*

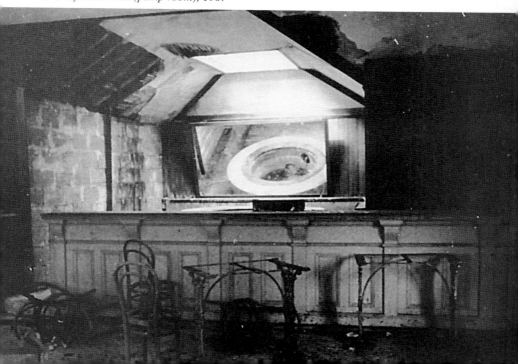

57. Halter-making: spinning the white thread (Mr. D. Jones)

58. Last plaiting (Mrs. Richards and her brother, Mr. Jones, at Post Office)

59. *Tombstone, Llanwrtyd Old Church*

60. *The hoof-prints*

61. *Moelprysgau, Tywi Valley*

62. *Aberceinciau, Irfon Valley*

above. Fanog, empty and decaying for many years, lies now beneath Llyn Brianne. The year's round of work there when Fanog was in its prime had a pattern which with minor variations was that of many Abergwesyn farms. Yet Fanog seems to have been 'special', too, a legend in its own lifetime, and worthy to be remembered.

'At the very end of the world the lonely homestead of Vanog...stands perched above the raging torrent. Homely white walls, a few wind-smitten shade trees, a front-yard full of collies taking their ease in these piping times between shearing and the autumn fairs, thousands of sheep upon the mountains round...as perfect a picture of pastoral isolation as could be found in Wales'. So wrote A.G. Bradley, who travelled the upper Tywi near the beginning of this century. Lonely in a sense Fanog must have always been, standing above its dramatic gorge and under the 'bumpy ridges' of mountain between Irfon and Tywi, a country of 'sheep and curlews and vistas of billowy solitude, blue and hazy'. Yet whether one took the rough track (an old county road) north from Ystradffin or south from Nantyrhwch, or dropped down on it from one of the paths over the hills, Fanog seemed always a destination rather than just a place on the way. Abergwesyn stories often begin 'Once, when I went over to Fanog...'.

The reservoir of Llyn Brianne meant the end of Fanog. Empty though it had been for years, while it stood it held encapsulated a vanished way of life. Tourists who drive along the road above the lake cannot know either Fanog's isolation — for no motor road ever passed near it — or the intensity of its life as a thriving farm, and, as we have seen, a centre of religious activity.

The first story of Fanog, that is of a farmhouse of that name on the site of the drowned eighteenth century house, dates from the late seventeenth century. A Scottish packman was murdered for his money by Dafydd Rhys Dafydd of Fanog. The crime was witnessed by the little servant-girl, whom Dafydd spared as long as she remained in the isolation of Fanog; but when she refused to be re-hired at the end of her term of service she was doomed. Dafydd killed her too. What had happened to the packman's body is uncertain; but one version of the story says that Dafydd's originality in disposing of the girl's corpse was his undoing. He stood her body upright behind a waterfall in the brook Coesnant, just south of Fanog. When it was discovered there some months later, the murderer was sent for trial, convicted and hanged. Another story has it that he confessed on his death-bed at Trawsnant.

Some of the history of the house built in the late eighteenth century we have already sketched — its days as the home of two separate Jones families, each of some distinction. Scattered entries in the parish registers show also the names of some of its early nineteenth century tenants. The last farmer of Fanog, who was there when Bradley visited it, was 'the charming and greatly- respected Miss Jones of Fanog — Jane Jones, spinster daughter of Thomas Jones the younger. She was named after an earlier daughter who died aged six, and had three other sisters, descendants of whom still live in the district. Jane was a capable and methodical farmer, who drove her work-people hard, and was considerably less generous with wages than she was with gifts to the Methodist cause. Every day she held a family service at Fanog; attendance was compulsory each morning and evening. The farm bailiff and a servant read a few verses of the Bible; then all knelt for prayers. Jane Jones died on 15 October 1916, aged seventy-two. Her funeral, led by her former shepherd, David Jones of Brongilent, was attended by most of her neighbours and connections for miles around. Many came fourteen or even fifteen miles to follow the coffin by the rough path over the mountain to Llanddewi Abergwesyn churchyard. Miss Jones is still something of a legend. She died intestate, her estate being divided between two sisters, a nephew and a niece. For the sale of her furniture, farm goods, cattle and ponies, held in September 1917, again a huge crowd gathered, coming on foot and horseback, some from a considerable distance.

Miss Jones ran Fanog to a system. The garden, the great pride of her bailiff Evan Davies, was planted early each year. Peat-cutting started on 1st May. If it had been a good spring, the peat was all carried to the peat-house before sheep-washing, which took place between 15 and 20 June, the lambs having been ear-marked at the beginning of the month. Shearing was at the end of June or beginning of July, and was of course a tremendous social occasion, when the cooking facilities in the house were supplemented by those in the *gegin* or out-kitchen, a building at right-angles to the front of the house, containing downstairs a large room with extra ovens for large-scale cooking, and above it a wool-loft. Before the shearing, the house was dazzlingly whitewashed, even the stones bordering the path and surrounding the flower-beds being whitened. There was a second shearing before the hay-harvest; usually about a hundred more sheep were gathered and shorn. Hay was harvested from three fields; in addition there was mountain hay to be cut, and some in later years from Pantyclwydiau. Dipping came next, at the beginning of September. In 1913 the last travelling sheep-dip, hired from Prytherch of Medical Hall, Llanwrtyd Wells, went over the hills to Fanog. A permanent sheep-dip was installed there in 1914. The mobile tub, supplied by Cooper & McDougall, was carried in its draining-pen, and drawn by a cob from Llanwrtyd to Ty'nyllan, Abergwesyn, by Llanddewi churchyard. Here the pony was changed for a heavier horse, to pull it up the old road between Ty'nyllan and the churchyard, up the hill and across the line of today's Forestry road, then higher up along a route more or less corresponding to the present road until, after the spot where the E.F.G. gate now stands, it turned left. The beginning of this track can still be followed through a ride of the forest. Then came the long haul over the right of way through the Rhyd Goch bog, and down to Fanog. The tub had to be hired for at least four days, allowing one for the journey, and taken back on a pre-arranged day ready for the next hirer.

A few ponies went over the hills to be sold at the big pony fair at Llangamarch on 15 October, to which buyers came from many parts of England as well as Wales. Geldings were broken in at about three years old and sold at four years. October was the month, too, for selling draft ewes, wethers and wether lambs. Then the potatoes had to be drawn — Fanog was very proud of these. They were placed in clamps, trenches in which they were covered with turfs, then earth, then rushes to provide a waterproof top layer.

November found the household busy making candles for the long winter nights ahead. *Mis Tachwedd* (Slaughter Month) was also the time for killing animals to salt down. The outside steps to the wool-loft formed a sacrificial slab for the killing of pigs. (These used to be kept by many Abergwesyn people.) The carcases hung from hooks in the house. At Fanog two pigs were usually killed on the same day. Another stone structure at Fanog, reminiscent of the days of long-skirted women riders, was the mounting-block at the upper end of the stable building.

In 1917 Jane Jones' bailiff, who had worked at Fanog for twenty-eight years, took over the farm, running it as efficiently as Miss Jones had done, and keeping up the family services every day except shearing- and gathering-days. A bachelor, a peace-loving man and a good neighbour, Evan Davies was noted for his startling resemblance to King Edward VII. He lived at Fanog until 1941, when he moved to Nantygwarog in Llanddewi Brefi; there he died three years later aged seventy-nine. Fanog had a few years in charge of a shepherd, during which time it became once more Llwynderw property, this time under Mr Glyn Hope. At last the house was abandoned and most of its land afforested. In 1972 the waters of Llyn Brianne crept up the walls and closed over Fanog. The summer of drought in 1976 saw a strange re-appearance of the mud-caked house from the dwindled lake. Since then it has surfaced several times in summers of drought. H.L.V. Fletcher's words about Nantgwyllt, the 'House Under the Water', whose garden walls similarly rose from Caban Coch lake in 1938, ring true of Fanog. 'An eerie, desolate landscape', he called it, 'just forgotten contours and mud, except that little streams, long lost, suddenly awoke and babbled cheerfully'. The old walls 'did not seem to belong to the sunlight anymore...many who knew the valley best felt more comfortable when the old places were hidden below the water again'.

Pentwyn, at the junction of the Tregaron mountain road with the Llanwrtyd- Beulah loop-road, is another important farm that for centuries formed a focal point for the life of the district, combining as it did the rôles of farm and inn. R.G. Jones wrote that the three taverns of Abergwesyn, including Uffern Bod and Cwrt y Rhagod, traditionally supposed to have been clustered in the neighbourhood of Pentwyn, pre-dated even the two mediaeval churches! They were undoubtedly rough and ready, probably riotous, and one can well believe Gwesyn Jones' disapproving allusion to week-long drinking-bouts. A local tradition gives the name of one of the taverns as Ty'r Harlot; it presumably doubled up as the local brothel. By Gwesyn Jones' time the taverns had been whittled down to one, at Pentwyn, which in the tithe schedule is simply called a farm, and in the Census returns is sometimes called Pentwyn, sometimes The Grouse Inn. Cliffe's *Book of South Wales'* (2nd edition, 1848) mentions the 'public house without a sign'. A young people's club was started there, but came to grief; there was too much drink, too near!

Pentwyn first emerges into written history in the eighteenth century, when a deed of 1726 lists it as one of the properties involved in the marriage settlement in 1694 of Richard Stedman of Strata Florida and his first wife Joan Gwynne. By 1776 we find Pentwyn, with other Llanfihangel farms, in the rental-books of the Nanteos estate. In 1788 it was sold to 'Mr E. Thomas', who, in view of the fact that Pentwyn now forms part of the Cefndyrys (Welfield) estate, seems likely to be Edward rather than Evan Thomas. In 1776 the tenant of Pentwyn was Rees Thomas; but the first details we have about the inhabitants of Pentwyn is Rees Gwesyn Jones' account in 1861 of the thrifty couple, Jack and Kitty Williams, who made a fortune from catering for drovers of sheep, cattle and horses, and harvest-workers on their way too and from the English border- counties. 'John Williams' appears in the tithe schedule as tenant-farmer of Pentwyn, then just over 448 acres. It is already called 'Grouse Inn' in the Census of 1841, which shows John and Catherine living there, he over eighty and she over seventy, with their son Evan, two men-servants and three female servants. John died before 1851; and Catherine had gone before 1861. The Williams children were respectable in the extreme; one, John, became an Independent minister. His parents did not 'profess religion' till they were old. Jack, aged eighty, was received at the same ceremony as his grandson, aged ten.

A sketch by Mrs Trahaerne, dating possibly from 1833, and not later than 1859, shows the inn-parlour, with the landlady in apron, shawl and almost oriental-looking headgear tending something in a skillet suspended over a flaming fire on a large open hearth. A young lady in a close-fitting bonnet-like cap, but holding a wide, beribboned straw hat, looks on, while a dark-clad man in a tall dip-brimmed hat sits somnolent on the opposite side of the hearth. The table is set with platters, jugs and mugs.

In 1861 Pentwyn was being farmed by Daniel Jones; he and his wife and young family had six work-people living in the house. By 1871 Rhys and Margaret Hope, two sons and a daughter, lived at Pentwyn; on Census day Rhys' mother Anne and nephew William were visiting there, and there were four employees and a lodger. In old Llanwrtyd churchyard a railed enclosure contains the graves of Rhys Morgan Hope, Esq., of the Grouse Inn, who died on 17 December 1905, of his son John Jones Hope of Llwynderw, and of his wife's kin, including John Jones of Trawsnant and Nantllwyd. Despite a story that Miss Clara Thomas had the inn's licence taken away, the truth is that Pentwyn did not cease to be an inn till many years after her death, and that because the Hope family wished to concentrate on the farm. Even in 1903 Bradley said that farming 'was a more serious matter to the landlord...than drawing corks.... Not that [the traveller] need fear any stint of simple refreshment'; but to call at the Grouse Inn at shearing-time, 'when 30 or 40 pairs of shears are hard at work for days together in the sheds...and thousands of sheep...are filling the valley with their persistent clamour' would make it clear that here 'wool and mutton reign supreme'. Bradley wrote that these original Welsh mountain sheep 'at four years old weigh about 9lbs a quarter, and at present prices produce almost nothing a head in wool'. Hill farmers here then, he said, would expect twenty per cent losses annually. Sheep wintered out and were given very little hay even in the worst weather. Farmers were said to work less harmoniously together on the open ranges than did those of Cumberland. Some ranges were under criticism for overstocking. Bradley said that the sheepwalks 'never actually [went] with the land'; we have seen that in Llanddewi Abergwesyn this does not seem to have been true, though there was a different situation in Llanfihangel.

Within living memory a number of improvised mechanisms were in use at Pentwyn. From the river Gwesyn, near the spot where Nant y Rhiw flows in, was constructed a wooden aqueduct (a raised channel still marks its course) to carry water along behind Tyhaearn bungalow to sluice-gates near a water-wheel, just below the old Iron Room (or the new bungalow which now stands near the site). Problems arose in winter, when the wheel sometimes froze up. The sluice-gates were operated by a wire which went across the road on poles to Pentwyn yard. There the wire was left hanging, and could be pulled to open or close the gates. Originally work was not done down by the wheel, but in the farmyard. A system of spindles and gear-wheels was driven by the wheel, and went under the road to emerge in the barn, where all the grinding was done. More spindles could be added to turn corners, so that a chaff-cutting machine, for example, could be used in its shed on the left past the gateway to the yard. Later, a shed was put up near the wheel for wood-cutting, and came to be used for some of the grinding. When the machinery was finally dismantled, parts were sold to a scrap-merchant, but the section under the road is still there. At some period unspecified, there is said to have been a shop in one of the buildings on the farmyard.

Perhaps the most noticeable change here during the present century has been the marked further dwindling in the number of farms. The many homesteads of the tithe schedule and the nineteenth century Census returns have become diminished to a handful. Nantybrain, the only farm left in Llanddewi, and Tymawr, Bwlchygorllwyn isaf and Llofftybardd in Llanfihangel are still occupied by Welsh farmers. Pentwyn was for some years worked by a Scot in partnership with the Cefndyrys estate, but has now reverted to the ownership of a native of the district. Glangwesyn is owned and run by an English farmer. Crug is farmed by an Irish artist. Llwyn Owen was long the home farm of Llwynmadog, and worked by an Englishman, but is no longer a farmhouse. The other farmhouses are demolished, or ruinous, or have survived but lost their function. The decline in farming was greatly accelerated by the arrival on the scene about the time of the Second World War of the Forestry Commission, with its tempting offers to struggling farmers of plentiful 'money in the hand' — offers at first resisted, later uneasily or avidly accepted. Similar offers followed from the Economic Forestry Group, the 'private woodlands' (now Till Hill). The Tywi valley was the first to yield farm-land to forest; the Irfon Forest came in 1950. The huge Nantyrhwch Forest of the E.F.G. now covers acre upon acre of the hills flanking the Tregaron road. The conversion of huge tracts of North Breconshire into forest seemed to open up possibilities of employment at a time of hardship. Many local people were torn between gratitude for the chance of work (though this was to prove, for most, sporadic only) and a deep sadness and resentment at the disappearance of farmhouses and farmland, and the familiar beauty of bare rolling hills and great skies, under the regimented hordes of conifers. It is especially ironical that some valleys, in which the difficulty of getting to and from their homes had increasingly irked a restless younger generation, have motorable Forestry roads now that the farmhouses those roads might have helped to survive are empty or demolished.

Now Llyn Brianne has drowned one of our valleys — an empty one, of subtle and varied beauty. Only 'people from off' protested. Perhaps local people, resigned to despoliation of living farmland, could hardly have been expected to feel as an outrage the end of something they themselves considered already finished. 'Wood and water,' said an old inhabitant, with sad fatalism, 'soon it will all be wood and water'. As he spoke, the hills loomed black against a sky glaring with the floodlights of the Tywi valley, labouring then towards the birth of the great dam.

Wood and water and holiday houses, one might then have feared. There was no local objection to the purchase of 'second homes', a decade or more ago, of houses that were conspicuously unwanted by the people of the district, and 'went for a song'. Now, enough new residents have moved into the area to work and make their homes for there to be good hope of continuing life for the little settlement. But it will be a different life from that of the 'old ways'. Despite valiant efforts by some of the immigrants to learn the language, it is hard to imagine life here in the future as distinctively Welsh. The network of kinship is still strong and real for the old families of the district, but of its very nature excludes newcomers. The fervent religion which gave life a supportive if rigid framework has little meaning for some of the incomers; though its rejection even by many younger members of old local families is ultimately more disruptive of the traditional structure of the community. The Welsh language is being fought for in classes for newcomers, and through the Welsh-medium unit or stream in local schools. It is under great pressure, not least that of the Celtic courtesy which dictates that a few English-speakers attending, for instance, a Welsh chapel's centenary, must have a service half in English for their benefit.

Now that the balance of population has swung so far towards incomers to the area, there has been a great change in attitudes from the pre-war days of the closed, inward-looking valley communities that could be found in some parts of the district — or possibly the change is in the degree to which such attitudes can be put into practical effect. In the 1920s and 30s the great majority of people who lived in valleys of the Cambrian mountains or their bordering districts were old families of the area. Some farming communities were so exclusive and so inbred that the marriage of a 'local' to a non-Welsh person, was a matter for grave debate, regret and suspicion. Even children born and bred in such a community to parents who had moved into it, could never hope to be anything but *dynion dôd* ('people who have come'). There was one law for the tightly-knit community of natives, and another for the incomers. The latter had to watch their step; but the real 'locals' played all games by their own rules, which they knew and understood. A man in his seventies recalls his boyhood in such a community, in which most of the farmers were tenants of a local estate, and were not as fortunate in their landlord as Abergwesyn people were. The landowner knew virtually nothing about them. Through his bailiff, he would try to find out, for instance, the exact financial state of a tenant whose rent he hoped to raise; but no-one knew anything, faces were blank, and silence closed round the man at risk. A rebellious incomer, who cared nothing about avoiding conflict with the landowner and very little about the sanctions of his neighbours, took the law into his own hands after he was refused some wooden posts for repair-work, and cut down two oak-trees. It was not only the bailiff who was horrified! The culprit's neighbours begged him to try and do things their way. 'We would have had an oak too,' they said, 'but we would have cut one down in a place where he would never notice he had one, and we would have chopped it up a bit at a time and taken it quietly!'

If we look back at the nineteenth century Census returns we find little evidence for Abergwesyn's having been a particularly closed society; in fact, despite its remoteness, there seems to have been a considerable degree of mobility. Some of the tenant farmers had not been born within the parish, or even in the county. Abergwesyn men had often married women from Cardiganshire, or from other parts of Breconshire, or further afield. (Eighteenth century registers show this to have happened then, too, and there was a corresponding movement out to other parishes of Abergwesyn brides.) Farm servants might come from the immediate area, but many, too, came from Cardiganshire, Carmarthenshire and elsewhere. Perhaps Abergwesyn's position as a key-point on the road over the mountains to the coast was a factor in opening it up and preventing excessively inward-turning attitudes. Nor, as we have seen, did Abergwesyn people have the experience of repressive landlords to leave a residue of bitterness.

Of course for accepted members of the rural community there has traditionally been no limit to neighbourly help. Mr David Jones tells the story of his Cardiganshire grandfather's experience at Bryn, Llanddewi Brefi, in 1896. (It was from Bryn that Mr Jones' father moved on his marriage in 1901 to Brongilent, Abergwesyn, carrying all his and his bride's possessions on a cart and breaking nothing, not even the glass-fronted dresser!) While Mr Jones' grandfather was at Bryn, his landlord decided to build a new farmhouse. For months the old man's son hauled stones, helped by neighbours from far and near. Help was given all the more readily in view of the old farmer's age. A local bard, a mason employed on the new house, sang

> Mae hen wr gwth o oedran
> Yn rhoi diolch am eich ffwdan.
> Ei ddymuniad yw pe gallai
> Iddo yntau gael eich talu.

(The old man, full of age,
Gives thanks for your trouble
And wishes that he could
Pay each one of you his due).

The post-war years saw a great increase in the acreage of Forestry Commission and 'private woodlands' planting, and a corresponding diminution in farmland. There have been some variations in stock, but the area is one of predominantly hill-sheep farming. Some farmers have experimented with break-aways from total dependence on Welsh mountain rams. Pentwyn keeps cattle once more. Bwlchygorllwyn isaf still has cattle. Cwmirfon has a dairy herd as well as sheep; though it no longer supplies its own milk to local houses. There has been a further reduction to zero-point in corn-growing, though some root-crops are planted. Some farms have carried out drainage and fencing programmes, and made new farm roads.

During the nineteenth and twentieth centuries there has been public road-building and road improvement, some of it welcome and necessary, some in recent years less so, and causing many to fear the compulsive highway-building which sees an idiosyncratic and beautiful little country road as something to be forced at all costs into conformity with a suburban standard. The old road from Llanwrtyd to Abergwesyn passed near the former Pwllybô farmhouse, which stood at the bottom of the steep cirque of hills behind the later house. This road was superseded in 1875 by one below the present house, and above the present road. Continuing thence to Nantybrain (sections of it can still be walked), the road went on to ford the Irfon, and followed the route described in Chapter 2. It is said that about 1850 there were thirteen gates on the old road from Llanwrtyd to Abergwesyn, turning for Tregaron at Pentwyn. The thirteenth, at Alltyrhebog, was replaced by a cattle-grid, the road at that point greatly widened, and an avenue of hedge-trees cut down.

Before the 1940s, though not totally impassable for motor traffic, at any rate in good weather, the Tregaron mountain road had the savour of high adventure. Many of today's motorists think that it still has! A *Western Mail* article of May 1933 wrote of the narrow, bumpy road from Abergwesyn village to Llanerch-yrfa, where a farmer was digging peat, while his wife and daughter stacked it by the side of a ditch. Geese promenaded near the three fords. After the Devil's Staircase, the stony road was crossed by little streams. The few farmhouses passed were dazzling with whitewash. Letters and articles in the *Western Mail* resulted in 'official notice being taken of the Tregaron-Abergwesyn road'. Officialdom bent its energies to making it 'part of the general highway system of the country'. In September 1933 the paper carried photographs of new bridges on the Tregaron road. Eventually it was surfaced; though as late as September 1956 an article referred to the Breconshire section of the road as 'two intermittently parallel series of potholes bridged by outcrops of naked rock', covered with 'thin oyster-coloured paste'. As long ago as 1760, Emanuel Bowen's Map of South Wales had a note by the Tregaron road at 'Foes Torr Cengl' — 'That part of the Road which goes over the Marsh or Bogg is generally out of Repare tho it might be kept in good order and made passable without any danger at a small Yearly expence'.

Edwin Davies wrote in 1909 of the coming of amenities to ease the life of Breconshire farmers — gas, electricity, better water-supplies and sanitation. There is still no mains water-supply to the farms and houses of Abergwesyn, though as most of the springs serving the inhabitants' needs are plentiful and good, this is not seen as a disadvantage; nor are there many complaints about the septic tank or cesspit drainage. Electricity is considered a great boon, and most houses have it. It was first brought to the village in 1963 at the instance of the late Mr Bevington Gibbins of Cwmirfon Lodge. Calor-gas and propane gas are used, too. Few local people understood the attraction of a more primitive lifestyle for some incomers of a few decades ago, who have rejected city standards and want to mark strongly the difference from all they had left behind. Natives of the district, who have in their youth known hardship, did not find it easy to comprehend a deliberate acceptance of life at subsistence level rather than energetic attempts to 'better oneself'. Yet perhaps for both old-established residents and idealistic newcomers there was not only regret for the passing of some things that were good, but a feeling for what could still be made of old fields, abandoned gardens, land that had been worked and could be worked again, ruins that could be rebuilt, human life always as ready to surge back as the encroaching wild is ready to oppose it.

13. Jobs Linked to Farm and Home

As well as the farmers, farm labourers, shepherds and farm servants who for centuries formed the greater part of the population of Abergwesyn, there were a number of people whose work was connected with that of the farms. Some of them lived here, some were itinerant. Among the most important and the most colourful of these were the drovers. From mediaeval times for centuries, Abergwesyn and the drovers were important to each other. The old taverns and later the Grouse Inn made a welcome stopping-place for rest, food and drink after the long plod over the hills from Cardiganshire. The Jonathan brothers' accounts (1839) show a disbursement of 15s 0d at 'Abergwesyn Tavern' (neither the lowest nor the highest of such sums). In the shoeing compound behind the inn the cattle were fitted with *ciws* (two-part iron shoes) for the next stage of their journey. Dr Moore-Colyer's article in *Country Life* (4 October 1973) mentions one of the well-known cattle-shoers of this district in the 1870s — Evan John Williams or Ianto Siôn Evans — and quotes a song about him composed by the itinerant poet Shelby (of Abergwesyn origin).

Some early Abergwesyn innkeepers are identified by seventeenth century Quarter Sessions records. In 1669, for instance, licences for tavern-keeping were applied for by Jonetta Williams, Thomas Prees and David Lloyd. Was this David Lloyd of Celsau, and David Lloyd the occupier of the three-hearth house? In 1671 John Williams and Evan Thomas applied for licences, in 1672 John Williams, Richard Lloyd and David Prosser, and in 1673 Jonetta Williams, Thomas Bowen and Evan Thomas. One brewer who in the nineteenth century supplied some of the public houses and taverns beloved of the drovers had an Abergwesyn home — Williams of Celsau, whose brewery was in Builth.

Some Abergwesyn men were drovers, like the Rhys Rowland who is said to have given his name to Carn Rhys Rowland, high over Rhiw Gareg Lwyd, and who surely must have been one of the Rowland family of the vanished Nantyrhiw farm on that hillside. At Blaennant, the ruins of which can still be seen at the edge of a plantation between the upper Gwesyn and Cnyffiad valleys, there lived Rhys Jones, once a drover, who became a roadmender. As an old man, he would mutter to himself, as he lifted stones to the side of the road, about the old days at the Northampton fairs. 'How much am I bid?' he would call to the passer-by or the empty air. In 1889 Blaennant was stricken by a diphtheria epidemic. Rhys and his wife Mary died on the same day in April, their twenty-eight year old daughter three days earlier.

The impact of droving on Abergwesyn was undoubtedly great —

the huge herds passing along: the hullabaloo of the drovers chivvying their beasts and shouting to warn farmers not to let their cattle get mixed up with the drove: the news and gossip the drovers brought: the commissions they undertook — all of it must have been a great surging-in of rich, loud life to the little village, of money to inns and smithies, of colour and noise and movement to the roads. Cattle-droving continued at least till the railways became established; sheep-droving went on longer, especially local droving to market or to 'tack'.

On a map (held at the National Library) of *Main Roads and Cattle Tracks in the Hundred of Builth* between 1800 and 1840, the only roads in this area to be marked specifically 'cattle-track' are those from Beulah, one north across Rhôs Saeth Maen to join one (not thus marked) running north-east to Rhaeadr, and the other south through Llangamarch to join the 'main cattle track for England', a continuation of the old Cefn Llwydlo route, through Tirabad, over the Epynt (stopping at the Drovers' Arms), and down to the ford and ferry of Cavan-Twm-Bach over the Wye at Erwood (Y Rhyd, The Ford). Certainly, however, some of the other tracks shown on this curious map were used by the drovers.

The main drovers' road through Abergwesyn is thought to have been the road from Tregaron and its continuation in the Cefn Cardis route, the Ancient Road. On the way along the dramatic valley between Llanerch-yrfa and Pentwyn corner the drovers passed, near Nant Serwydd, a field called Pant yr Efail Fach (Hollow of the Little Smithy). Could it have been an ancient shoeing-field, pre-dating the better known one at the Grouse Inn? From Pentwyn the drove would ford the Gwesyn and climb Llethr Dôliâr and Rhiw Garreg Lwyd, passing along Cefn Gardys or Cardis to Aberanell and what is now Beulah village, thence going north to Newbridge and Radnorshire en route for England, or taking the Epynt route, on which they would link up with cattle from points south. The Cefn Cardis route, wrote Mr John Rowland in the *Western Mail* in 1933, was also used by the *porthmyn defaid* (sheep-drovers), driving sheep from Abergwesyn to Garth.

Toll-gate dodging was not necessary in Abergwesyn, far from turnpike roads, but finding short cuts over the hills, where the cattle could spread out and feed on the rough grass, led to the use of other now forgotten routes. A *Western Mail* article of 1933 referred to a Tregaron tradition that some Pembrokeshire cattle were brought through Llanddewi Brefi (south of Tregaron) over the mountains to Soar y Mynydd in the Camddwr valley, and there shod. Crossing the Tywi at Pantyclwydiau (the outbuildings only of which now survive, below the new road past Llyn Brianne), they turned up Rhiw'r Ych (Ox Road, Ox Hill — *rhiw* can mean a slope, a farm driftway or a drovers' road) and over the right of way through what was then the Rhyd Goch bog (now forest), past Cerrig Bara Chaws (Bread and Cheese Rocks) to Llwynderw and Penybryn and thence down through Abergwesyn. At Pentwyn they joined cattle and cattlemen coming down the Tregaron road from Penyrhyddfa, where two droves had met. One had come from Tregaron over the 'main' drovers' road, one from Pontrhydfendigaid. This one, having travelled along the old road from Strata Florida, had turned up Ffordd or Rhiw y Porthmyn behind Nantystalwyn, crossed the hill and come down the upper Irfon valley.

Sometimes part at least of the huge drove joining up at Penyrhyddfa, after crossing the Irfon by the 'Irish' fords at Llanerch-yrfa, would climb the dramatically steep and rocky Rhiw Gam, the Crooked Way, just to the south of the farmhouse, on the further side of Nant y Fedw, and continue along the top of Esgair Irfon between the Irfon and the Gwesyn. It is said that some then followed a route older than the Cefn Cardis one, descending into the Gwesyn valley above Pwll y March (Stallion's Pool, marked on the 2 and a half inch O.S. map). Somewhere near there, according to tradition, there was once a smithy with a large enclosure, where at one period the smith's many children helped look after the cattle on overnight stops. The tithe map shows a large isolated field at this point — Cae Mawr, in 1842 belonging to Blaennant. Investigation on the ground reveals its boundaries and at each end a small building near the stream. The drove would then continue across the Miller's Ford and up the slope to pass Trysgol, going on along the hillside into the upper Camarch valley, fording that river and passing over the high plateau past the cairns (one now grass-covered) on Carnau hill, to Bwlch y Ddau Faen and down to the Rhiwnant en route for Rhaeadr.

One route was described to R.J. Moore-Colyer by a Llanddewi Brefi man — that for cattle and sheep from Nantystalwyn 'across the Drygarn' to Rhaeadr via Rhiwnant and the Elan valley. Dr Moore-Colyer comments that not even aerial photographs reveal an established track over Drygarn. The modern O.S. map shows clearly this elusive route as a right of way from the upper Irfon valley via Llanerch-yrfa up the Nant y Fedw valley, near Drygarn Fach and over Drygarn Fawr, to join the Carnau-Nant Paradwys track near Bwlch y Ddau Faen. One farmer, Dic Davies, claims to have found *ciws* in the upper Camarch valley. The 1800-1840 map marks a track across the headwaters of the Camarch and on to the Claerwen valley. The fact that it is not labelled 'cattle-track' means little, for neither is the Cefn Cardis road. (Incidentally, the Claerwen-Camarch track on this map continues across the Abergwesyn-Beulah road and the Cefn Cardis track and follows a line parallel to the Cerdin valley to emerge on the Abergwesyn-Llanwrtyd road just below the old church — probably where a track still comes down from the house Penybanc. This route is now obscured by Forestry plantations.)

It is interesting that the reputed drovers' route through Bwlch y Ddau Faen passed the old house (now a ruin in the Forestry), variously called Lle'rtaihirion and Llett(y)au hirion ('Place of the longhouses' and 'Longhouses' or 'shelters'). The track marked on the tithe map shows this particularly clearly. Both the plural and the use of the term *Llet(t)y*, implying shelter, may have significance here, especially as the house was at least in recent times, and possibly earlier, flanked by Scots pines, still a landmark rising above the plantations. Toulson and Godwin refer to their planting by farmers wishing to let the drovers know of accommodation to let. In some areas, Radnorshire for instance, the trees might of course be 'Charlie trees', marking a house of Jacobite sympathisers; in others, simply a waymark or shelter-belt.

Names on the map, or in the memories of the old, are often clues to old routes, including those of the drovers. Cae'r gôf (Smith's field), a ruined farmhouse on the hillside above the upper Cerdin, seems to the present inhabitants of Abergwesyn so unlikely a place for a smithy that an alternative name has been suggested, Cae'r Ogof (Field of the Cave). But if the house once stood near a track down the Cerdin valley or across the hills above it, we have no need to invent an even more unlikely cave to account for the name. There is Pant yr Efail, too, at Esgairgarn, the remains of which stand just above the modern lakeside road where it cuts across the Gwrâch valley. Not far to the east of the cairn above this ruin, and running at right angles to the head-waters of the river Culent above the lead-mine, roughly southwest-northeast in the direction of Nantybrain, is a section of old trackway, wide and grass-grown, that emerges from the boggy plateau-land of Cefn Blaencwmhenog. The track seems wide enough, and for a short distance clear enough, to be part of an old route of importance in its day, whenever that may have been; and it is intriguing that it runs along hills above a 'smithy hollow'.

The eastern bank of the Tywi, from which valley the herds climbed the hills between that valley and Abergwesyn, has Nant yr Ych (Ox), Rhiw'r Ych, Esgair Bustach (Bullock) and Nant y Bustach. It is unlikely that one track only was used, though Rhiw'r Ych appears to have been the main one. Then, in the Gwesyn valley, nearly opposite Trysgol, Nant yr Ychain flows into the Gwesyn. As we have seen, it is a point higher upstream which is associated with the descent of the droves into that valley. Nant yr Ychain may take its name from local cattle pastures, or from its source near the old track along the ridge, a route possibly taken by cattle diverging from the Gwesyn-Camarch-Claerwen route in order to descend to Abergwesyn at Pentwyn yard.

Troedyrhenrhiw, a house which once stood on Llwynmadog land, was named from its position at the foot of a track leading to the old road (hen rhiw) along Cefn Cardis — old already at the unknown time when the house was first named. The ridge and the road along it were called after the 'Cardis', the men of Cardiganshire who drove their herds along it; though even before their day it is likely that, nameless or by some ancient name, the ridgeway was known to very early inhabitants indeed.

Unlicensed droving, whether on a large scale or small dealing for a quick turning, was an offence. Joseph Thomas of Llanwrtyd, for instance, in 1686 was presented at the Quarter Sessions 'for being a petty drover'. In the last three months he had 'bought several cattle in the county and sold some within five weeks contra formam statuti'.

Smiths did not, of course, ply their trade solely for the drovers. As Geraint Jenkins wrote in *Brycheiniog* (vol. XIV) 'the rural neighbourhood was an economic as well as a social entity'; any skill the farmer needed to call on was usually to be found within the village community. There was therefore an economic network holding the community together, as well as those of kinship and tradition. The little modern bungalow of Ty Gôf (smithy) near old Abergwesyn Post Office stands near the site of the 'house, smithy, shop and garden' called in 1842 Troedyrhiwafallen. 'Pantfallen' seems to have been an alternative name. Sometimes the blacksmith, perhaps his assistant, lived at nearby Glangwesyn. In 1855 the blacksmith John Lloyd had lived at the mill, an arrangement similar to that of the Cnyffiad valley blacksmith who in 1871 lived at Ty'nycwm near another mill. We remember Tal-a-Hen's statement in 1888 that most farms of the area cut down on blacksmith's bills by doing much of the work themselves. Nearer Llanwrtyd, in the late eighteenth century there was a David Evans, blacksmith, at Cwmirfon farm; he probably worked in one of the buildings on the yard, recorded in a list of old houses as 'Efail y Gôf, on Cwm Irfon yard'.

The shop referred to at Troedyrhiwafallen in 1842 was followed in later years by that at Ty'rfelin, now better known as Old Abergwesyn Post Office. In the late nineteenth century the Ty'rfelin shop was kept by the Davies family, who were followed there by Mr Isaac Price, father of the later postmistress, Mrs D. Jones. In 1881 the 'grocer' William Price lived at One Gwesyn Terrace, now part of Ty Gwesyn, on the site of the mill. In 1891, Thomas Davies was there. In 1851 Morgan Price, a shopkeeper, was a lodger at Nantyneuadd, below the Trysgol oakwoods. His fellow-lodger was a nineteen year old 'mantua-maker', Elizabeth Hamer, a native of Cwmdauddwr in Radnorshire. Their landlady, Gwen Williams, aged seventy-eight, was a pauper hose-knitter. At Celsau in 1861, seventeen year old David Williams was a shop-assistant, perhaps at Beulah nearby.

The district was well-served in the mid nineteenth century by masons. Besides John Davies of Pantfallen, who by 1843 was calling himself a mason (if indeed he was the former blacksmith of that name) there was an Edward Richards, mason, over the mountain at Cae'r gôf in 1841, with his wife, baby son and two children surnamed Evans. He seems to have moved to Bwlchygorllwyn isaf by 1861, by which time three sons were following in his footsteps. Down at the Aberanell end of Abergwesyn, in one of the two Penybont cottage, lived in 1841 another mason, William Davies. Another, Evan Bebb, lived in 1854 at Nantyneuadd. The Camarch valley had in 1868 James Price at Penycae.

By 1871 Abergwesyn had more masons, surely, than at any time in its history. They were probably employed on the Victorian church, which was completed in that year. Many of the houses had them as lodgers. There were masons from Carmarthenshire, one at Pentwyn, one at nearby Ty isaf: a Dudley man at Bwlchygorllwyn uchaf: a Shropshire mason at School Cottage, and two more at Trawsgyrch: an Oxfordshire man at Abergwesyn Mill: and at the smithy, three Cardiganshire masons and two 'wallers', one born at Lampeter and one at Hay. Llanddewi had its share too. Elizabeth Probert, who kept a lodging-house at no. 2, Nantybrain, had Charles Allen and William Jones from Llandeilo and George Jones from Brecon staying there. A pauper family at Ty'nyllan were housing a mason from Llanfair-ar-y-Bryn: Thomas Wesley, of Birkenhead, lodged at secluded Brongilent. A number of these lodgers were married men, away from home for short-term employment. The building of the church probably accounts too for the presence at the same time of some bricklayers and their labourers, at Ty isaf, School Cottage and Bwlchygorllwyn isaf. One such labourer, at Ty'ncelyn, Jacob Jones, was the son of the house, and may have been permanently employed in the area. All these building-workers had vanished by 1881.

Melin Abergwesyn, the Gwesyn Mill, used to stand where now Ty Gwesyn is found, opposite the Post Office. Parts of its timbers survive in the southern end of what was once a small row of cottages. The mill pool occupied the Old Post Office garden. A water-course leading to it from the river can be traced across a field behind the Old Post Office. A deed of 1726 refers to 'Bron Wessyne with the water corn grist mill there-unto belonging called Gwessynne Mill'. A cottage called Brongwesyn once stood on the side of the upper Gwesyn valley, on Tymawr land. There is only a barn there now, with traces of an old garden. The Nanteos rental-book of 1776 has a note, 'Mill vacant and down'. By 1781, Abergwesyn Mill was in use, it seems, as the tenant was Morgan Williams. In the 1840s The Mill, Abergwesyn, was worked by Roderick Williams. By 1850, the man in charge there was Hezekiah Herbert, born in Carmarthenshire, with a Llanwrtyd wife. In 1851 his mill is called Tymawr Mill. The Census of 1861 called it Brongwesyn Mill; in 1868 Ann Lewis' baby David was baptised from Tymawr Mill. No

Abergwesyn or Tymawr Mill appears in the Census of 1881. The list of old houses known to people still living in 1907 gives a Melin Fel (Grist Mill) on Tymawr land, as well as a house Brongwesyn. We have found the 'Miller's Ford', below Trysgol, remembered as the crossing-place of the drovers, but no evidence has yet appeared to suggest a mill further upstream than the one at the present Ty Gwesyn. Was there a mill on the Cedni in 1861, when William Lloyd, miller, lived at Penycae? He does not seem to have been farming there. In 1851 there had been a miller of that name at Llwynmadog; the nearby mill does not appear to have been working at the time.

There are late seventeenth century and early eighteenth century references to a Llanfihangel Abergwesyn water corn grist mill which seems from the context to have been Melinycwm, near Llwynmadog. The Census returns call it Ty'nycwm Mill or Cwm Mill, and show that at some time after 1841 it fell into disuse. It was being rebuilt in 1851, but not until 1871 do we find it occupied and working again. The mill-pools are marked on the tithe-map as on Ty'nycwm land, one each side of the road. The 1890 O.S. map shows the 'mill race' from Ty'nycwm running parallel to the Cnyffiad. Near the mill marked 'Melin-y-cwm and Saw' is a ford and a 'spout'. In 1841 the miller, in his late thirties, was Rees Davies. Working for him was Thomas Jones, aged between fifteen and twenty, and Erasmus Jones, twenty or over, a millwright, all Breconshire-born. One later miller of Melinycwm was consulted by Miss Clara Thomas about her pet dog, which had lost its appetite. Judging the fat little creature to be pampered and overfed, the miller starved it for two days, earning a handsome tip when Miss Thomas welcomed back her ravenous pet. The same man, put out by the fact that one of his customers, the Pantycelyn minister, hardly ever spoke to him, topped up one of his sacks of ground corn with sawdust. The minister came to complain, volubly, to the delight of the miller, who had achieved his object.

By 1900 North Breconshire still had corn mills working at Abergwesyn (presumably Melinycwm), Llanwrtyd, Beulah, Garth, Llanfihangel, Bryn Pabuan, Llanafan fawr, Llangamarch, and two at Builth.

The old mill-building of Melinycwm (later part of a trout-hatchery) was sometimes used as a carpenter's workshop. As we have seen, there was a sawpit there about 1890. In 1851 a sawyer from Llanafan, John Davies, lived in one part of Dôlberthog in the lower Camarch valley. In 1861 he was called 'carpenter', and his son John was now the sawyer. By 1871 John junior had moved, and his father and eighteen year old brother were sawyers. The tithe schedule shows a *cae llêf* (sawpit field) on Dôlberthog. A sprinkling of carpenters served the needs of the district in the mid-nineteenth century. Thomas Richard lived in the other part of Dôlberthog in 1851. Another Thomas Richard, carpenter, was to be found at Ty'ncelyn. John Thomas, London-born, lived at Cwmcywydd, just below the Ancient Road, over the ridge of hills south of Ty'nycwm. At Dôliâr in the Gwesyn valley was the carpenter Roger Prytherch; William Jones, and later John Williams, occupied one of the Penybont cottages at the other end of Llanfihangel. The carpenters lodging at Ty isaf in 1871 may have been employed on the church. One at Tymawr was a 'visitor'. The Culent valley had in 1851 David Jones, Carmarthenshire-born, living at Nantycrâf. In the Tywi valley were Edward Edwards and his son Thomas at Ty'nygraig. The distribution of these craftsmen (at any rate before 1881, when the Census reveals far fewer of them) reinforces the impression one gets of some at least of the Abergwesyn valleys as having been, cerainly till the mid-nineteenth century, little sub-communities of their own.

Carpenters were undertakers too. One who lived at Abergwrâch earned a reputation for quick and reliable work, for example when he made a coffin for a funeral from Brynbrith farmhouse near Soar y Mynydd. The two sons of the farm, wild lads and drinkers, had dallied so long on the way to Abergwrâch that the carpenter did not get his instructions till ten o'clock on the night before the funeral. Nevertheless, the coffin was made and delivered on time.

As well as the craftsmen living in Abergwesyn itself, there were others who could be reached nearby, like the Beulah wheelwright whose photograph can be seen in *Brycheiniog*, vol. XIV. After the First World War there was still a saddler's shop at Llangamarch, and till recently there was a basket-maker at Llanafan fawr. Pigot's directory of 1830 shows in Builth three saddlers, three wheelwrights, two coopers, one currier, two tawers, nine joiners, two tanners and other craftsmen. Llanwrtyd had its carpenters and masons too, its wheelwrights, tailors, shoemakers and dressmakers; and the lower village of Pontrhydyfere had in 1841, for instance, smiths, carpenters, shoemakers and a tailor among the occupations shown.

Within living memory, a chimney-sweep lived at Clynglas above the wooded Gwrâch valley, now an inlet of Llyn Brianne. His work would take him as far as Llethr farm over the Cardiganshire hills. Clynglas was isolated; every three weeks, half a sack of flour would be brought from Abergwesyn shop over Bwlch y Dôrfa on pony-back. Philip, the sweep's son, was mentally backward but of enormous physical strength. Tragedy came when Clynglas caught fire, and Philip's mother was trapped alone in the house and burnt to death. 'I would rather have lost my best cow than my Mari,' was her husband's comment!

There was a 'cobbler' at Ty'ncelyn in 1871. An early shoemaker,

Rhys Jones of Nantycrâf, master of the Rev David Williams in his apprentice days in the 1790s, is said to have been highly eccentric, and so, indeed, to have been typical of the people of Abergwesyn, 'an original race..., who had cultivated their own individuality from generation to generation without let or hindrance, and where every man, woman and child was an entirely new edition of humanity'. Jones' workshop in the Culent valley was a 'parliament' for the local young men, who, like David Williams, learnt there to discuss nice points of theology and debate the affairs of the world. David himself became a good shoemaker, choosing well-dressed hides and working skilfully and conscientiously to produce 'shoes and boots...impervious to the thin penetrating water of the spongy meadows and weeping sidelands of the neighbourhood'. The 1881 Census shows Evan Williams, a shoemaker, at Dôlberthog in the Camarch valley; he was the son-in-law of the sawyer John Davies.

Tailors often worked in the houses of their customers, sometimes staying for several days, and were no doubt as efficient at gathering and retailing news as were the drovers, though their information was more local. The 1841 Census shows John Rice, tailor, living at Ty'nyllan by Llanddewi church with his family and two non-Breconshire girls in their late teens, probably sewing-girls. At Nantystalwyn in the Tywi valley two young tailors, Rees Jones and John Evans, were with the farmer and his family at the time. In 1861 John Rice, tailor, was at Nantyneuadd in the Gwesyn valley.

Elizabeth Theophilus, at Pantfallen in 1851, was a dressmaker. Her mother Jane, who lived with her, was a housemaid. Dressmakers, like tailors, often spent some days with their customers, making clothes for the family. In 1861 we find the spinster Caroline Smith, a London-born dressmaker, aged fifty-two, at Llanerch-yrfa, where no doubt her skill was much in demand for Mrs Williams and her eleven children, certainly for the four girls. There were two dressmakers from Cardiganshire staying at Nantyrhwch in the Tywi valley in 1861. Catherine Herbert, a locally-born dressmaker, was in 1871 a visitor at Alltfelen, where lived Mr and Mrs Davies with their five daughters and three sons and Mrs Davies' blind mother aged eighty-one. At that time a Radnorshire dressmaker, Elizabeth Lewis, was lodging at Ty isaf, if only because Edward Lewis, staying there too, was probably her husband. The nineteen year old Catherine Jones, dressmaker, at Abergwesyn Mill, was a daughter of the house, as in 1861 was an even younger dressmaker, Anne Richards, at Penybont near Beulah. We find Catherine Herbert again in 1881, at Cefngilfach with her brother, and in 1891 at Nantygarreg. Another dressmaker, aged eighteen, in 1881, was a daughter of Llofftybardd farm, and a twenty-one year old 'needlewoman' lived at Cefnmorarth. The remote lead-mining area of the Culent valley seems an unlikely spot to find a dressmaker; Cardiganshire-born Leah James lived there in 1881 with her mother and ten-year-old son, at Penygwaith. By 1891 Leah was alone. A dressmaker was again visiting Nantyrhwch in Cwm Tywi in 1881. The 1891 Census shows the Glangwesyn farmer's eighteen-year-old niece as a dressmaker, as was the fifteen-year-old stepdaughter of David Davies, Alltfelen. 1881 is the first year in which the census records a 'post boy', aged fifteen, at Penybont Cottage.

Servants at the larger houses were by no means always or even mainly local people. At Llwynmadog in 1851, for instance, Mary Oliver, the forty-five year old clerk, was from Montgomeryshire, and Mary Watkins, the twenty-five year old housemaid, from Disserth, Radnorshire. Their male colleagues were from even further afield. Thomas William Crowhurst, the butler, aged thirty-seven, came from Cranham, Herts.; Lachlan McKinnon, aged thirty-one, the gamekeeper, was born in Firie; and William Hopkins, the twenty-one year old coachman, came from Middlesex. One of the now-destroyed Penybont cottages was the home of the Llwynmadog laundress — Sarah Davies in 1851, Mary Davies twenty years later, and Mary Thomas in 1881. Indeed, local tradition called the house 'the Llwynmadog laundry'. Another later laundress, a freelance washerwoman, lived at Cefnmorarth, on the hill above the hanging woods of Llwynmadog. Before the First World War she used to be seen walking to the Grouse Inn every Monday to do a day's washing for one and six. She would 'pick and steal' to eke out her earnings and get food for her six children. Attempts to frighten her out of her misdeeds with ghost stories and tales of retribution all failed — 'If she saw the devil', said one man who remembered her, 'she would call him brother!'

The roads of Abergwesyn have been trodden over the centuries by countless travelling vendors and workers, among them tinkers, jobbers, butter-merchants, packmen, craftsmen itinerant or semi-itinerant, and seasonal workers (such as harvesters going to and from England). Among the latter were Welsh women walking to London and the Home Counties, in early summer, to seek work as gardeners or servants. A Welsh article based on the reminiscences of Mr Evan Jones of Ty'nypant, Llanwrtyd concerns the adventures of Ruth Siôn Watcyn of Penywern, Abergwesyn, who walked to London in the eighteenth century with a group of Cardiganshire girls, and survived unharmed a meeting with a debonair highwayman. She became first a gardener and then lady's maid to Lady Goodrich. Ruth was visited in London by her father, who travelled with a drover and traced his daughter by singing her name aloud in Ludgate. After Lady Goodrich's death, Ruth returned, the richer by a pension, to Abergwesyn, and took up her life as a quiet, respected local woman (though with a romantic aura of the great world about her) and a sober black-clad worshipper with her two sisters at Pantycelyn chapel.

The writer describes the Cardiganshire girls approaching Abergwesyn along the drovers' road, on their way to earn money for themselves and their parents by their summer work. They were simply but neatly dressed, barefooted, to save shoe-leather, until they reached the Wolf's Leap in the Irfon valley. There they put on their shoes before reaching the village. Models of industry, they knitted stockings as they walked! (Hannah Whitney told Kilvert of three such Cardiganshire women she remembered, who 'used to pass by the house every March walking to London to weed gardens'.) Ruth Watkins, defending Abergwesyn against her friends' criticisms of its quietness, claimed that the Grouse Inn was always busy, full of drovers from Tregaron, theological students from Ystrad Meurig on their way to and from Oxford and Cambridge, ministers and clergy, travelling harvesters. The Cardiganshire girls, however, thought little of these mild excitements, and lured Ruth to London with stories of'my lord this, my lady that, a banquet one night, a ball the next, and we in the midst of it all'. The first day's walking took them well on the way to Hereford; the walk to London was done in less than a week, through Hereford, Caerleon, Oxford, Abingdon, Reading and Windsor, on the outskirts of which took place (so says the story) the encounter with Wil Rhandirmwyn, a highwayman later to be hanged, who claimed a kiss from one of the girls and tossed her a silver guinea in return.

As well as direct selling of surplus butter by the farms, there once used to be selling through middlemen, travelling butter-merchants, in this area. There as Jac y Menin (Jack the Butter), who died in the 1830s, and his brother Josi y Menin. Abergwesyn people also sold butter to the growing industrial areas of south Breconshire and north Glamorganshire. D.L. Wooding recorded that Margaret, wife of David Davies of Lle'rtaihirion, walked when she was over sixty from the Camarch valley via Brecon to Llanelli ironworks with nine pounds of butter on her back.

Other itinerants included cloggers. Alders growing between Llanwrtyd and Abergwesyn were used by them up to 1939 for making clog-soles. The wood, cut in spring and summer, had to be left to season. Geraint Jenkins writes that there had been generations of these craftsmen, and that many of the later ones 'were natives of the Llandovery district...during the spring and summer months they wandered from grove to grove in lowland Brecknock with a few simple tools, living in roughly-built huts or tents'. Alder is a water-resistant wood, a quality necessary for footgear 'widely used on farms, factory floors, and mines'. The clog-soles were not made simply for local use —

they went to clogging-factories in the North of England.

The roads and paths used by all these travellers were looked after in haphazard and piecemeal fashion until comparatively recent times. By the Local Government Act of 1894 minor roads became the responsibility of local councils; and from then on the figure of the council roadman comes on to the Abergwesyn scene, clearing and patching up parish roads which were still rough tracks by modern standards — and none the worse for that, one is tempted to think, comparing the curlew-haunted solitudes of the old road over Elenydd with the summer confrontations of angry car-bonnets on that road today, over mountains stubbly with spruce!

When Mr Evan Evans of Bryndolau retired in 1968, Abergwesyn found itself for the first time for many years without a resident road-man and at the mercy of the litter-hurlers. Mr Evans' father, also Evan Evans, and also a roadman, moved to Bryndolau from Tyhaearn, nearby, with his wife and family of sixteen children. We have come across Rhys Jones, the nineteenth century ex-drover roadman of Blaennant. Penyrhyddfa, by the Devil's Staircase, was the home of more than one road-worker, including John Edwards, formerly a shepherd for the Robertses of Llwynderw, who lost his job when Llwynderw was bought by John Jones Hope. John Edwards then worked on the Tywi valley road. In 1911 he was followed at Penyrhyddfa by another roadman, the colourful William Rogerson. William was born in Manchester, surnamed Smith. He ran away from home, took to a wandering life, changed his name to Littler, under which name he came as a farm servant to Trawsgyrch, where he met and married Elizabeth, also a farm servant, and about that time changed his name to Rogerson. He had no Welsh, she no English, and for the whole of their life together they communicated in a strange pidgin dialect of their own. Their son's speech was permanently affected by it.

William and Elizabeth lived first at Llwyndêl, a cottage near Rhiwnant farm in the Claerwen valley, at the time when the first dam was being built in the nearby Elan valley. They made money by unlicensed selling of beer to the workmen. It is said that they had difficulty getting the drinkers out of their small house, and were helped by a lodger, who would put wet peat on the fire and a sack on top of the chimney to smoke out the customers! Thence the Rogersons moved to Tyhaearn in Abergwesyn, afterwards to Cenfaes, and finally to Penyrhyddfa. William worked on the Tregaron and Tywi valley roads from Penyrhyddfa via Nantystalwyn up to the Cardiganshire border at Moelprysgau, and downstream as far as Trawsnant. One day when he was at work a 'toff' walking up the road stopped to make some disparaging jokes about its roughness and remoteness. 'When are you getting the roller up here?' he asked. Without a smile, Rogerson answered 'Coming next week by post!' — just the sort of deadpan and deflating quip beloved of Abergwesyners.

Mrs Rogerson was short and very fat. She used to walk down to Abergwesyn shop each week, and sometimes to Llanwrtyd; despite her figure she was such a brisk walker that even much slimmer people found it hard to keep up with her. Many of her purchases she carried in her skirt, which she held up, displaying an elaborate petticoat. Her pidgin Welsh-English greatly amused everyone. A titbit remembered with relish is her report to Mrs Watkins of Gwesyn Cottages on Mrs Davies' pullets, which had started to lay."Huwch! Huwch!'' she exclaimed excitedly. 'Mrs Davies Shop told him cocks laying! If lies, him lies!' William Rogerson died on 2 March 1931; his body was carried on a gambo for burial at Pantycelyn. Elizabeth followed him on 20 May that same year. She died suddenly, on the field where she and her hot-tempered son were planting potatoes. John was questioned by the police, but no more was heard about the mystery of his mother's death. He sold up and left in September for work on Pantyfedwen farm near Pontrhydfendigaid. John, too, died suddenly a year later, aged twenty-six, and was buried at Strata Florida.

A few more exotic occupations are mentioned from time to time in old records and reminiscences of Abergwesyn and the other North Breconshire parishes. Morgan Williams of Nantycerdin, Llanwrtyd (1797-1875) was a falconer, who got his splendid savage birds from the Pembrokeshire coast. He kept a falcon and a fox as pets. Pwll y March (Stallion's Pool) in the Gwesyn valley was once sounded by an old local fathomer, and found to be 'seven ropes and a halter' deep (about fifty-four yards). Water-diviners are used nowadays in rural Wales and elsewhere, as they have been over the centuries.

Consurwyr ('conjurors', soothsayers) and charmers may be pooh-poohed by some of the younger generation, but are remembered, at least by many of the old, who are interested to note, in the light of present-day knowledge, how the advice of the 'wise man' often coincided with modern health rules. Farm-wives seeking advice on soured cream and failed butter, for instance, might be given a programme of ritually-repeated washings of their pans and implements. Old family recipes for salves and herbal medicines are still surrounded with a certain mystery. In the past, conjurors were thought to 'call spirits from the vasty deep'. To deny all of them some powers inexplicable by common-sense standards is to be bigoted indeed. The argument about the supernatural or non-supernatural origin of these powers is not dead yet. Certainly some 'wise men' seem to have had hypnotic talents, and to have been adept in suggestion. People of this district knew well the wonders attributed to the Harries family of Cwrt-y-Cadno in North Carmarthenshire, who used a mirror to impart secret knowledge to enquirers gazing into its uncanny light. John Lloyd printed in his *Historical Memoranda* an account of the prosecution for witchcraft in 1789, at Brecon Quarter Sessions, of Daniel Jones of Llanafan fawr, who had been consulted by Thomas Daniel, of a farm as far away as Ystradfellte, about the milk troubles of his father's cows. Thomas had been asked by Daniel Jones to advertise his fortune-telling and his skills in recovering lost and stolen goods.

The late Don Gardner, in an article in *Country Quest* (February 1970) referred to an old woman of Nantystalwyn, a clairvoyant, who 'used to tell the fortunes of the mountain women for the few pence they could spare'. She foretold the death of William Williams of Pantseiri, the 'King of the Mountains', in the same year that one of his Welsh Black cows, grazing on summer pasture in the Tywi valley, would give birth to a white calf. She was proved right when both the birth and the death occurred in 1773.

14. Local Industries

(i) The Woollen Industry

Theophilus Jones tells us that 'from the latter end of the sixteenth to the beginning of the eighteenth century great fortunes were acquired in Brecon, and the vicinity, by the manufacture of woollen cloths'. The *State Papers (Domestic)* have references to the Breconshire woollen industry, for example a grant of the 'alnage of cloth' there and elsewhere by James I in November 1606 to the Duke of Lennox, who by December was dealing with demands about 'fees for the alnage of the new draperies with exceptions thereto by the worsted weavers, dornix weavers, and knit-stocking makers'. The following June he appointed Roger Powell his deputy Alnager of Cloth for counties Monmouth, Carmarthen, Pembroke, Cardigan, Glamorgan and Brecknock.

The drab, coarse cloth exported through the markets of Brecon and other border towns was given the name of 'brecknocks'. The wool of the thousands of sheep grazing on the mid-Welsh hills was from very early times gathered and spun, knitted or woven, at first domestically, and later in woollen mills. Geraint Jenkins, whose *'The Welsh Woollen Industry'* (1969) should be consulted for the story of woollen manufacture in this area, points out that the cloth produced was often rough and undressed, the comparative scarcity of the element *pandy* (fulling-mill) in Breconshire place-names bearing out this statement. There is a Cae Pandy farm near Builth; but Nantyrarian was at one period a fulling-mill, and Geraint Jenkins lists Llanganten and Llangamarch among Breconshire villages where fulling was done. There was, too, a 'dye works and mill at Wernwyn, Llanddewi'r Cwm.

The Breconshire woollen industry in general declined by the mid-eighteenth century, by which time its rivals, Gloucestershire and Wiltshire in particular, were in the ascendant. The Breconshire Agricultural Society, founded in 1755, tried to re-animate the trade by offering prizes for the best woollen yarn and length of cloth, but in vain. Howell Harries' community at Trefecca, too, fought against the tide; but by the early nineteenth century, as W.E. Minchinton wrote, 'woollen manufacture survived in the county as only a very small-scale industry with some people continuing to weave fabrics for their own use or for their neighbours...on a quasi-barter basis', fleeces being brought to the mill (or house) and the weaver being paid in spun yarn.

The growth of demand for flannel in industrial South Wales brought a prosperity in which Breconshire had but a small share. Late nineteenth century modernisation (for finer cloths) was not to the advantage of small water-driven mills, which could not afford the new machinery. Nowadays the only woollen mill still working in Breconshire is the Cambrian Factory, Llanwrtyd, run by the British Legion and employing a number of disabled people. It has its own small shop by the mill, selling quilts, blankets, clothing and small gifts. Many visitors each year are shown over the modern work-rooms and dye-plant, and a room containing an old hand-loom in working order. The only other Breconshire woollen mill now working anywhere is also from Llanwrtyd — Esgairmoel. It has been re-erected at the Folk Museum, St Fagan's. Here too can be seen weaving in progress on an eighteenth century loom, and a range of operations performed on nineteenth century machines.

The history of the North Breconshire woollen industry does not follow quite the same lines as its general history in the county. Abergwesyn and the other parishes of the Hundred of Builth seem always to have produced their spun yarn and woven cloth mainly for local use, though, as we shall see, some Abergwesyn stockings were peddled in the industrial areas further south. Domestic spinning and weaving, which had declined in most of the county by the later years of the eighteenth century, continued here till the end of the nineteenth century, though it remained for most workers, as in earlier times, what Geraint Jenkins calls it, 'an adjunct to animal husbandry', which brought 'little prosperity to...the isolated cottages and farmhouses'. It would have been carried on here mainly in the slack days of winter in the house or in a shed. In an area as remote as this there must have long been a need for local craftsmen and local products, if only because travelling to market was often so difficult.

Llysdinam, the district between Llanafan fawr and Newbridge-on-Wye, was once a centre of the woollen industry. Theophilus Jones wrote that 'old surveys of the manor and ancient presentments' treated the 'weavers of Inam' (one of the ancient commotes) as a body corporate, separately assessed for payment of chief rent to the lord of the manor. He conjectured that the old court of Penllys on its green ridge was the place from which the law was administered for this curious community-within-a-community, 'under regulations of their own and subject to charters of their own adoption, or by grants from the lords'.

Books, traditions, Census returns yield the names of a few individual workers in the woollen industry of Abergwesyn and its surrounding area. In the eighteenth century, Rees Jones, a tailor's son, was at work as a weaver in Llanddewi Abergwesyn. The Rev David Williams' family had for generations combined weaving with farming. His ancestor William Williams came from the Tywi valley a little further south. In the next generation, Roderick Williams moved to Lluestyfedw on the land of Blaencwmhenog, a remote farm in the fastnesses of the hills beyond Llanwrtyd old church. Thence sprang David's own family of Nantydderwen and Maesygwaelod. David was breaking with family tradition when he chose the craft of shoemaking. David Davies of Bwlchygorllwyn was called 'weaver' at his marriage in 1825. A Roderick Williams, weaver, aged thirty-eight, born in Llanwrtyd, was living at Bwlchygorllwyn uchaf, Llanfihangel Abergwesyn, in 1851, while over the hills to the south of the road to Beulah, at lonely Esgairlas, the 1851 and 1861 Census returns record the 'wool weaver' Rees Davies. A twenty-nine year old daughter and sons of fourteen and twelve were employed at home. By 1871, at the age of fifty-nine, Rees was a pauper. In the Camarch valley lived the 'cotter and weaver' Isaac Arthur at Cluniau bach. He was still there in 1881, but his son David was now the 'woollen weaver'. By 1891 he was a farmer only.

Although by the mid-nineteenth century there were several woollen 'factories' in the area, it is probable that Isaac Arthur, Rees Davies and Roderick Williams worked at home, for these are farmhouses; in 1842 Bwlchygorllwyn uchaf was a farm of over 100 acres and the other two of about 200 acres. The weaver-farmers would have made lengths of cloth for garments, and *carthenni* (blankets or shawls). The word means 'shrouds', too, and links us to the days of 'burying in the wool'. Geraint Jenkins says that the Llanwrtyd district was long known for a particular type of plaid *carthen* in brown and grey. That does not sound much like the intense, jewel-like colours of the bales of finished cloth on the shelves of today's Cambrian Factory.

One 'spinner wool' appears in the Abergwesyn Census returns, a seventy year old grandmother at Bwlchygorllwyn uchaf in 1861. The other domestic workers in the woollen industry were the stocking-knitters. Abergwesyn had a number of these. Older women today remember home knitting of long, warm, durable socks for their menfolk. The earlier stocking-knitters worked as well to sell their wares both locally, at nearby markets, and also, through stocking-merchants who acted as middlemen, as far afield as the South Welsh valleys when these became industrialised and heavily populated. In Breconshire generally there was a decline in hose-knitting in the later years of the eighteenth century. John Clark wrote in his *View of the Agriculture of Brecknockshire* (1794) that the stockings were 'sold at the markets at around 8d a pair', and worked out that even a very industrious woman could hope for a profit of only one shilling a week on the making of her weekly quota of four pairs. She would have to card, spin and knit the stockings, and needed a pennorth of oil for each pound of wool. With this meagre return she had to support herself in food, clothes, fuel and rent, and at some times of the year the shilling would buy only a gallon of wheat out of all her requirements. Yet, as Theophilus Jones points out, in the Hundred of Builth stocking-knitters survived much longer, whether because of lower expectations or lower expenses, or better profits on a better product, is not clear. Richard Fenton, who visited Llanwrtyd in May 1804, found in the lower village (Pontrhydyfere, later Llanwrtyd Wells) a 'concourse of peasants, mainly women' who had come to sell their 'very coarse stockings' to the merchants who had gathered to meet them.

There is a story of two knitting-women of Cwmdu, on the Cardiganshire bank of the Tywi opposite Llanddewi Abergwesyn, who were probably the last people to occupy this little farm, about the 1850s. The farms on the Caron bank seem to have been linked for some aspects of their work. We have seen earlier that Hafdre housed in its stables the horses of Bronyrhelem; and earlier, Cwmdu kept on its land the dry cattle of Hafdre. The two women, probably sisters, looked after these cattle, and possibly lived rent-free for doing so. Every June they used to trudge the mountains, wool-gathering (literally — though, imagining the repetitive job under the great skies, one sees how the connotation of absent dreaming arose). This wool they would spin at home into yarn for knitting stockings and *carthenni*. One Sunday evening, weary, they went to bed in the early evening, and waking just after a late sunset thought it was early Monday morning. Setting off on another wool-picking expedition, they met Mr Thomas Jones of Hafdre, who bent brows of displeasure on the Sunday workers; they were as shocked as he was when they found what day it was. (There are other stories which show how seriously Sabbath-breaking was taken, such as the one about the farmer of Esgairanell on the slopes of Epynt, who absent-mindedly rode over one Sunday to Cefnbrith Mill with a load of corn to grind, only to be greeted with a scandalized cry of 'O Esgairanell! Esgairanell! What is this!'.)

Census returns for 1841 show many woolpickers staying at farmhouses of the Camddwr and Tywi valleys and the Mountains of Dewi: Brynglas had no fewer than sixteen! By 1851 they were all gone.

Gwenny and Esther were two old stocking-knitters of Llety Graig, Llanddewi Abergwesyn, a little square ruin still perched on a shelf of the hillside opposite the Tregaron road, about halfway from the road-junction to Llanerch-yrfa. There is a certain pathos in the sight of this tiny building with a small platform of old garden in front of it, and superb desolation all around. Perhaps Gwenny and Esther were the Gwen Jones and Esther Davies who lived at Digiff, a little further downstream in 1841 and 1851. They were paupers then, both born in Llanwrtyd. Gwen had been a servant, Esther a farmer's wife. The grandmother of Mr T.M. Hope and of the late Mr J.R. Hope of Pentwyn remembered them at Llety Graig, busy with their knitting; one of them, she said, had a blind eye. Probably the 'cottage labourer' Margaret Davies of Nantyfleiddast, too, was a stocking-knitter, if not a spinner or a weaver. In Llanfihangel we have found the seventy-eight year old pauper Gwen Williams, hose-knitter, up at Nantyneuadd in 1841. Ten years later the Census returns show six knitting-women in the parish — thirteen year old Margaret Jones at Cluniau Siân: Elizabeth Meredith, a seventy-three year old pauper, at Cenfaes: Charlotte Davies, aged forty-nine, born in Llanafan, living at Penycae bach: a seventy-three year old widow, Anne Richard from Caeo, at Ty'ncelyn: a spinster, also Anne Richard, aged thirty-eight, at Fron fach near Llwyn Owen: and Anne Williams, aged fifty-nine, in one of the Penybont cottages. The year 1861 found Elinor Morgan knitting at Cwmcywydd, Mary Richard, the carpenter's wife, at Penybont, and Ann Thomas at Dôliâr, with her daughter Elizabeth helping.

Another knitter was Rachel, who lived at little Ty Pica, beside the lane leading northward from Trawsnant in Cwm Tywi. Her landlord was the John Jones we have already met. Rachel used to accompany her packman husband to sell her stockings in South Wales. Into each mining town she would precede him, praising his wares and beating up trade by purchasing several pairs herself. Rachel was a forceful woman, and no respector of persons. Furious with her landlord, who had 'borrowed' her pony for shepherding, she pushed him down the hill! Eventually Ty Pica was badly damaged by fire and Rachel had to leave.

Mr J.R. Hope knew of a 'hosier' called William Jones, who once lived at Abergwrâch further up the Tywi valley. Probably he was the one lodging at Cribin nearby in 1861, when David Davies, the son of the house, was also a stocking-merchant. William Jone's gravestone in Llanddewi churchyard says that he died in 1879 aged seventy-three, outlived by his wife Elizabeth. William appears in the Census returns for 1871, at Abergwrâch. He used to carry stockings from Cwm Tywi for sale in Merthyr, draping them between the prongs of a large fork. Another hosier lived at Penyrhyddfa in 1870; on 1 September Gwen, John, Betha and Thomas Jones were baptised, children of this David Jones and his wife Margaret.

The earliest woollen mill, run by water-power, to open in the immediate vicinity was Esgairmoel, built about 1760, as Geraint Jenkins writes, as a weaving-shop by Richard Rhys Winston of Esgairmoel isaf farm. In the early nineteenth century it was equipped with carding and spinning machinery. In 1946 this mill and the Cambrian Factory were the only two left in Breconshire. The rebuilding of Esgairmoel at St Fagan's took place in 1953. There is an interesting account of it, as a typical rural Welsh mill, in 'The Welsh Woollen Industry'. In the early 1880s, Isaac

Williams, who had worked at the Cambrian Mill, took over Esgairmoel from the Winstones as tenant of the Pugh Jones family then at Esgairmoel isaf. Isaac was followed by his son Rees in 1936.

To Esgairmoel local people brought their fleeces and had the wool spun and woven for their families' needs. The manufacturer also bought fleeces at the weekly Builth market and sold his products there on his own stall. The mill produced mainly white blankets, cloth for suits, knitting-yarn, shirt-flannel and *carthenni*. After the railway came, goods went to Builth market, and raw wool came back, by train.

Further away, just outside Builth, another early mill was Nantyrarian, first a fulling-mill at the end of a row of eighteenth century weavers' cottages; later it was equipped with carding and spinning machinery, and till the mid-nineteenth century supplied yarn for weaving. Kelly's first *Directory*, of 1830, says that in that year 'the only manufacture' at Builth was 'that for flannel, the establishment for which [was] on the River Wye'. The Builth manufacturer was Charles Lawrence. Pigot's *Directory* referred to two woollen mills at Builth. One of these must have been Nantyrarian, which is on the Irfon.

Nearer Abergwesyn, about 1804 was built Dôlaeron Woollen Factory, across the Camarch from the former Penybont cottages, in what is now Beulah. Now converted into a house, the old mill stands by the riverside between Eglwys Oen Duw and the farmhouse of Dôlaeron, which used to flaunt an astonishment of peacocks, strutting by the road under tall trees. About 1822 the mill was taken by Benjamin Wooding, who after some time at a Cardiganshire mill came back and settled there. He was the father of the David Lewis Wooding who married Marianne Jones of Llwynderw. This mill appears in Geraint Jenkins' list of the most important ones in Breconshire from 1830 to 1914, and was one of the nine left by the 1920s.

The Cambrian Mill, Llanwrtyd, followed the early nineteenth century Maesygwaelod Mill. Lewis's *Topographical Dictionary* mentions in 1833 only 'one large factory' in Llanwrtyd, dealing with all stages of the manufacture and giving employment to many people. The Cambrian Factory was founded in the 1820s, and Geraint Jenkins takes this to be the one Lewis refers to, though it is not clear why Esgairmoel is not also mentioned. In 1927 the Cambrian Mill was equipped by the British Legion with new machinery, including the first 'dobby loom' in Wales, and henceforth employed a quota of disabled workers. In the 1940s a large new three-storeyed mill was erected alongside the older building.

Lewis's *'Topographical Dictionary'* refers also to 'a small manufacture of fine flannel' on the river Irfon at Llangamarch, 'employing only about a dozen persons'. This bears out a local tradition of three or four small 'factories' there, supplying cloth to Cefn Gorwydd nearby, said to have been a hamlet of tailors. Jenkins lists Penrhiw (Llangamarch), Llysdinam and Llanlleonfel mills as operating between 1830 and 1914. The *'Topographical Dictionary'* refers to a few people engaged in woollen manufacture in Llanlleonfel village, 'on a very limited scale'. Lewis notes that down the Wye valley, at Glasbury, about sixty persons were 'employed in an extensive establishment for sorting wool', with north windows 'to avoid too strong a light'. According to the requirements of the staple, different qualities of wool were apportioned to clothiers, hatters, hosiers and so on. Lewis thought that Breconshire cloth-manufacture in his day was 'confined to the weaving of yarn spun in private families, into what are called *hanner gwe*, i.e. half-woven or raw cloth'. It was 'sometimes brought to the fairs and markets, rolled up in pieces of 26 to 32 yards long and about one and a half yards broad'. These were 'milled and dyed in England'. Not all the 'small manufactures' we have heard of fell into this category, however — Lewis himself noted that 'fine flannel' was the product of Llangamarch, for instance. Nor, after such factories as Esgairmoel, Nantyrarian and Dôlaeron were equipped with the newer machinery, would yarn have invariably been spun at home.

(ii) Mining

Another industry which at one time brought lively activity to Abergwesyn and its neighbourhood was metal-mining, chiefly for lead. The old track up the south-eastern bank of the Culent valley from Nantybrain (passing on its way the bracken-choked mouth of a solitary adit) is known as Heol y Mwyn (Mine Road). It is many years now since the derelict lead-mine to which it leads was last worked. A.G. Bradley, who passed it about 1902 on his way over to the Tywi valley, found it abandoned and silent except for 'the weird groaning of an old and rusty pump'. One can still see the rust-covered heads of great iron pipes that sink from view into the eerie depths of more than one uncovered shaft. A dropped stone ricocheting from the pipe wakes disturbing echoes; not for some time does the far-off sound of a splash drift up the clammy tunnel. Dark water fills the trench where a huge wheel once laboured round. Nameless pieces of iron, gritty with rust, protrude from the debris of stone sheds. The site of Pengwaith house can be pointed out by those who know the valley; one of the trees that used to mark it fell a few years ago. The spoil-heaps of the old mine loom up along the narrow stream, giving a barren, lunar air to the upper part of the valley. Further downstream, the valley is green or russet or brown as the seasons turn; here it is grey. This desolation is all that now remains of a mine that it was once hoped would rank 'among the first mines in Wales, both for stability and profit', and that the parents of men still living remembered in its later days as 'Number 8E, Rhandirmwyn'.

Nantymwyn itself (at Rhandirmwyn) was a well-known lead-mine, the property of the Earl of Cawdor. One Abergwesyn mine-captain, a certain Morgan John, at a period when the Culent valley mine had fallen on hard times, is said to have spurred on the workmen and gulled the shareholders by 'salting' his mine with buckets of lead from the more prosperous concern at Rhandirmwyn.

Part of the Culent valley mine's story can be pieced together from paragraphs in the *Mining Journal*. On 4 May 1844 came the congratulatory announcement that 'the lead-mines on the Nantbran estate... (of which P. Vaughan, Esq., is the proprietor) have been let to a company who intend immediately to commence operations'. Referring to Nantymwyn, the writer says that the same productive veins probably extend 'under the Nantbran lands'. 'P. Vaughan' was Philip Vaughan, a Brecon solicitor who had acquired some of the Llwynderw estate; he had earlier acted for Peter Jones in raising mortgages on Llwynderw property. The *Mining Journal*'s correspondent hoped that the proprietor and lessees, and the 'labouring population' of the surrounding district, would all benefit from the new Abergwesyn venture.

It was not the first time that interest had been shown in the potential mineral wealth of the area. A mine near Llanwrtyd had, writes W.J. Lewis in *'Lead-Mining in Wales'*, produced at some time during the eighteenth century some tons of ore sold at £12 per ton. Theophilus Jones wrote about 1800 that a small amount of lead-ore had been discovered at Llanwrtyd, but was 'so anomalous in its dip and progress' and had such great problems of expense in transport that the search had been abandoned. G.W. Hall in *'Metal Mines of Southern Wales'* lists a mine, Nant Gyrnant, roughly one and a quarter miles west of Llanwrtyd Wells, where an opencast working can be seen, and not far away a shaft and an adit in what appear to be trial workings. He wonders if this could be Castle Rock, Llanwrtyd, which appears in a list of mines in 1875. Perhaps it was an attempt to re-work the eighteenth century mine. The Clwyd-Powys Archaeological Trust survey (1993) calls it eighteenth - nineteenth century — 'a south-west striking lode with pyrite, chalcopyrite, galena and blende mineralisation', and says 'the later extension of opencast workings was made by two winzes and a south-west adit. Trials and a shaft are noted on Banc y Dinas, and a shaft at SN 8606 4736, and a level at SN 8603 4742. There are tramway track beds from shafts and adits, and 'an intact manual winch and pump above a winze in the bottom of the opencast adit'.

In 1831, when Llwynderw was offered for sale, 'veins of lead-ore' were among the attractions mentioned in the *Hereford Journal*. Judging from the situation of the properties listed, the lead-deposits meant may well have been those later known as the 'Irfon Mine'. Samuel Lewis in his *'Topographical Dictionary'* of 1833 wrote that the hills on Llanfihangel Abergwesyn were thought to contain lead, and that lead-ore had been found in Llanddewi, but in his day was no longer worked. One of five people from whom a deposition was taken in 1823 was Susannah Edwards of Pengwaith Cottage, Llanddewi Abergwesyn. We have seen that this was a house near the Culent valley lead-mine; 'Pengwaith' means 'head, top or end of the workings'. Possibly an earlier mining venture had given the house its name; we do not know whether this venture was still in progress in 1823. Pengwaith may have been the house of a manager or accommodated workers at the mine. It is doubtful whether any such venture aroused keener expectations than did that of 1844.

By 26 July 1845 the ore from the Nantbran Lead Mines was said to yield 80% of lead with a small proportion of silver, having been assayed by Messrs Johnson & Co. of Hatton Garden. The mines were being opened as quickly as possible in the confident expectation of their proving 'very productive, and...highly remunerative'. The shares were at a premium already. For the next few years 'anticipations' were 'crowned with the most complete success'. The manager, Peter Paul Couch, initiated an annual Christmas dinner of roasted bullock and good ale for the workmen. But Couch resigned in 1849. In a letter to the *Mining Journal*, he wrote of his indifferent health, and the feeling that the mines should have a resident manager, not one living in Surrey. His brother had been elected as his successor. However, in view of Mr Couch's acidly polite reference to the visit to the mines, arranged by the directors in their manager's absence, of a mining expert, one may suspect undercurrents of dissension. Mr Couch expressed his pride in the development of the Abergwesyn mines, and his intention as a holder of over two hundred shares to 'keep a watchful eye' on their welfare.

Couch refers to himself as a Cornishman. Local tradition insists that in Abergwesyn as elsewhere in mid-Wales, a large body of Cornish miners was brought in to supplement local labour and to provide 'know-how' superior to that of most Welsh lead-miners. W.J. Lewis cites one Welsh inspector of mines who criticised the Welsh miner's 'failure to interest himself in the technicalities of his work'. Couch speaks in his letter of 'ample accommodation, contiguous to the works...now provided for 50 to 100 miners'. Such a miners' barracks does not show up on the Census returns. 'Contiguous to the works' suggest Pengwaith or its neighbourhood. (The most recent house on the site was of timber and corrugated iron. It appears in the Census returns for 1881 and 1891, the house mentioned in 1823 being no longer there by 1841. The later Pengwaith was demolished in 1917, at the same time as the great water-wheel.) Or was the forgotten miners' barracks at Nantybrain itself, where the tithe map of 1848 shows a building no longer there, to the west of the house and outbuildings? Some of the miners were lodged in the scattered farmhouses of the area, but this arrangement may have obtained more widely in the later, less ambitious phase of the mining. Fifty to a hundred is a large number of workmen to have been accommodated in such a sparsely-populated district. Immigrant miners living under barrack conditions were more riotous than local work-people; Nantybrain has its stories of violence. The south-facing wing of the house, known at one period as Ty Capten, the Captain's House, was the scene of a catastrophic fight in which one of the furious men, Jenner, was killed.

Couch wrote enthusiastically in 1849 of what had already been done, and what more could be done, at the mine — the 'great size of the veins (...champion lodes)': the sinking of a shaft and the driving of levels: the 'water-pumping engines' which 'will allow of the mines being sunk 100 fathoms deep': the 'engine-shaft' passing 'through the lode from the 30 to 40 fathoms level, thereby investing this mine with a character' of great and unusual stability. A crusher and other cleaning machinery were being erected, and a team of wagon-horses had been provided by the company to carry away the ore for smelting. But, he wrote, 'if it should be determined to smelt the ore on the spot, it may be done at a trifling cost; there being countless thousands of tons of peat lying waste'. The terms of the lease provided for using this 'for all purposes connected with the mines'. Fire-clay, stone and water-power were there in abundance.

By March, 1850 the crusher was still not erected, for on the third of that month the *Mining Journal* quoted the agent's February report on 'Abergwessin (Nant-y-Criar) [sic]', which said 'it was desirable to have a crusher erected', for 'some hundred tons of lead ore were laid open,...and immediate returns could be made'. The reading of the report had taken place on 2 March at 'a special meeting of adventurers held at Gregory's Hotel, Cheapside'. The statement of accounts showed a balance of £1,200. 'Mr Evan Hopkins stated verbally his opinion of the property, which was satisfactory'. The agent described the lode as '14 feet wide, carrying a leader of lead under the hanging wall, more than one foot of big, solid ore, and the whole lode saving work'. The three existing directors were to be increased to seven , and the mines venture was to be prosecuted 'with the greatest vigour' — a resolution which may imply some lack of vigour in the immediate past!

By May the rumblings of doubt and dissension had grown louder. In its final report on the Abergwessin Silver-Lead Company's activities, the Mining Journal stated that at 'an adjourned meeting of shareholders' on 1 May, with George Pell, Esq. in the chair, 'an angry feeling at first seemed to pervade amongst some of the proprietors', though eventually they decided on 'co-operation for their mutual benefit'. So far from being vigorously prosecuted, mining operations had been at a standstill, 'several of the shareholders having declined to pay up their calls, because the deeds relating to the property had not been deposited with the company'. The 'difficulty was now obviated', and the shareholders had promised to honour their pledges. Mr Vaughan moved the adoption of the report. The chairman's explanation of the trouble was mentioned but not reported by the *Journal,* which simply quoted his hopes for prompt payment of debts, and vigorous application to work. The secretary, Mr Spiller, read 'very lengthened' and satisfactory reports of the mines from 'Mr Evan Hopkins, Captain Ennor and Mr Dean', and a long desultory conversation ensued, about the original constitution of the company, from which it appeared that 'great irregularities had occurred in the transfer of shares, etc.' — but a temporary happy ending was achieved by appointing two extra members to the committee, 'all of whom pledged themselves to devote their energies to the company'.

The Abergwessin Silver-Lead Mining Company then disappears from the *Mining Journal,* but not so mining from the Culent valley. Frank Couch, presumably Peter Paul Couch's brother, was the Cornish manager of the lead-mine who, as the Census returns show, lived at Nantybrain in 1851. There too were his Cornish wife and fourteen year old daughter Ann Geiger Couch. At Crug, across the Irfon, lived a thirty year old Meirionydd-born lead-miner, William Roberts, married to a Cardiganshire woman. Their lodger was a Cornish miner, the widower Oliver Willboly. Ten years later, there were two lead-miners lodging with the farmer Rees Prothero at Digiff — a Pembrokeshire man, Jonathan Thomas, and Robert Davies, born at Merthyr Tydfil. In 1863 a new mining-venture started in the Culent valley with the advent of Josiah Harris and the re-christening of the mine as 'Newton'. The *Mining Journal* reported a fine lode (the Red Lode) and plenty of ore piled on the dressing-floors. The Builth registration of births of Abergwesyn miners' children during the 1860s show Morgan Jones at Doliar in 1863, John Jones (a lead- and copper-miner from Pembrokeshire) at Digiff in 1865, and Morgan Jones (the same one?) at the Mill in 1868. By 1871 the mine was known as East Nantymwyn, and in that year was taken over by a new company, after some sub-division of the land originally leased. The mine-agent, fifty-four year old John Motherall, a married man from Devon, was a boarder at no. 1, Nantybrain. G.W. Hall refers to the company's purchase from the Tuckingmill Foundry of a thirty foot by two foot six water wheel. Higher upstream a smaller wheel had been used — its remains in the wheelpit can still be seen. The new wheel was installed when there was a hope of deepening the shaft; this was not immediately done, for it proved to have been sunk partly in weak ground. A new shaft and adit were begun sixty fathoms to the south, an extension of flat rods from the wheel being made for pumping out the shaft. Both shafts are still to be seen, with their pump heads. It was decided eventually to concentrate on the old shaft. Captain Robert Northey was in charge in 1875. After the raising of six tons from a pocket of ore in the old shaft, which had now been deepened to thirty-five fathoms, Captain Northey urged the directors to have confidence in the mine and offered to work for six months for nothing — in vain. There had been gross mismanagement, a committee of enquiry found, the mine having been bought for £6,000 without a visit, as a pig in a poke! Directors and shareholders had no conception of the bleakness and remoteness of the Culent valley, the difficulty of transport, and the scarcity of skilled labour. The keeping of accounts left much to be desired.

G.W. Hall refers to the 'adjoining property' of Nantybrain being worked by a Mr Powell at this time; apparently the venture was close enough to East Nantymwyn for water from one to flood the other. Older Abergwesyn people not many years ago remembered their parents' stories of the days in the latter part of the nineteenth century when Heol y Mwyn (a metalled track) was still busy with wagons bringing ore from 'Number 8E', and Cornish miners were billeted on local farms — Carregyfrân is said to have been one of these. Report number 75/14 in a mineral reconnaissance of Central Wales by the National Environment Research Council refers to the Culent valley mine as 'Abergwessin (or Nant-y-brain: Irfon River: Trawsnant: Newton: East Nantymwyn), a lead-mine last worked in 1883 at a maximum depth of 64 metres'. (In 1881 a miner, Morgan Jones, lived with his family at Number One, Iron House in Abergwesyn.)

The small Irfon Mine, referred to by W.J. Lewis as having been worked by Andrew Williams in 1856, may be identical with the Cefn Coch Mine, now hidden by conifers, overlooking the Tregaron road from high on the opposite bank of the Irfon. There remain above the waterfall of Nant Byr the ruins of a small stone building (an ore-bin), a filled-up shaft at SW 5357 8402 with a projecting pump, a water-wheel pit, and above the working a pond and leat formed by damming a stream. The beginnings of an adit are to be seen at the foot of the waterfall. Cefn Coch was a lead and copper mine. An agent's report in the 'Mining Journal', dated 30 November 1860, speaks of a 'well-timbered shaft', then ten and a half fathoms deep, 'secured by an experienced miner', and a lode 'containing lumps of copper and fine lead ores'. He considered that a wheel nine feet by two feet would be necessary. There are traces of tramways. The N.E.R.C.'s report indicated that the mine was not worked after 1860, and that its maximum depth was twenty seven metres.

Rhys Gwesyn Jones wrote in 1861 that much copper and lead had been mined in Llanwrtyd parish, and it was expected that much more would be mined when the railway came. He thought that the well-waters sprang up near valuable veins of copper, and that the next generation would see a great increase in miners' houses here, as the mountains of the area held riches of lead, copper, some silver, and even gold!

Another silver-lead deposit near the Culent valley mine was on the land of Trawsnant, Llanwrtyd, which W.J. Lewis mentions as worked by the Trawsnant Silver Lead Mine Company. It began, he says, 'as a grant to some Leicestershire men to search for ore under Trawsnant farm' in 1846. This mine was abandoned in 1850, and later claimed by the Abergwessin Company. Josiah Harris obtained a lease on it from Morgan Pryse Lloyd in 1863. There was much litigation, some record of which can be found in the Glansevin MSS in the National Library of Wales. The mine changed hands three times between 1862 and 1872, but remained unproductive, Lewis tells us.

Just to the north-east of Llanfihangel Abergwesyn, over Bwlch y Ddau Faen, was the mining area of the Rhiwnant valley, on the borders of Breconshire and Radnorshire. Here, wrote Edwin Davies about 1909, the Nantycar lead-mine had been worked with 'considerable plant' till 1890, when the lord of the manor of Builth ended its life by selling it to the Birmingham Corporation to ensure the purity of their new reservoirs. G.W. Hall describes the north mine (predominantly copper) on the south side of the Claerwen just above its confluence with the Rhiwnant. He thinks that 'shallow workings existed in the eighteenth century, or even earlier'. There is a local tradition that Nantycar was known to the Romans. Theophilus Jones wrote of a failure, about the turn of the eighteenth-nineteenth centuries, to follow a vein of copper near Nantycar, but said the iron vein was 'steady and uniform'.

In the mid-nineteenth century the north mine at Nantycar, and Dalrhiw copper and lead mine on the opposite bank of the Rhiwnant (where 'the remains of workshops and cottages may still be seen'), enjoyed brief acclaim, but failed about 1854.

After the north mine closed, the south mine was developed, but was disappointing; the company was wound up in 1859. Later tenants tried their hand on a private basis. Hall writes that about 1883 Nantycar was abandoned for Nantygarw, higher up, 'remotely situated in the heart of the moors', whose silence today accentuates the stillness of disuse. Nantygarw was probably reached by the Claerwen-Rhiwnant farm-

Nantycar track. Some mining continued till 1899, possibly using a water turbine and steam or gas engine. The reservoir ended the enterprise.

At all these solitary sites are remains of some of the characteristic lead-mining structures and apparatus — shafts and adits; tramway beds: wheel-pits; pumps; leats; crusher houses; jiggers (for separating the ores by jolting them in water-covered sieves); buddles (sloping hutches over which washing-water flowed); ore bins; picking, washing and dressing floors. The Clwyd-Powys Archaeological Trust's survey found at Nantygarw North a platform for, probably, a horse-driven winding-frame. Nantygarw is particularly rewarding. As well as the shaft, adit and wheelpit, there is a leat running over a mile from Llyn Carw, that loneliest of little moorland lakes, and the home of legendary red trout. A 'precipitous miners' track' blasted out of Craig Rhiwnant is 'a spectacular piece of engineering', though eroded now by blocked culverts. 'Fragments of a smithy, mill buildings, barracks and offices remain'.

Hall points out that these 'mountainous western parts of Breconshire' are the only mineral-rich area of the county, except for pyrite in Cwm Dyfnant, Llangamarch and at Park Wells, and the 'curious deposit' of copper at Talachddu in the Old Red Sandstone area. Theophilus Jones reminds his readers that the veins in the Hundred of Builth were thought sufficiently important in the time of Edward I and II for commissions to be issued, such as that 'de minera Ballivum de Built', to Hoel ap Meurig (7 Ed. I), the King's bailiff (to whom the castle and manor of Builth were demised at £1000 a year), and similar commissions in later reigns, providing for the care of these minerals for the King's use.

Jones wrote about 1800-09 of unsuccessful attempts to mine coal at Llanwrtyd. Only non-combustible 'black Jack' and blackish slate had been found, and mineralogists laughed at the idea of coal being discovered there. A local 'collier' was married in Llanwrtyd in 1825. In 1861 Gwesyn Jones said that there was a strong local tradition of coal having been found downstream from the bridge by the old church. Despite the pooh-poohing of geologists, he thought the surrounding hills did contain traces of coal or its substratum of chalk. In 1881 a Llanwrthwl-born coal-miner, Thomas Jones, was living with his father-in-law at Coedtrefan; and at 3, Nantybrain in Llanddewi was the coal-miner Edward Morgan, a son of the occupier. Possibly they had returned from South Wales.

(iii) Quarrying

Quarrying in the past has given employment to a number of Abergwesyn men. There is still a working quarry in Builth, or rather at Llanelwedd, the adjoining parish. It was referred to by Samuel Lewis in 1833 as producing clay slate, rich in trilobites, and also hard volcanic stone. Nearer home, a quarry on the hillside opposite the old church of Llanwrtyd was till recently worked at intervals for road-making stone as it became needed. There was a slate-quarry near Cwmirfon; the remains of the powder-house are hidden in the trees on the steep slope behind the farmhouse. At the Beulah end of the Camarch valley are the starkly impressive remains of Penceulan Slate Quarry, possibly once a mine, for it has cave-like adit-entrances gaping among trees, and one alarming vertical shaft plunging from the valley-bottom. The hills of slate loom greyly in drizzle or gleam blue-grey in shade on a sunny day. Across the river, below the still-occupied farmhouse of Llednant, are the ruins of little Sychnant, said by the late Mr Aneurin Jones of Llednant to have been the home at one time of a bailiff of the quarry.

Penceulan was one of the important quarries of the area in the nineteenth century. D.L. Wooding recorded that in 1829 tiles produced there were selling at a shilling a hundred. The 1851 Census shows two quarrymen lodging at the adjacent farmhouse of Penceulan — William Jones, a twenty-five year old Denbighshire man, and Robert Owen, aged thirty-eight, born at Llanllefni, Caernarfonshire. By 1871, Caernarfonshire slate-quarryman, Owen Jones, who in the late 1850s and early 1860s was at Cefnmorarth, was farming at Penceulan, possibly working at the quarry next door as well. He and his family had two lodgers working there, both North Welshmen. Evan Jones, quarryman, lived there in 1881, and another, John Davies, at Cefnmorarth. At the next house downstream, Dôlberthog, lodged in 1871 a slate-dresser, also born in North Wales. (What Cornwall was to the Abergwesyn mines, North Wales was to its quarries — a source of expert labour.) David Davies, husband of Sarah, the Llwynmadog laundress, at one of the Penybont cottages in 1851, worked at the Cwm Irfon slate-quarry. Local people remember that a slate-quarryman at that quarry, Thomas Jenkins, a native of Strata Florida who married a local girl, died at Llanwrtyd as recently as 1935.

As well as the better-known quarries which regularly employed Abergwesyn people, there are small quarries in the hillsides of the area, some no doubt the result of hacking out stone for the building of a farmhouse nearby, some worked for a short time at a period now uncertain. One local account of the building of Llwynderw states that most of the stone came from Llanelwedd quarry, and the tiles for the roof from near Trecastle; another has it that the roofing-tiles came from a quarry near Cefngilfach in the upper Camarch valley, a version which suggests that the craggy outcrops upstream which the O.S. two and a half inch map marks 'Chwarel Ddu' (Black Quarry) were indeed that, or were near to a quarry.

(iv) Timber

Long before the planting of so many Abergwesyn hillsides with conifers, the district had another industry concerned with trees — the felling and exporting of hardwood timber-trees, in particular oak. After the death of David Jones of Llwynderw in February 1810, five hundred and fifty-eight oaks and forty ash on Fanog land were advertised for sale by auction at Builth. In February 1813 the *Hereford Journal* advertised a timber auction to be held 'at the King's Head in the town of Builth'. Included in the lots were one hundred and twenty-eight oak trees, most of them 'fit for Naval purposes', on Aberanell demesne: one hundred and forty-one equally good, on Llwyn Owen: six hundred on Llofftybardd: five hundred and eighty-one on Llanerchneuadd and Cefncendu: three hundred and eight on Wynllan: four hundred on adjacent Penceulan: eighty-one 'adapted for Naval purposes' on Llednant farm, opposite, and three hundred and twenty others on the same farm. Not only the Navy , but the new industrial areas of the South, were buyers of timber, which was sometimes carried by sea from the nearest port. The advertisements quoted here are merely random examples; there were certainly many more, as the area was rich in timber on the slopes below the high moors. The oakwoods which remain on some Abergwesyn valley-sides today give us some idea of the abundance and beauty of yesterday's woodlands.

15. Recreation

(i) Local Amusements

It would take a thoroughgoing cynic to doubt every one of the repeated assertions by older people of the Abergwesyn neighbourhood that though in their youth working hours were long and hard, and money short, nevertheless in the main people enjoyed life, and knew how to savour their leisure moments and such diversions as came their way.

Some of these diversions were from time immemorial found in the home itself, or part of the cycle of the farming year, like the much-enjoyed shearing-feasts, and the planned or impromptu gatherings round the hearth, for gossip and story-telling, singing, games and knitting. Tal-a-Hen describes in the *Red Dragon* (1882) the knitting-parties which in this district in the late eighteenth century and early nineteenth century made a convivial glow in the long winter evenings. The knitters met in rotation at the various farmhouses. 'The stockings, which were sold to a subordinate army agent for the use of soldiers, fetched a good price'. Three pairs could be made on large pins by a good knitter in the course of a long day, the writer claims. To prepare for the party, the women of the house would polish the solid oak furniture and the pewter plates and dishes, sweep down the cobwebs, and build a huge fire of peats around a 'gnarled root of bog-timber'. Ghost-stories brought a pleasant shiver to those sitting in the heat of the fire. The knitters were regaled with 'solid yellow pudding' of finely-mashed potatoes mixed with flour and milk, and cooked in a close-lidded round pot hung over the fire.

Even before it was finally undermined by the coming of 'the wireless' in the 1920s, the custom of *dechreunos* (beginning of the night), which had persisted here as in other similar districts, was gradually dying. Once, in each valley, families would take it in turn to keep open house after the day's work, which was synonymous with the ending of the light. Each evening, when the nights drew in towards winter, there would be one house casting a welcoming light into the darkness of the valley until bedtime came at about nine o'clock. This was the one in which the gathering of neighbours was taking place. If one were not the host of the evening, it was unusual to have a light — even candles, let alone a paraffin lamp. One is reminded of the 'grudged candlelight' of Harri Jones' poem about the Llanafan-Llanfihangel Bryn Pabuan district. Firelight was considered enough. When supper — usually a bowl of soup — was to be prepared and laid, the fire was poked into vigorous flame.

Some people still remember their youth on the now-dead farms of the Tywi valley, for instance, as a time of gaiety, company and life, when young people rode or walked of an evening from farmhouse to farmhouse, alighting on one hearth or another in a chattering, laughing crowd, perching for a while to gossip and play cards before taking off again into the darkening solitudes.

Another informal gathering, prescribed by custom and quietly enjoyed in recent times by the men-folk of the area, was the Sunday roadside meeting. One such meeting-point was at the road-junction near Cynala in Llangamarch, where each Sunday at mid-afternoon a small group of men would gather to stand smoking and chatting by the hedge. In Abergwesyn favourite meeting-places were Llwynderw turn, and the roadside near Pantycelyn, to which, while their elders were in chapel, the farmers' sons and young farm-workers of the Camarch valley would come over the pass to meet with those of Alltfelen and other farms on the hither side of the hill, and enjoy gossip and racy stories.

In the days before the repeated religious revivals of the nineteenth century continued the work started by the Methodist Revival, the sports loved by men of the Hundred of Builth, as elsewhere, were often violent, sometimes cruel. Theophilus Jones said that before 1800 the most popular Breconshire sports were throwing the bar, wrestling and running, and that these were being followed in his day by hunting, ball-games and drinking, the latter accompanied by drunken singing! Local tradition claims that one of the delights of North Breconshire men in the eighteenth century was 'fencing with staves', quarter-staff fighting, and that it was not until the latter part of that century that the 'Cardis' became proficient at this. We remember the story of the fight at Tregaron Fair in 1785, in which the Jones and Watkins gentry-families were involved. Funeral pomp and drunken aggressiveness merged in the later incident of a post-funeral fight at Pentwyn Inn in 1809. An age of soccer violence and prevalent vandalism can understand the thinness of the line separating partisanship in sport from open violence, and the element of sport in the violence itself. Bare-fist fighting and savage wrestling were for many years features of Breconshire fairs and other gatherings; certainly fighting of all kinds seems to have been not only a favourite sport of Abergwesyn men, but part of the ordinary stuff of life! It was linked to the fierce or stupid addiction to drink long shared by gentry and workpeople alike, here as elsewhere. Until the work of the revivalists in this area, and in particular the long ministry of the Rev David Williams in this area, and the gentling and genuinely civilising influence (on Llanddewi at any rate) of Elizabeth Jones of Llwynderw, Abergwesyn had a reputation for extreme violence, in which no doubt its sport shared to the full. It is sad to read of the old Abergwesyn harper becoming convinced that his music was of Satan, but less sad to learn of some diminishment in cruelty, savagery and sottish drunkenness.

One of the bloodier sports long very popular in and around Abergwesyn was cock-fighting. The 'Welsh Main' was especially brutal. Specimens of the formidable spurs worn by the cocks can be seen together with other items from the apparatus of cock-fighting at the National Museum of Wales. Those who could afford them would get silver spurs to reduce the danger of infected wounds. Steel was second best. It is not known whether cock-fighting (or, for that matter, churchyard games) took place in the two churchyards at Abergwesyn, but it is very probable that it did, as these were considered lucky places for the meeting, the north or devil's side of the church being preferred. The sacred soil was thought to protect the birds against spells cast by rival owners. Cock-fighting long resisted the discipline of the revivalists. Indeed, some of the most ardent local reformers seem to have been at heart devotees of the sport. D.A. Griffiths tells the story of Thomas Jones of Tanyrallt, a stocking-trader who sold to ships the stockings he travelled round to buy. One day, on his way to Llandovery on business, he found the bridge over the Irfon by Llanwrtyd church had collapsed. As the water was high, he had to cross by Llanwrtyd Mill, where at the time David Williams' father was living. There Jones saw a cockerel he knew would make a wonderful fighter. He persuaded Rhysin Siôn, an old man and a neighbour, to talk Isaac, David's brother, into catching the cockerel, promising to buy it or share the profits he was sure it would make. When its absence was noticed, Isaac kept quiet. However, when Rhys, his father, went in a few days' time to the Beulah smithy, he was told of his bird's success in the Llanafan cock-pit, and though he was an opponent of the sport, could not help a thrill of pride at this triumph over the famous Llanafan fighting-cocks!

Well into the nineteenth century cock-fighting remained highly popular. The bird's comb and wattles and the feathers at the throat and under the wings and breast were cut off. The spurs were removed and artificial ones, needle-sharp, were fitted. Often a written charm from a local 'wise man' was inserted into a special socket in one of the spurs. An aficionado of the sport told Griffiths of a little cockerel he bought for a guinea from Vaughan of Pontardulas Mill near Tanyrallt, and entered for a competition at Disserth, Radnorshire. (There were many cockpits once at the various inns of the district, one of the last Radnorshire ones to survive being that at Llanelwedd, adjoining Builth.) The gallant little cockerel was to fight for a three guinea watch for its owner. Salt was spread like snow over the cockpit, to break spells. The narrator's bird was thrown from the bag into the pit, and almost at once ripped out the bowels of his first opponent. The second took longer to dispatch, and by the time the third appeared the little cockerel was weakening. Yet after a protracted and bloody struggle he won again, and secured the watch for his master. After a few days' rest he was the winner at Rhaeadr of £7 in bets and prize-money.

The sums of money changing hands in these contests were small compared to the high play of the cockfights frequented by the gentry. W.H. Howse writes that 'the Gentlemen of Radnorshire were matching their birds against those of the gentlemen of other counties in the 1750s, and continued to do so for at least another 60 years'. Each side had thirty cocks or over fighting in the main, at four or five guineas a battle, and the stake for the final fight to decide the champion might be fifty to a hundred guineas.

Another savage sport, to which a field near Penyrhyddfa by the Devil's Steps was devoted — hence its name, Cae Meirch (Stallions' Field) — was stallion-fighting. It is not known when the last fight took place, but one may conjecture that in such a remote place the sport would have died hard.

The *Gwyl Mabsant* (Parish Wake, feast-day of the patron saint) was once a major event in parish life. D.A. Griffith writes that the Llanwrtyd one used to be held in the grounds of Dôlycoed House, about May Day (not on St David's Day) and was enlivened by dance-music played by Daniel the Harper from Cilycwm in North Carmarthenshire. The week-long feast began on Sunday, and featured football and other games by the day, singing and dancing by night, and much carousing at all hours. Boys and girls would come and stay till the fun was over or their pockets empty. Other North Breconshire parishes, too, had their feasts, in preparation for which young people would take dancing lessons at five shillings a quarter. The *Gwyl Mabsant* in Abergwesyn is said to have ended about 1800 to 1810 for the same reasons as those noted by the Anglican historian of the Vale of Clwyd, the Rev Elias Owen — 'the dissipation, the brutal fights and bickerings'. What he said of North Wales is as true of mid-Wales — the feasts 'included much that was innocent and pleasurable...dancing, penillion singing, games and sports, and trials of strength... Hospitality was profuse, and distant friends were welcomed to every house in the parish'. But, while fostering 'parish patriotism', the feats 'often generated antagonisms between parish and parish, which lasted longer than the wakes', and led to savage fighting, as indeed they did in parts of England. Gradually, as Brian James pointed out when writing of the feasts of the Vale of Glamorgan, 'respectable' people deserted the wakes, which degenerated into the riotous preserve of the wilder members of the community.

Another event referred to by D.A. Griffith as part of the local scene which the nonconformist revivals were gradually to transform was the *cwrw bach* (small beer). A man in straitened circumstances would brew small beer and let everyone know of the occasion. All the young people of the district would congregate to buy the beer and little cakes, to shoot and to draw lots for a pig, a sheep, a watch and so on. It must have been like a tipsy benefit bazaar with assorted raffles. But, says Griffith, it encouraged wantonness!

So, possibly, did the old-style wedding festivities of the area, about which Griffith is intriguing rather than expansive. He extends his disapproval to the old funeral rituals as well, either subconsciously feeling their echoes of 'Popery' — the ritual meal which has been compared to a Low Mass, and the *offrwm* (offering) to the clergyman — or disliking their tendency to end in drinking and brawling. 'Monstrous' is his word to describe the old practices. They were like night-birds, he says, that could not live in the daylight of the Gospel. Such local traditions of old wedding customs as have survived are scanty, but seem harmless enough. A partial list has come down to us of a characteristic 'bidding' (solicitation of marriage-gifts) for the wedding of John Jones of Pwllybô in 1847. The sums given (on the pages which remain) range from 10s 6d (from John's father) to 1s 6d, the most usual amount being 2s or 2s 6d. Vague surviving stories of 'races' at weddings suggest that the district shared the customs once prevalent in rural Wales, of a feigned horseback abduction of the bride and a pursuit over the hills ending in her 'recapture' and arrival at the church.

However incongruous it seems to think of a funeral as a form of recreation, in the wider sense it is, and has always been, just that in the Welsh countryside. It is the summing-up of a life, a not-to-be-missed occasion for widely-scattered relatives, friends and neighbours to meet, to share a meal and a few hours of rest. More than most family gatherings it lends itself to parody, and is open to the suspicion of lugubrious hypocrisy. Yet it has great cathartic value, and few who have heard the great hymn 'O fryniau Caersalem' echoed back to an Abergwesyn graveside from the hills across the river will deny even today's diminished ritual a poignant beauty.

One of the most macabre entertainments was a visit to a public hanging. Earlier executions took place near the scene of the crime, as did the hanging in August 1789 on Garth Hill of Lewis Lewis the younger for the murder of Thomas Price on the hills nearby. Later, public hangings were carried out on a scaffold raised between the walls of Brecon Gaol and the river. Spectators, including some from the Abergwesyn area,thronged the bridge and the river-bank at the hanging in April 1845 of Thomas Thomas of Maesyradwy, Carmarthenshire for the murder of a carrier on the highway in Trecastle. There was a great crowd in April 1849, too, of ten thousand to twenty thousand according to one spectator, for the execution of another convicted murderer. Not till the 1850s did these public hangings cease.

Even after David Williams' ministry and the efforts of other reformers had started to bear fruit in huge congregations, it was long before the traditions of revelry, the endless potations and the ready aggressiveness were modified. The chapels were too small to hold the Communion Sunday crowds, but after chapel those crowds would move on to the taverns. At Llanwrtyd, young people thronged to hear David Williams, then spent the rest of the day at the Dôlycoed Hotel or the New Inn. Perhaps they were not actually members of the chapel, Griffith suggests! Gradually, however, the revivalists won the day. The pendulum swung from eighteenth century licence to the total restrictiveness of the Welsh Sunday as our immediate forebears knew it, and which in its turn bred a new reaction.

With the Gwyl Mabsant gone, emphasis shifted to other treats, such as the many fairs, including those at Builth, Garth, Newbridge, Brecon and Llandovery. A few who could afford to went as far afield as Chester and Wrexham fairs, and if they had no gig of their own to take them to a coach town were prepared to walk great distances to get the coach. This willingness to work hard at pleasure died hard hereabouts. Sid Wright, staying in 1947 at the Rhiwnant farm over Bwlch y Ddau Faen, was amazed at the journey undertaken by a daughter of the farm for a day out at Aberystwyth fair. He details her homeward route — '15 miles by bus up the Ystwyth valley to Ffair Rhôs, followed by an eight-mile walk over the hills by the Teifi lakes to the Claerwen Farm', where her brother met her with a spare pony, on which she rode the remaining eight miles, and said the trip was well worth it.

Hunting, which Theophilus Jones referred to as growing in popularity at the beginning of the nineteenth century, has never lacked its following in Abergwesyn. The local hunt, the Irfon and Tywi, is now based in Llanafan fawr. Out of season, when a fox has been attacking sheep, a small band of mounted farmers can be seen setting out in a businesslike way equipped with guns, and spades for digging out, and accompanied by a tail-waving straggle of amiable, shaggy, eccentric hounds and a yapping of minute terriers.

Hare-coursing was popular early in this century; the school logbooks refer to an annual match 'in the neighbourhood'. Sheepdog trials are still a favourite event. In 1979 the Abergwesyn sheepdog trials were revived for the first time for many years, and have since then become once more an annual event, including refreshments at the old schoolroom. This occasion of sport and feasting has replaced the former village winter party in the schoolroom. The sheepdog trials are held, as in former years, in a field of Tymawr farm. The Llanwrtyd trials take place near the Abernant Lake Hotel.

Sport is no longer habitually violent here. The ball-playing which Theophilus Jones noted is popular in various forms. Llanwrtyd has its football team, while inns still offer a range of games including darts and quoits, the latter no longer played with horseshoes but with rubber rings. Llanwrtyd has an annual Show, too, and a Carnival, while the school treats of earlier years have been followed by school parties, plays and sports which involve parents and other friendly adults as they have always done.

The great event of the district in July is the Royal Welsh Agricultural Show, held on its permanent show-ground at Llanelwedd, adjoining Builth. It is an event in which the whole local community feels involved, a meeting-place of friends, colleagues and long-separated kinsfolk, and one to which come a host of visitors from further away. To its obvious importance for the dissemination of farming know-how, for the efficient advertising of new products and the upholding of standards in stock and crops is added the opportunity of a long day out in congenial company, with a variety of show-ring events and peripheral displays — an opportunity rarely missed by Abergwesyners, most of whom make a point of going to Builth for at least one of the show-days.

Sales have always provided entertainment, especially the larger sales, auctions of property, furniture and farm- stock. To the pleasure of a day out is added the interest of studying the prices fetched, even if one has not gone to bid.

Miscellaneous events of the nineteenth century — a lecture on mesmerism, with demonstration, at Builth in 1850, the visit of an American circus to Brecon in 1851, early railway-trips, the treats and parties of the church, chapel and school, can all be paralleled (except perhaps for the thrill of a quite new form of transport) in today's assorted fare. The main difference is in the freshness of the entertainments then, the trouble taken to get to them, the savouring of them, the storing-up, and, on the other hand, the comparative taking for granted now. 'Comparative' only, for there is still a powerful will to enjoy, and the sense of wonder is not dead.

One of the best-loved recreations of Abergwesyn and the nearby parishes, as indeed throughout Wales, has always been music, from the dance-music of the harpers and fiddlers who make an occasional appearance in old registers and lists of tenants to the choral singing of church and chapel, of mourners at the graveside, of village choirs, and of family and friends at home. Concerts and *eisteddfodau* have from their inception attracted an eager audience, and the relative merits of the competing choirs and soloists are still a talking-point in the district. Some families treasure a boxful of the little bags that used to be presented to local eisteddfod winners. Something of this musical activity and its local celebrities will be referred to in the next section, and in the following chapter.

(ii) Tourism and the Spa-Country

For years, for centuries, even, some of the men and women of North Breconshire have spent part at least of their working lives in the tourist trade. Many people, some from the cities, some from a dissimilar countryside, have come to explore the remote Hundred of Builth, or simply to rest here: to enjoy its beauty and peace, to puzzle over its enigmas, to feel the frisson of its wildness. Among the visitors, of divers types and occupations and nowadays of divers nations, are writers, painters, bird-watchers, fishermen, golfers, botanists, motorists, cyclists, walkers and trekking enthusiasts. Some of the old farmhouses and cottages have become 'second homes', some are let to holidaymakers in summertime. Bed-and-breakfasting is a useful addition to farmhouse incomes. There are Youth Hostels in the fastnesses of the Elenydd. Builth, Llangamarch and Llanwrtyd have a number of hotels, Abergwesyn till recently had one at Llwynderw.

In the past, however, what drew many of the visitors to the Builth area was the pursuit of health. Theophilus Evans, clerical grandfather of the county historian, wrote in 1732 of a tradition that 'about two or three hundred years ago' the *ffynnon drellwyd* (stinking well) of Llanwrtyd had enjoyed a 'greater repute, especially in all scorbutic cases, than the Bath', and surmised that its long neglect might be accounted for by a former lack of suitable accommodation for 'the valetudinarian sick'. It was Theophilus Evans himself who publicised in a letter of 1732 to the editor of the *St James' Chronicle* the virtues of the 'stinking well', which he himself had tested after seeing a cheerful and healthy frog pop out of its noisome and unknown depths. Finding his scurvy greatly improved, he made known to others the healing powers of what was to become the Dôlycoed Well, and thus launched Llanwrtyd, or rather Pontrhydyfere, on a new life as the busy little spa of Llanwrtyd Wells, the 'Matlock of Wales'.

Builth and Llangamarch, too, bear the suffix 'Wells'. The official guide to Builth states that its reputation may date back as far as Roman times, and that 'during the 18th and 19th centuries this was a much visited small spa'. Edwin Davies was surprised that Jones did not mention the Builth spring; in fact he did, but it was in his account of Llanfihangel Bryn Pabuan parish, where the Park Wells were situated, in the grounds of the old Williams mansion of Parc ar Irfon, about one and a half miles from Builth town. There were saline, sulphur and chalybeate springs close together in a handsome pump-room. Theophilus Jones called it an unfashionable spa, and thought the waters less efficacious than those of Llandrindod, but quite good enough for half of those who frequented watering-places 'to dissipate their property and waste their time'. In 1830 Dr Daubeny, professor of chemistry at Oxford, referred to the Builth springs as 'more newly discovered' than those at Llandrindod, and twice as strong. Not far away from Parc were the Glannau Wells, chalybeate and sulphur. Lewis in 1833 praised the 'well-established' Parc springs, but thought it a pity that Builth did not provide more accommodation for visitors. In June 1870 Kilvert met Powell, the Clyro blacksmith, 'hobbling' from Hay. Powell talked of trying the Builth mineral waters for his rheumatic and gouty foot. Probably about that time visitors needing a Builth doctor would have been cared for by Dr Bennett, who, wrote Kilvert in May 1871, was attending Morris, the sunstruck Llysdinam waggoner, who had 'brain inflamation'. The doctor was 'shaving his head, bleeding, leeching, blistering, fomenting with gin and vinegar and water. Blister on the nape of the neck, leeches on the forehead, hot bottles to his feet, mustard plasters to the calves of the legs'. Ice for Morris' head was ordered from a Hereford fishmonger.

The frog which played its part in the rediscovery of the Llanwrtyd springs is matched by a pig in the Llangamarch story. In a year of drought, a cottager, searching for his 'grunter', tried as a last resort the dried-up bed of the river. There was the pig, cooling itself in a little water that issued from the parched ground. The cottager, thirsty, scooped up a mouthful of water, but hastily spat it out. His story of the evil-tasting spring led to an analysis being made of its properties. Poole writes that the Llangamarch wells had in his time (the 1880s) ''long enjoyed a respectable though somewhat local reputation'', having been recommended by Dr Thomas of Llandovery, and also by Dr Prestwood Lucas of Brecon. Not till 1833 was a complete analysis made, by Dr Dupré of the Westminster Hospital, who pronounced the really interesting ingredient to be the rare barium, a specific for heart disease, and found otherwise only at Kreuznach in Germany. 'The railway communication is excellent,' said Poole, 'and Llangamarch has evidently a very cheerful, if not prosperous, future before it', with its 'several good private lodging residences' to supplement the Cammarch Hotel. Poole, and Edwin Davies (who wrote about 1900), mention the part played in publicising the Llangamarch spring by William Smith, agent for the Maitlands of Garth House. Soon after 1900 the Lake Hotel appeared, with its 'ornamental grounds'; it offered shooting and fishing. The barium spring had given Llangamarch 'some celebrity.... A well has been constructed upon the rock and machinery erected' for raising water for baths, and for drinking. It had 'a peculiar saline taste' and was 'very slightly opalescent'. Bradley, passing through about 1902, through Llangamarch 'a delectable little watering-place'. It remained little, despite the scarcity-value of its waters, and as a spa gradually fizzled out, like the others in mid-Wales, towards the mid-twentieth century; though David Verey was hard on it when he called it in 1960 the 'dreariest' as well as the 'smallest' of spas! Llanwrtyd held no appeal for him, either; and indeed one cannot but agree that disused and sheep-fouled pumprooms are 'depressingly forlorn'. But the fishermen and walkers, the trekkers and kite-watchers, still come to the spa-country, knowing little and caring less about the trickle of disused healing-waters. Only Llandrindod, the Radnorshire spa which had its time of glory as a more fashionable spa than these, has made attempts to revive public interest in the virtues of its wells.

Llanlleonfel, though never developed as a 'Wells' village, has its sulphur spring on the slope of the hill on which the church stands. Here went the servants from Garth House, when they were told to fetch water from Llanwrtyd. It was easier and pleasanter to laze on the hill and bring back water from their local spring.

To return to Llanwrtyd ('Town', to Abergwesyn people): after Theophilus Evans' publicising of his own cure, the Wells gained in reputation. The *Hereford Journal* in January 1771 carried an advertisement of the lease of Dôlycoed by Mr William Davys, who would consider 'only qualified inn-keepers' as tenants of 'that well-known and accustomed House', to which 'Company' resorted 'for the benefit of those incomparable waters, called Llanwrtyd, or Stinking Wells'. The house, outbuildings and 'exceedingly fruitful' walled garden with 'Wall-fruit' could be let with 'any quantity of Land to the amount of 300 acres'. On 9 June 1779 the same journal advertised the Dôlycoed Hotel, run by William Gardener, who is said to have been formerly the Garth butler. He had 'laid in a fresh stock of Liquors and much improved his accommodation.... The waters [were] now in the highest perfection'.

In 1804 Richard Fenton, touring Wales, found in Llanwrtyd Wells (he was already using the name) 'a most romantick beautiful retirement'. The Dôlycoed was a 'fine river-House' with very good food. For a light luncheon he was given roast chicken and custard pudding, for which the proprietor did not want to make any charge, as Fenton ate so little! There were two good large oak-wainscoted rooms downstairs, and upstairs 'a number of small tidy bedchambers', enough for twenty-five to thirty beds. Fenton sampled the springs, the 'small run' of chalybeate and the sulphur well with its rotten-egg aroma. Llanwrtyd was quite his favourite mid-Welsh spa; the Builth springs were too far from the town, while Llandrindod he thought 'a miserable place'. About that time the Rev. John Evans called Llanwrtyd a 'celebrated spa for the South Walian gentry': a spa remote and difficult of access, and (he thought) with bad accommodation, yet 'well-frequented during the summer months, and full of gaiety'.

In 1817, Lord Dynevor, writing to persuade his friend Charles Abbot to try the cure at Llanwrtyd for a severe bout of erisypelas, was uncomplimentary about the accommodation. 'Very poor,' he called it. 'Neither wine, spirits or beer are to be had within several miles' (a surprising statement), 'and mutton and trout is your only food, very good bread and excellent water. The House is very old and not well furnished but the beds are not bad and you live in common all together'. However, he had high praise for the non-purgative sulphur-water of the 'great well', and mentioned the 'strong chalybeate spring' nearby. ('Funnon bwrlwm' and other springs are referred to in deeds of 1812 relating to the property of the Jones family of Dôlycoed.)

The first edition of the O.S. 1 inch map (1833) marks Llanwrtyd village by old St David's church. It was Pontrhydyfere, at a meeting of roads further downstream, which was developed into modern Llanwrtyd Wells, though no great change took place till the railway arrived in 1867. The lower village had started to gain a little in importance almost one hundred years earlier, when about 1770 the fairs were moved there from old Llanwrtyd by order of the Gwynnes (lords of the manor), it is said in consequence of a quarrel between two local families; possibly the affair had been kept up as a 'faction fight', which Gwynne hoped to defuse by distancing the excitement of the fair from the home-ground of the angry families. Lewis in his *'Topographical Dictionary'* of 1833 tells us that since the discovery of the sulphur spring Llanwrtyd had become 'during the summer season, a place of resort for respectable families'. These were catered for at the Dôlycoed, which had recently been enlarged. 'The village,...pleasantly situated on the bank of the Irvon, [derived] an air of cheerful activity from the resort of visitors, and [had] been greatly improved'. But by 1850 Kilsby Jones was complaining of Welshmen's lack of enterprise in developing the village, advertising the Wells and providing amenities to entice English visitors. It was probably much the same 'thoroughly Welsh' village that charmed C.F. Cliffe in 1848 — 'a primitive bridge, and less "runs" of water — a nest of rude thatched cottages on a rocky strand, with their peat-smoke curling upwards...wild round brown hills, with bluffs that *suggest* much — an air of profound repose'. One could 'rough it' at the Belle Vue Inn, or find comfort at the Dôlycoed, *'the* "Boarding House"', which then charged £1. 15s per week for board and lodging 'at the first table, including the use of the waters' amid 'prettily laid out grounds', or £1. 3s at the second table. It also provided self-catering accommodation. The season here began in May.

A.G. Bradley writes that it was not until the mid-nineteenth century that the Dôlycoed well was enclosed. By the time that he visited the place about 1902 there was 'a fine pumphouse' in the grounds, where 'gaseous waters' could be seen bubbling up. After it fell into disuse, the spring still pulses from the earth; the great basin, with a slanting mirror above it, behind the counter in the derelict pump-room, was furred with fungus-like deposits and blue with the mineral salts which are apt to dye baths and wash-basins in this country of springs. The slabs around the top of the basin were patterned with a profusion of little fossils.

Before the coming of the railway, the nearest point which could be reached by public coach was Builth. Kelly's *'Directory'* for 1830 shows that every Tuesday, Thursday and Saturday afternoon at two o'clock during summer the 'Imperial' from Newtown to Merthyr Tydfil via Brecon called at the Upper Lion. The coach from Merthyr to Newtown through Llandrindod Wells called on the same days at 11.00 a.m. Carriers' carts left Builth, one for Brecon and one for Hay, and on Friday another went to Newtown. The railway, coming from Llandrindod in 1867 and continuing to Llandovery in 1868, brought increased custom and prosperity. In 1867 there were plans for a brickyard, a billiard-hall and a library, none of which, however, materialised, though brickworks flourished for some time at Garth and Cynghordy not far-away.

It was claimed that Llanwrtyd's sulphur water was the best in all Britain except possibly for the wells of Harrogate. The geologist Roderick Murchison thought Llanwrtyd ought to be enjoying a world-wide reputation. Pryse's 'Handbook to the...Mineral Springs' (1874) quotes Dr Blenkinsop, once of Abergavenny, who wrote in the *Gentleman's Magazine* of the virtues of the sulphur spring, the water of which 'sits easily on the stomach and passes quietly through the kidneys'. It was of value for treating 'a stomach impaired by drinking spirituous liquors', and a diuretic useful in kidney and bladder complaints, as well as for 'lowness of spirits and inveterate scurvy'. Both sulphur and chalybeate springs were analysed by Mr Herepath, who considered them successful in cases of dyspepsia, skin diseases, gravel and nervous debility. Dr Garrod, F.R.S., said the chalybeate spring was valuable for poverty of blood and during recovery from many 'chronic afflictions'. Dr Lingen, who first went to Llandrindod in 1858, agreed, but warned against treating mineral waters as a universal panacea. Dr Macpherson added to the list of successfully treated complaints 'bronchial irritation and threatened tuberculosis'. 'Patients usually begin with drinking two or three glasses of the sulphur water at a quarter of an hour's interval before breakfast, and two or three wine-glassfuls of the chalybeate in the afternoon'.

An anonymous physician recommended delicate patients not to drink more than five or six glasses a day, but said that more robust people might take as many as eight. Those with stubborn skin complaints might 'adopt, with precaution, the practice of the Welsh peasantry, of drinking as much as the stomach will bear with impunity'. The sulphur water was best on an empty stomach, the chalybeate on a full one. Epsom salts or 'lenitive electuaries' might be taken. A course of treatment should last at least three weeks, and might take up to three months. Bathing in the waters might increase the good done by drinking them.

The 1874 'Handbook' refers to the 'animated and enjoyable scene' at the recreation ground near the Dôlycoed pumprooms — cricket, croquet, quoits and archery in progress, while the less active visitors talked, read, sketched, and of course drank the waters. 'All are thoroughly enjoying themselves; for whether it be from the extreme purity of the air, the beauty of the scenery, or the invigorating and exhilarating effect of the waters, time never seems to hang heavy at Llanwrtyd'. In the village were to be found hardly any 'persons listlessly wandering.... The village itself bears the aspect of cheerfulness, cleanliness and comfort', combining the amenities of town and country. The little guide-book recommends the walk or drive to Abergwesyn and the Wolf's Leap, and whets the appetite of botanists with a reference to the Osmunda Regalis fern at Abergwesyn, rare river-plants and grasses on the banks of the Irfon and Wye, reindeer-moss on nearby hills, and stag's horn moss on Moelfre not far away. Today, rescued from Forestry ploughing by the pleas of a 'summer resident', the globe-flower flourishes in a field near Pwllybô.

As the spa gained in reputation, other hotels and boarding-houses grew up in the lower village near the station. Pryse's 'Handbook' advertises the Neuadd Arms, a 'family and commercial hotel and boarding house', which had recently been built in the square. A week's board and lodging with chambermaid and waitress was £1.15s. A private sitting-room was 2s 6d a day, and servants might be boarded for a guinea a week. 'An omnibus passes the door to meet every train'. The Belle Vue family and commercial hotel, proprietress Miss Sarah Owen, called itself 'old established' in 1874. It offered 'home comforts combined with moderate charges', good stabling, lock-up coach-houses and free fishing. The Dôlycoed was now run by Benjamin Jones. It had 'recently undergone thorough repair, [was] elegantly furnished, and replete with every convenience', and proud of its situation by the 'celebrated Preserved Trout Stream' of the Irfon, and within three hundred yards of the Springs, which were free to its guests. It, too, was served by the train-omnibus. First table here had now gone up to £2.10s per week; dinner was at three o'clock, and at one o'clock for the cheaper commercial table. A warm bath was two shillings, a cold bath one shilling. 'Superior apartments' were advertised by David Williams at Britannia House, 'pleasantly situated overlooking the River Irfon'. Any new book or periodical could be ordered from Thomas Lewis, bookseller, stationer and local newsagent.

Captain Penry Lloyd, the second of three surviving sons of John Lloyd 'the Poet', one of the Lloyds of Dinas, further developed Llanwrtyd as a spa when he opened the Victoria Wells in 1897, Diamond Jubilee year, and provided a new road to the village. Another spring was struck in 1908. Captain Lloyd had retired to live first at Cwmirfon Lodge, the family holiday home in his youth, and later built himself a new house in the village, Ffynnonau (Wells). He was greatly liked and respected by visitors to the Victoria Wells and by many local friends, who put up to his memory a monument which still stands by the old Wells buildings, where Penry was often to be found walking and talking with visitors to his beloved wells. He provided for them a bowling green, croquet lawn and skittle alley. A county councillor and a leader in the Volunteer movement, a man of many interests and activities, who was described at eighty-two as 'physically one of the finest men' in Brecon and Radnor counties, Penry Lloyd was genuinely missed by Llanwrtyd and the whole district when he died in March 1913. Between four hundred and five hundred people gathered in front of Ffynnonau to see the funeral cortège move off via Victoria Wells to the old church near Dinas.

The first of the Victoria Wells was sunk to a depth of seventy-six feet in felspar rock. Eventually there were four — sulphur, magnesium, lithia saline and chalybeate. Hot and cold electric baths were advertised for weak nerves, neuritis, rheumatism and anaemia. There was also a solarium. In 1922 a mineral spring was found on Henfron farm, just outside the village on the Llandovery road, and developed by John Price; here, too, a pump-room was built.

One of the chief attractions of Llanwrtyd Wells during the summer months used to be its music, the *eisteddfodau* and concerts for which a pavilion was specially built. The first eisteddfod is said to have been held in August 1863 on Dôl John. The *Hereford Times* carried reports of these events, like the eisteddfod of July 1866, for which a pavilion holding 4,000 people was necessary. Addresses included one by the president, W. Campbell Davys, Esq., of Neuadd Fawr in North Carmarthenshire, of a family which had intermarried with Jones of Dôlycoed. The forceful Rev Kilsby Jones of Glenview also made a speech. In the evening there was a concert. Not all the *eisteddfodau* were housed in a custom-built pavilion. In an article in the *Brecon and Radnor Express* Canon

Jones-Davies quotes from the *County Times* of 10 July 1869 an account of the Llanwrtyd eisteddfod on 30 June of that year, when at 'the beautiful and much-resorted [sic] wells of Llanwrtyd' a large gathering of people from 'Brecon, Builth, Rhandirmwyn, Trecastle, Llandovery etc.' crowded on a glorious day into a suffocating little chapel to hear music, recitation and adjudication.

Concert-performers and competitors in the eisteddfod, coming from many parts of Wales, were often very talented. These events, like the morning prayer-meetings in local chapels, were for the benefit of visitors. Local farm-people were busy with summer work; residents of Llanwrtyd were occupied with looking after the influx of summer guests. It was only these guests who had the leisure to enjoy regularly the social events of the season; local people joined in as an occasional treat. Those who can still remember those summer days speak of the 'good spirit' prevailing, the singing for singing's sake, performers out to please and listeners out to enjoy. There was some ceremony in the proceedings, even a 'chairing of the bard', complete with a presentation miniature chair in china. Visitors chose a committee to organise the events and raise and distribute prize-money.

Despite the early reference to Llanwrtyd as a summer resort of 'respectable families' — 'respectable' with the older implication of substantial and socially desirable — and the continuing function of the Dôlycoed Hotel as a house for the more genteel, it was mainly as a working-class spa, above all a haunt of South Wales miners and their families, that Llanwrtyd Wells later developed. The tall boarding-houses were crammed with such holiday-makers, who ate their meals in shifts, and on a fine night, after returning from the evening dose of the waters, would sit out at the street's edge and sing Welsh hymns and songs till bedtime. A.G. Bradley in 1903 thought the 'shady walks' round the pump-rooms an ideal place for seeing Welsh people at their ease. 'Five or six times a day, before and after every meal, the long procession of patients and holiday-makers traverses the half-mile of road which connects the village and the Dôlycoed grounds'. There were people 'of all ages and almost all classes', about half of them speaking Welsh, and most in a cheerful, garrulous mood. Baptist preachers playing croquet, North Welsh parsons discussing 'Church statistics and the price of sheep', young men spontaneously singing part-songs as they strolled along, Cardiganshire farmers 'talking chapels and crops', their wives knitting and gossiping, old men enjoying a joke, all were there, some of them drinking so heavily of the waters as to suggest they were doing it for a bet. The 'barman' said they paid by the day and liked to get their money's worth. Sometimes in the evening Tom Roberts, the Builth harper, would play Welsh airs under a tree outside the pump-room, and the young people (or those not too strictly puritanical) would dance. By ten o'clock silence had returned; the village guests had all gone back to bed, singing part-songs on the way. (Recently, a local family, sitting by the fire with a solfa hymn book to sing their favourite hymns, lamented the present decline in the old skill of spontaneous part-singing, rare now here even in chapel services.)

Golf could once be played at Llanwrtyd; the 2½ inch O.S. map marks a 'Golf Course (Private)' about half a mile north-east of the Abernant Lake Hotel, on ground then that hotel's property. Now a track, wide at first, leads into a wasteland past the boundary-ridges of forgotten farms, and loses itself in the grassy lands towards Prysiau Fawr. There was a good race-course, too, at Llanwrtyd, near the lake, between the river and the present Glanirfon bungalow. The ground formed a natural grandstand. Mr David Jones of Abergwesyn remembers hearing on a still day, from his childhood home of Brongilent, voices and music coming up the valley from the loudspeaker at the racecourse. It still existed in 1938. His brother-in-law, Mr Fred Richards, created a local record by winning the point-to-point five times.

Llanwrtyd as a spa was dying by the 1930s. The workers of South Wales had tasted holidays further afield, and mid-Wales had lost its glamour for them. Gone were the days, described by a Llanwrtyd shopkeeper some years ago, when as a boy in the small market-town of Llandovery he would be unable to sleep for excitement at the thought of next day's Sunday School Treat — a trip to Llanwrtyd Wells. The Second World War brought a renewal of life, in a different form. Bromsgrove School was evacuated to the village, taking over empty hotels and boarding-houses. A Czech school followed. When South Welsh towns began to be bombed, Llanwrtyd Wells was one of the places in mid-Wales that became the refuge of families who had been bombed out, or feared they might be so. With peace, this temporary life departed. Soon, the holiday trade revived. Walkers and campers came as ever, and now trekking became popular; Llanwrtyd proved an ideal centre for exploring the Abergwesyn hills and valleys and other beauties of North Breconshire and North Carmarthenshire. Along the old tracks and the narrow roads, throughout the summer months, pass the colourful files of riders, penetrating recesses of the countryside that otherwise only walkers see. Those walkers now enjoy at Llanwrtyd several major events of their own, in which walks are of lengths graded according to individual stamina or perseverance, the Lord Crawshay Memorial Walk, the Drovers' Walk, the International Four Days Walk, the Real Ale Ramble and the New Year Walk. There are a number of other popular annual events. An old-established one is the Man Versus Horse Handicap, sometimes enlarged to admit mountain bikes; the Abergwesyn hills and valleys provide a large part of the course, and even in rain attract crowds of onlookers. Perhaps the most extraordinary 'happening' (stranger even than 'Morris in the Forest') is the Bog-Snorkelling Championship, greatly enjoyed, as it caters for the messy toddler who lurks in adult hearts. For horse-enthusiasts there are in autumn the Red Dragon Long Distance Rides, and for cyclists the International Four Days' Mountain Bike Rides.

Guests are welcome here, and not only for the cheerful ringing of tills that comes with holiday-time, but for the life and interest they bring to a sociable village that grew up around the holiday trade. Chatter and pleasant bustle, new things to talk and laugh about, adding to the store of topics mulled over in the winter months: foreign voices on Heart of Wales Line trains, rucksacks piled by the seats: visiting cars parked by the Cambrian Factory: newcomers poring over maps in the square: memento-hunters strolling over the bridge: passers-through idling with a pint of beer in the sunshine, and scrutinised by a watchful group of elders of the village — it is all part of the ceremony of summer, enjoyable still. 'We shall have the visitors soon', people start saying in early spring; there is summer in the words.

The spa-country has not been without its visiting celebrities, a few famous, and many acclaimed more locally. We must include among them the anonymous visitors who heard 'Sospan Fach' being enthusiastically rendered by a group of impromptu singers at Llanwrtyd, and took it home to Llanelli, where it became the team-song and the best-known of all the 'anthems' of Welsh rugby crowds. It is said to have been written by a young theological student on holiday at Llanwrtyd Wells.

One of the most famous visitors to North Breconshire was Lady Hester Stanhope, who stayed for a time near Builth, took the waters at Llanwrtyd, and knew Abergwesyn well. Born in 1776, the eldest child of the third Earl Stanhope, Lady Hester lived at Chevening till she was about twenty-four, when she left home for her grandmother's house in Somerset. There, Kinglake tells us, she passed some of the time breaking in vicious horses for local people. Later she moved to London, and managed her uncle William Pitt's household in Montagu Square. She was good-looking, efficient, imperious, eccentric and sharply witty, and inspired perhaps more fear than love. At her uncle's death she continued to live in his house on the pension he left her, but in 1810, grief-stricken at the death of her brother and that of her beloved Sir John Moore, and disenchanted with fashionable life, she left Britain forever.

The stories told of her visits to North Breconshire in 1808 and 1809 show her adventurousness, aggressiveness and love of organising, and the sheer oddity of the woman who was later to become a chieftainess of the Druses on Mount Lebanon. Bradley writes that another London visitor to Builth in 1808, Lord Kensington, called in (or had thrust upon him) the help of Lady Hester when his child swallowed an ear-ring. 'Builth, with the exception perhaps of the local chirurgeon, looked on with admiration and bated breath' — but we are not told whether the child survived. Lady Hester was only too fond of physicking her neighbours and dependents and 'prescribed vigorously for the sick of Builth' and the area around. Her patronage probably helped the growing popularity of the Llanwrtyd spring, too.

While she was staying at the Royal Oak Hotel in Builth, the thirty-two year old Lady Hester 'formed violent attachments to one or two persons in the place, taking them long hours on horseback with her through the wild parts of South Wales, their baggage strapped on pack-horses'. She was fond of the journey through Abergwesyn into the wilderness of Elenydd, and in the rigours of these uncompromising hills found a foretaste of the remoteness she was later to court in more exotic surroundings. One of her chief favourites was a talented young man, an artist of about twenty years of age, Thomas Price, a clergyman's son, born at Pencae'rhelem near Llanfihangel Bryn Pabuan church. He later took orders, and under his bardic name of Carnhuanawc became well-known throughout Wales as a scholar, writer, translator, musician, naturalist, antiquarian and *eisteddfodwr*. Some of his drawings were used by Theophilus Jones as illustrations for the *'History of Brecknockshire'*. Carnhuanawc's chief work was probably his *'History of Wales and the Welsh to the death of Llewelyn ap Gruffydd'*.

During her visit of 1808, Lady Hester saw and liked the farmhouse of Glanirfon at Cilmeri, the village where now stands a memorial to Prince Llewelyn the Last of Wales, who was killed nearby in 1282. After Sir John Moore's death the following winter, Lady Hester made arrangements through Thomas Price's father, the Rev Rice Price, to leave London for Glanirfon, and in a long series of letters sent detailed instructions about how to kill her mutton, mix paint and choose wallpaper. As her personal servant she engaged the daughter of the vicar of Glascwm in Radnorshire.

Lady Hester arrived in spring in quasi-royal procession. She lived at Glanirfon as a very great lady, her stay there foreshadowing her later years of queening it over the Mount Lebanon tribesmen. 'She kept a coach at Builth, two saddle-horses and a carriage at Glanirfon, and reigned a Lady Bountiful among the simple folk of the Wye and Irfon valleys. She distributed cloth and flannel generously, and in return seems to have asked only the privilege of physicking the natives to her heart's content'.

After leaving England in 1810, Lady Hester wandered through the

Middle East and eventually settled at the lonely villa of Djoun in the hills beyond Sidon. She is said to have laid claim to spiritual powers. For a while she held absolute sway over the Druse tribesmen, who venerated her; but she died poor, helpless and deserted.

Another famous traveller to have explored the regions round Abergwesyn was George Borrow, who during the mid-nineteenth century referred in his unpublished notebooks (quoted by F. James Johnston in *Country Quest*) to coming over the mountain road from Tregaron to Pentwyn (where he is thought to have breakfasted on at least one occasion) and to leaving Abergwesyn up the hill towards Beulah. He may well mean by this the ancient road up Rhiw Gareg Lwyd and on to Aberanell, though he could also have followed the road past the mill and smithy and up the 'pitch'. Another article in *Country Quest*, by E.H. Stuart Jones, describes an encounter at the Foelallt Arms, Llanddewi Brefi between a taciturn and suspicious Borrow and his admirer Kilsby Jones. All the latter could get out of Borrow was a grudging admission of having spent the previous night in Abergwesyn. Borrow then collected carpet-bag, umbrella and 'formidable stick', bowed to the company 'and stalked out of the room with giant strides'.

We have already mentioned Anthony Trollope's friendship with Mr and Mrs Williams of Llwynderw. Other famous visitors to the Llanwrtyd area included Madam Patti. The Hamar family of the old-established grocer's shop in Builth Wells supplied delicacies for some of the lavish parties at the singer's home, well to the south, Craig y Nos.

16. Scholarship and the Arts

Llanwrtyd Wells in its heyday was quite a musical centre. The popular concerts and *eisteddfodau* were mainly summer events; but the area could boast resident musicians of some distinction. Such a musician was John Thomas, born in Cardigan in 1839, who married the Llanwrtyd postmaster's daughter, an ex-pupil of Kilsby's school at Glenview. John became postmaster himself up to his death in 1921. The pleasant old *llythrdy* where he lived has now been knocked down for road alterations. A National Eisteddfod prize-winner on more than one occasion, John Thomas composed a number of hymns and anthems, many of which have remained popular. He was awarded an honorary M.A. by the University of Wales in 1920, in recognition of his services to the musical life of Wales. His grave is in the old churchyard of St David's, Llanwrtyd. There too lies Dr David Christmas Williams (1871-1926), of Sunny Bank, Llanwrtyd, who studied music at Cardiff under Dr Joseph Parry, and himself became a tutor in the South Wales College of Music, and an organist and choirmaster at Penarth, and later at Merthyr Tydfil. As conductor, composer and *eisteddfodwr*, too, he is remembered with pride.

Beulah has its musical traditions and its names well-known throughout Wales and beyond. J.W. Parson Price was born in Beulah in 1839, though the family soon moved to Aberdare. He went to America, and after five years on the stage married and settled for a time in Kentucky, where he became a singing master, a career in which he later distinguished himself in New York. Parson Price had a great respect for his uncle David Price, born in Beulah in 1800 and buried there in 1883, an excellent musician and conductor who was precentor at Troedrhiwdalar for many years at a time when the district was rich in whole families of talented singers and instrumentalists. Then, too, there was John Price, born at Llangamarch in 1857; he moved to Ty Cornel, Beulah, when he was five. That was the year, as an article in *Brycheiniog*, vol. III, points out, when Curwen's Tonic Solfa system of reading music was introduced to Wales, and immediately became very popular, offering as it did the opportunity of reading vocal music at first sight. This 'brought choirs into being in almost every village', and started 'the golden age of choral singing in Wales', the age of the *Cymanfa Ganu* (Singing Festival) and the fullest blossoming of the *eisteddfodau*. The leader of all this activity in Beulah was 'Alaw Buellt', Daniel Jones of Llwyncus, singer, conductor and bard. Beulah choir became one of the finest in Wales. It was first with Daniel Jones, and later with a Brynaman teacher, that John Price studied singing and the fundamentals of composition.

After two years in America, John Price returned to Beulah as a carpenter on the Llwynmadog estate. He and his wife made their home at Dolfari, in the village. John Price worked hard for music in the Hundred of Builth, taking solfa classes, adjudicating at local *eisteddfodau*, conducting choirs and helping with music festivals, but above all writing music, mainly tuneful part-songs and hymns, with which he won many prizes, including that of the Tonic Solfa Association of Great Britain. John Price died in April 1930. Carved on his headstone in Beulah chapel burial-ground is the title of one of his best-known part-songs — 'Clyw, f'enaid, clyw' ('Hark, hark, my soul'). There is a local tradition of harp-playing and composing for the the harp. The second Sackville Gwynne, Esq. of Glanbrân was in the second half of the eighteenth century an expert on the triple harp. He was praised by his friend Carnhuanawc as one of the two finest performers of his day. He composed for the harp, too; some of his melodies such as 'Glanbrân' must have been well-known in this district. He brought the North Welsh harpist John Richards from Llanrwst to spend his last days at Glanbrân. The nineteenth century, too, saw harpists welcomed at that house, among them John Wood Jones as resident harpist.

Jane Williams ('Ysgafell') in her collections of Carnhuanawc's work refers to Samuel Davies ('Hen Sarn') of Builth, who at the turn of the eighteenth and nineteenth centuries accompanied open-air dancing, and could play his 'one row' harp while walking. The late nineteenth saw the rise to fame of John Roberts, again of Builth, who was summoned to play the harp before Queen Victoria.

In recent years Mrs Lisa Chamberlain (author of children's stories under the pseudonym Philadelphia Lee) taught operatic singing in the Builth area, and brought concert opera to the Wyeside Arts Centre. 'The Wyeside' has a cinema and a theatre which has housed a variety of entertainments, including performances by peripatetic drama companies such as Theatr Powys.

Some of the scholars and writers who spent part at least of their lives in the Hundred of Builth we have come across in earlier chapters. There were Thomas Huet, Biblical translator and cathedral precentor, who is buried at Llanafan fawr, and who built Tymawr in Llysdinam: the great hymn-writer William Williams of Pantycelyn, curate of Llanwrtyd and Abergwesyn: Charles Wesley, also a celebrated hymn-writer, who married Sarah Gwynne of Garth House: 'Carnhuanawc', the Rev Thomas Price, Lady Hester Stanhope's young dragoman, who became a man of many-sided learning, an artist and a writer: the poet and classical scholar, John Lloyd of Dinas, and his nephew of the same name, rather less of a poet, but a student of and writer upon Breconshire history.

Llangamarch is particularly rich in such associations. Llwyneinon in that parish was the home of Theophilus Evans, already mentioned, the author of *'Drych y Prif Oesoedd'* and grandfather of the county historian, Theophilus Jones. A historic house is Cefnbrith, a whitewashed farmhouse of the longhouse type on the slopes of Epynt; it may stand on the site of an even older longhouse. There in 1559 was born John Penry, the Puritan martyr. In 1587, deeply indignant and hurt at the Church's neglect of his countrymen, Penry published *'The Aequity of an Humble Supplication in the behalf of the country of Wales, that some order may be taken for the preaching of the Gospel among the people'*. Salesbury's translation of the New Testament had been found difficult, so that many Welshmen still had no access to the Bible. Penry pointed this out, and also criticised the appointment of non-Welsh-speaking clergy to Welsh parishes, clerical absenteeism, and the dearth of preachers. The *Supplication* brought its writer into conflict with Archbishop Whitgift. Penry's later connection with the Marprelate tracts is unproven; nevertheless his association with the printing-press which produced among other works his *'Exhortation to the governours and people of Wales'* and *'View of such publike wants and disorders as are in the service of God in Wales'* gave authority (ultra-sensitive then to criticism of the established church) enough excuse to hound him and finally arrest him on a charge of sedition. Sir Thomas Phillips wrote in *'Wales'* (1849) that his trial disgraced the name of English justice. A few days after his conviction he was hurried out of the King's Bench prison in Southwark into St Thomas Waterings, and there hanged. A week before his death, Penry wrote 'My loyalty to my Prince did I never forget'. He sent Queen Elizabeth a farewell message — 'I am a poor young man, born and bred in the mountains of Wales. I am the first, since the last springing of the Gospel in this later age, that publicly laboured to have the blessed seed thereof sown in these barren mountains.... I leave the success of these my labours unto such of my countrymen as the Lord is to raise up after me.... I never took myself for a rebuker, much less for a reformer of states and kingdoms.... Great things in this life I never sought for.... I do from my heart forgive all those that seek my life'. Penry left a Bible to each of his four little girls, the eldest of whom was only four. It was, he said, all he had.

Cefnbryn, also at Llangamarch, is considered by some authorities (others favour Abernant, Carmarthenshire) to have been the birthplace in 1593 or 1594 of a man who hated Puritans — 'odd crack-brained schismatics...[who] make it nothing to interpret every tittle of the Apocalypse'. This was James Howell, the first Historiographer Royal; the post was given him by Charles II in recognition of his support for the Royalist cause. He spent nine years in the Fleet prison as a 'dangerous malignant, much disaffected' to Parliament, but came to terms with the new régime during the 1650s. James Howell's father was, as we have seen, Thomas Howell, curate of Llangamarch, and later rector of Cynwil and Abernant. 'If ever soul entered heaven, his is surely there', wrote James on hearing of his father's death. James' elder brother became royal chaplain and then bishop of Bristol; two of his younger brothers were London businessmen. J.D.H. Thomas in *Brycheiniog*, vol. IX, emphasizes that, coming as he did from a remote Welsh countryside, and 'getting on' conspicuously in the great world, he was in general (though not in all the quirky variety of his career) representative of many of his countrymen in seventeenth century Wales. Not many of them, however, could have matched his versatility; he was among other things in his time steward at a glass-factory, traveller and diplomat, ambassador's secretary, and spy. Howell was also a prolific writer, among his works being the allegorical poem 'Dodona's Grove': a historical study of the Venetian state: another on the 'Pre-eminence and Pedigree of Parliament': and above all his collection of letters, *'Epistolae Ho-elianae'* (*'Familiar Letters'*), which were enjoyed by many distinguished writers of later generations, and were one of Thackeray's two favourite books. Howel met with criticism too. J.D.H. Thomas quotes Carlyle's description of him as 'a quick-witted, loquacious, scribacious, self-conceited Welshman'.

Howell never forgot Wales, nor his interest in the Welsh language, though he wrote that one of his imperfections was that he was 'not versed in [his] maternal tongue exactly as [he] should be'. Yet the 'old British' had not quite been driven out by English — 'the cask savours still of the liquor it first took in'. Many of his letters concern languages and the correspondence of each to the temper of the nation which speaks it. Though among his many skills was that of a translator, he was alive to the shortcomings of all translations, which he thought 'like the wrong side of a Turkey carpet...full of thrums and knots, and nothing so even as the right side'. Writing on 'the original mother tongue of the countries of Europe', including Welsh as the 'prime maternal tongue' of Britain, he dealt with its dialects of Cornish and Armorican (Breton), its relationship with Irish (which he thought had the accent of a subjugated race), and the occurrence of Welsh words in the New World. He makes it clear, however, that it is English which he considers his own language.

Some of Howell's correspondents lived in Wales; J. Davies, near the Hereford border, Howell begs to send a good cheese from that country of fields so lush that, 'as they say here,....if one should put his horses there overnight, he should not find them again the next morning'. To Howel Gwyn, Esq., his 'much endeared cousin', he sends a Welsh epitaph on Prince Madog, 'found in the West Indies...near upon six hundred years since', and discourses on the name Howel, the kings of Armorica who bore it, its persistence in the France of his day, and Welsh place-names which contain it.

Howell had a Welshman's warm family feeling. In February 1637, he wrote to Dr Thomas Prichard that he must go to Bath for treatment for his arm, 'and then I think I will take Brecknock in my way, to comfort my sister Penry, who I think hath lost one of the best husbands in all the thirteen shires of Wales'. In a fanciful will he composed in the Fleet prison, he left his 'best natural affections' to 'the Lord B[ishop] of B[ristol], my brother Howell, and my three dear sisters, to be transferred by them to my cousins their children'. Being 'always naturally affected to woods and Groves', he asked a dear friend to plant a little tree on his grave.

An eighteenth century clergyman and writer, Joshua Thomas, was born at Penpiod in Llanlleonfel. The late Onfel Thomas wrote in *Brycheiniog*, vol. V, that this Oxford Welshman, who as well as his incumbencies held the chaplaincy to the Earl of Powys, was best known for his translation into Welsh of several standard works, especially J. Scott's *'Christian Life'* (1752). Among the subscribers were many of the Gwynnes, including Mrs Charles Wesley (Sarah). Joshua Thomas, a 'genial Christian', as Onfel Thomas called him, settled in Merthyr Cynog not far away; he died in 1759 and was buried in Llanlleonfel.

Penrhiwllwynyfynwent, in Llangamarch, was the birthplace in 1807 of Rhys Price, a Congregational minister and a writer. His family moved while he was young to Llanwrtyd. A self-educated man, a solitary and a book-lover, by trade a weaver, Rhys was ordained in 1835 and later moved to South Wales. His book *'Llysieu-lyfr Teuluiaidd'* (*'Family Herbal'*) was, says the *'Dictionary of Welsh Biography'*, long a standard work. Rhys wrote also some 'didactic revivalist poems'. He died in 1869.

Builth can claim a connection with Thomas Jeffery Llewelyn Prichard, an English-language writer who considered himself the first Welsh novelist, on the strength of his *'Twm-Shon-Catti'*. He wrote also *'Heroines of Wales'* and the *'Llandrindod Guide'* (1857) and planned further guides to other watering places, including Llanwrtyd Wells. Prichard is said to have kept a bookshop in Builth in the mid-nineteenth century. He married a Builth wife. He led a varied life; amongst his occupations was that of travelling actor. He died in Swansea from burns after a fire at his house, shortly after the charity of his neighbours had rescued him from destitution. A valuable account of his life and work is to be found in the articles on him by Sam Adams in *The Anglo-Welsh Review*, vol. 24, and in *Brycheiniog*, vol. XXI.

Another Builth mini-celebrity, forgotten now, was Dr John Downes, a surgeon, whose three-volume book, *'The Mountain Decameron'*, was published in 1836. Lord Glanusk called it 'a morbid book'. Dr Downes loved rambling around the countryside equipped with a small tent; sometimes he took his two sons on these expeditions. He died in 1860.

A twentieth-century writer who was born and brought up in Builth is Hilda Vaughan, novelist, short-story writer and dramatist, whose parents' house there was The Castle (not to be confused with the remains of the real castle). A descendant of the Vaughans of Llansantffraed yn Elfael in south Radnorshire, Hilda Vaughan was married to the novelist Charles Morgan, and mother of the present Lady Anglesey. Several of her novels, certainly the earlier ones, are set mainly in the countryside of the Hundred of Builth, though the place-names are fictitious. 'Llangantyn', for example, is not the real parish of Llanganten, but a fictionalised Builth. *'The Battle to the Weak'* (1925) has as its background in part the hills near Builth, in part the Cardiganshire coast. *'Here are Lovers'* (1926) also takes the Builth area as its setting, as does *'The Invader'* (1928). *'Her Father's House'* (1930) moves south to the Radnorshire side of the Wye valley below Builth. The later short-story *'A Thing of Naught'* returns to the North Breconshire countryside for the main part of the action. A study of Hilda Vaughan by C.W. Newman is to be found in the Writers of Wales series (University of Wales Press, 1981).

Llanafan fawr boasts an excellent children's novelist in Alison Morgan, whose perceptive books, including the well-known *'Fish'*, *'Pete'* and *'Ruth Crane'*, as well as being good stories set amid local scenes and activities, and with characters true to the area as it is today, develop unpretentiously the theme of growing up, of the attainment of self-knowledge, and the acceptance of responsibility. The books contain realistic descriptions of local events, such as an eisteddfod in an Epynt chapel (*'At Willie Tucker's Place'*) and a village show (*'Ruth Crane'*). *'Leaving Home'* and its sequel, *'Paul's Kite'*, mark a departure from the North Breconshire background of Alison Morgan's earlier novels; they take the young central character to Swansea and then London. *'Paul's Kite'* won the Guardian Book of the Year Award. *'Eyes of the Blind'* travels in time as well as place to Judaea at the time of the Assyrian invasion of 701 B.C. The short novel, *'The Wild Morgans'* is a story of the days of great sheep droves from Abergwesyn over the Epynt to Brecon. It will be interesting to see what form this versatile writer's next venture will take.

Llanwrtyd had a Celtic scholar of distinction — Kilsby Jones' one-time pupil, Thomas Powell (1845-1922), of 4, Irfon Terrace, an editor of *Y Cymmrodor* and first lecturer in Celtic Studies at University College, Cardiff. His Llanwrtyd house at one time had a bookshop named after him on its ground floor.

Geufron, on the eastern slopes of Y Garn, near Llanwrtyd, was the home of a young and unhappy Welsh poet, 'Dafydd ap Gwilym from Builth', born 1804. Poole says that he was 'the son of humble parents, and a tailor by trade'. A Calvinistic Methodist who was intended for the ministry, Dafydd became an Independent; he preached at Gelynos, Llanwrtyd. Then the greater financial rewards of the Church ministry tempted him to change again, and he started to attend college at Ystrad Meurig. His college career ended disastrously; he was accused of horse-stealing, and he is said to have been broken in health and spirit thereafter. Later he went to Merthyr Tydfil, some say to work as a tailor, some to translate Harvey's *'Meditations'* into Welsh; probably he did both. The translation is considered a fine one. Dafydd returned to Geufron to die at the age of about thirty, and was buried at Llanwrtyd.

A twentieth century English-speaking poet of the area, and one with Abergwesyn connections, was T. Harri Jones of Cwmcrogau in the Hirnant valley not far from Llysdinam Rhôs. He drowned in Australia in 1965 at the early age of forty-four. His four published volumes were *'The Enemy in the Heart'* (1957), *'Songs of a Mad Prince'* (1960), *'The Beast at the Door'* (1963) and *'The Colour of Cockcrowing'* (1966). His *'Collected Poems'* were published by Gwasg Gomer in 1977. Self-consciously an exile from Wales for the latter years of his life, Harri was always an exile from happiness. He emigrated to Newcastle, New South Wales, in 1959, to lecture in English at the university there, after realising the poor prospects of such an appointment in Wales; but he could not forget the countryside of his early childhood. He writes movingly in many of his poems of the stern, beautiful, passionate land of North Breconshire, sometimes with a desperate nostalgia. His love for it was tormentedly mingled with rebellion against the 'violent unsleeping eye' of the 'only god' that was his — 'the ancient thunderer': against the years of toil weighing down his forebears, 'the quiet men, the burdened women,/ Aloof as foxes', in 'a broken landscape of regrets': against the hypocrisy of chapel deacons, type-figures of repression he sets in contrast to the blazing gorse-fire of sexual love. 'Cwmchwefri Rocks', across the hill from his childhood home, could seem hostile, like 'the stern face of God', something to forget in a goddess-woman's arms. Walking on the rocks 'above even the last sheep-droppings/ And bits of rabbit-fur and peewit feathers', he could see how faith in the impossible was needed to make men 'mow meadows and milk cows' below in the 'sideland farms', in 'such unlikely places'. That was the sort of faith his great uncle Daniel Jones had, who, 'riding, wet to the waist, through the bracken,/ In search of old, thin sheep scarce worth the saving', still 'felt he could prophesy like Isaiah' –

Or he would see somewhere towards Abergwesyn
The city that had no need of the sun, neither
Of the moon, to shine in it.

Harri had Abergwesyn grandparents, who lived at the lonely farmhouse of Llanerch-yrfa below the Devil's Steps. His grandmother is said to have been a fine horsewoman. Of her and Thomas Jones, his 'father's father', he wrote in the poem 'My Grandmother Died in the Early Hours of the Morning' —

A little woman was dead, a little old woman
Who had long confused me with her youngest son.
I did not even think, How small she looks,
And certainly had no thought of her life of labour,
Nor wondered how she who had always been old to me
Had once been whatever beauty the world has
To the old man I now led out of the room,
Out of the house, up the narrow road,
In the dawn he could not see for tears, taking
My hand in his as he'd done when I was small,
Both of us wordless against the dawn and death.

One of Harri's other relatives, Huw Jones, lost an eye in a fight with Rees Williams, the shepherd of Nantystalwyn, who was jailed for six months. The Daniel Jones of 'In Memoriam' is said to have been something of a *bardd gwlad*. He and his wife lived at Llanerch-yrfa till 1897, then went to even more lonely Cefngilfach for a year's shepherding at Trawsgyrch before they moved on to Llanafan. Daniel had twelve children —

always
He had to go back to the cramped house, to too many
Sons and daughters, unprofitable husbandry.

Harri wrote

I hope
That when I am an old man, as he when last
I saw him, I too can continue picking the hostile
Stones off my sour fields, and riding wet to the waist
Through the recurrent bracken, and still
Lift my head to sudden visions and prophesyings.

It was not to be. Harri Jones died still young, far from the ugliness and the ecstatic singing of Pisgah chapel, from the Chwefru and

the small hill Allt-y-clych,
The hill of bells, bedraggled with wet fern
And stained with sheep.

Another modern poet came to Llanafan fawr shortly before his death in January 1974 — Cyril Hodges, who bought a cottage near Troedrhiwdalar. A business-man, half-Scot, half-Cornishman, who grew up in Cardiff and passionately espoused the cause of Wales, both culturally and politically, Cyril Hodges was a prolific writer, sometimes completing a poem a day, according to Meic Stephens in *Poetry Wales*. He was an eager book-buyer and supporter of Anglo-Welsh magazines. His help to the National Eisteddfod, the Welsh Language Society and Plaid Cymru was practical and generous. Meic Stephens writes that till just before his death Hodges was full of projects, including plans for the Llanafan house, which in 1970 he described in 'Letter to Skyros from Troedrhiwdalar' —

This house is old and small, and painted white
In the manner of the land; indeed, is less
House than bwthyn huddled against the road
To watch the letting of the tack in its mean
Restricted acres.

In the poem Hodges identified with those who, living in this uncompromising countryside, have always to 'make a little peace' with their land — the 'frozen avalanche' of the hills, the 'barren threat' of the horizon, the 'snarl' of the desert waste.

Poetry has not been in recent Welsh tradition an esoteric thing, an art for the few. For many years the Eisteddfod has offered the opportunity of fame among their Welsh-speaking countrymen to those who in open competition win the cherished Chair or Crown, and encouraged many others to foster their gift and submit work for adjudication. And behind these bards or potential bards has traditionally existed a whole hinterland of *beirdd gwlad*, folk-poets, whose Welsh verses were the pleasure of their neighbours and the pride of their families. One such was Gwenallt's uncle, who lives in his nephew's well-known poem 'Rhydcymerau' (translated by Anthony Conran). It mourns the passing of a Welsh way of life in a countryside now choked by forests — a life that gave birth to such poets.

My Uncle David used to farm Tir-bach,
And was, besides, a poet, the countryside's rhymester;
His song to the little cockerel was famous in those parts...
It was to him I went for the summer holidays

To watch the sheep and fashion lines of *cynghanedd,*
Englynion, and eight-line stanzas of eight-seven measure...
In our family we'd a real nestful of poets.
And by this time there's nothing there but trees.

There were undoubtedly many such *beirdd gwlad* in Abergwesyn and its neighbouring parishes, who are now forgotten, like the anonymous bard who gave its name to Llofftybardd farmhouse, and William John the Poet, who was buried in Llanfihangel Abergwesyn on 31 March 1752. But some are still remembered, such as Edward Lewis of Penycae (Iorwerth Camarch), who died as recently as December 1947. Mr D. Jones of Abergwesyn Post Office cherished a poem written for his shepherd father by Iorwerth Camarch — '*Abergwesyn rhwng mynyddoedd*' ('Abergwesyn among mountains'). 'Dark as a bag', he said, were the nights through which Lewis walked the hills to tend his sheep, and composed verses as he went. Daniel Jones of Llanerch-yrfa we have already met, and the 'travelling bard' Shelby, who wrote amongst other verses one about the cattle-shoer Ianto Siôn Evans in the 1870s. A recent Welsh article in the *Brecon and Radnor Express* refers to an earlier poet, Shelby Price (ap Rhys), who spent part of his life travelling with the drovers. He was born in Abergwesyn at Llanerch-yrfa about 1760, states the article, and died in 1842 at Rhaeadr, where his widow was a member of Kilsby Jones' Independent congregation. Rough though his verses may have been, Shelby Price was a master of impromptu composition; no-one was quicker with the riposte to another's challenging stanza. According to local tradition he took a lively part in the notorious fight in 1809 after an Abergwesyn funeral!

Theophilus Jones refers to a anonymous Abergwesyn poet who affixed some satirical verses beneath the Latin inscription on a board at Llwydlo fach alehouse on the Breconshire/Carmarthenshire border in Tirabad. Jones also makes several references to Edward Richards, the 'Sweet Swan of Ystrad Meurig' in Cardiganshire, founder of the grammar school there, scholar, critic, antiquary, and a poet whose pastorals take their inspiration from the great sheepwalks of the upper Tywi on Abergwesyn's western borders, and the North-west Breconshire moorlands. Jones says that Richards, who 'predicted in one of his pastorals that he should die deserted and abandoned...was found dead in his bed, his doors locked, but without keys, and no human being within the house'.

In the mid-eighteenth century 'Walter Morgan of Caemawr, a poet', from the Llangamarch side of the Cerdin valley, married Margaret Jones of Nantystalwyn. Llanafan had its Welsh poets too. Theophilus Jones refers to a late fourteenth century poet said in an Ashmolean MS of

Lhuyd's to have been of that parish. He was known as 'Mab y Clochddyn', the Sexton's son, and was probably the same person as Macclaf ap Llywarch. In the first volume of the Myfyrian Archaeology is a poem by him in praise of Gwenhwyfar, wife of Hywel ap Tudur ap Gruffydd. He sounds more like a professional bard than a folk-poet. Who, one wonders, was the seventeenth century Rees David Gitto (he appears in the old parish register of Llanafan) who earned the English nickname of 'The Poet Laureate'? Nineteenth century Llanafan poets included the parish clerk and Guardian of the Poor, and, from 1858, Builth registrar, David Davies, at whose funeral in 1861 was sung a hymn he had recently composed; a verse of it was also engraved on his tombstone at Troedrhiwdalar. Other hymns of his were well-known locally.

North Breconshire, despite its great beauty, cannot claim an association with any painters as famous as John Piper in the Vale of Clwyd or Graham Sutherland in Pembrokeshire. It can boast a slight link with Thomas Jones of Pencerrig, Wilson's pupil, whose sobriquet 'The Artist' seems to indicate that such people were unusual hereabouts. Thomas Jones was related on his mother's side to the Jones family of Cribarth and Llwynderw, and amongst his paintings — not one of his best — is one of Llwynmadog in Abergwesyn, as well as others, more attractive, of Pencerrig and its neighbourhood. Mrs Trahaerne's watercolour sketches of Abergwesyn and Llanwrtyd are of historical interest and not without period charm, but can be fairly compared only with other such pictures by 'accomplished' ladies. Paintings and photographs of local interest are featured in some of the exhibitions at the Wyeside Arts Centre at Builth. Recently this Centre housed an exhibition of the work of the Abergwesyn artist and sheep-farmer Sean Milne, who is particularly noted for natural history studies and illustrative work. The sculptor Ted Folkard, whose 'Saint David' stands in old Llanwrtyd church, has already been mentioned. Another example of his work is an interesting 'Madonna and Child' at Llanfaes church, Brecon. Some of the best work of the South Welsh painter Bernice Carlill is to be found among her mid-Welsh landscapes, including a number of the Abergwesyn area.

This is a district of folk-art, too, verging on craft, the visual impulse having found expression in such forms as the carving of ornament and inscriptions on tombstones and memorial tablets (local burial-grounds contain interesting examples, some at Pantycelyn having traces of colour) — or the carving in wood of lovespoons, walking-stick handles and shepherds' crooks in recent times, for instance, by Mr Powell of Llofftybardd farm. Some members of the Lewis family of Penycae in the Camarch valley — a family now scattered and dwindling — have been skilful horn- and wood-carvers, beautifully shaping the grip of walking-stick and the crook of shepherds' staffs into animal faces, fish or springing horns. Mr David Jones' father was a skilled basket-maker and wood-carver (he could make the traditional love-spoons). For his baskets, some of which were big enough to hold thirty pounds of potatoes, he used complete rounded twigs, rather than split wood favoured by some basket-makers. Another of his skills, which his son learnt and exercised was the making of horsehair halters. Not only has the finished product the beauty of functional appropriateness, but the making itself, with its slow progression of 'the scattering' (separating out the horsehair, black and white), the spinning of the thread, and the repeated plaitings, is itself a gravely and precisely performed ritual, a work of art.

17. Stories

Till the coming of 'the wireless' in the 1920s one of the chief diversions of Abergwesyn people, as we have said, was conversation and the exchange of stories, especially when family and friends gathered round in the long winter evenings. The enjoyment of such evenings has not died, but was even keener in days when it was so much harder to get professional entertainments. People relied more than they now do on what memory and native wit could provide. Even before television came, radio and better transport had caused a break in the old tradition of storytelling, which had been handed down from the earliest times. The Hundred of Builth still has a rich variety of stories, and there are noted raconteurs still living; but it is hard to imagine many of the younger people passing on the matter or the art to their children.

There are stories of the marvellous, stories of violence, and funny stories galore, many of the latter concerned with eccentric local characters whose doings have been wondered over and laughed at for years. These tales depend very much for their effect on the manner of their telling; they are essentially oral. A written version is feeble deprived of the story-teller's changes of pace and volume, his 'long face', his twinkle of the eye, raised eyebrow, quizzical glance at the listener. Such are the stories of 'Billy Boy' of Tafarn y Mynydd on the Epynt. Once, sleeping in the manger at Pentwyn, Billy heard a man who was dossing down on the floor below him grumbling about the cold. 'Come upstairs to bed, then!' cried Billy. He had two faithful dogs, Constable and Stick, and used to be allowed the sheeps' heads which were left for the crows. Once, at the Cammarch Hotel, he tucked into a good meal of fish caught by two guests. 'What am I to tell the gentlemen who caught the fish?' shrieked the distraught serving-maid. 'Tell them another gentleman ate them!' said Billy. His wish was to be buried at Abergwesyn. 'How are you going to get buried over there?' asked a Llangamarch neighbour. 'I'll go there the night before!' was the reply.

Then there was Jacob the Miser, who was so mean he would even salt chickens and rabbits and hang them to be eaten bit by bit. Butter he stored in a scalded chamber-pot. Once he bought half a pound of butter at Beulah, and after walking two miles up the road towards his roadside cottage of Nantygarreg decided that he had been cheated, and that the lump of butter was underweight. Back he trudged to Beulah, and insisted on having his little parcel re-weighed, only to find that it was in fact half an ounce overweight! When the First World War broke out, Jacob was willing to join up. He had weapons, he said — his axe, and his shepherd's club with a spear projecting from it. His spade and clogs would be useful, he thought, for digging trenches, but when the Germans advanced he had every intention of 'setting his clogs on fire' with the speed of his retreat!

Thomas Edwards was a shepherd who once lived at Cwmbach, a little house near Cwmirfon farm, and later worked at isolated Moelprysgau in the upper Tywi valley. Finding meat had been taken from the salted carcase of a pig in the dairy, and seeing the marks of a polecat in the snow outside, Thomas set off after breakfast to follow the tracks. After trudging for miles over the snowy hills, he found the animal had gone to earth in Ciloerwynt Rocks in the Claerwen valley. Resignedly he plodded back mile after mile to Moelprysgau, arriving late in the evening, and set a trap by a hole in the dairy wall. After only a few minutes, the polecat was in the trap.

The funeral of Edwards' first wife at Llanddewi Abergwesyn took place on a day of heavy drifting snow in January 1886. Many of the mourners were unable to get home that night. Farmers suffered great losses during three terrible days of storm. Edwards' second marriage was happier than his first. His employer was downcast one day over the loss of a pig, a loss thought to be particularly unlucky. 'No, boss,' said Edwards. 'It is good luck. The first pig I lost, I buried Jane. The second I lost, I married Elizabeth.' At Elizabeth's funeral in Strata Florida, Edwards was a silent and lonely figure. After the service, he looked down at the coffin lying in the grave, whistled his dogs, and walked away.

In many stories of discomfiture and misfortune, a wry irony takes the place of more genial humour. A well-to-do farmer of Abergwesyn in the last century lived for a time in the Elan valley. Hearing that his bank at Rhaeadr was 'going smash', he went into town to demand his money. 'Certainly,' said the bank manager, 'you can draw it out if you like; but remember, it's quite safe here. Nothing is going to happen to the bank!' So the farmer decided to leave his money where it was; but in less than a week the bank failed, and the money was lost. Hot-tempered at best, the victim was a man to avoid for many a day.

Human greed is remembered and mocked at in local stories, such as the one about a one-time tenant of the Tywi valley farm of Ty'nygraig, who stole 100 sovereigns from Hafdre, about a mile further up the valley. One of his neighbours warned him that he was suspected of the crime, so one dark night he crept along to Hafdre with the money, quietly opened the door, hurled the sovereigns into the house and rushed away. But when the money was found, £1 was missing!

Downstream, on the same bank as Hafdre, the ruins of Nantyneuadd, near an old track over the hill to the Camddwr valley, lie now in the forest, above Llyn Brianne. The farm was an old one —

seventeenth century deeds show it to have been rented then from the Vaughans of Trawscoed by Rees Prichard of Llanddewi Abergwesyn, Gentleman. Here lived in later days William Roberts, who died in 1936 aged ninety-four. He was a larger-than-life character of whom many stories are told. One of the sons of Blaenglasffrwd, a lonely house off the old road to Strata Florida, Roberts had in his youth the reputation of 'a bit of a joker' and 'a bit of a rebel'. His boisterous practical joking included creeping up behind the farm-women as they were doing the laundry in the stream, and pushing them in — more fun for him than for his victims. There was more than a hint of violence in William Roberts' nature. He was once fined £5 for threatening to kill his neighbour at Tywi fechan; there are those still living who can point out the desolate spot where he had dug a grave in readiness.

A farm-girl at Blaenglasffrwd became pregnant by William's younger brother. She bore her child in the barn; shortly afterwards she milked the cows, and finished her other tasks. Then, helped by young Roberts, she managed to get on to a pony. With the new-born child, the couple rode over the bleak hills, past Soar-y-Mynydd in the Camddwr valley, and down the Doithie to the girl's parents' home at a spot near the present dam. By that time it was late evening. Mother and child spent the night in the stable; by morning, the baby was dead. The girl crept to the house door and was taken in and put to bed. Ill though she was, she recovered, and later married her lover.

William Roberts in his later life at Nantyneuadd was a formidable man, of enormous physical strength, who is remembered as 'one of the old type' — there were giants in those days! Once he fell from his horse on the hillside near Bronyrhelem, and gashed his head badly on a rock. Streaming with blood, he rode downstream, and tried to persuade Mr Davies of Fanog to sew up the wound with cotton and save a doctor's bill! However, on this occasion he was forced to have the doctor — fortunately, as the cut needed sixteen stitches. Mr Roberts spoke very little English, and his English farm-lad no Welsh, but somehow they understood each other. Roberts' daughter was bilingual. She came to a tragic end the year after her father's death, drowning in the dipping-tub in the yard.

Roberts had to undergo a good deal of teasing. It must have been like bull-baiting. Once he had a dozen 'Cardi stacks' in his field overnight. A few mischievous lads packed them together to look like six in the moonlight, and were delightedly convulsed when the deluded Roberts rushed about bellowing for his buxom wife to come and see what had happened.

Of Daniel Jones, the poet-shepherd, the story is told that when after leaving Trawsgyrch he sought to rent Penrhiwmoch, near

Troedrhiwdalar, on the Llwynmadog estate, Miss Thomas' agent asked what was his occupation. 'Shepherd,' was the answer. 'Carrying a club and leaning on it!' scathingly commented the agent. 'And what about your wife — what was she? — 'A school-teacher.' 'Oh damn!' exclaimed the agent, 'that's worse still!' He was none too serious, it seems, for Miss Thomas proved a most generous landlord to Daniel and his huge family, who were greatly helped, too, by Daniel's securing a post during the First World War as an officer of the Ministry of Agriculture.

The late Mr J.R. Hope of Pentwyn used to tell a story of his grandfather, John Jenkins of Penybont farm, whose best friend was the then shepherd of Fanog. This man, Charles, finally got his father's permission to emigrate to Australia, and asked John to take him to Liverpool on a horse-drawn cart. When they arrived at the port, Charles tried to persuade John to sell the horse and cart and come with him; but John felt unable to agree, and turned back, journeying homeward through Welshpool, Newtown and Builth. One year after John died, a letter came from Australia to the Congregationalist minister at Llanwrtyd, asking whether any of the Jenkins family of Penybont were still alive. A Llanwrtyd cousin wrote back to say 'yes', and some time later a parcel arrived. It contained two black emu's eggs, each about the size of two teacups placed together. One was at Pentwyn for many years till eventually it was broken.

It is interesting that several Abergwesyn legends are, in their essentials, archetypal stories which can be paralleled in other parts of Wales, indeed sometimes in other parts of Europe. We have mentioned the 'drinking stone' which gave its name to Dôlmaen on Pentwyn, and which is said to have later done duty as a gatepost; and the story of the change of site for Llanfihangel church has been discussed. Then there is the 'hoofprints' story. On a rocky outcrop of the hillside above Alltyrhebog are two impressions in the shape of hooves, made, so local tradition tells, by a magic pony that leapt across the Irfon from Llwynderw mountain, and landed with fore-hooves against the rock. The fact that one of the Pentwyn people in years gone by is said to have carved the first hoofprint, and the second one is known to have been added by one of the the Hope family, has not affected the handing down of the classical story of the magic horse, one of many which performed such feats in various parts of Wales. T. Gwyn Jones in his *Welsh Folk-Lore* quotes a reference to the horse of Mari Lwyd, warrior-princess of Glamorgan and Gwent, who left his hoofmarks on a rock at Rhyd y Milwr near the source of the Rhymni. Elias Owen writes of another wonder-horse which covered two fields in two leaps at Llanfor near Bala, and imprinted a stone by the river.

The first of several murder-stories told about derelict Moelprysgau concerns a haunting of many years' standing. The family who lived there at some unspecified but early date, possibly pre-Reformation, were plagued by the ghost of a murder-victim, and sent to Strata Florida for a 'religious man' (a monk of the abbey?) to help lay the ghost. He took a handful of fine sand and threw it into a deep pool, ordering the spirit to enter the pool and not to leave it before collecting every grain of sand. It is still at the endless task, for the water of the pool between Moelprysgau and Penybwlch is coloured to this day, local people claim, as though by churned-up sand. This tale of exorcism has features in common with a number of traditional ghost-stories: the idea of the haunting being the result of guilt and violence, and the faith of the persecuted family in the powers of the 'religious man'. T. Gwynn Jones writes that long after the Reformation people revered Catholic priests for their 'magic' powers; and after the spread of Dissent the Anglican clergy inherited this reputation. Later, nonconformist ministers, too, became invested by popular imagination with strange gifts — like Henry George of Pembrokeshire, who died about 1880, and was thought to have a familiar spirit.

The method of exorcism used in the Moelprysgau story is a familiar one — binding the spirit to an impossible labour. Gathering sand was a favourite task. Other ways of disposing of a spirit included sending it to the Red Sea and allowing it to travel back at the rate of the length of a barley-corn yearly, or shutting it up in a box and burying it under water. Sir John Wynne of Gwydir was thought to have been deposited under the Swallow Falls, to be 'punished, purged, spouted upon, and purified from the foul deeds done in his days of nature'.

In 'Portrait of the Wye Valley', H.L.V. Fletcher has told the true story, based on documents at the National Library, of an eighteenth century murder trial, that of Lewis Lewis the Younger for the murder of Thomas Price on the hills of Llanafan fawr. This factual account co-exists locally with a folk-version of the same story, stressing the murderer's unavailing attempts to dispose of the body. It was the head that caused the trouble. Wherever he put it, down the well or in the oven, it would spring out. This classic story of the indestructibility of part of a corpse (in some Welsh tales it is the heart) may be compared with the trial evidence. The murderer and his accomplice did in fact fail to reduce the body entirely to ashes, and one of the bones left recognisable after burning was part of Price's skull. It seems that the orally-transmitted story tends to conform to a type, while retaining elements of what actually happened. The type-story has moral implications; the head or heart (where the victim's self or soul abides?) proclaims the murderer's guilt, like Abel's blood crying out for vegeance.

Another archetypal story, one of fratricide and belated recognition, is told of a little house, probably a *hafod-ty*, in the far north of Llanfihangel Abergwesyn. No track follows the desolate windings of the upper Irfon to the still visible ruins of Aberceinciau by Nant y Gorlan. Centuries ago — one version says 'in the time of the Crusades' — this belonged to the two Pely brothers. (Some say there was a third brother, who was killed by a wild horse; he was dragged by the halter, which he could not disentangle from his wrist). One brother, having made his fortune in distant lands, rode home, happy in the thought of enriching his family. He found no-one at Aberceinciau but a maidservant, who gave him a bundle of rushes for his horse — the only fodder to be had in that wilderness — and told him that William Pely had gone to Abergwesyn. He rode back down the Irfon and made for the village along the drovers' road. At a roadside well, still a damp place pointed out by local people, the brothers met, but did not recognise each other. William saw only a well-dressed gentleman, ripe for plundering, and killed him on the spot. As he was stripping the corpse in search of booty, he found a familar mark on his victim's body. Realising with horror whom he had killed, he ended his own life. The two bodies were found lying at the edge of the well, which from then on has been known as Brothers' Well.

Just over the hills to the north, stories of the parishes of Llanwrthwl and Cwmdauddwr echo some of the themes in this Abergwesyn legend, as well as that of the 'time of the giants' mentioned by Lhuyd's seventeenth century correspondent. Well before the drowning of the Claerwen valley the Radnorshire historian Jonathan Williams recorded a cryptic inscription on a huge stone set in the ground at Abernant-y-Beddau, the confluence-point of Nant y Beddau (Stream of the Graves) with the Claerwen, now below the lake. His is the only evidence that this stone ever existed, but this is a district which he knew well. The lines ran —

> Mae tribedd tribedrog
> Ar Llanerch dirion feillionog,
> Lle claddwyd y tri Chawr mawr
> O Sir Frycheiniog,
> Owen, Milfyd a Madog.

> (There are three graves
> On a pleasant clovery glade,
> Where are buried the three great giants
> Of Breconshire,
> Owen, Milfyd and Madog.)

As to dating, Williams lists the stone after his account of the ruins of Capel Madog and its connection with Strata Florida Abbey, calling it 'the next piece of antiquity that occurs in point of time'. It seems, then, that he considered it a post-mediaeval monument, though we may wonder whether the inscription was added to an ancient standing stone. Just before the valley was flooded, T. Thornley Jones wrote (1951) that near the confluence 'close to the ford ... there are certainly some mounds which look like graves. Several large stones are lying about, but [not] any large standing stone'. One stone bore a few small crosses. Another stone, 'probably marked in the same way', had been removed and used in the walls of 'the new Nant-y-beddau farmhouse', an isolated house perched high on the valley-slopes. This stone bore what seemed to be Roman characters. Certainly in 1970 there lay just by the front wall of the house a blunt-ended stone, broader at one end than the other, and about two foot six inches long. On the broader end were deeply-incised marks of varying length, possibly made with a wedge-shaped tool. Mr Price, then of Nantybeddau, stated that this stone was brought from 'the graves', which he said could be clearly seen in a rectangular enclosure near the confluence. Nantybeddau once had a Norwegian visitor who considered the stone at least 1000 years old, and thought the marks showed an affinity to an ancient Scandinavian script. T. Thornley Jones thought that the 'Stream of the Graves' commemmorated earlier burials than those at the ford. There is a tumulus on the hill near the source of the stream, and at Nantybeddau itself were the slight remains of a round barrow and cist. Further north we find Esgair y Beddau (Ridge of the Graves) near the source of the Clettwr.

Another story of this spot repeats a Breconshire theme. Some nineteenth century lead-miners are said to have started to dig up the graves to look for giant-sized bones (and, perhaps, treasure?). They were terrified by a violent thunderstorm and left the task unfinished, as might be seen in 1951. A similar story of desecration and a warning thunderstorm is told of the little lake Pant y Llyn, in the north Epynt hills just above Builth, where interrupted diggers of the eighteenth century, trying to find traces of a buried town, are said to have left the marks of a drainage-channel.

We have noticed that in one version of the Brothers' Well story the Pely brothers are said to have been three in number. Three brothers — three giants — fratricide, suicide, in various permutations the themes and the number recur. Some think the giants buried at Abernant y Beddau were identical with the three gigantic brothers of Llanerchycawr, the ancient Llanwrthwl longhouse, not far away. One or two of them, caring for their sheep up the valley, quarrelled and fought fiercely and long at Nantybeddau. At last they dropped to the ground exhausted, and there the third brother, finding them helpless, vented his own murderous grudge against them both, killing them where they lay. Then came remorse for his deed, and inevitable suicide. The inscription has been connected with this story, and it has been noted that in Williams' transcription the words 'Llanerch' and 'Cawr' are singled out by initial capitals — a cryptic clue to the home of the three buried giants — or gigantic brothers? Sceptics hold that the inscription (if it ever existed) suggested the story.

'Feillionog' (clovery) is puzzling. It is so inappropriate to the Nantybeddau area, one of rough grass and stones. Was it used fancifully, as Thornley Jones suggests, to match the triad-like verse and its triple subject with a triple-leaved plant? or could it refer to a spot to which the huge stone was a signpost? Owen, Milfyd and Madog are called *Breconshire* giants. Were they buried near their home, the 'Giants' Glade', and did the longhouse get its name from some dim memory of these legendary figures? Possibly the fratricide story came later, a fusion of half-forgotten legend with a local murder-story, as may have happened too with the tale of Brothers' Well. Not far to the east of Llanerchycawr the boggy source of a stream is called Pwll Tri Beddau (Pool of Three Graves) on the slopes of the Ridge of Three Graves. And could *car* in Nantycar, by the old lead-mine, about one mile upstream from Llanerchycawr, be here a corruption of *cawr* (giant)?

Lhuyd noted about 1690 that Llanddewi Abergwesyn had a rock Carreg Cethin, 'supposed to be so called from one Rys Gethin a famous Herwr [outlaw] and since ye hold of one Moilsin as famous a Raparee'. There is a Twll Rys Gethin in Craig Alltwineu above the Irfon Valley between Abegwesyn and Llanwrtyd. If Rys was indeed, as some say, a lieutenant of Owain Glyndwr, this places him about the turn of the fourteenth-fiftennth centuries. The name of Lewsin ap Moelin is still dimly remembered here as a noted freebooter of the sixteenth century. He had a cave in the rocks above Nantystalwyn, and another in Craig Irfon below Llanerch-yrfa, now known, from its echo, as 'Tonc Padellau' (Clashing of Pans). Once, closely pursued by the Law, he leapt over the river Irfon a little above the Wolf's Leap, at a spot called thereafter 'Naid Lewsyn' (Lewsyn's Leap). It is not surprising to find stories of the marvellous and supernatural told in a lonely, hill-folded village like Abergwesyn, but one should add that the staunchest sceptics are to be found among natives of the district, some of whom perhaps fear to be thought naïve, 'behind the times', if they admit to a belief in the occult — and the most credulous among the incomers, a few of whom claim to have had strange experiences of lights and presences in the mountain night. Tales of the *ladi wen* (white lady) get a more sympathetic hearing from some of those in flight from what they judge the banalities of suburban life than they do from certain mid-Welshmen born and bred, who more readily attribute such manifestations to a trick of the light or the shadowy appearances of white calves or ponies. But not all natives are sceptical, by any means, and some of the more persistent and convincingly-told stories are those of death-omens, especially those presaging the actual funeral. Such were the tales of phantom funerals that were seen passing over the hills from lonely Blaennant before an epidemic claimed lives there in the last century; and the many tales of corpse-candles or phantom lights, in churchyards, before the house where lived a man or woman shortly to die, or moving along the route later to be taken by the funeral procession. Lhuyd's Llanafan informant wrote in the late seventeenth century 'There is usually seen here Corp's Lamps goeing before Burials'. Griffith Thomas of Cefngilfach, who was buried at Abergwesyn in 1784, was returning from Rhaeadr market with some iron pots for his son Thomas, who was shortly to marry, when at the crossing of the river Camarch he stumbled into the river, flooded by tempestuous rain, and was drowned. Next day his body was found downstream near Fedw, where, it was said, not long before he and William Arthur of Blaenycwm had seen a 'spectral light' on their way home from taking sheep to Llwynmadog.

Stories of miraculous cures include those about the *llaethfaen*, the 'milkstone' that cured hydrophobia. At Dinas, Llanwrtyd, is a small chalky white stone said to have come from Llanafan, and to have been handed down through generations. Scrapings from it used to be taken in milk as a remedy against the bite of a mad dog. People travelled many miles to use such a stone, like the one owned by the Thomases of Welfield (now Cefndyrys), Llanelwedd. Tradition said that it dropped from heaven on a clear summer's day. Its help continued to be sought up to about 1880. Herbert Vaughan refers to seeing at Llwynmadog one which was still used in that area in the early twentieth century; but as we have seen Miss Clara Thomas vetoed discussion of the supernatural, so 'there was a strict taboo on the whole subject of the *llaethfaen* and its uses'. The Llwynmadog stone was one of two reputed to have been found in the ground by a rabies victim who fell asleep on a hill and dreamed that a remedy lay under his head.

Nowadays superstitious beliefs are sufficiently singular to be remembered as idiosyncrasies. Mr D. Jones, formerly of the Post Office, Abergwesyn, remembered, for instance, that when he used to cut the hair of Thomas Davies of Penybryn, he was never allowed to burn the clippings, but had to throw them in the river.

There are many stories of haunted houses in the area, though they are rarely specific. Little Ty Bwci, which once stood on the hillside above the now ruinous Brongilent, took its name from a *pwci* (puck), a mischievous sprite even the thought of which was enough to terrify the little servant-girl of Brongilent on her way to fetch water from the spring. Ty isaf (Ty'nyddôl) has vanished, too, from its site near Pentwyn ford; that was another haunted house. As for the mansions, Llwynderw and Llwynmadog, and others further away, like Garth House, each has its ghost, rarely detailed more fully than 'a lady in white' or 'a lady in old-fashioned clothes'.

An unusual tradition of a haunting concerns a long upper room or 'gallery' of Dinas farmhouse, Llanwrtyd, the old home of the Lloyd gentry family. A young girl is said to have been unwilling to sleep in this room, which she claimed to be haunted by manacled slaves, kept here on overnight stop in their journey from Bristol, where they had disembarked, to some destination unspecified.

Some of the hauntings were by the ghosts of murder-victims; in particular there are a number of murdered packmen, such as the one we heard of at Fanog. Kilvert's tale of the 'haunted swamp-surrounded house' of Llanshifr in South Radnorshire, where the skeleton of a 'Scotch pedlar... murdered for the sake of his pack' had been found in the moat, can be paralleled by several tales of the Abergwesyn area. Moelprysgau, scene of the early exorcism story, later witnessed the killing by its unscrupulous tenant Evan Edwards and his wife of a packman they buried under the floor of the house. The victim's grey horse wandered the moors till it was impounded for the lord of the manor. Another packman was murdered at Gilwern, near the river Camarch near Beulah. A 'conjuror' employed to lay his ghost incarcerated it for a while in a tobacco box under a long flagstone before the door. But after some years, in the mid-nineteenth century, manifestations began again — unexplained sounds in the passage, on the staircase, in a room at the head of the stairs. Gilwern as it now stands is not the same old straw-thatched house it was then, and the former doorway no longer exists. The last farmer is now dead, and no-one seems to know whether the murdered Scotsman still troubles the peaceful-looking house in its wooded valley.

Vistors who carry away from Abergwesyn a memory of beauty, friendliness and peace are not deluding themselves — these things are here. So is violence — in the grimmer aspects of the landscape: in storm, snow and flood: in the hardness of the hill-farmer's life for many centuries: in the assault of these things on the mind and nature of humans living often in great isolation. Many stories of the Hundred of Builth tell of murder, suicide, robbery and pillage — crimes of passion and crimes of greed. Moelprysgau, that particularly isolated farmhouse of the far upper reaches of the Tywi, and scene of two murders we have already mentioned, saw also two other killings, both by the packman's murderer, Evan Edwards. His brother Thomas he murdered for his share of the family inheritance. While they were washing horses in Llyn Cripil in the Claerwen valley, Evan called Thomas's attention to a salmon and pushed him into the water, repeatedly thrusting him back in, cutting the rushes to which his brother desperately clung, and finally crushing his head with a stone. In later years Edwards kept a mistress at Pontrhydfendigaid. His wife, not surprisingly, doubted his stories of riding over there to attend church, and one day followed him and prevailed upon him to go home with her. They had one horse; she, pregnant at the time, rode behind. Near Pen Bwlch Rhyd y Meirch on the old road to Strata Florida, she began again upbraiding him. Goaded, he stabbed her in the belly, and left her writhing in her blood by the track. She was found dead the next morning; a cairn, Carn gerrig, was raised near the spot. Edwards confessed and was hanged. The story is told in an elegy by David Thomas of Bronberllan.

It is said that only one of the houses of the upper Tywi was not the scene of a murder! Howell Harris wrote in his diary on 26 August 1739 of travelling towards Tregaron from Abergwesyn and passing after leaving Dôlgoch 'a house where a man was slain by his servants; and by another house where a man slew his wife, stabbing her in the heart, and it was her oath, that if such and such a thing was not so, may a knife be in her heart'. Harris must have followed the old track branching off the Abergwesyn-Tregaron drovers' road and striking out along the upper Tywi for Strata Florida. The second house he mentions is obviously Moelprysgau. The first is Nantystalwyn. Here in 1697 lived Humphrey Jenkins, grandfather of a celebrated red-haired matriarch Gwen Nantyrhwch. Mr Jenkins employed a serving-man, a boy, a housekeeper and a servant-girl. He had made someone a loan of £40, a large sum then; when his debtor returned the money, the presence of this tempting prize proved too much for the three older servants, who plotted to murder their master and steal his money. Only the boy was ignorant of the plan.

One day Humphrey Jenkins returned home thirsty. Soon after swallowing a drink brought by the servants, he fell ill. Alarmed by the swelling of his body, and suspecting poison, he drank salad-oil in an attempt at first-aid, and shouted to the boy to saddle his horse. But it was too late. While the boy was fetching the horse, the other servants overpowered their sick master, strangled him with a stocking, carried him upstairs and put him in his bed. Presumably the boy was told that Mr Jenkins had changed his mind. For two days the corpse lay in the bedroom, the door of which the servants locked from the inside, climbing out through the window. The boy was mystified by his master's absence, but he was kept busy with shepherding and other work, so that he had little opportunity to pry. Meanwhile the others ransacked the house for the money. After two days, there was a knock at the door. Daniel Prydderch, Humphrey's friend, was told 'Mr Jenkins is sleeping — he's been sleeping for two days, and we can't open the door. We don't know what to do!' Prydderch ran upstairs and shouted urgently through the bedroom door, but silence lay heavy on the stuffy air. Filled with foreboding, he fetched neighbours who helped him break open the door. There lay the missing man, dead on the bed. In the room was found the key of the empty safe.

The funeral was hastily arranged. No-one suspected foul play (strange, surely, in a strangling case) and for two years there was quiet. Then the two maids quarrelled violently over their shares of the money. Spite, fear and even a qualm of conscience caused the younger maid to confess and implicate her fellow-servants. The housekeeper appeared in the local court for questioning, the young girl giving evidence against her. Later the older woman was convicted of murder at Brecon Great Sessions, and hanged on 3 May 1699. The girl who had turned King's Evidence was a minor and was released. The third murderer, the manservant, disappeared; he was hunted through the whole of Britain, in vain.

Nearby parishes have their stories, relished by Abergwesyn people. A favourite and very lurid one is that of John Evans, a drover, who in 1825, aged twenty-six, was sentenced to death at Brecon for the murder at Tirabad of Margaret Williams, otherwise Peg of Ffrydie. Peg, who was pregnant, had been kicked and beaten 'in and upon the Head, Neck, Throat, Breast, Back, Belly, Sides and other parts of the body, and strangled with both hands, her neck being dislocated'. John Evans' motive, never definitely established, was believed to have been fear of Peg's 'swearing to him' her coming child — that is, swearing before a magistrate that he was its father. He had already had one child by Peg eight or nine years ago, and was almost certainly the father of another by her, an eighteen month old boy who lived with his mother. It was claimed that John's intended bride had refused to marry him if he had another child by Peg; but this rumour was contradicted by one of John's witnesses.

David Rowlands of Penrhiw, Llangamarch, whose wife Eleanor was John Evans' sister, stated before magistrates that he had gone on Sunday evening to a prayer-meeting. After supper he went to bed; so did Eleanor and a six-year-old girl, another child of the prisoner. After midnight, John Evans pushed open the back door, and called desperately to Rowlands to go out with him. Evans picked up a spade, muttering that 'she was dead enough'. In answer to his brother-in-law's horrified questioning, Evans said it was Peg he meant. Mounting his horse, he struggled to lift the corpse on horseback before him, alternately swearing and begging Rowlands for help. The latter, afraid of both 'the Prisoner and the Corps in his heart', put the dead hand into that of Evans and backed away. 'Come here, come here, for God's sake!' cried Evans. Between them they got the body on to the horse's back. Rowlands went a little way with Evans, then ran home by Llwynyfynwent wood. He sat on the bed and cried.

On Monday morning Thomas, Evan and Elizabeth, Pegi's brothers and sister, reported her disappearance to Rice Davies of Glandulas, where she had been a servant. They suspected John Evans, and told how John had visited Pegi on Saturday night in her loft-bedroom at Ffrydie on the Epynt. Next morning Elizabeth upbraided her sister for allowing her lover in the house when their father was very ill. Peg told her she had arranged to meet John on the Epynt on Monday morning and elope with him. Rice Davies, at first incredulous, met with Evans and taxed him with being at Ffrydie. Evans brazened it out, but a neighbour claimed to have seen him leaving Ffrydie on Saturday night. Soon Colonel Gwynne gave permission for Evans' arrest, and a huge 'posse', the whole parish in fact, rose up and went after the suspected murderer. Evans leapt on his brother's horse near his home, Troedrhiwyddon, now a ruin in the forest, and galloped off towards Llandeilo'r Fan. The pursuit ended at last when Evans plunged into Cilieni brook, pulled out a knife and threatened to destroy himself. He was finally taken alive. Then followed a search by hundreds of people, it is said, for Peg's body. Help is said to have been sought from the *dyn hysbys* Harries of Cwrt-y-Cadno, who showed to a Tirabad man, in a mirror, a vision of Evans trampling down with bare feet the earth of a new-made grave near Penrhiw, in a dingle of Llwynyfynwent wood. Here, after a four-day search, Peg's battered body was found. Evans was hanged for his crime.

There are those who claim that the reason why hard facts about the Hundred of Builth are hard to come by is that until comparatively recent times this was such a lawless countryside that it was to the advantage of its inhabitants not to let news get out to the world beyond the hills. It is still to some extent a hidden land. Stories of the days before the influence of religious revival, and the gradually growing effectiveness of law and order, suggest a life in which robbery and violence were almost a commonplace. Greed and revenge were perhaps the commonest motives. They are not unknown today, nor restricted to lonely countrysides!

We have come across one of the local *causes célèbres* of the eighteenth century, the murder of Thomas Price of Llanafan fawr by 'Lewisin Simin', who was hanged at Garth in 1789 near the scene of his crime. In the same year, Thomas James ('alias Thomas of Troedrhiwcadarn') was killed at Maesygenffordd Inn — now replaced by Garth Inn — by John Price junior of Cwmchrefru, Gentleman, Evan

Evans of Melinygarth, and David Price of Maesllêch, farmer, each of whom was accused by the widow Elizabeth of striking, beating and kicking the victim with his hands and feet 'in and upon the head back belly and sides and other parts of the body down unto and upon the ground' so that he died 'instantly' of these 'mortal strokes wounds and bruises'. The verdict was manslaughter. The killers here were local minor gentry and substantial yeomen — the Prices of Cwmchwefru and Dôlfelin lorded it in Llanafan for generations. The James family was ill-starred — Thomas James's daughter married John Price of Llanafan, a shepherd who came of an Abergwesyn family, and who was killed in his turn in 1826 on the Daren hill in Llanafan fawr. Rees Lewis of Rhandirlaes was accused of the murder. Rees, standing on an old peat-path, had told a witness that John Price had 'put his dogs to bark and disturb the sheep upon the walk'; Rees threatened to kill the dogs. Further evidence showed that Rees had been seen at the crucial time going towards, and later running from, the Daren,where he had no sheep depastured, and no reason to be. Early Sunday morning, John's son Peter, on his way to prayer-meeting, met his father going up the Daren, to look after the sheep of William Jones of Gilwern. He seemed well. He was probably carrying 16 shillings in a grey fustian purse. Later, Peter went up the hill to call his father down to dinner, and found him dead, face down on the ground, mouth and face bloodstained and swollen, and handkerchief knotted tight around his neck.

By Sunday evening news of the murder had reached most farms in the district. At four or five o'clock on Monday morning, John Williams, servant at Erwddôl, went to the barn to fodder the cattle, and saw Rees on a field-path nearby. 'Where are you going?' asked John, and was told 'I am going about my own business'. 'I have something to do with you,' said John, seizing Rees by the collar. Rees seems to have allowed John to take him to Tanyrallt, home of the Rev. David Williams, where the latter enlisted the help of the servant and a neighbour. 'They say you murdered John Price Pantoilw,' said John Williams. 'Put to me if you think so,' sullenly replied Rees. 'I am not afraid of you,' said John. 'I will make a greater fag with you than Jack Pantoilw if you put to me!' Rees made little real resistance to being taken into custody. An innocent man who knew there could be little hard evidence? Or a guilty man brazening it out, but knowing the game was up? The trial evidence, with its crude rendering of local idiom into English, shows that between the time of the murder and Rees' apprehension by Williams, he was glimpsed by curious witnesses running through fields, through an alder-copse, across the river Dulas — pausing, looking about him, going on again. He seems to have been on the run for hours, but in no very effective way, addled perhaps by a dark awareness of what he had done and the impossibility of escape.

Tales of fights and feuds indicate a state of near-vendetta violence among some of the 'tribes' of the North Breconshire valleys. The word 'tribe' is in fact used by older people to describe the old family networks — the Cochiaid Cwm Tywi, the Siminses, the Shelbyites, the Gythoed and others: their loyalties, territories, ferocious quarrels. It is said that, at one inter-tribal affray, among the women who came to cheer on their menfolk was the pregnant wife of one of the combatants, carrying one child in her arms and with another dragging at her skirts. The tribal names are mentioned guardedly. Present-day descendants are not always anxious to publicise the connection, yet still cherish a deep pride in kinship, a loyalty that can be fiercely defensive. Constantly the listener feels that some nuance has escaped him, some association has not been appreciated. 'So you see, on her mother's side she was a —' a name follows, nods are exchanged. The full significance one does not see; one never will.

Some stories of violence have a more explicit social element. The nearest point to Abergwesyn to experience serious Rebecca riots was the Rhaeadr-Cwmdauddwr area, where toll-gates were attacked in 1843. John Davies, who was at the time bailiff for Thomas Lewis Lloyd, referred in letters to several affrays, including the one when 'a party of Rebeccaites sawed off the posts of the Cwmtoyddwr Toll gates, broke the Gates to atoms and then threw the wood into the river'. The forty or fifty men in women's dress were thought to be all from Llanwrthwl and Cwmdauddwr. A later incident which is the theme of a favourite Abergwesyn story was called by *The Aberystwyth Observer* of 17 October 1868 'The Arson Case — Rebecca Riots on Moelprisce'. But it could ony be so termed in a general and derivative sense, the Rebecca formula having been adopted by those attempting to redress a variety of social grievances. In this case it was enclosure by a landlord of mountain grazing traditionally used in common by the farmers of the district.

The story tells of Stephen Lloyd of Pantybeudiau, an ancestor of Mrs D. Jones, formerly of Abergwesyn Post Office. Over the desolate mountain of Esgair Garthen flanking the Claerwen valley stretched in those days the huge sheepwalks of Moelprysgau, owned by the Nanteos estate. Neighbouring farmers had long used it for grazing sheep and cattle. To prevent them from claiming right of common, Colonel Powell and his tenant built an isolated cottage, Pantybeudiau, and installed Stephen Lloyd in it as shepherd to keep off trespassers. One night when Lloyd was away from home to attend a funeral, his young wife Elizabeth had only her small baby and ten-year-old sister Mary for company. After midnight she was awakened by the dogs' barking, and heard the swish of feet approaching over the tussocky ground. No house was near, no help possible. Loud knocks at the door were followed by the crash of breaking windows. Elizabeth lit a candle, but it was blown out when the door was lifted off its hinges. Terrified, she cried for mercy into the windy dark. 'Come out!' shouted the unseen attackers. 'Where is your master?' She begged for time to get her sister and the baby out of bed; but the men burst in — a great mob of them it seemed. One hustled Mary outside, another grabbed an armful of clothes from the hanging press and thrust them after her. Elizabeth took up the baby and went out. Lights flared in the blackness. Furniture was dragged out; pots, pans, treasured china from the dresser were thrown on the dunghill. With a bar and pick-axes, the men pulled down the little house and set fire to its remains and to the hayrick and peat-stack. The flames revealed about fifteen men, some with coats turned inside out and all with blackened faces, in the manner of Rebecca rioters. They scattered the remaining stones, and disappeared into the darkness of the waste. Only the turf-stack was still glowing when the young woman set out, the baby in her arms and the little girl clinging to her hand, on the long walk through the night to seek shelter. A reward was later offered for information, but the guilt of the suspects was never proved. The ruins of rebuilt Pantybeudiau can still be reached along the west bank of the Claerwen reservoir, not far above the shore of the lake. Elizabeth is said to have been very ill after her ordeal, but she survived, as did the little girl and the baby.

There is a footnote to the story of that night in 1868. The 1871 Census returns for Llanfihangel Abergwesyn show, at Lle'rtaihirion in the Camarch valley, Stephen Lloyd, aged thirty-three, a Cardiganshire-born shepherd, his wife Elizabeth, two-year-old son Stephen, eight-month daughter Jane, and the family's young 'general servant, domestic', Elizabeth's thirteen-year-old sister, Mary Morgan. By 1881, Stephen and Elizabeth had five more children, daughters of eight, three and two, and sons of six and four. Mary Morgan was no longer there.

In Abergwesyn, with its stories, its ruins, its will to go on living, 'then' marches only a shadow-pace behind 'now'. And 'to come'? The marks on hillside and valley-floor of centuries of home-building, fencing, pasturing, digging, draining, roadmaking, ploughing, growing, storing, should bring hope as well as regret, speaking as they do not only of all that is gone, but of the land's potential, and of the achievement and ever-renewed vitality of man.

Bibliography

A. Maps

Atlas Brycheiniog (1960)
Bowen, Emanuel: Map of South Wales (c.1760, NLW)
Estate maps of some farms of the Crosswood and Nanteos estates (1781 and 1819, NLW)
Estate map of Celsau by Meredith Jones (NLW)
Main roads and cattle tracks in the Hundred of Builth (c.1800, NLW)
O.S. Historical Maps
O.S. preliminary drawings (1820-21)
O.S. one inch maps (from 1833)
O.S. two and a half and six inch maps
Rees, William: Map of South Wales and the Border in the Fourteenth Century (reproduced by O.S., 1932)
Rees, William: Historical Atlas of Wales (1959)
Saxton: Map of Radnorshire, Breconshire, Cardiganshire and Carmarthenshire (1578, British Museum Maps, c7.cl)
Tithe maps of Llanfihangel and Llanddewi Abergwesyn (1842 and 1848, NLW)

B. Printed Books

Bennett, R.: Early Life of Howell Harries (trans. G.M. Roberts)
Beynon, T. (ed): Howell Harries' Diaries
Beynon, T. (ed): Howell Harries, Reformer and Soldier 1714-73 (1958)
Beynon, T. (ed): Howell Harries' Visits to Pembrokeshire
Beynon, T. (ed): The Circulating Welsh Charity Schools (from Welch Piety)
Bowen, E.G.: Settlements of the Celtic Saints in Wales (1954)
Bowen, E.G.: Saints and Seaways (1977)
Bradley, A.G.: Highways and Byways in South Wales (1903)
Bund, J. Willis: The Celtic Church in Wales (1897)
Clark, J.: View of the Agriculture of Breconshire (1794)
Cliffe, C.F.: Book of South Wales (2nd edn, 1848)
Colyer, R.J.: The Welsh Cattle Drovers (1976)
Davies, C.: Welsh Folk-lore (1911)
Davies, L. & Edwards, A.: Welsh Life in the Eighteenth Century (1939)
Davies, W.: General View of the Agriculture of South Wales (1815)
Dawson, D.H.: Churches of Breconshire (1909)
Dictionary of Welsh Biography
Dodd, A.H.: Life in Wales (1972)
Dodd, A.H.: Studies in Stuart Wales (1952)
Edwards, W.R. (ed): Cofiant a Gweithiau Rhys Gwesyn Jones, D.D. (1902)
Evans, J.T.: Church Plate of Breconshire (1912)
Fenton, R.: Tours in Wales (1804-13)
Fletcher, H.L.V.: Portrait of the Wye Valley (1968)

Giraldus Cambrensis: Itinerary through Wales (Everyman edn., 1908)
Griffiths, D. Avan: Cofiant y Parch. David Williams (1877)
Grimes, W.F.: Guide to the Prehistory of Wales (1939)
Hall, G.W.: Metal Mines of Southern Wales (1971)
Haslem, R.: Powys (Buildings series; 1979)
Howell, D.H.: Land and People in Nineteenth Century Wales (1977)
Howell, E.J.: Wales, vol.3 (1943) of Land Utilisation Survey, ed. D. Stamp
Howse, W.H.: Radnorshire (1949)
Hughes, J.: Methodistiaeth Cymru (1854)
Hughes, P.G.: Wales and the Drovers (1943)
Jenkins, D.C., (ed): The Diary of Thomas Jenkins of Llandeilo
Jenkins, D.E.: Calvinistic Methodist Holy Orders (1911)
Jenkins, J.G.: The Welsh Woollen Industry (1969)
Jones, E.: Cymdogaeth Soar-y-Mynydd (1979)
Jones, F.: The Holy Wells of Wales (1954)
Jones, G.H.: Celtic Britain and the Pilgrim Movement (1912)
Jones, J.: History of the Baptists in Radnorshire (1895)
Jones, O. & Walker, D. (eds): Links with the Past (1974)
Jones, T.: History of Brecknockshire (Glanusk edn., 1909)
Jones, T.G.: Welsh Folkore (1930)
Kelly's Directories (from 1830)
Kilvert, F.: Diary (1870-74)
Leland, J.: Itinerary in Wales (ed. Lucy Toulmin Smith, 1906)
Lewis, E.T.: North of the Hills
Lewis, S.: Topographical Dictionary (1833)
Lewis, W.J.: Leadmining in Wales (1967)
Lhuyd, E.: Parochialia (Arch. Camb.)
Llewelyn, A.: Wales (Shell Guides, 1969)
Lloyd, J.:Historical Memoranda (I, 1899& II, 1904)
Lloyd, J.E.: History of Wales to the Edwardian Conquest (3 edn., 1939)
Llywelyn-Williams, A.: Crwydro Brycheiniog (1964)
Macfarlane, A.: Reconstructing Historical Communities (1977)
Mais, S.P.B.: I Return to Wales (1949)
Malkin, B.H.: South Wales (1807)
Morgan, E.: Life and Times of Howell Harris, Esq. (1852)
Morgan, V.: Life and Sayings of the late Kilsby Jones (1896)
Nash-Williams, V.E.: The Roman Frontier in Wales (ed. Jarrett, 1969)
Nash-Williams, V.E.: Early Christian Monuments in Wales
Nennius, ed. & trans. John Morris (1980)
Newman, C.W.: Hilda Vaughan (1981)
Nicholas, T.: Annals and Antiquities (1875)
Owen, E.: Welsh Folklore (1896)
Owen, G.D.: Elizabethan Wales (1962)
Parry-Jones, D.: Welsh Upbringing (1948)
Phillips, T.: Wales (1849)
Pigot's Directories

Poole, E.: History of Brecknockshire (1886)

Pryse, T.: Handbook to the Radnorshire and Breconshire Mineral Springs (1874)

Rees, T. & Thomas, J.: Hanes yr Annibynwyr Cymru (1875)

Rees, W.: South Wales and the March, 1284-1415 (1924)

Roberts, G.M.: Y Pêr Ganiedydd (1949)

Roberts, G.M. (ed): Selected Trevecka Letters [of Howell Harries]

Sylvester, D.: The Rural Landscape of the Welsh Borderland (1969)

Thomas, T.G. & Jones, J.: Brecon and Radnor Congregationalism (1912)

Thomas, R.: Y Duw Bô'r Diolch (1983)

Toulson, S.: The Drovers' Roads of Wales (1977)

Vaughan, H.: The South Wales Squires (1926)

Verey, D.: Shell Guide to Mid-Wales (1960)

Wales, R.C.R.H.M.: Brecknock: Hillforts and Roman Remains (1986) H.M.S.O.

Wheeler, E.M.: Prehistoric and Roman Wales (1925)

Williams, A.H.: Introduction to the History of Wales (1926)

Williams, D.: Modern Wales (1950)

Williams, D.H.: The Welsh Cistercians (1970)

Williams, G.: Welsh Reformation Essays (1967)

Williams, G.: Religion, Language and Nationality in Wales (1979)

C. Journals, etc

Abergwesyn Observer (17 October 1868)

Anglo-Welsh Review (24)

Archaeologia Cambrensis

Brecon Naturalist (27 and 28)

Brecon & Radnor Express (Chwilio'r Cilfachau and Museum News)

Brycheiniog

Clwyd-Powys Archaeological Trust Powys Metal Mines Survey (193)

Country Life

Country Quest

Cymru

Y Diwigiwr (August 1861)

Gentleman's Magazine

Hereford Journal

Hereford Times

Journal of the Historical Society of the Presbyterian Church of Wales

Journal of the National Library of Wales

Mining Journal (1844, 1845, 1849, 1850)

Montgomery Collections (54)

Montgomery News

National Environment Research Council (Institute of Geological Studies) Report No. T5/14

Old Wales

Poetry Wales

Radnorshire Society Transactions

Red Dragon (1882)
Western Mail

D. MS Sources

Builth Registry records
Parish Registers and Bishop's Transcripts
Records of N.S.P.R.E. and British Society
Log Books of Abergwesyn School
Church in Wales records
Tithe maps and schedules
Probate records
Collections of deeds and estate papers (N.L.W.)
Quarter Sessions records
Great Sessions and Assizes records
Health Tax returns
Census returns
State Papers
Religious Census, 1851
Papers of David Lewis Wooding (courtesy of Mr P. Owen)
Letters of Roberts family (courtesy of Mr B.D. Clarke)
Notes of Capt. Christopher Pearce and other papers (courtesy of Mr M. Bourdillon)
Bidding list (incomplete) of John Jones of Pwllybo

E. Monumental Inscriptions